Everyday English 1500–170

A Reader

Edited by Bridget Cusack

Edinburgh University Press

© Bridget Cusack, 1998

Edinburgh University Press
22 George Square, Edinburgh

Typeset in Ehrhardt and Futura
by Norman Tilley Graphics, Northampton
and printed and bound in Great Britain
by Cromwell Press, Trowbridge, Wiltshire

A CIP record for this book is available from
the British Library

ISBN 0 7486 0776 5

Contents

Preface

This Reader aims to put into the hands of students some typical examples of non-literary documents written in English between 1500 and 1700, the Early Modern English period. Some degree of linguistic naïveté characterises each.

The people whose words are captured in these documents spoke and wrote an English like and yet unlike our own. We can understand what they are saying in a much more immediate way than when we attempt to read a text from the Middle English or Old English period, but we constantly come across linguistic features different from ours. It is because of the combination of these two factors that the Early Modern period is considered by many the most rewarding place to begin research on historical change and development in English.

We have ample access to works of literature from the period; the plays of Shakespeare alone are a source of enormous and valuable information for the historical linguist. But at the same time any literary work must carry with it an element of doubt as to how close it brings us to the language of the real-life people of the time. Moreover, there is normally at this period a link between authorship and linguistic conformity, and where in its own day a text was printed and published, the English of any author who wrote idiosyncratic English was often tidied, even if only in spelling and punctuation, to conform with what was beginning to be perceived as a norm.

In 1589 George Puttenham, in *The Arte of English Poesie*, discussed what kind of English a poet ought to write in. He answers his own question: *the most vsuall of all his countrey*. But then he goes on to qualify this. Do you live in the country? Then you are *poore rusticall & vnciuill*, so your language is no use. Is your town a small coastal port? Then your language is spoiled by the *straungers* there. Are you *of the Inferiour sort*? Then you *doe abuse good speaches by strange accents or ill shapen soundes, and false ortographie*. Are you an academic? Then you *vse much peeuish affectation of words out of the primatiue languages*. Do you enjoy reading? Then you probably share language *out of vse*. Are you from the North (or even Scotland) or the West? Then your English is neither *Courtly* nor *current*. So, having dismissed most of the population, Puttenham concludes *ye shall therfore take the vsuall speech of the Court, and that of London and the shires lying about London within lx. myles, and not much aboue*. The documents transcribed here are manuscripts in which the English of people representing many of the social groups that Puttenham rejects is on record, simply because the documents have happened to survive and are now in the care of a library or record office. The texts are arranged in groups,

Abuse, Accounts, Depositions, Journals, Letters (grouped into men's and women's), Memoirs, Presentments and Wills. Each group is introduced by discussion of the nature of that particular kind of document and of linguistic matters arising, and each is accompanied by an annotated photograph of a typical manuscript.

In such a collection of documents it has not been possible to give extensive coverage to every area, every type of text and every decade within two hundred years. For quick reference the tables at the end of the book list the texts by place and by date. More specialist studies are called for to investigate the many areas of interest which begin to emerge even when only sixty-four short documents are offered as data.

A brief discussion of ways of using these texts for investigating the English language of the sixteenth and seventeenth centuries has been provided, with a select bibliography of useful books. As a starting-point for using the texts, and others like them, for elementary study and small-scale research, a set of suggested Topics for linguistic investigation is appended to each of them, and the Introductions to each section deliberately range more widely than the small set of texts in each group.

While preparing this Reader, I have often felt like a privileged eavesdropper in Early Modern England. I hope that many others will find in these documents as much of interest as I have done.

Bridget Cusack
Brixham, 1997

Acknowledgements

For their kind permission to publish the documents in this volume (on all of which copyright is reserved) the editor would like to thank the following:

The Controller of Her Majesty's Stationery Office for Crown copyright material held in **The Public Record Office**: Texts 1, 11, 18, 19, 28B, 37 (with photography permission), 38, 47. The Keeper of the Records of Scotland for material held in **The Scottish Record Office**: Texts 21, 23, 43. **The British Library**: Texts 12, 15, 22, 28A, 33 (with photography permission), 34, 44, 48, 51, 52; and **The Churchwardens of St Nicholas with St Mary, Strood** for material held in the British Library: Text 12. The Trustees of **The National Library of Scotland**: Text 53. The Supreme Judicial Court Division of Archives and Records Preservation for material held in the Judicial Archives, **Massachusetts State Archives**: Text 32. **Bristol Record Office**: Texts 49, 50, 63. **Cornwall Record Office**: Text 16. **Cumbria Record Office (Kendal)**: Text 13. **Devon Record Office**: Text 59; and **Diocese of Exeter** for material held in the Devon Record Office: Texts 5 (with photography permission; photograph by Focus Photography), 6, 24, 26, 27; and **The Parish of Ashburton** for material held in Devon Record Office: Text 9. The Governors of **Dulwich College** Texts 39, 41. The Right Reverend The **Bishop of Durham** and the **Durham Diocesan Registrar** for material held by **Durham University Library**, Archives and Special Collections: Text 3. The County Archivist, East Sussex County Council, for material held in **East Sussex Record Office**: Texts 14, 35. **Edinburgh University Library**: Text 36. **Essex Record Office**: Texts 8, 30, 55 (with photography permission), 56. The Right Reverend The **Bishop of Gloucester** for material held in **Gloucestershire Record Office**: Text 64 (with photography permission); and **The Rector and PCC of Minchinhampton** for material held in Gloucestershire Record Office: Text 17. **Centre for Kentish Studies**: Text 40. The **Lord Kenyon** and the County Archivist, **Lancashire Record Office**: Text 46 (with photography permission). **Lincolnshire Archives** (and on behalf of **Diocese of Lincoln**): Texts 20, 60. The Right Reverend The **Bishop of London** for material held in **Greater London Record Office**: Text 62. St Giles and St Columba's **Kirk Session, Elgin** and **Moray Record Office**: Text 7. Kenneth F. Arnold, Clerk, **Northampton County Circuit Court, Eastville, Virginia**: Text 29. **Northamptonshire Record Office**: Text 58 (with photography permission; photograph by Peter Moyes). Library Committee of The **Religious Society of Friends** in Britain: Text 54 (with photography permission). **St Andrews University Library** and the Scottish Record Office: Text 2. **Scottish Borders Council Museum and Gallery Service**: Text 21 (with photography permission). **Somerset Archive and Record Service**: Texts 42, 49. **Southampton Archives Services** (and on behalf of **Southampton City Council**): Text 31. **Stratford-upon-Avon Town Council** for material held by **Shakespeare Birthplace Trust**: Text 57. **Wigan Archives Service**: Text 35. **Company of Merchant Adventurers of the City of York**: Text 10 (with photography permission; photograph by Ken Shelton). **York University, Borthwick Institute of Historical Research** (and on behalf of **Diocese of York**): Texts 4, 61.

Investigating the English of the Sixteenth and Seventeenth Centuries

From the texts assembled here a number of investigations into the English Language of the Early Modern period may be made, some major and others small-scale.

One central area for study is to compare the language of these naïve documents with that of more formal texts. A second research field is to draw comparisons between this everyday language and that depicted at secondhand in the literature of the time, especially where literary and 'real' language meet in the writing of contemporary dramatists. A third important approach to the material is to explore to what extent it confirms the accounts of non-standard language made by those people, expecially in the seventeenth century, who wrote about the regional and social dialects of their day.

Since the texts span 200 years, diachronic studies of changes and developments within the Early Modern period suggest themselves, as well as consideration of the English of the period in relation to Middle English and Modern English. As the texts come from a number of different areas of England, together with Scotland and America, the regional variation which is rarely shown in more formal texts is frequently illustrated here, and can be viewed either synchronically or with reference to the history and later development of different dialects. Because many of these texts identify the age, sex and social standing of the speaker/writer and set out the context of situation within which the language is used, much of the material lends itself to socio-linguistic study.

Some investigations will cover several aspects of the language, others may give particular attention to some particular area, graphics, punctuation, spelling, pronunciation and phonology, morphology, syntax, vocabulary and semantics, or to some one topic within one of these, such as the phasing out of þ and ʒ, the introduction of full stops, the evidence of spellings in regard to the vowel in *sea* or the consonants in *fight*, the use of *thou* and *you*, why some texts have *makes* and others *maketh*, what constitutes a single sentence, regional use of loanwords from Scandinavian languages, the factors which determine which of a number of words for the same thing is employed.

In every case, the results of such analysis may be compared with the results yielded by parallel studies based on data provided by more formal texts, so that our conclusions about how English worked in the Early Modern period may take account of the unique evidence with which texts of this kind furnish us.

Select Bibliography

Studies of Early Modern English

Charles Barber, *Early Modern English* (André Deutsch, London 1976; reprinted Edinburgh University Press, Edinburgh, 1997).

Manfred Görlach, *Introduction to Early Modern English* (Cambridge University Press, Cambridge, 1991; originally published in German as *Einführung ins Frühneuenglische*, Quelle and Meyer, Heidelberg, 1978).

Roger Lass (ed.), *The Cambridge History of the English Language* Vol. III, covering period 1476–1776 (Cambridge University Press, Cambridge, forthcoming 1998).

Particular Aspects of Early Modern English

David Cressy, *Literacy and the Social Order: Reading and Writing in Tudor and Stuart England* (Cambridge University Press, Cambridge, 1980).

Giles E. Dawson and Laetitia Kennedy-Skipton, *Elizabethan Handwriting 1500–1650* (Faber & Faber, London, 1968).

E. J. Dobson, *English Pronunciation 1500–1700*, 2 vols, 2nd edn (Clarendon Press, Oxford, 1968).

E. J. Dobson, 'Early Modern Standard English', *Transactions of the Philological Society*, 1955, pp. 25–54; reprinted in Roger Lass (ed.), *Approaches to English Historical Linguistics* (Holt, Rinehart & Winston, New York, 1969), pp. 419–39.

Kenneth Hudson, 'Shakespeare's Use of Colloquial Language' in Kenneth Muir (ed.), *Shakespeare Survey* 23 (Cambridge University Press, Cambridge, 1970), pp. 39–48.

Jean F. Preston and Laetitia Yeandle, *English Handwriting 1400–1650* (Pegasus Paperbacks, Binghampton, New York, 1992).

Vivan Salmon, 'Elizabethan Colloquial English in the Falstaff Plays', *Leeds Studies in English* New Series Vol. I (University of Leeds, 1967); reprinted in V. Salmon and E. Burness (eds), *A Reader in the Language of Shakespearian Drama* (John Benjamins, Amsterdam, 1987), pp. 37–70.

Vivan Salmon, 'The Spelling and Punctuation of Shakespeare's Time' in Stanley Wells and Gary Taylor (eds) *William Shakespeare, The Complete Works, Original-Spelling Edition* (Clarendon Press, Oxford, 1986), pp. xlii–lvi.

Margaret Williamson, *Colloquial Language of the Commonwealth and Restoration* (The English Association, Pamphlet No. 73, 1929).

H. C. Wyld, *A History of Modern Colloquial English*, 3rd edn (Blackwell, Oxford, 1953).

Literary English of the Early Modern Period

N. F. Blake, *Shakespeare's English: An Introduction* (Macmillan, London, 1983).

S. S. Hussey, *The Literary Language of Shakespeare* (Longman, London, 1982).

C. T. Onions, enlarged and revised R. D. Eagleson, *A Shakespeare Glossary* (Clarendon Press, Oxford, 1986).

A. C. Partridge, *Tudor to Augustan English: A Study in Syntax and Style from Caxton to Johnson* (André Deutsch, London, 1969).

Gert Ronberg, *A Way with Words: The Language of English Renaissance Literature* (Edward Arnold, London, 1992).

W. W. Skeat and A. L. Mayhew, *A Glossary of Tudor and Stuart Words especially from the Dramatists* (Clarendon Press, Oxford, 1914).

General Histories of English which include the Early Modern Period

A. C. Baugh, *A History of the English Language*, 4th edn revised T. Cable (Routledge, London, 1993).

N. F. Blake, *A History of the English Language* (Macmillan, London, 1996).

Denis Freeborn, *From Old English to Standard English* (Macmillan, London, 1992).

Roger Lass, *The Shape of English: Structure and History* (Dent, London, 1987).

Dick Leith, *A Social History of English* (Routledge & Kegan Paul, London, 1983).

T. Pyles and J. Alegeo, *The Origins and Development of the English Language*, 3rd edn (Harcourt Brace Jovanovich, New York, 1982).

Barbara Strang, *A History of English*, 2nd revised edn (Methuen, London, 1972).

Martyn Wakelin, *The Archaeology of English* (Batsford, London, 1988).

Studies of Particular Aspects of English which include the Early Modern Period

N. F. Blake, *Non-standard Language in English Literature*, André Deutsch, London, 1981).

David Denison, *English Historical Syntax: Verbal Constructions* (Longman, London, 1993).

Geoffrey Hughes, *Swearing: A Social History of Foul Language, Oaths and Profanity in English* (Blackwell, Oxford, 1991).

Charles Jones, *A History of English Phonology* (Longman, London, 1989).

Charles Jones (ed.), *The Edinburgh History of the Scots Language* (Edinburgh University Press, Edinburgh, 1997), Part I: The Beginnings to 1700.

Suzanne Romaine, *Socio-Historical Linguistics* (Cambridge University Press, Cambridge, 1964).

Suzanne Romaine, *Language in Society: an introduction to sociolinguistics* (Oxford University Press, Oxford, 1994).

D. G. Scragg, *A history of English spelling* (Manchester University Press, Manchester, 1974).

Mary Serjeantson, *A History of Foreign Words in English* (Kegan Paul, London, 1935).

Grant G. Simpson, *Scottish Handwriting 1150–1650* (Aberdeen University Press, Aberdeen, 1986 reprint).

Peter Trudgill, *The Dialects of England* (Blackwell, Oxford, 1990).

Elizabeth Closs Traugott, *A History of English Syntax* (Holt, Rinehart & Winston, New York, 1970).

T. H. Visser, *An Historical Syntax of the English Language* (E. J. Brill, Leiden, 1963–73).

The Period 1500–1700

Some Books on Social-Historical Background

Madeleine Bingham, *Scotland under Mary Stuart: An Account of Everyday Life* (Allen & Unwin, London, 1971).

Carl Bridenbaugh, *Vexed and Troubled Englishmen 1590–1642* (Oxford University Press, London, 1968 (1976 paperback)).

F. G. Emmison, *Elizabethan Life: Home, Work & Land* (Essex Record Office Publication No. 69, Chelmsford, 1991).

Antonia Fraser, *The Weaker Vessel: Woman's Lot in Seventeenth-Century England* (Weidenfeld & Nicolson, London, 1984 and later paperback editions).

John Guy and John Morrill, *The Tudors and Stuarts*, Vol. III in Kenneth O. Morgan (ed.), *The Oxford History of Britain* (Oxford University Press, London, 1984 (revised text 1992)).

Rosemary O'Day, *The Longman Companion to The Tudor Age* (Longman, London, 1995).

Ralph Houlbrooke, *English Family Life 1576–1716* (Blackwell, Oxford, 1988).

Keith Wrightson, *English Society 1580–1680* (Unwin Hyman, London, 1982).

Joyce Youings, *Sixteenth-Century England* (Penguin: *The Pelican History of Britain*, London, 1984 and later reprints).

Reigns of Kings and Queens

England		Scotland	
1485–1509	Henry VII	1488–1513	James IV
1509–1547	Henry VIII	1513–1542	James V
1547–1553	Edward VI	1542–1567	Mary
1553–1558	Mary I	1567–1603	James VI
1558–1603	Elizabeth I		

Union of Crowns

1603–1625	James I (VI of Scotland)
1625–1649	Charles I
1649–1660	Commonwealth
1660–1685	Charles II
1685–1688	James II (VII of Scotland)
1689–1702	William III and Mary II

Editorial Policy

The Texts

The texts have been transcribed from manuscript. Since the aim of this collection of texts is to allow readers to deal for themselves with the interpretation of original texts, the transcription has been done with the minimum of editorial interference. Where there is doubt about a reading, this is noted in the Manuscript section of the Notes to that Text.

Some of the documents have never before been printed, others have been edited, mostly for the use of historians, and often a long time ago under the auspices of one of the many bodies which since the nineteenth century have dedicated themselves to making old records available, especially for the study of local history. The tradition of editing is to be meticulous, but since editors' principal interest has normally been the subject-matter, they have very rarely felt any obligation to retain those features of the language which make the texts, as they have seen it, unnecessarily tough for a modern reader, that is the virtual lack of punctuation and, in its absence, the uncertainty about where one sentence ends and another begins. Historical linguists investigating Early Modern English syntax and the perception of syntactic structure have consequently been unable to draw the data they need from such editions. Moreover in many cases, the freaky and difficult spellings that characterise so many of the texts have been eliminated. As recently as 1983, the editor of some sixteenth-century correspondence states as editorial policy:

> Abbreviations have been extended, and punctuation and spelling have been modernized throughout – this is particularly useful ... since she uses some very idiosyncratic, or phonetic forms.[1]

Just the kind of spellings which a historical linguist would wish to see, as possibly revealing the pronunciation of the writer. Silent expansion of abbreviations has also given spurious definition to many features, such as the expansion of the symbol signifying ambivalently 'there is a plural ending here which consists of vowel + *s*' to a firm Southern -*es* or Northern -*is*. The policy of the present edition is to allow readers to see for themselves. Also noted (see details below) are those places in the manuscripts where the writer has had a change of mind, deleting or correcting or adding to what was first written. In some texts these changes are of great interest.

The **characters** þ and ȝ are retained, and **u**, **v**, **i** and **j** transcribed as used in each text. The distinction between the two **allographs** of **s** and of **r** has not been retained in either case, but may be seen in the illustrations.

Capitals have been kept as in the manuscripts, with **ff** transcribed in this form, although it might be considered a way of writing capital F. None have been added.

Punctuation, including the now–obsolete oblique stroke /, has been kept as in each manuscript, and manuscript **paragraphing** has also been retained. None has been added. However, the style of **account-keeping** has been standardised.

Superscript short-forms have been retained as in the manuscript. **Abbreviations** have otherwise been expanded, but all letters supplied by the editor in the expansion of an abbreviation have been italicised.

Angled brackets indicate places where letters or words have been lost because of damage to a manuscript. Anything printed within such angled brackets is conjecturally supplied by the editor, as in **wa<s>**. Angled brackets also sometimes indicate a problem such as a space left in the manuscript or a totally illegible word; here the capitalised note within the brackets describes the problem, as in **<BLANK>** or **<ILLEGIBLE>**.

Curly brackets indicate letters or words written above the line as a correction or afterthought on the part of the writer. Thus **bro{a}d** and **to {soche} a lyke place**.

Letters or words crossed through indicate that they are deleted in the manuscript, but still legible, as in ~~that~~. Where a deleted word is replaced by a word inserted above the line, both are indicated, as in ~~taking~~ **{talking}**. Where the word deleted is rendered illegible, this is indicated by using ~~mmmm~~.

Square brackets indicate material which has been editorially added for information, nearly always the folio number, set at the start of the page, thus [f. 1v]. Where the date of a manuscript is given in square brackets, as in [1518], this is because the date is conjectural rather than set down in the document.

With the exception of initials used as marks, all **personal marks** used instead of signatures by people unable to write have been denoted by **X**, irrespective of the actual shape.

The Glossaries and Notes

A † **dagger** against a word indicates that the lexical item appears to have been in dialect rather than universal use. However, dialect forms and spellings have not been noted in this way.

The equals sign has been used where a familiar word needs glossing because its spelling makes it difficult to recognise, as in *fowlies* =foolish. Some such words also need further glossing, thus *marro* =morrow, next day.

Where reference is made to an entry in one of the dictionaries listed below, the lexical item is set in capitals, in the form under which it appears in that dictionary, thus *gissune* **childbed** (CSD **JIZZEN**).

Abbreviated titles for reference works:

OED: J. A. Simpson and E. S. C. Weiner (eds), *The Oxford English Dictionary*, 2nd edn (Clarendon Press, Oxford, 1989).

WRIGHT: Joseph Wright (ed.), *The English Dialect Dictionary* (Froude, London/ Oxford 1898–1905).

DOST: W. A. Craigie, A. J. Aitken and J. A. C. Stevenson (eds), *A Dictionary of the Older Scottish Tongue from the Twelfth Century to the end of the Seventeenth* (Oxford University Press, London and, later, Aberdeen University Press, Aberdeen, 1937–).

CSD: Mairi Robinson (ed.), *The Concise Scots Dictionary* (Aberdeen University Press, Aberdeen, and, later, Chambers, Edinburgh, 1985).

WEBSTER: Philip Babcock Gove (ed.), *Webster's Third New International Dictionary of the English Language* (Bell, London, 1961).

The Introductions

Where extracts from the texts in this collection are quoted, brackets and italics are edited out. Where extracts are quoted from material edited elsewhere, the text is presented as in that edition, even though in virtually all cases the editorial policy was different from that for this volume as set out above.

Note

1. Joan Thynne (ed.), *Two Elizabethan Women: Correspondence of Joan and Maria Thynne 1575– 1611*, Wiltshire Record Society, Vol. XXXVIII (1983), Introduction, p. xxxiv.

Abuse

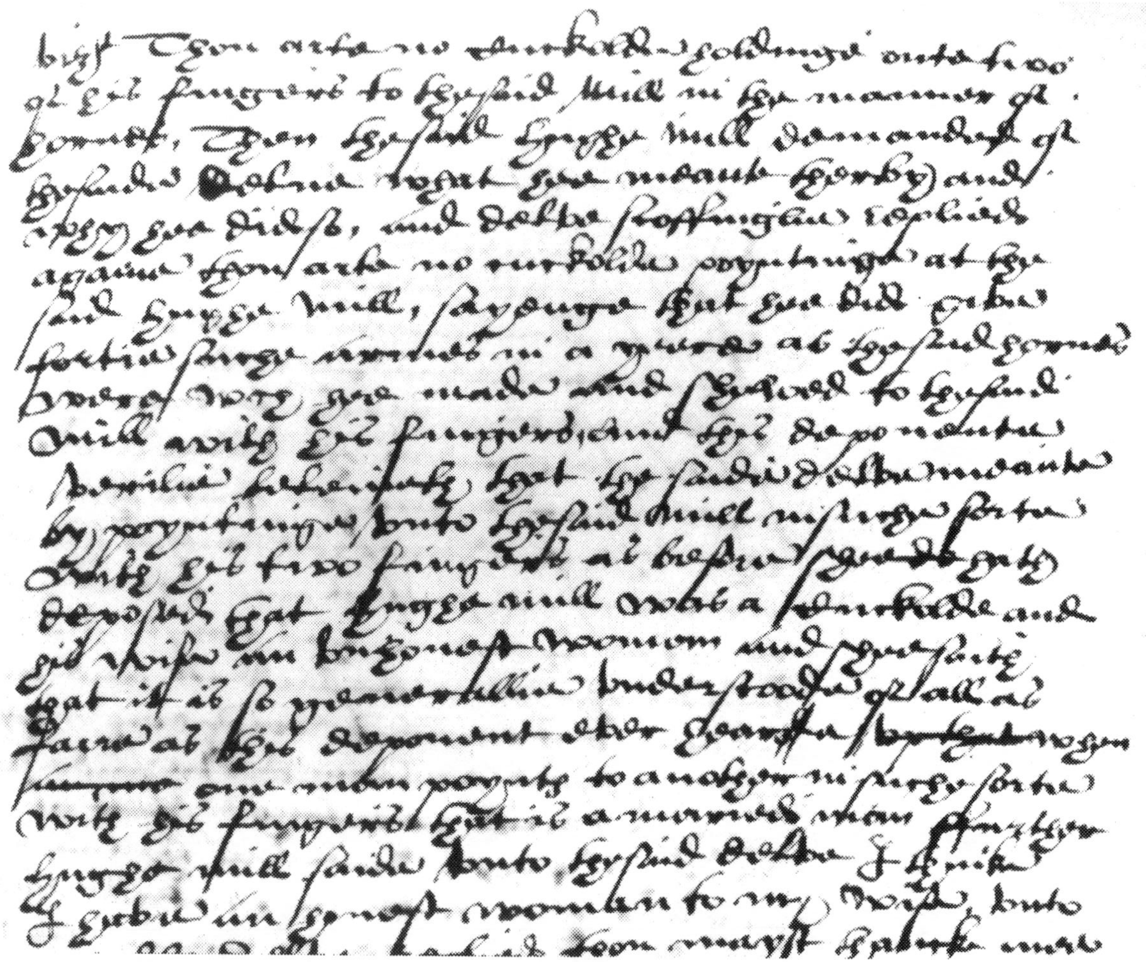

Plate I

Text 5A
William Delve: Devon 1615

Devon Record Office Manuscript Chanter 867 f. 129r
Edited text 5A/11–23

vi*delice*t Thou arte no Cuckolde holdinge oute two
of his fingers to thesaid Mill in the manner of
hornes, Then thesaid Hughe Mill demanded of
thesaide delue what hee meante therby and
5   why hee did so, and delve scoffinglie replied
againe thou arte no cuckolde poyntinge at the
said Hughe Mill, sayenge that hee did give
fortie suche armes in a yeare as thesaid hornes
were wch hee made and shewed to thesaid Mill
10   with his fingers, and this deponente
verilie belieueth that the saide delve meante
by poyntinge vnto thesaid Mill in suche sorte
with his two fingers as before shee ~~do~~ hath
deposed that Hughe mill was a Cuckolde and
15   his Wife an vnhonest woman and she saith
that it is so generallie vnderstoode of all as
farre as this deponent ever hearde ~~vp that~~ when
~~anyone~~ one man poynt*es* to another in suche sorte
with his fingers that is a married man ffurther
20   Hughe mill saide vnto thesaid delve I thinke
I have an honest woman to my wife, vnto

Allographs: Long and short forms of *s*: (5) *scoffinglie*, (14) *deposed*, (2) *his fingers*.
Characters *u* and *v* operating as allographs: (11) *beleiueth*, (12) *vnto*, but see also (7) *give*.
Capitals: Note different shape of capital in (1) *Cuckolde* compared with (6) *cuckolde*, but
size only criterion for deciding about (2) *Mill* and (14) *mill*; use of *ff* in (19) *ffurther*.
Abbreviations: (9) *w^ch*, (18) *poyntes*; extreme example in (1) *videlicet*.
Punctuation: Some use of commas, e.g. lines 3 and 5.
Alterations: Deletion in lines 17–18 with following text suggesting that the correction
to *when* is made at the time.
Problems of interpretation: Ambiguity of minims in (11) *meante*, (12) *in* and (15)
vnhonest resolved as *n* because of context. Is the *ch* in the short-form (9)*w^ch* really super-
script? Is the last character in (18) *poyntes* an *-es* abbreviation-symbol or a simple *-s*?

3

Introduction to Abuse

Documents recording verbal abuse set down in written form words alleged to have been spoken, for which the speaker is now being charged with defamation,[1] words *to discredite and disgrace* the complainant (5C/17), *obprobrious wordes* (1/8) or *vngodly speiking* (2F/5–6).

The specific abuse is always retailed via witnesses,

> And this shee knoweth to bee true because shee was present the tyme and place afor said and heard and sawe all the premisses (5B/30–31).

Whether or not defamation documents give us true records of what was said by the accused depends therefore on witnesses' truthfulness and also on their power of recall. Several of the texts included here are witnesses' statements presenting the recall problem very clearly. In Text 1 when a witness is asked whether or not he heard Warneford call Bridges a *croked nose knave* he thinks back to *almost twelmoneth ago* and remembers hearing the abusive words *shyte vpon his Croked nose*. When asked whether the accused said he would *sett the sayd Sr Iohn Bridges by the heles*, i.e. hang him, the same witness agrees that he heard him say *he wold one day shake a halter* at him. In Text 5C the careful Vicar elaborates his evidence with convoluted attempts to offer the best his memory can produce. He says that the words spoken were,

> I have heard somme saye, that thou art a bastard, or I have heard saye that thou art a bastard, or somme saye, thou art a bastard: but w[ch] of these particular wordes the said Adrian Sweete then and there vttered, he this deponent doth not otherwise remember, but he sayth, that he is certayne That the said Sweete sayde vnto Poweninge aforesaid these wordes, with somme of the former, or of the same meaneinge: thou art a bastard.

It is scarcely surprising that many 'quotations' end with the escape-clause *or wordes to the like effect* (8/21).

Contemporary recognition was given to the fact that what someone said might be wrongly interpreted out of context. In 1590 a lawyer[2] pointed out that a man might call another a robber, a cut-throat or a murderer without any serious malicious intent to slander him, because he meant, in context, that he had 'robbed' him at the card table, taken 'cut-throat' interest on a loan or 'murdered' partridges.

Other arguments might centre around precise wording and its significance. In 1541 Sir Thomas Wyatt was accused of having spoken treasonable words about Henry VIII,

4

that same wiatt being allso Imbassadore maliciously falcely and traytoursly saide y[t] he feryd that the kinge shulde be cast owte of A Cartes arse and that by goddis bloude yf he were so he were well served and he wolde he were so.

In his own defence Wyatt argues,

> yt is a smale thynge in alteringe of one syllable ether with penne or worde y[t] may mayk in the conceavinge of the truthe myche matter or error/ for in thys thynge I fere or I truste semethe but one smale syllable chaynged and yet yt makethe agreat dyfferaunce, and may be of an herer wronge conceaved and worse reported and yet worste of all altered by an examyner/ Agayne fall owte, caste owte, or lefte owte makethe dyfferaunce, yea and the settinge of the wordes one in an others place may mayke greate dyfferaunce tho the wordes were all one/ As a myll horse and a horse myll,

and he claims that his actual, non-treasonable, words which have been either mistaken or, more likely, misrepresented were,

> he is lefte owte of the cartes ars and by goddys bloude he is well served and I am glad of yt.

Even his supposed oath *by goddis bloude* was maliciously added,

> by cawse I am wonte some tyme to rappe owte an othe in an erneste tawlke looke how craftylie theie have put in an othe to the matter to mayke the matter seme myne.[3]

Although in the texts collected here the men and women whose alleged words are in question did not have the resources to defend themselves in this style, sometimes the texts, such as 2B and 2C, record their attempts to deny outrageous language by admitting minor verbal indiscretions.

It is principally in abuse documents that we find vocabulary intended to be offensive. It is usually immediately clear why the words have been considered opprobrious. In 1614 a case was brought against a woman who was offered some rushes from a field belonging to neighbours and who refused,

> sayeing That she would have none of the Cuckholdlye knavs rushes, (meaneing the articulate Richard Howe) neither of the balde arsse whores, (meaneing the articulate Clement Howe the wife of the said Richard Howe) ... w[ch] wordes were very slaunderous.[4]

But some simple terms, where the insult is not so apparent to a modern reader, were evidently as likely to cause a scene, as in the riposte *If thou call me knave Ile call thee whore* (5B/8–9). Particularly rich lexical stores can be exploited where historical and geographical accident made a wider vocabulary available, producing phrases such as *noughtie pak* (3H/3), *fals smayk* (2E/5), *skabbit Lowne* (7/4) or *grandgorie Lipper swonjour* (7/20. As well as actual insults, lexical items which appear peripherally may also show colloquial local usage. Thus Northern speech is recorded as employing *lasse* (3F/3 and 4/21) while a South-western speaker has *wench* (6F/6). Also Northern are *steg* 'gander' (3H/4) and *yawd* 'mare' (3I/9), while in Scots we find items such as *harnes* 'brains' (2B/1), *thyg* 'beg' (2E/4) and *luggis* 'ears' (2E/5). Further colloquialisms appear to be

non-regional, such as *long of* (8/8), *nay mayry* (3H/5) and *Sirra* (5B/7).
   Spoken grammar is also on record here, both syntax,

> hast minde (5B/26)
> yea that he was (6F/5)
> a mans wife of our towne (6F/6),

and morphology,

> the King is a coming now (8/20)
> she would haue holpe (8/28),

and sometimes forces a modern reader to rethink ideas of what is informal/informal, such as the question framed without *do*-support in *call thou me goose steiler* (3H/5) or the subjunctive recorded in *if thou call me knave* (5B/8).
   In the majority of these texts the prominent morphological material is the evidence on second person forms. Of particular interest is the selection of *thou* to be more insulting, especially when the abuse is directed to someone normally addressed with a polite *you*, as when William Morton

> oppinlie in ye public essemble manest boistit and Iniurit the said minister in ye pulpot saying thir wordis following or siclyik in effect My brothir is and salbe vicar of crayll quhen thow sal thyg thy mayt fals smayk I sall pul ye owt off ye pulpot be the luggis and chais ye owt of yis town (2E/2–6).

Furthermore, when *you* forms are employed, these records show to what extent the distinctive subject-form *ye* was still used. The second-person singular verb forms associated with the *thou* pronoun, both in present and in past tenses, are also well illustrated, often showing how colloquial speakers handled cumbersome preterites, producing reduced forms such as in *thou … wentes to leache* (5A/26–7).
   Phonological detail is occasionally noted, where the clerk puts on record what he heard, writing down, for example, the Durham pronunciation of 'woe is me' as *waies me* (3F/3).
   The settings from which these documents come are important. The commonest frame in England is that of the Church Court,[5] dealing with immorality rather than crime, and presided over by the local Archdeacon or his appointee. Texts 3, 4, 5 and 6 are all from Church Courts, the manuscripts having been preserved among the records of the relevant Diocese. The definition of defamation demanded that the speaker had in a public place and in the presence of others accused someone of immoral behaviour, thus depriving him or her of his or her good name.
   This had spin-off on the structure of witnesses' statements, producing sentences which are introduced by subordinate constructions detailing the when and where of the alleged incident. Sometimes these are relatively simple,

> about the ende of Maye Last past he this deponent goeinge along of the streete in Tottnes Towne towardes the bridge of Tottnes articulate (5B/3–5)

but they can extend,

on a workday about a fourtnyghte before or after may day last, about one or two of the clocke in the after noone, ... this parte comynge into the hous of one peter dighton in northgate in wakefield and beinge an alehous wher he had bene in the mornynge of the same day (4/4–9).

Moreover, for the present-day sociolinguist the picture drawn usually gives an interesting context of situation for the reported abusive or defamatory words, providing clues as to the relationship between situation and choice of language, as when (6E) the case against George Bailey is based on his spreading the story of what he claims to have been told by Sloccombe as they relieved themselves in the backyard of the local alehouse.

So many cases of defamatory verbal abuse were handled by Church Courts that much of the paperwork generated by each case was organised by the use of standard documents with a set pro-forma framework, in Latin, prepared in advance with blanks left at appropriate places into which the details of the particular case could be entered. Texts 3 and 6 are of this type; in each case the names of the defendant and the complainant and the English words alleged to have been used are entered on an identically-worded Latin document, used to set out a summary of the case in advance. The detailed depositions of witnesses will be forthcoming later, and here only the abuse itself is on record. It is noticeable that these formal summaries give the alleged defamatory words in both second and third person form, it being more important to make sure the charge sticks than to specify whether Agnes Ellis said to Christiana Brooke *thou art a whore* or whether, in mentioning her to someone else, she said *she is a whore*, for both are equally actionable.

In Scotland it was the local Kirk Session which heard cases concerning verbal abuse. Texts 2 and 7 are from Kirk Session records, minuting instances of people reproved for their language, and occasionally describing the penalty prescribed by the Elders and Brethren who made up the Session,

> Thairfor yᵉ sessioun ordanis him to cum publicle vpon sonday nixttocum and mak humiliacioun for ye said wikked and vngodly speiking (2F/4–6).

Often a more precise description is given, instructing the guilty party to stand at church, wearing a white sheet and carrying a candle, and publicly to take back his or her wicked words. While a few refused and others had the penalty commuted to a fine, many conformed.

Settlers in the New World took with them from England both the habit of verbal abuse and the mechanism, transferred to secular courts, of complaint about defamation,

> the said Turner, since the beginning of June last, hath reported and said that the said Charles Stockbridge is a cocally rogue, and that Abigaill, his wife, is as very a strumpett as any in New England, and that the said Abigaill is a brasen faced whore, and that her husband is a coccally raskall ... The jury found for the plaintiffe one hundred pounds damage, and the cost of the suite.[6]

It is doubtful whether the enormous damages awarded were actually paid.

In Text 8 an abusive fishwife is brought before the secular court at the local Quarter

Sessions. This may be because as the seventeenth century proceeded, and especially in the Commonwealth period where this text falls, the boundaries of Church and State business become confused but it is also because the abuse of which she is accused centres round political rather than personal vituperation, and that, evidently, her calling her neighbour a *roundheaded rogue* has provoked a serious and dangerous disturbance in the town, especially since she added

> many other reviling words whereby a great tumult was raised in the said towne insomuch that this Informant was constrained to take a Marsh forke from a Marshman to defend himselfe from hurt & violence, wch. was like to bee offered to this Informant by reason of the said vproare and tumult.

Where fisticuffs, or worse, were the eventual outcome of verbal abuse, and if the parties were of higher social status and greater wealth, the case might end up by an appeal by the aggrieved party being made at national rather than local level, to the Court of Star Chamber, where the case would be laid before the King and Privy Council. This is the setting of Text 1, where the complainant and the accused are both Yorkshire gentry.

Whatever the type and level of the Court where abuse cases were heard, the records that have come down to us have always come via the clerk who set down the case. Tension between spoken language and the written form used by the clerk sometimes produces a very clear contrast, as where the clerk soberly and wordily spells out the import of the simple obscenities which he has just recorded,

> this pricke hath fuckt Ioan Pecke many tymes (meaning thereby that the said Iohn Slocombe was and is a man of dishonest life and Conversacion and that he had the carnal knowlege of the bodie of the said Ioane Pecke (6E/4–7).

In this instance we can discern where the clerk's language begins. Deciding in most other cases is more problematic. How far did clerks write down the spoken language just as they heard it?[7] For example, in one South-western text we have on record the two second-singular preterite forms *vntrust* (5A/26) and *wentes* (5A/27). These spellings tell us something important about the popular rendering of the awkward forms which formal usage of the period would employ here, that is *untrussedest* and *wentest*. Then in another text from the same area, we have a parallel form recorded as *heldest* (6D/3). Is this because this speaker was more careful, or because *heldest* is less difficult to say than *wentest*, so that it was not colloquially shortened, or is the inflexion supplied by the clerk from his knowledge of good usage, irrespective of what he heard spoken?

In many cases, the clerk does not aim to present the spoken language directly, but feels that it is appropriate to turn it into indirect speech. Accordingly, third-person forms are used,

> Super primo et secundo articulis dicit that for his owne parte he takethe W^m hobson articulate to be an honest man of good and honest Lyefe and conuersacion/ And so hathe he harde him accompted and taken amonges his neighboures (4/1–4),

and past tenses are also introduced where direct speech undoubtedly used present tenses, [she said] that Ianet his wyff was apoky & noughtie drab (3A/2–3).

However, there appears to be ample evidence that clerks felt obliged to retain wording and phrasing. This happens not only where the words are important because they form the accusation of abusive slander, as in phrases such as *he doth keepe thee ... as common as the high waie* (6C/3–4) or *she was euer kend for nought all the daies of hir lyff* (3E/2–3), but also where the idioms are from witnesses, as with *in ye fore end of the harvest* (3I/2). An interesting instance of total dedication to recording the precise words uttered occurs where a witness begins to use one phrase, but changes his mind, and the clerk is careful to change his record accordingly,

> deponit et dicit That ~~in~~ {vppon one of} the ~~Christmas holy~~ twelve days in the feast of Christmas Last past (5C/4–5).

Two further factors interact with the spoken words on record here. Firstly, the clerk was bound to certain extent by agreed conventions as to how his record should be phrased, the pattern often being based on the established Latin formula traditionally employed for the same purpose. It is no accident that in Text 1B the highly trained Star Chamber clerk introduces one witness with the formulaic style,

> Roger wikes of Ashebury in the Countie of bark gent of thaige of L^ti yeres or ther aboutes sworne and examined the day and yere aboue writton deposith and sayeth to the first article (1B/4–6)

and then employs exactly the same phrasing for the introduction of the next witness (1B/26–8).

Secondly, there is an interesting relationship between the clerk's own language and the language he is putting on record in that many texts show that the clerk shares the same local dialect which the complainant, accused and witnesses all use. This is particularly evident in the Scots texts. To what extent the clerk's spoken language was dialect modified by upbringing, education or travel is less clear, and to what extent he is in the position of speaking dialect but writing a less regional variety is also debatable, but often we can identify occasions when his local ear picks up small points. One such can be identified from the accounts of two cases, one in Durham and the other in Devon, in which witnesses use the same euphemism for sexual relations. While the South-western clerk records what he hears as *I might have had to doe with her if I wolde* (5A/24–5), the Northern clerk records local *at do* for Southern *to do* in the phrase *he ... had had ado wth hir, & might when he wold* (3C/2–3).

Notes

1. There are extremely helpful discussions of defamation, in Martin Ingram, *Church Courts, Sex and Marriage in England, 1570–1640* (Cambridge University Press, Cambridge, 1987), Chapter 10 'Sexual Slander' (pp. 292–319), and in J. A. Sharpe, *Defamation and Sexual Slander in Early Modern England: The Church Courts at York*, Borthwick Papers No. 58 (Borthwick Institute of Historical Research, University of York, 1980).

2. Quoted in R. H. Helmholz, *Select Cases on Defamation to 1600*, Selden Society 101, 1985, p. 81.

3. British Library MS Harley 78, f. 7v and 10r and v. For full text see Kenneth Muir (ed.), *Life and Letters of Sir Thomas Wyatt* (Liverpool University Press, Liverpool, 1963), pp. 187–208.

4. Case of *Howe* v. *Fathers*, 1614. Devon Record Office manuscript Chanter 867 f. 101r (Consistory Court records from Diocese of Exeter).

5. For details of procedures see Anne Tarver, *Church Court Records: An Introduction for Family and Local Historians* (Phillimore, Chichester, 1995), Chapter 6 'Defamation', pp. 113–124.

6. Case brought in October 1669; Nathaniel B. Shurtleff (ed.), *Records of the Colony of New Plymouth in New England; Judicial Acts 1636–1692* (White, Boston, 1857 and reprint, AMS Press, New York, 1968).

7. For a much fuller discussion of this matter, see Introduction to Depositions pp. 92–98 below.

Text 1

John Warneford: Wiltshire 1555
(Public Record Office Manuscript STAC 3/4/9)

Text A: Questions put to witnesses

[f. 19r] Item whether you euer hard the sayd warneford saye that he wolde sett the sayd Sr Iohn Bridg*es* by the heles./

Item whether youe euer hard the sayd warneford saye, the sayd Sr Iohn was a croked nosed Knave or a vylleyn knave, or any other raylynge word*es*./

5 It whether youe euer hard the sayd warneford say that the sayd Sr Iohn was a very cowarde, or that he was so pr*o*uyd at Bullaigne/ And a keper or maynteyner of thef*fes* or and that he was a theff hymself/

Item whether you hard the sayd warneford speake eny other lyke obprobrious word*es* of the sayd Syr Iohn, and what suche word*es* wer, where & when they 10 were spoken, and what nomber of p*er*sons were by./

Text B: Replies

[f. 27r] Witnessis on the p*art* and bihalf of Sir Iohn Abridges Knight agenst Iohn warneford gent swo*r*ne and examined the xxviijth of Octob*er* Anno MCd vj^{ti} quinto

Roger wikes of Ashebury in the Countie of bark gent of thaige of L^{ti} yeres or 5 ther about*es* swo*r*ne and examined the day and yere abou*e* writton deposith and sayeth to the first article/ ~~he~~ That he neuer hard the said warneford speke or say eny suche word*es*/ ne yet {any} other wo*r*des sounding to eny suche intent/

To the ij^d he sayeth he hard not the said warneford speke eny suche word*es*/ but ~~sath~~ sayeth that almost twelmoneth ago he ~~y~~ hard the said warneford saye to 10 Thom*a*s Stevyns and to this depo*n*ent ~~taking~~ {talking} then of Sr Iohn abridges/ Mary said the said warneford shyte vpon his Croked noose/. At wich tyme the said warneford Rayled vngoodly vppon the said Sr Iohn calling hym knave And that he wold one daye shake a halter at the father and the [f. 27v] Soone/ meanyng Sr Iohn abridges & his soo<ne>

11

15   To the iij^d he sayeth that he never herd the said warneford say or report that s*ir* Iohn Abridges shuld be a cowardly Knave & that he was so pr*o*ved at ~~Bulloyng~~ Bullaign/ or that he was a thieff/ But reme*m*berith well/ that at Seuyngton about a twell monyth ago he hard the said warneford saye in his howse in the pr*e*sence of this depo*n*ent and ~~one~~ Thom*a*s Stevens thelde<r> & Thomas

20   Stevyns the young*er* th<at> in his conscience Sr Iohn abridges wa<s> accessory to his soones s*er*u*au*nt*es* that were arrayed of felony/

To the Last he sayeth he hath not herd ~~S~~ the said warneford speke eny other opprobrius word*es* or Rayling word*es* of the said Sr Iohn Abridges more then he hath now declared vppon this his examinac*i*on to his now reme*m*braunce/

25   Roger wykky*es*

[f. 28r] Thom*a*s Stevyns of Chisilden in the Countie of wilts gent of thaige of xxv yeres or ther aboute*s* swo*r*ne and examined the daye and yere aboue w*r*iton deposith and sayeth to the first article

That he hard the said warneford saye that if he had a iust cause he durst set the

30   said s*ir* Iohn Abridges by the heles/ and wold do it/ wiche word*es* this depo*n*ent hath hard hym speke about halff yere ago he being in his howse at Sevington/ otherwise he Denyeth this Article/~~That~~

To the ij^d he confessith that he hath herd the said warneford speke dyu*er*s tymes many Rayling word*es* of the said Sr Iohn/ and that ~~th~~ he was a croked nose

35   Knave/ and shite vppon his Croked nose/

To the iij^d he sayeth he doth not reme*m*ber that eu*er* he hard the same warneford spek eny such word*es* or eny such like as be mencioned in this article/ but this depo*n*ent doth reme*m*ber that he hard the same warneford ~~said~~ saye of s*ir* Iohn Abridges that he thought in his constiens that the same s*ir* Iohn ~~was~~ did

40   su*m*what Lene w^t ~~the~~ {his soones} s*er*u*au*nt*es* that ware arreyned of felony/

[f. 28v] To the Last he sayeth that he dyu*er*s and soundrey tymes being in company w^t the said warneford hathe hard hym speke dyu*er*s evill & opprobrius word*es* of the said s*ir* Iohn/ Rayling also ~~o~~ vppon hym/ And that trusted one day to shake a halter to hym/ wiche he spake ~~in his house~~ about a twell moneth

45   a<go> in his howse in the pr*e*sence of dyu*er*s p*er*sones/ whois names he doth not now reme*m*ber/ And sayeth the same warneford is a gret Raylor vppon the said s*ir* Iohn/ for the wiche this depo*n*ent hath ben dyu*er*s tymes sory and yet is And more at this tyme he doth not Reme*m*ber

Thomas stepynse

Notes

Text

From the records of the Court of Star Chamber. The Papers relating to this case, of which a selection is presented here, are edited in F. E. Warneford (ed.), *Star Chamber Suits of John and Thomas Warneford*, Wiltshire Record Society, Vol. XLVIII, 1993.

Manuscript

The gaps in the manuscript, conjecturally filled, are where letters at the right-hand end of lines on verso pages are impossible to see because of tight binding.

Some of the writer's corrections of his first spellings are of interest: (B11) *sath* changed to *sayeth*, (B16) *Bulloyng* changed to *Bullaign*.

In (B21) *arrayed* appears to be an error, in view of (B40) *arreyned*; but the confusion might be either the witness's or the clerk's.

In some instances word-initial *w* is largish, and could be argued to be a capital. However the large letter is not confined to proper names, and also appears medially in (B18) *twell monyth*, so it has been treated as lower-case.

Note that most endings in *es* are derived by expansion of abbreviation, on the pattern of full forms such as (B4) *yeres*.

Although the letters *c* and *t* are often confusable at this date, *constiens* (B39) appears to be spelled with *st* rather than *sc*. It could, however, be argued to be *conshens*.

Glossary

(A1)	*Item* (shortened to *It* in l. 5)	Word inserted to mark beginning of new member of a list
(A1–2)	*sett … by the heles*	put in the stocks
(A4)	*vylleyn*	criminal
(A4)	*raylynge*	abusive
(A6)	*very*	utter
(A10)	*by*	present
(B2)	*examined*	questioned
(B7)	*sounding to*	suggesting
(B9)	*twelmoneth*	a year
(B11)	*Mary*	Exclamation of indignation (see note)
(B12)	*vngoodly*	roughly
(B13)	*halter*	hangman's noose
(B20)	*in his conscience*	in his honest opinion
(B28)	*article*	numbered question put to witness
(B40)	*sumwhat*	to some extent
(B40)	*Lene w¹*	?sympathise with (OED LEAN does not have this phrase)
(B40)	*arreyned* (and (B21) *arrayed*)	=arraigned, accused

Place names

(A6)	*Bullaigne*	Boulogne

Explanatory notes

(A6) *Bullaigne*: Boulogne was besieged by English troops in 1544, and held, though under pressure from France, until 1550. Sir John a Bridges was Deputy-Governor.

(B11) *Mary*: Probably at this date, and as the spelling here suggests, an exclamation based on *St Mary*, though later the etymology was lost and the word became *Marry*.

Background

John Warneford bought from Lord Thomas Seymour, to whom he was Steward, the lordship of Sevenhampton in Wiltshire near the Berkshire border, together with part of the manor. The remainder was bought by Sir John a Bridges, a man of higher rank and greater power. The two men and their households were in constant conflict, especially over territorial rights, and each considered that the other was maintaining a vendetta against him. Warneford brought a case against Bridges in the Star Chamber for harass-ment of all kinds, and Bridges counterclaimed that he was the one harassed. Among other things, Bridges alleged that Warneford had many times uttered abusive language concerning him. These witnesses, both gentlemen and able to sign their own names to their depositions, are replying to interrogatories based on what Bridges alleges Warneford has been saying about him. The reports reflect the care that was taken in a court of this level to establish whether or not the accusation of defamation was true and what exactly had been said by questioning different people about what they remembered having heard.

Topics for linguistic investigation

1. Variant spellings and the information they yield.
2. How we can tell what parts of speech the following are: (A4) *vylleyn*, (A6) *very*, (A10) *by*, (B11) *shyte*, (B13) *vngoodly*, (B24) *now*, (B30) *wiche*, (B40) *sumwhat*, (B41) *Last*.
3. The use of *do*-support.
4. The semantic history of *knave* and *villain*.

Text 2

Margaret Murdo and others: St Andrews, Scotland 1560–61 and 1593

(St Andrews University Library Manuscript CH2/31/6/1)

Text A (26 April 1560)

[f. 11r] Margaret murdow delatate for Blasphemous saying*es* aganist the Sacrament of the body and Blude of christ sayand thir wordes in the oppin fische mercat ȝe gif ȝo^r Supper quhome to ȝe pleas I traist to god ȝe salbe fayne to Steale fra that Supper and dennar or this day tolmonth.

Text B (2 May 1560)

[f. 11r] Iohne Law Said the divell knok owt Iohne knox harnes for quhen he wald se him hanget he wald gett his Sacrament. Iohne Law grant*tes* that he said god give knox be hanget?

Text C (2 May 1560)

[f. 11r] Williame petillok dwelland be este thomas martynes Said the divell ane kirk will I gang to and the devill burn up the kirk or I come In to It. and It wer gude that knox war kend the gayt quhare fra he come. williame granttes thir wordes the divell cayre the kirk.

Text D (16 July 1561)

[f. 24r] thai called vpon ye sayd m^r alex*ander* as p*ar*son yarof desyring hy*m* to co*n*cur w^t thame according to ye admonicion mayd by ye sup*er*inte*n*dent m^r alex*ander* ansuerit and sayd he wald do na thing in yat behalue nor obey ony admonision or com*m*and of that fals dissaitfull gredy & dissimblit smayk for he wes ane of tham that maist oppressed smored & held down ye word of god and now he is cu*m*in to it and profess*es* ye same for grediness of gayr lwrkand & watchand q^{ll} he maye se ane other tym and farther ekit & sayd befoyr ye sam p*er*son*n*is abowe wrytty*n* or I war not rewe*n*ged of that fals smaik I had lewer renu*n*c my p*ar*t of ye kyrk of god

5

15

Text E (8 October 1561)

[f. 28v] And albeid he maid his protestacion that na man suld be offended therby
Newertheles wylia*m* mortoun of cambo oppinlie in ye public essemble manest
boistit and Iniurit the said minister in ye pulpot saying thir wordis following or
siclyik in effect My brothir is and salbe vicar of crayll quhen thow sal thyg thy
5   mayt fals smayk I sall pul ye owt off ye pulpot be the luggis and chais ye owt of
yis town

Text F (6 March 1593)

[f. 239v] The qlk day Ihone downy messinger being accusit for speking publicle
vpon y*ᵉ* hi*ᵉ* calsy to M*ʳ* robert 3uill techear in yis co*n*grega*cioun* on reuere*n*tle
thir word*is* saying y*ᵗ* he suld swyffe in dispyte of y*ᵉ* mi*n*ister quhen he plesit and
speir na tyding*is* at ye mi*n*ister Thairfor y*ᵉ* sessio*u*n ordanis him to cu*m* publicle
5   vpon sonday nixttocu*m* and mak humili*acioun* for ye said wikked and vngodly
speiki*n*g

Notes

Text

From the Records of the Kirk Session of St Andrews, Scotland. The text has been
edited by David Hay Fleming (ed.), *St Andrews Kirk Session Register 1559–1600* (2 vols,
Part I: 1559–1582, Part II: 1582–1600), Scottish History Society, Vols 4 and 7, 1889 and
1890.

Manuscript

Final *n* has a lengthened right stroke, which has been taken as empty, in (C2) *burn*, (D2)
admonicion, (D5) *down*, (E6) *town*.

The writer sometimes adds a flourish to final *s*. This too has been taken as empty,
although it could be argued that it represents *ss*. Thus (A1) *Blasphemous*, (A3) *pleas*, (D5)
wes, (E5) *fals*, (E5) *chais*.

The question-mark at the end of Text B could be an elaborate colon, and does not
mark a question; but at this period exclamations are similarly marked.

In (A1) *aganist* the three minim strokes could be read to give *against*.

Text F, thirty years later than the others, is in a very different hand. It favours
abbreviations, and uses 3 in its capital form. In (F3) *quhen*, the final letter might be read
as *r*, but 'where' is more usually spelled *quhair*.

Glossary

(A1)	*delatate* †	denounced
(A3)	*fayne*	glad
(A4)	*this day tolmonth*	a year from today
(B1)	*harnes* †	brains

(C2)	*gang* †	go
(C2)	*or* †	before
(C3)	*kend* †	shown the way to
(C3)	*gayt* †	road
(D2)	*concur*	co-operate
(D3)	*in yat behalue*	in regard to that
(D4)	*dissimblit* †	deceitful
(D4)	*smayk* †	rogue
(D5)	*smored* †	smothered
(D6)	*gayr* †	money
(D7)	*q^{ll}* †	(for *quhill*) until
(D7)	*ekit* †	added
(D8)	*had lewer*	had rather
(E1)	*albeid*	although
(E2)	*essemble*	assembly, congregation
(E2)	*manest*	=menaced
(E3)	*boistit*	threatened
(E4)	*thyg* †	beg
(E5)	*mayt*	food
(E5)	*luggis* †	ears
(F1)	*messinger*	=messenger, carrier of official documents
(F2)	*calsy* †	paved street
(F3)	*swyffe*	have sex
(F3)	*in despyte of*	in defiance of
(F4)	*speir* †	ask
(F4)	*tydingis*	permission (OED only in sense 'news')
(F4)	*sessioun* †	Kirk Session, Committee of minister and elders
(F4)	*ordanis*	decrees
(F5)	*nixttocum* †	=next-to-come, next
(F5)	*humiliacioun*	an act of self-abasement

Topics for linguistic investigation

1. A comparison between the Scots spellings and the way Southern English texts of the same date spell the words (A2) *Blude*, (A3) *fische*, (B1) *quhen*, (C3) *war*, (D8) *abowe*, (E3) *boistit*, (E5) *be*, (F2) *calsy*, (F4) *sessioun*.
2. The Southern English equivalents of: (A2) *thir*, (A3) *mercat*, (C1) *dwelland*, (C2) *kirk*, (C3) *quhare fra*, (E4) *siclyik*, (E4) *sal*, (F3) *swyffe*.
3. The inflexions used for various forms of verbs, including auxiliary verbs.
4. The extent to which different source-languages provide the words used in colloquial and in more formal Scots as on record here.
5. A survey of some Northern English texts to find non-Southern linguistic features shared with these Scots extracts.

Text 3

Margaret Dawson and others: Durham 1570
(Durham University Library Archives and Special Collections Manuscript
Durham Diocesan Records Volumes V/2 and VII/2)

Text A

[Vol. Book VII/2 f. 97v] gilbertus ~~gilling~~ gyllesse con*tra* margaret dawson vx*or*
georgij in c*aus*a diffamac*ionis* vi*delicet* that Ianet his wyff was apoky & noughtie
drab/

Text B

[Vol. VII/2 f. 100r] Elizabeth Robson con*tra* Isabell ~~agnet~~ knops in c*aus*a
diffamac*ionis* vi*delicet* that she is a hoore & a harlott/

Text C

[Vol. VII/2 f. 102r] Ienett dalton con*tra* Robertu sairgan in c*aus*a diffa*macion*is
vi*delicet* {he said} that he the said Rob*er*t had had ado wth hir, & might when he
wold & A hore to ride of ye one syd of ye cart & he ye other

Text D

[Vol. VII/2 f. 104r] margar*et* atkinson con*tra* agnet bylle vx*or* Robert in c*aus*a
diffamac*ionis* That she was an harron hoor & badd hir goo follow ye flennem*m*es
& marinall*es* as she had don

Text E

[Vol. VII/2 f. 105r] m*ar*garet dawson vx*or* georgii con*tra* ~~y~~ Ianet gyllis vx*or*
gilb*er*ti in c*aus*a diffamac*ionis*/ vi*delicet* that she was abarrell drome/ & y^t she
was eu*er* kend fo^r nought all the daies of hir lyff

Text F

[Vol. VII/2 f. 122v] Margaria nicolson singlewoma*n* con*tra* agnete blenkinsop
vx*or* Robert in c*aus*a diffamac*ionis* vi*delicet* hyte hoore a whipe and a ~~era~~ cart/

18

& a franc hoode/ waies me foᵣ yᵉ my lasse wenst haue a halpeny halter foᵣ yᵉ to goo vp gallygait & be hanged/

Text G

[Vol. VII/2 f. 132r] Iohannes highton Smith con*tra* y̶ georgii ffenwick gei*ger* in *causa* diffa*macionis* vi*delicet* That he was amainsvorn*n*e man & yᵗ he wold so pr*o*ve h*y*m

Text H

[Vol. V/2 f. 79v] Agnes ~~wheitle~~ wheitly vx*or* Robt ... dicit yᵗ as yis ex*aminate* was comy*n*g foreth ~~whi~~ wᵗʰ hir skeill she hard bullma*n* wyffe call styllynge noughtie pak/ who answerd what nowtynes know yᵉ by me/ I am neyth*er* goossteler noᵣ ~~stek~~ steg steiler I wold yoᵘ knew ytt/ and *yen* bullma*n* wyff said
5   what noughty hoore call thou me ~~nowghtie~~ goose steiler/ nay mayry I know the foᵣ no such saith stillinge wyff but I thank yᵒ foᵣ yoᵣ good reporte whill*es* yᵘ & I talk further/

Text I

[Vol. V/2 f. 125v] George Colson de gillygatt Tayler etat*is* xvij ano*rum* ... saith That i*n* y*e* fore end of harvest Isabell Robson was fettinge a cruse of drink out of y*e* aile house and one of ~~hus~~ hudspeith sones said to hir that she wold be a pretty rop*er*s wyffe/ and she answered & said yt she dyd not passe yf all ropers
5   wer hanged and the said Raiff being i*n* his fathers loft boune to bedd hering thois word*es* pra*i*ed yᵗ bett*er* might be yᵣ happ then hanging/ and said yf they had ben hanged that tok one yawd i*n* wethe of their own/ they had not ben sytting wher they were syttinge at y*e* tyme ex*amined* whither wilson named y*e* said Robson at yᵗ tyme or at any others to be a yawd steiller ye or no r*espon*dit
10   negative/

Notes

Text

From the records of the Consistory Court of the Diocese of Durham. More extracts from the volumes from which these brief extracts are taken are edited in James Raine (ed.), *Depositions and other Ecclesiastical Proceedings from the Courts of Durham*, Surtees Society, Vol. 21, 1845.

Manuscript

The records of these defamation cases are in Latin, but the words which the accused person is alleged to have uttered are written in English.

The Latin text, being almost entirely formulaic, is usually highly abbreviated. The English material uses a few common abbreviations, and in Text I employs a less usual *y* with horizontal stroke over it to represent the definite article which in the other texts is written *y*ᵉ or *the*.

The surname of the accused woman in Text D is written *Byllye* in other cases in this manuscript.

Glossary

(A2)	*poky*	infected with the pox
(A2)	*noughtie*	wicked
(A3)	*drab*	slut
(C2)	*had ado with*	had to do with, had sexual relations with
(D2)	*harron*	=arrant out-and-out
(D2)	*flennemmes*	=Flemings
(D3)	*marinalles*	sailors
(E2)	*barrell drome*	See note
(E3)	*kend* †	well-known
(E3)	*nought*	wickedness
(F2)	*hyte* †	contemptuous interjection
(F2)	*hoore*	=whore
(F3)	*franc hoode*	hat for immoral woman (see note)
(F3)	*waies me fo*ʳ	=woe is me, I am sorry for
(F3)	*wenst*	do (you) want
(F3)	*halpeny*	=halfpenny, cheap
(F3)	*halter*	hangman's noose
(F4)	*gallygait*	Gallogate (name of street leading to town gallows)
(G2)	*mainsvornne* †	perjured
(H2)	*skeill* †	pail
(H3)	*naughtie pak*	wicked baggage
(H3)	*nowtynes*	wickedness
(H4)	*steg* †	gander
(H5)	*mayry*	=marry, indeed
(H6)	*whilles*	until
(I2)	*fore end* †	beginning
(I2)	*harvest*	Autumn, harvest-time
(I2)	*cruse*	jug
(I4)	*passe*	care
(I5)	*loft*	upstairs room
(I5)	*boune to* †	ready for
(I6)	*happ*	fortune
(I7)	*yawd* †	mare
(I7)	*in wethe of*	?in mistake for
(I8)	*examined*	questioned
(I9)	*ye*	=yea, yes

Latin

Typical structure:

Mary Smith *vxor* ('wife') of John *contra* ('against') Jane Brown *vxor* of Peter *in causa diffamacionis* ('in a case of defamation') *videlicet* ('namely')

In Text H: *dicit* says

In Text I: *etatis xvij anorum* seventeen years old; *respondit negative* replied in the negative.

Explanatory notes

(E2) *abarrell drome*: 'barrel' and 'drum' are both presumably in reference to shape and size, but additional sexual innuendo seems likely since the phrase is being claimed to be defamatory.

(F2) *a whipe and a cart/ & a franc hode* the words picture the punishment for a woman convicted for sexual immorality: being whipped, being carried through the streets in a cart as a public spectacle (also referred to in Text C), and being forced to wear some distinctive head-gear.

For *franc hode* (=french hood) with this sense OED has only this example.

Background

Case-outlines, quoting the alleged defamatory words.

Topics for linguistic investigation

1. The forms and use of second person personal pronouns.
2. The constructions: (D2) *badd hir go follow yᵉ flennemmes*, (F3) *wenst haue a halpenny halter*, (H4) *I wold yoᵘ knew ytt*, (H5) *call thou me goose steiler*, (I7–8) *they had not ben syttyng*.
3. The etymology of (A3) *drab*, (F3) *lasse*, (G2) *mainsvornne*, (H2) *skeill*, (H4) *steg*, (I5) *boune*, (I5) *loft*, (I6) *happ*, (I7) *yawd*.
4. An analysis of the local features in the reported speech in F2–4.
5. Linguistic features that these texts share with Scots.

Text 4

Roger Jackson: Yorkshire 1597

(Borthwick Institute of Historical Research Manuscript CP.G/3227, Hobson *v.* Jackson 1597)

Super primo et secundo articulis dicit that for his owne parte he takethe W^m hobson art*iculate* to be an honest man of good and honest Lyefe and conu*er*saci*on*/ And so hathe he harde him accompted and taken amonges his neighboures yet not w^t standinge he sayeth that on a workday about a

5 fourtnyghte before or after may day last, about one or two of the clocke in the after noone, what other more certayne day or tyme he rememb*ereth* no^r call to his Remembraunce this p*ar*te comynge into the hous of one peter dighton in northgate in wakefield and beinge an alehous wher he had bene in the mornynge of the same day, and fyndinge the art*iculate* Roger Iackson ther, whome he had

10 lefte ther in the same mornynge this ex*amina*te asked the sayd Roger Iackeson whether he dwelte ther or not/ who sayd he dyd not. And then this p*ar*te asked the sayd Roger Iackson for the art*iculate* W^m hobson, whether he was ther or not who had promysd to mete this ex*amina*te ther agayne/ about that tyme, to whome Roger Iackeson sayd it is no matter where m^r hobson be (meanynge W^m

15 hobson art*iculate*) for he fuckes {and sardes} bothe Alen Sugdons wyfe of Stanley and her doughter I do not thinke so quothe this ex*amina*te for I take Sugdens wyfe to be a very honest woma*n* and if she be a woma*n* of that dispoisyci*on*, she deceyues me & many more And for her doughter, she is to yonge to be of suche besunys, quothe Roger Iackeson, her doughter is aboue

20 thirtene yeres olde & then I will take no chardge of her ~~I g~~ W^m hobson had a pece of golde of myne wch he gave to the lasse meanynge the sayd Sugdens wyfes doughter, if I had that agayne lett him fucke and sarde where he will in the develes name

Notes

Text

From among the cause papers relating to cases at the Consistory Court of York Diocese. The text printed here has not been edited before, though this case is mentioned, with brief quotation, by J. A. Sharpe, *Defamation and Sexual Slander in Early Modern England: The Church Courts at York* (Borthwick Institute of Historical Research, University of York, York, 1980).

Manuscript

The text is confused in l. 6, and restoration problematic. The context demands a *not*, and an ambiguous abbreviation makes the verb-form uncertain. The text might be conjecturally restored (using the 3rd singular present inflexion favoured by the clerk, though not by the deponent) as *he remembereth not* but the transition to *no^r call* is then unlikely though not impossible. Alternatively, there has been omission of *doth not*, and the verb-form is *remember*, giving *he doth not remember no^r call*.

In l. 20, the clerk appears to have begun to write *I gave* and then changed to a different construction, presumably following a change of phrasing on the part of the deponent, who is here recalling what he heard Roger Jackson say.

Glossary

(2, 12)	*articulate*	previously mentioned, said
(2)	*honest*	(sexually) moral
(3)	*conversacion*	behaviour
(3)	*accompted*	estimated
(7)	*parte*	=party, person
(10)	*examinate*	person being questioned
(15)	*sardes* †	has sexual relations with
(16)	*quothe*	said
(20)	*chardge (of)*	responsibility (for)

Latin

(1) In response to the first and second matters raised he says ...

Background

The evidence of a witness in the case against Jackson.

Topics for linguistic investigation

1. The differences between sixteenth century and PDE use of prepositions in: (8) *in*, (18) *for*, (19) *of*, (19) *aboue*.
2. Identify the various clauses and the links between them in (4–11) *on a workday ... he dyd not*.
3. The semantic history and later development of the words *conversation, party, charge*.
4. Why does attention need to be drawn to the curious incident of the entry on *fuck* in editions of OED prior to 1989?

Text 5

William Delve and others: Devon 1615 and 1618
(Devon Record Office Manuscript Chanter 867)

Text A (1615)

[f. 128v] Iana Bradmeade vxor willie*lmi* Bradmead de Sundford vbi nata fuit
eta*tis* sue xxxij vel xxxiij annorum aut de circiter testis admiss*us* iurat*us* &c
p*ar*tes litigan*tes* bene novit vt dicit … Ad secundum articu*lum* libelli deponit et
dicit That aboute Candlemas last past as neere as shee can remember there was

5   a fallinge oute betwene Hughe Mill and Elinor his wife the parties agent*es* in
this cause and William delve defendent in ~~th~~ their village or towne next
adioyninge vnto the p*ari*she Churche of Sundforde {& within the said paryshe}
and neere vnto the dwellinge houses situate within the said village and amongst
divers and outragious speches wch past betwixt them thesaid william delve

10   spake these followinge of thesaid Hugh mill ~~with an intent to sla~~ in a slanderous
manner and verie disgracefullie [f. 129r] vi*delice*t Thou arte no Cuckolde
holdinge oute two of his fingers to thesaid Mill in the manner of hornes, Then
thesaid Hughe Mill demanded of thesaide delue what hee meante therby and
why hee did so, and delve scoffinglie replied againe thou arte no cuckolde

15   poyntinge at the said Hughe Mill, sayenge that hee did give fortie suche armes
in a yeare as thesaid hornes were wch hee made and shewed to thesaid Mill with
his fingers, and this deponente verilie belieueth that the saide delve meante by
poyntinge vnto thesaid Mill in suche sorte with his two fingers as before shee
~~do~~ hath deposed that Hughe mill was a Cuckolde and his Wife an vnhonest

20   woman and she saith that it is so generallie vnderstoode of all as farre as this
deponent ever hearde ~~vp that anyone~~ when one man poynt*es* to another in suche
sorte with his fingers that is a married man ffurther Hughe mill saide vnto
thesaid delve I thinke I have an honest woman to my wife, vnto w^ch ~~dle~~ delve
replied thou mayst thancke mee for it for I might have had to doe with her if I

25   wolde, for shee vntrussed my poynt*es* and then hee spake vnto ~~Agn~~ Elinor Mill
Hughe Mills wife hast minde when thou vntrust my poynt*es* and thou quothe
the said delve speakinge still vnto thesaid Elinor went*es* to leache for thyne
vncomelie part*es* and neither part*es* meaninge therby ~~as this~~ that shee was a
whore and that shee had bin cured of some filthie disease, ~~vt dicit Et aliter nescit~~

30   ~~deponere vt dicit~~ {And this shee knoweth to bee true because shee was present
the tyme and place afor said and heard and sawe all the premisses present also
Iohn Bradmead And Amy Stephens and divers others in the ~~presence and~~
hering thereof et al*ite*r nescit deponere}

24

Text B (1615)

[f. 181r] Rich*ard*us Sampson de Totton Shoemaker vbi mora*m* fecit p*er* dece*m* annos vlte elapsus seu circ*iter* testis admissus &c etat*is* 34 annoru*m* seu circ*iter* … Ad 2. ar*ticulum* deponit et dicit That about the ~~Las~~ ende of Maye Last past he this deponent goeinge ~~from~~ {along of the streete in} Tottnes Towne towar*des* the bridge of Tottnes ar*ticu*late did heere these word*es* of anger and malice passt betweene the parties articulate, v*idelice*t the Libellate Amey Nyell sayd vnto the ~~articulate~~ Libellate Walter Weaver Sirra ~~doest~~ remember thou callest mee whore yea quoth the s*aid* Walter Weaver, If thou call mee knave Ile call thee whore, wch word*es* the s*aid* Weaver did speak in greate anger and mallice, ~~and with a purpose to discredit in the pre~~ Et reddit ca*usa*m sci*enti*e sue quia p*res*ens fuit also then and there Elinor Tuckeninge, and at Least twenty oth*er* persons whose names he cannott nowe declare because he tooke noe such particular notice of them vt dicit et al*iter*.nescit dep*one*re. vt dicit./

Text C (1618)

[f. 402r] Robertus Holdesworth Cl*er*icus artiu*m* mag*ister* vicarius p*er*petuus ecclesie paroch*a*lis de Modberye: Exon*iensi* dioces*ii* vbi stetit vicarius p*er* decem menses seu circ*iter* test*is* admissus &c … Ad secundu*m* ar*ticu*lum Lib*el*li deponit et dicit That ~~in~~ {vppon one of} the ~~Christmas holy~~ twelve days in the feast of Christmas Last past he this deponent ~~w beinge~~ {was} in the vicaridg house of Modbery ar*ticu*late together the Libellate Peter Powneinge and ~~Adrian~~ the Libe*ll*ate Adrian Sweete, ~~in the~~ and then and there in the hall of the s*aid* house he this dep*one*nt heard a greate falleinge out in ~~wor~~ angrye word*es* betweene the s*aid* Poweneing and Sweete and amongst oth^r word*es* the foresaid Adrian Sweete spoke these word*es* to the s*aid* Peter Powneinge, ~~videlicet~~ three or fower tymes, v*idelice*t I have heard som*me* saye, that thou art a bastard, or I have heard saye that thou art a bastard, or som*me* saye, thou art a bastard: ~~&~~ but wch of these particular word*es* the s*aid* Adrian Sweete ~~vttered~~ then and there vttered, he this dep*one*nt doth {not} otherwise reme*m*ber, but he sayth, that he is certayne That the s*aid* Sweete sayde vnto Poweninge aforesaid these word*es*, {with som*me* of the former, or of the same meaneinge:} thou art a bastard: wch word*es* were so spoken to discredite and disgrace the s*aid* Powneinge and were often vttered in greate anger vt dicit et reddit ca*usa*m sci*enti*e sue vt prius because he was p*res*ent ~~and~~ the tyme and place aforesaid and heard and saw the p*re*misses, p*res*ent also then and there Iohn Phillipps ~~&~~ and Richard Hynde his contest*es* vt dicit et al*ite*r nescit dep*one*re. vt dicit./

Notes

Text

From the book of witnesses' depositions relating to cases heard at the Consistory Court of the Diocese of Exeter 1613–1619, case of *Mill & Mill* v. *Delve* (Text A), case of *Nyell* v. *Weaver* (Text B) and case of *Powning* v. *Swete* (Text C). The texts printed here have not been edited before. For other material from the same source see Text 27 below.

Manuscript

A photograph of lines A12–23 from this document, together with a commentary, appears as Plate I on pp. 2–3 above.

The correction from *articulate* to *Libellate* in B7 is because the two terms, both meaning 'said', are not interchangeable, since *Libellate* is more appropriate when the person previously mentioned is one of the principal parties in the case.

The deletions and corrections in Text C could further reflect the scrupulosity in wording his evidence already apparent in the vicar's testimony lines 11–16.

Glossary

(A4)	*Candlemas*	Feast of Purification of Our Lady, 2nd February
(A4)	*last past*	last
(A5)	*parties agentes*	people bringing the suit
(A6)	*cause*	case
(A14)	*againe*	in reply
(A15)	*fortie*	dozens of (imprecise large number)
(A15)	*armes*	?gestures (not in OED or WRIGHT in this sense)
(A19)	*vnhonest*	(sexually) immoral
(A22)	*sorte*	manner
(A24)	*had to doe with*	had sexual relations with
(A25)	*vntrussed*	unfastened
(A25)	*poyntes*	laces holding up hose
(A26)	*hast minde*	=have (you) mind, do (you) remember
(A27)	*leache*	physician
(A28)	*vncomelie*	indecent
(A28)	*neither*	=nether, lower
(B5)	*articulate*	already named, said
(B6)	*videlicet*	(Latin) namely
(B7)	*Libellate*	already named, said (See note on Manuscript above)
(B7)	*Sirra*	Contemptuous form of address
(C5)	*deponent*	witness
(C21)	*contestes*	joint witnesses

Latin

(A1–4) Joan Bradmeade wife of William Bradmead of Sundford where she was born, 32 or 33 years of age or thereabouts, admitted as a witness, sworn etc. who, according to her, knows the disputants well ... To the 2nd article in the accusation she testifies and says (A33) and she knows nothing more to testify

(B1–3) Richard Sampson shoemaker of Totnes where he has lived for the last 10 years or thereabouts, admitted as witness etc. 34 years of age or thereabouts ... To the second article he testifies and says

(B10–11) And he reports this matter of his own knowledge because he was present

(B21) as he says, and he knows nothing more to testify, as he says.

(C1–4) Robert Holdsworth, Clerk in Holy Orders, Master of Arts, Perpetual Curate of the Parish Church of Modbury in the Diocese of Exeter where he has held the position of Vicar for ten months or thereabouts, admitted as a witness etc. ... To the second article of the accusation he testifies and says

(C18) as he says, and he reports this matter as above

(C21) as he says, and he knows nothing more to testify, as he says.

Background

The Vicar who testifies in Text C is also called on as witness in other cases; the record of one in January 1617/18 states his age then as 32.

Topics for linguistic investigation

1. Add present-day punctuation to Text A to mark syntactic structure.
2. Identification of the various forms of verbs associated with 2nd person singular personal pronouns.
3. The use of the prepositions: (A7) *vnto*, (A9) *betwixt*, (A20) *of*, (A23) *to*, (B5) *of*, (C8) *in*.
4. Survey other texts (both in this book and more widely) for evidence of communication by body-language at this period.

Text 6

Sybil Pennacott and others: Devon 1615 and 1629
(Devon Record Office Manuscripts CC4B and CC5)

Text A (1615 Sybil Pennacott)

[CC4B/9] Gett thee in whore, pray for the parson thy pott boyles the better for him

Text B (1615 Elizabeth Earle)

[CC4B/13] I hope to haue the whore whipt ere it bee longe

Text C (1629 Elizabeth Oxenham)

[CC5/98] Thou art or shee is (Loquendo ad d*ic*tam Ioanna*m* weeks seu de eadem) a whore, and thou art or shee is my husband*es* whore, meaning & naming her husband Iames Oxenham of South Tawton, ... and he doth keepe thee or yo*w* or her as com*m*on as the high waie, et vlterius (loquendo ad d*ic*tam

5   Ioannam Weeks seu de eadem) thou art or shee is a drunkard, and thou fellest or shee fell drunke from thine or her horse in Ockhampton markett

Text D (1629 Agnes Ellis)

[CC5/160] Thou art or she is (loqu*en*do ad d*ic*tam Christiana*m* seu de ead*em*) a whore & my husbands whore & I came and found my husband dealing wth thee or her, & thou heldest vpp or shee held vpp thy or her smocke wth thine or her ~~mmmmmm~~ teeth

Text E (1629 George Bailey)

[CC5/196] Thou or he (Loquendo ad d*ic*tum Iohan*n*em Slocombe seu de eodem) didst or did pisse or make water in the widdowe Tylles backside, and thou didst shewe me or he did shewe me (the said George Baily) thy pricke or his pricke, and saidst or said, this pricke hath fuckt Ioan Pecke many tymes

5   (meaning thereby that the said Iohn Slocombe was and is a man of dishonest life and Conversac*i*on and that he had the carna<l> knowlege of the bodie of the said Ioane Pecke

Text F (1626 George Saunders)

[CC5/167] I was never whipt, loquendo ad di*c*tum Tho*m*am Peryan seu de
eodem) and then being asked who was whipt whether Thomas Peryan the partie
agent were whipt, he the said Saunders al*ias* fford answered goe looke. and then
being againe demaunded whether Thomas Peryan were whipt or no, he the said
5 Saunders al*ias* fford answered, yea that he was, he was whipt in the Castle at
Exeter for lying w^t a wench that nowe is a mans wife of our towne (meaning of
the towne of Sidmouth) and also meaning that the said Thomas Peryan was a
man of dishonest & incontinent life

Notes

Text

From the papers outlining cases to be heard by the Consistory Court of the Diocese of
Exeter. The cases from which they are taken are: (Text A) *Agnes Westcott* v. *Sibyl
Pennacott*, (Text B) *Elizabeth Fleshman* v. *Elizabeth Earle*, (Text C) *Joanne Weekes* v.
Elizabeth Oxenham, (Text D) *Christiana Brooke* v. *Agnes Ellis*, (Text E) *John Slocombe* v.
George Bailey, (Text F) *Thomas Peryan* v. *George Saunders*. The texts printed here have
not been edited before.

Manuscript

The texts are from Latin documents with the alleged defamatory words in English. The
writing, spacing and overall style suggests that the Latin has been prepared in advance,
and that the names, dates and English sections have been inserted later. This is
particularly clear in Text D where the Latin is neatly and formally written in Roman
hand while the English insertions are scribbled in in Secretary hand.

In D4 the erased word is illegible, but the form *thine* which precedes it suggests that
it began with a vowel or *h*, but the initial letters showing through the deletion appear to
be *de*.

Glossary

(D2)	*dealing w^{th}*	having sex with
(D3)	*smocke*	shift, under-petticoat
(E2)	*back side*	back yard
(E5)	*dishonest*	(sexually) immoral
(E6)	*conversacion*	behaviour
(F2–3)	*partie agent*	person bringing the suit
(F4)	*demaunded*	asked
(F8)	*incontinent*	lacking (sexual) self-restraint

Latin

(In all texts) *loquendo … eodem* or *eadem* speaking to or about the said **X**; (C4) *et vlterius*
and further.

Explanatory notes

In Texts A–E the alleged quotations are worded, as the Latin introductions state, to cover the possibility of being either directly addressed to the person who is bringing the suit, or uttered in a comment to some third party.

In Text E the charge is that George Bailey had defamed John Slocombe by saying that he has heard Slocombe boast of his sex-life. There is therefore quotation within quotation.

Topics for linguistic investigation

1. The form and use of the second person personal pronouns and verb forms employed.
2. The differences from present-day syntax in: (A1) *Gett thee in*, (E3) *thou didst shewe me*, (E5) *meaning thereby*, (F3) *goe looke*, (F5) *yea that he was*, (F6) *a mans wife of our towne*.
3. How and why the vocabulary of E1–4 is different from that of E5–7.
4. A comparison between the language of Text E and that of the discussion of a similar topic in Text 24 below.

Text 7

Andrew Wanes: Elgin, Scotland 1619

(Moray Record Office Manuscript CH2/145/3; Scottish Record Office
Microfilm CH145/3)

[f. 143v] Vitness admitted and Sworne in the actioun betuix Androw wanes and
Elspet Cumming spouse to Iames petrie.

William Cobane deponit that Androw Wanes said to Elspett cumming, scho was
als lyk ane witche as he was lyk a skabbit Lowne also, callit hir wagaboind, and
5 that his mother Lent hir meill to baik penny Cakis that held hir housband in the
countrey and helpit to mak wp the pack again

James Nauchtie deponit Androw Wanes said to Elspett cuming spous to Iames
petrie that scho was als lyk a witche as cairling, as he was lyk a grandgorie Loun
and choppit on hir teithe and said thair was lytill good in hir face, also that he
10 said hir harlatorie had almaist garit hir housband Leawe the countrey.

Isobell patersone deponit Androw Wanes callit Elspett Cumming witche
carling.

[f. 144 r] Margarat brander deponit scho hard no thing of the bisines

*   *   *   *

[f. 144 v] Thomas milne deponit he hard no thing of the bisines

15 Walter fraser deponit he hard androw Wanes say I sie the devill quhan I sie the,
thow hes bein a great pairt of the wyt of my seknes.

Ianet ogilvie deponit androw Wanes said scho was als lyk a witche as he was lyk
a grandgourie Swonjour

*   *   *   *

[f. 145r] Hew Kay deponit he hard Elspett Cmming call androw Wanes
20 grandgorie Lipper swonjour that thow art I sall hawe a mendis of the ather by
slicht or be micht.

31

Androw Kempt deponit he hard no thing

Ianet Ogilvie deponit scho calld him grandgo*urie* swonjour

Notes

Text

From the records of the Kirk Session of Elgin, Scotland. The documents presented here are only some of those in the case of *Wanes* v. *Cumming*. Extracts from this and other Elgin Kirk Session cases appear in Stephen Ree (ed.), *The Records of Elgin*, New Spalding Club No. 35, Aberdeen, 1908, Vol. 2, pp. 160–61.

Manuscript

Where *s* is word-final it is sometimes written as long-*s* with an additional flourish. This has been treated as empty, thus (8) *als* and (1) *Vitness* where the second *s* is written in this way.

In (8) *Loun* the final *n* is looped back. This has been deemed empty, but might be an abbreviation for a further *e*, as in the full spelling (4) *Lowne*.

The rendering of the name of the accused presents minim-stroke problems. In (2) *Cumming* there are five minims (for *um*) before the *i*, and an abbreviation-stroke over it adds a second *m*. In (7) *Cuming* there are only two minims (for *u*) and an abbreviation-stroke over. In (19) *Cmming* there are six minims and no mark of abbreviation.

Glossary

(3)	*deponit* †	testified
(4)	*skabbit* †	covered with scabs (implying syphilis)
(4)	*Lowne* †	rogue, idler
(8)	*cairling* †	old hag
(8)	*grandgorie* †	infected with syphilis
(9)	*choppit (on)*	?mumbled (with)
(10)	*garit* †	made
(16)	*the wyt (of)* †	the person to blame (for)
(18)	*swonjour* †	rogue, layabout
(20)	*Lipper*	=leper
(21)	*slicht*	cunning
(21)	*micht*	=might, force

Topics for linguistic investigation

1. A comparison with Text 21 (from Selkirk 1540) in respect of the spellings: (1) *vitness*, (1) *admitted*, (3) *scho*, (5) *the*, (9) *good*, (13) *hard*, (16) *great*, (16) *pairt*.
2. What the representation of long vowels does and does not tell us.
3. The etymology of: (3) *deponit*, (4) *skabbit*, (4) *Lowne*, (4) *wagaboind*, (8) *cairling*, (8) *grandgorie*, (10) *garit*, (18) *swonjour*, (21) *slicht*.
4. A reconstruction in direct speech of the exchange of abuse between Wanes and Cumming, taking into account the various witnesses' evidence about it.

Text 8

Margaret Edwards: Barking, Essex 1645
(Essex Record Office Manuscript Q/SBa 2/57 Item 13)

[f. 1r] Essex sc*ilicet*/ The Informac*i*on of Robert White of the parish of Barking
yeoman taken vpon Oath the 28th day of Iune 1645 before S^r. Henry Mildmay
K^{tt}. & William Toppesfeilde Esqr. two of his Ma*iest*ies Iustices of the peace for
the said County.

5   The Inform*a*nt s*ai*th, that two Monethes since or thereabouts going along
ffishers streete in the towne of Barking vpon his occasions, Margaret the wife
of Thomas Edwards of the same ffisherman in a violent & outragious manner
called him roundheaded rogue, and said. It was long of such roundheaded
rogues as hee was, that they were brought into such a condic*i*on, vsing many
10   other reviling words whereby a great tumult was raised in the said towne
insomuch that this Inform*a*nt was constrained to take a Marsh forke from a
Marshman to defend himselfe from hurt & violence, wch. was like to bee offered
to this Inform*a*nt by reason of the said vproare and tumult./

The Informac*i*on of Edmund Palmer of Barking Draper taken vpon Oath vt
15   supra./

The Inform*a*nt s*ai*th that two Monethes since or thereabouts hee being then
Constable & going to demaund of Thomas Edwards of Barking ffisherman
some Money due vpon a rate; Margaret the wife of the said Edwards said to this
Inform*a*nt (vid*elicet*, That a Company of yo^w had brought a Popish Preist to
20   towne; but (s*ai*th shee) the King is a coming now, and then wee shall haue a
course taken wth. yo^w & such as yo^w are: Or words to the like effect./

The Informac*i*on of Nicholas Cleere of Barking Mealeman taken vpon Oath vt
supra./

Who s*ai*th, that this day sennight, going out of the Markett, hee heard
25   Margarett the wife of the said Thomas Edwards say; That Mr Peter Witham
Preacher of Barking placed there by the Parliam*ent* wth. the approbac*i*on of the
Assembly of Divines, was a Papist Dogg, And further s*ai*d, That if shee had bin
there (meaning att the buryell of one Margarett Spence) shee would haue holpe

33

to haue torne him in peices like a Papist dogg as hee was. /

30   Wm Toppesfeilde

[f. 2r] The Informac*i*on of Iohn Vaughan of Barking ffisherman taken vpon Oath on the 28th day of Iune 1645 before s^r. Henry Mildmay, K^tt. & William Toppesfeilde Esq: &c.

Who s*ai*th, that hee hath heard Margaret the wife of Thomas Edwards of
35   Barking a fores*ai*d ffisherman raile oftentimes against the Parliam*en*t, and hath wisht the King to bee here with all his Company, and then (*said* shee) they would quiett yo^w all, a Company of Round headed rogues as yo^w are; wishing the Parliam*en*t were all hangyd, railing & traducing the people y^t came from Church neglecting & despising the ffast daies appointed by the King &
40   Parliam*en*t, & allsoe is a comon stirrer vp of tumults & comotions.

                                                          Wm Toppesfeilde

Notes

Text

Informations taken by Essex Justices of the Peace for the local Quarter Sessions. For a photograph and transcription of f. 1r (lines 1–30) see Hilda P. Grieve, *Examples of English Handwriting 1150–1750* (Essex Record Office Publications No. 21, Chelmsford, 1954).

Manuscript

The writer frequently puts a full stop after an abbreviation. This has been omitted where the abbreviation is expanded, as in *saith* from *s^th.* in l. 24.

A form of *l* shaped like a capital appears occasionally, but since it is used medially in (22) *Cleere* and (35) *raile* as well as initially in (8) *long*, it has been treated as lower-case.

Glossary

(5)	*since*	ago
(6)	*occasions*	affairs, business
(11)	*constrained*	forced
(12–13)	*offered (to)*	attempted (against)
(18)	*rate*	local tax, such as poor-rate
(20–1)	*a course*	steps
(24)	*this day sennight*	a week ago today
(28)	*holpe*	helped (strong past participle)
(38)	*traducing*	slandering
(40)	*comotions*	public disturbances

Topics for linguistic investigation

1. The history of (8) *long of* and (24) *sennight*, and their development from general to dialect use.
2. In what other texts of the mid-seventeenth Ccntury are the verb construction *is a coming* (20) and the past participle *holpe* (28) attested?
3. The extent to which the vocabulary and phrasing of lines 5–13 can be attributed to Margaret Edwards, Robert White or the clerk.
4. *Papist* and *Roundhead*: Find further examples of hostile names (from all periods) used by opponents of religious, political or other groups, and investigate their derivation.
5. *Two Monethes since*: Words meaning 'ago' used in texts from other areas.

Accounts

Plate II

Plate II

Text 10
Thomas Darby: York [c.1520]

Company of Merchant Adventurers of York Manuscript Estate and Tenancy
Papers 2 f. 1r
Edited text 10/8–26

   ffyrst I hayff payd ʒow for farme y^t I was yowre

   Tennand the spays off xxxviij ʒers _____ iij$^{xx\ li}$ xvj^{li}

   Also I mayd Rep*ar*acio*n*s off the same rentt

   off my nawnne gudd*is* wylk I had neu*er* A penne

5   A lowyd for bott payd my farme _____ x^{ii}~vj^{ii}~ {xlvj^{li}}

           Su*mm*a y^t ʒ^e hayff off me in farme

          w^t rep*ar*acons is _____ vj^{xx} ij^{li}

   Thes ar the gudd*is* that I hayff left be hynd me

   It*em* the glasyng off the wyndows in the hall and parlor Cost me _____ iij^{li} xiij^s iiij^d

10 It*em* the syllorryng and pallorryng off parlor _____ xxvj^s viij^d

   It*em* for syttyng A lyght in parlor syde _____ x^s

   It*em* for makyng off A chymnay w^t ij stows _____ xxvj^s viij^d

   It*em* for A nownd in the butt*er*e w^t ij hawm*er*ys _____ x^s

   It*em* for two hovyns in the kycchyn _____ xiij^s iiij^d

15 It*em* for A rang*is* w^t a chymnay in the kycchy*n* _____ xx^s

   It*em* for A kowttyng hows w^t A Bay wyndow in the schop _____ xiij^s iiij^d

   It*em* for the bynkk*is* in the hall w^t a dubyll hek I bowght

     thame off nycholis beu*er*lay _____ x^s

   It*em* A Par kays in the ware hows _____ x^s

Characters: Use of ʒ in (2) *ʒers*, (1) *ʒow* (but also *ʒowre*). Use of *y* in (1) *y^t* but not in (3) *the*.

Allographs: Two forms of *r*, tailed variety in (5) *farme*; short form in (10) *syllorryng and pallorryng*; both in (10) *parlor*. Long and short forms of *s*, e.g. both in (2) *spays*. Little evidence as to a system for *u* and *v*, either being used medially for [v], thus (14) *hovyns* beside (18) *beuerlay*. Final character in numerals realised as *j*, e.g. (2) *iij*.

Capitals: Use of *ff* in (1) *ffyrst*; not used here for proper names, (18) *nycholis beuerlay*.

Abbreviations: (12) *w^t*, (1) *y^t*, (6) *ʒ^e* (nothing omitted here); (8) *guddis*, (3) *Reparacions*, (13) *buttere*, (16) *kycchyn*.

Punctuation: None.

Typical spellings: (16) *schop*; (8) *guddis*; (4) *nawnne*; (2) *spays*.

Problems of interpretation: Is the letter *A* in e.g. (11) *A lyght* a capital? Is (16) *kowttyng* a spelling for 'counting', or is the reading *kowccyng* 'cooking'? or *bowttyng* 'bolting'?

Introduction to Accounts

Accounts are a form of written communication, generated by people who are account-able to someone for the details of how money is spent: a tradesman to his customer (Text 15), a steward to his employer (Text 11), a mayor to his borough (Text 16), church-wardens to their parishioners and diocese (Texts 9, 12 and 17), the people fitting out a ship to the port for which they have been acting (Text 14). In some cases the work has not yet been done, as in Text 13, where experts have been commissioned to inspect farm-buildings and then submit their estimate of the cost of repairs needed, while in Text 10 the writer submits details of personal expenditure in the hope that the recipients of his accounts will agree to reimburse him as having acted in their interests. Occasionally a document may record expenditure for purely personal reference, but one could argue that in these cases the writer is, as in a private diary, writing to himself, so that he can keep track of his money.

As written communication, however, accounts have a different basis from that of letters. Letters are addressed to a named person, usually appearing somewhere in the text as *you* or *thou*. Accounts, with certain exceptions such as those intended for the eyes of an employer or customer (Texts 11 and 15), were frequently written to be read by a group to which the writer was responsible. Such a group might not even be totally literate, so that the contents were, presumably, read to them for their information and approval. In 1609 the Churchwardens of St Oswald, Durham,[1] presented their accounts to the leading parishioners; the group signed their approval in the account-book, but out of the twenty laymen present, eight signed by making their mark.

In the writing of accounts the writer and those for whom he writes are in shared possession of certain data, so that much of the reference is by mutually understood allusion, which may disadvantage outsiders such as present-day readers. The Tailor's bill (Text 15) has no need to specify more than that the dresses are for *three of yor daughters* (15/19–20), but the text yields additional information for the social historian when the ages of the three girls are discovered from other documents. Similarly, Thomas Darby's account of building works done in his house (Text 10) does not have to say where the house is, since both he and the Guild know, nor do the Churchwardens of Ashburton need to spell out to their parishioners the nature of the trouble *contra eos de Bikenton hoc anno* (9A/18–19) or who William Austin or John Gye was (9A/43–4).

In closer verbal detail, too, accounts are often obscure in that things referred to are unfamiliar to modern readers unless they happen to have a specific knowledge in, say, costume or bell-ringing or naval gunnery. However, it is worth distinguishing between terms which would have been generally understood at the period and those which even at the time would have caused difficulties for many. We need equally an explanation for *sepulcar* (12/45), *boge barrel* (14/16) and *tastes* (15/12), but when the lexical items are considered in the context of their own time, it seems likely that everyone would know where you would find an Easter Sepulchre and what you did with it, but it is doubtful whether Sir Robert Spencer could have said what *tastes* were, though his elder daughters probably knew, and doubtful whether those same girls would have been able to define a *boge barrel*.

While vocabulary in accounts is wide-ranging, syntax and morphology are governed and limited by the nature of the material. Some accounts are accompanied by other sorts of writing, such as Darby's framework of argued appeal (Text 10) or the memo on church seating written in the Minchinhampton account-book (Text 17), but as for the accounts themselves, they typically have a repeated syntactic pattern of *(paid) ((to) so-and-so) for such-and-such*,

> payd to vmffray ffor a horsse hyd (12/12)
> p^d for apare of shoes for mathew dier (16/11)
> for pesyng of belropis (9/13)

or else *bought (of so-and-so) such-and-such*,

> bought of goodwyfe mylles a vyrkyn of buter (14/54)
> bought 6 galand vynger (14/52).

Variety in syntax resides almost entirely in the structure of the NP functioning as *such-and-such*, which is frequently heavy with post-modification,

> caryag off a pasty off redder from Iohn agaunte to þe park (11/31–2)
> iiij brode yeardys of blacke for my ladys grace slape (11/9),

though occasionally clauses are introduced to explain the circumstances of a payment,

> for lyme to the stepell when he was rowcaste (9A/21)
> rewardyd to þe keper off marshode park whan my ladys grace was ther (11/21–2)
> gaue to ffrancies willes when Hee went to bresto (16/9).

These patterns were established by customary usage when accounts were drawn up in Latin, and in Text 9, where Latin is still used for many entries, either independently or macaronically mixed with English lexical items, the parallels are obvious, as where the later accounts have the entries,

> for makyng of wex (9B/33)
> Ipayde to will Erl for makyng of the Cownttys (9C/30)

but in 1500–01 the equivalent entries read,

> pro facturo ceri (9A/11)
> willielmo Erle pro facturo computi (9A/7).

It is very possible that the preference for following nominalised present participles with prepositional phrases rather than direct objects is strongly influenced by the fact that the English *-yng* forms equate with Latin nouns which show their verbal origins less clearly. More than a hundred and sixty years later the Minchinhampton accounts still have,

> Payd ffor drawing out of the transcript and keeping of our accoumpts and partchments (17/35–6)

alongside,

> payd Thomas Lord pro mending the Clock (17/11).

Accounts are not the place to look for much that is a syntactic commonplace elsewhere. Sentences with a full NP + VP structure are extremely rare and there are neither questions nor exclamations. The range of morphology is also restricted. Finite verbs are few, and those that do appear in dependent clauses are usually 3rd person preterites,

> 3 saymen yt Lost there ship (16/8).

and where pronouns appear 3rd person forms are also the norm,

> to my ladys grace at poltimore for her offreng (11/3)

The accounts of Mayor Joshua Baudon are unusual in that he is accounting for his own expenditure, so that 1st person forms occasionally appear,

> for my Charg for goinge to size and Hors hier (16/27),

and in the same way Churchwardens may mention expenditure which involved them personally,

> payd ffor owr dyneris at the vysytacyon (12/8).

Those texts which extend beyond the itemisation of expenditure naturally add more syntactic material, and the two texts which are making a case, in the one instance (Text 10) for reimbursement and in the other (Text 13) for money to be expended at some future date, are less tied to the traditional modes of presentation. On the other hand the Churchwardens of Strood (Text 12) move from accounting to making an inventory, and in this section the syntactic patterns are of an even more limited type. The notes about seating at the end of Text 17 have yet another formulaic style.

Most accounts come from named people, even when they are acting, as in the case of churchwardens, as office-bearers rather than as themselves. Often, however, it is uncertain whether the named 'writer' is the actual writer of the document or whether an amanuensis was employed. Some accounts are holographs, and among the texts collected here both Thomas Darby (Text 10) and Joshua Baudon (Text 16) seem to have written for themselves. For the person keeping accounts for the Countess of Devon (Text 15), to be sufficiently literate and numerate for accounting was evidently a requirement of his job, but whether the Tailor presenting his bill to Sir Robert Spencer wrote it himself or employed a clerk is unknown. Who wrote the accounts for the fitting out of the Rye Ship (Text 14) is equally uncertain, but at the end of the estimates for repairs at the Appleby farmstead (Text 13) the document itself suggests, in the handwriting of the text and the four names, three of them 'signed' by marks, that at least three of the four surveyors are illiterate, with the fourth, or possibly an independent clerk, setting down the agreed opinions of all. The accounts from churchwardens present an extremely interesting case in this respect, for the men themselves were in a very special situation.[2]

Each church elected its churchwardens annually, some churches having a tradition of a single year in office, others making sure of continuity by using a system where one of two (or two of four) churchwardens were re-elected for a second year. Churchwardens had many responsibilities,[3] and in the course of time even more were heaped on them by both church and state. Their accounts often include a note of expenses incurred in the course of their duties, such as attendance at the Archdeacon's Visitation of their area, *Item payd ffor owr dyners at the vysytacyon* (12/8).

Prominent among their tasks, and highlighted by their description of themselves as *custod[es] bonorum instancie parochianorum ecclesie parochialis* 'keepers of the store of the goods of the parishioners of the parish church' (9A/2), was seeing to the proper maintenance of the church fabric and contents, and since this necessarily involved payment for workmen, materials and items bought, they were accountable to their parishioners for this as well as other expenditure. When churchwardens were sworn in, soon after their election, the job-description to which they publicly swore included detailed instructions about accounts,

> yow shall yeilde and give up at the yere's ende a faithefull and true accompte of all somes of money church implementes furniture and books as then shall remayne and delyver to your successors. So God you helpe by Jesus Christ.[4]

This immediately raised a problem, since the writing of presentable accounts demanded skills which were not a requirement for election to the office.

Churchwardens were usually drawn from the solid middle rank of society, farmers, tradesmen and craftsmen (only occasionally women). For gentry to hold the office was rare. Since the need for writing skills might well be small in reference to their work, it could not be relied on. It was therefore standard practice to have the accounts drawn up by someone who was suitably skilled, and it is normal everywhere throughout the Early Modern period for churchwardens' accounts to record a fee paid for this,

> item Ipayde to will Erle for makyng of the Cowntys (9C/30, Ashburton, Devon 1503)
>
> Itm payd for ye wrytyng of our books of a counte ye yer (Halesowan, Worcestershire, 1548)[5]
>
> Item given for writinge our busines about the church and kepinge our booke as haith bene accustomed (St Oswald, Durham, 1592)[6]
>
> Payd ffor drawing out of the transcript and keeping of our accoumpts and partchments (17/35–6, Minchinhampton, Gloucestershire 1664).

While successive churchwardens came and went, the person writing the parish's accounts might continue to be called on. Thus the Ashburton accounts were written by

William Erle not only in the three years quoted as Text 9, but for the whole period 1485 to 1507.[7] He was the local baker, and had served as churchwarden himself. Since wardens of the churches in every hamlet needed accounts written, the person called on was inevitably local, whoever in the village was willing, available and sufficiently literate. The diarist Roger Lowe (Text 35) was all of these, and notes several times that in spare moments from his work as apprentice-shopkeeper he did writing for other people, among whom were the Churchwardens of his home-village, Ashton-in-Makerfield,

> I was this afternoone with William Chadocke and Thomas Heijes casting vp their accounts and after I had done with them I came to shop and shutt it vp (35/30–31).

Since literacy and fluency in written English were virtually self-assessed in those who took on the clerk's role, churchwardens' accounts are often particularly interesting for spellings which reflect pronunciation rather than convention. Thus (9A/38) *Sirpellys* 'surplice', (9A/35) *yeate* 'gate', (12/27) *cristymes* 'Christmas', (12/17) *sholl* 'shovel', (12/22) *allow* 'hallow', (17/14) *varmins*, (17/22) *Parrotor* 'apparitor'. Such spellings often suggest local pronunciations, and since both churchwardens and the people they got to write their accounts on their behalf were local, and the documents were for submission to local people this is scarcely surprising. Texts may similarly illustrate local morphology, as in the use in the Ashburton accounts of the past participles *Ipaide* and *Ibofte* (9B/25 and 32), demonstrating that the Old English ʒe- prefix survived to 1500 in the South West. Regional lexical items may also appear, and since church expenditure was more or less on similar things everywhere, accounts can provide comparative data. Bounty-payments for the killing of what were deemed to be vermin, animals and birds that destroyed crops and so on, show entries relating to rewards paid in a Lancashire parish[8] for the killing of *malpes*, *mouldiwardes* and *hurchantes*, that is bullfinches, moles and hedgehogs (urchins), while in Devon[9] bullfinches appear under quite a different name in an entry recording payment for *3 hopes heddes*. The same two parishes furnish a further small example in their entries for roof-repairs. While Lancashire[10] makes payment *for slatinge the church*, the Devon text substitutes *helyng* (9A/25 etc.). A Durham parish[11] reports repairs to *the church garth wall*, where Southern texts use other words.

Where churchwardens use their account-books for other purposes, such as notes, it is not their regular writer who makes the entries, and so there may be even less approximation to a written standard, so that such extra pieces of text are often of exceptional interest to the linguist. The memorandum about John Manning's seat, probably written by Manning himself, in Text 17 lines 37–44 is of this type. A minor example from elsewhere is the Warwickshire village[12] where churchwardens used careful and large capitals to write inside the cover of their account-book,

CLIFTON SVPERDONSMORE IN THE COVNTI OF WORWICK RICHARD LEA AND THOMAS HVIT CHVRCH WORDONS THE YEARE 1634. WITH OUVR ANDS WEE DID PVT IN .9. LEAVES IN TO THIS BOOKE.

Moreover, in the accounts of people other than churchwardens, regional characteristics of all sorts may be marked, as other texts here show. Joshua Baudon of West Looe (Text 16) has spellings that suggest that in 1664, the English spoken in Cornwall had not raised the vowel in *sea* to [i:], while York pronunciation of the early sixteenth century may be deduced from spellings used by Thomas Darby. such as *layth* and *knaws* (10/38–9). It is interesting that phonetically-interesting spellings often crop up where the writer of the accounts has to deal with a word which he may use frequently in speech but rarely sees written down, such as a local place-name; thus Baudon's written forms *Bodmond*, *Hanavore*, *shilling game*.

Notes

1. J. Barmby (ed.), *Churchwardens' Accounts of Pittington and other Parishes in the Diocese of Durham from 1580 to 1700*, Surtees Society, Vol. LXXXIV (1888), p. 153.
2. The classic discussion of these is in J. Charles Cox, *Churchwardens' Accounts from the Fourteenth Century to the Close of the Seventeenth Century* (Methuen, in series 'The Antiquary's Books', London, 1913).
3. For further consideration of some of these, see Introduction to Presentments, pp. 280–288 below.
4. Quoted by A. Tindal Hart, *The Man in the Pew 1558–1660* (John Baker, London, 1966), p. 63. This book has an invaluable chapter on 'The Churchwarden and His Accounts'.
5. Frank Somers (ed.), *Halesowen Churchwardens' Accounts (1487–1582)*, Worcester Historical Society (1957), p. 95.
6. Barmby, *Churchwardens' Accounts*, p. 33.
7. Alison Hanham (ed.), *Churchwardens' Accounts of Ashburton, 1479–1580*, Devon and Cornwall Record Society, New Series, Vol. 15 (1970), p. vii.
8. F. A. Bailey, *The Churchwardens' Accounts of Prescot, Lancashire 1523–1607*, Lancashire and Cheshire Record Society, Vol. CIV (1953), p. 108.
9. Hanham, *Ashburton*, p. 159.
10. Bailey, *Prescot*, p. 111.
11. Barmby, *Churchwardens' Accounts*, p. 140.
12. Cover-illustration in A. Gooder, *Plague and Enclosure: A Warwickshire Village in the Seventeenth Century*, Coventry and North Warwickshire History Pamphlets No. 2, University of Birmingham and the Coventry Branch of the Historical Association (1965).

Text 9

Churchwardens of Ashburton: Devon 1500–1503

(Devon Record Office Manuscript 2141A/PW1)

Text A (1500–1501)

[f. 32v] Compu*tus* Ioh*anni* paty Thome Schabetor Ioh*anni* Clyffe ac Thome
arscote custod*um* bono*rum* instan*cie* parochiano*rum* ecclesie *pa*rochial*is* de
aysb*er*ton a festo S*anc*ti Ioh*anni*s ante portam latina*m* anno d*om*ini mill*esi*mo
ccccc^{mo} vsq*ue* ad idem *fes*tu*m* anno d*om*ini mill*esi*mo ccccc^{mo} p*er* vn*um*
5   ann*um* integru*m*

*   *   *   *

[f. 33v]

Item will*ie*lmo Erle p*ro* facturo computi	ij s iiij d
Item p*ro* emendac*i*one le Schyppe de argento	xiij d
Item p*ro* Sirpos	iij d
10 Item p*ro* trussyng Gurdell*ys* and a Spereschefte	vj d
Item p*ro* facturo cer*i* in di*uersis* tempor*um* anni	iij s j d
Item in Soluc*i*one diu*ersis* homi*ni*b*us* that caste [f. 34r] the Stepell & for ther expenc*ys* when they made the Bergyn	iij li viij d
Item in Soluc*i*one pet*ro* mayne p*ro* worke	ij s iij d
15 Item in Soluc*i*one p*ro* lyme Sack*ys*	xvij d
Item p*ro* mending of a bell whele & for cariage of Tymb*er* and for woode	ij s ij d
Item in expenc*ys* apud Exceter & london cont*ra* eos de Bikenton hoc anno	iij li viij s
20 Item p*ro* ropis	xiiij d
Item for lyme to the stepell when he was rowcaste	xvj s viij d
Item for Bokett*ys* for a lyme Seffe for helyng stonys & for pergettyng of þ^e churche howse and for lathis lathenaile & pynnys	v s iiij d ob
25 Item for helyng and rowcastyng of the ameltorijs	iiij s ix d
Item for Tynne for the orgonys	xvj d
Item for wexe	~~xx~~ viij s iiij d
Item Ipaide to the plum*m*er	v s j d
Item for tymb*er* naylis makyng of belropys andfor grese	

46

30	to the bell*ys* _____	iij s
	It*em* It*em* for wenscote for Belcoler*ys* and Bokell*ys* for	
	pavyng of the church and for mendyng of the chetell _____	iiij s ij d
	It*em* for paynty*ng* of þᵉ churche howse for mendyng of	
	a be{l}stocke for a lant*er*ne for mendy*ng* of a Sege for	
35	mendyng of a locke & a lacche & cache for þᵉ yeate _____	iij s iiij d
	It*em* for pesyng of ropis and Tymb*er* to þᵉ orgonys	
	for ij Skynnys to the Same & for glew and nailys to	
	þᵉ Same and for mendyng of Sirpell*ys* _____	iij s vij d
	It*em* for ij albys for child*er* _____	iiij s
40	It*em* to will Grey for mason worke_____	xj s ob
	It*em* to will knoll and denbolde for worke _____	vj s ix d
	It*em* to Schaptor for cariage_____	ij s
	It*em* d*omi*no will*ielm*o austyn in no*mi*ne rewardi de comput*i* __	xij d
	It*em* to Iohn Gye _____	xxxiij s iiij d
45	It*em* to Rogg*er* Edwarde for stonys_____	iiij s

Text B (1501–1502)

[f. 34v] Comp*ut*us Ioh*ann*i Clyffe Thome arscote Ioh*ann*i Sperke & Will*ielm*i denbolde custod*orum* bonor*um* instanc*ie* p*ar*ochianor*um* ecclesie p*ar*ochial*is* de aysberton a festo S*anc*ti Ioh*ann*is ante portam latina*m* anno d*omi*ni mill*esi*mo Quingentesimo p*ri*mo vsq*ue* ad id*em* f*estu*m anno d*omi*ni mill*esi*mo Quin-
5   gentesimo Sec*un*do per vnu*m* annu*m* integru*m*

*   *   *   *

[f. 35v]

	It*em* Will*ielm*o Erle p*ro* factur*o* comput*i* _____	ij s iiij d
	It*em* Ioh*ann*i Gye p*ro* orgonic*is* _____	xiiij s viij d
	It*em* p*ro* lyme_____	iij s
10	It*em* p*ro* lathis _____	xv d
	It*em* p*ro* Schyndelstonys helyng pynnys ovys Bord*ys*	
	and helyng _____	ij s vij d
	It*em* for pesyng of belropis_____	jd ob
	It*em* for mason ys hyre abowte the yeate _____	x s
15	It*em* for pegg*ys* ryngg*ys* and gemeys a bowte þᵉ saide yete____	ij s vj d
	It*em* for pavyng _____	xviij s
	It*em* for straw and Thachyng to Ric*hard* willia*m* ys howse____	iiij s ix d
	It*em* for makyng of wex _____	xxiij d
	It*em* for coler*ys* to þᵉ bell*ys*_____	xx d
20	It*em* for ruschis & pesyng of ropys_____	ij d
	It*em* for helyng of þᵉ dormer of the churche yeate_____	xv d
	It*em* for schyndelstonys walstonys and crest*ys*_____	iiij s j d
	It*em* for makyng of a whele _____	ij s vj d

Item for a barr*e* for the churche yeate ———————— xxd

25 Item Ipaide to the glasier for mendyng of glass*e* ———— vj s ix d
Item to the same glasier for a bargyn that ys made bitwene
the parysch & hym to repayre the glass*e* yereli that ned^t ——— iij s iiij d
and so eu*ery* yere while he lev^t
Item for bord*ys* and tymb*er* ———————————— iij s viij d

30 Item to Iohn mayne for his labo*ur* ———————— iiij s
Item for yreworke to þ*e* same ———————— xiiij d
Item for wex Ibofte that yere ———————— xv s j d ob
Item for makyng of wex ———————————— xx d
Item Symon Bullocke for mendyng of bokys ———— xvj d

35 Item for a Surpell*ys* ———————————— viij s viij d
Item for yre worke & masyn worke and drayng of
stonys & frankencense ———————————— iij s ij d
Item Ioh*anni* Sop*er* p*ro* le churche yeate ———— xxvj s viij d

Text C (1502–1503)

[f. 36r] Comp*ut*us Ioh*anni* Sperke Will*ielm*o denbold Ioh*anni* p*ri*diaux &
Joh*anni* Noseworthy custod*orum* bono*rum* instan*cie* p*ar*ochiano*rum* ecclesie
p*ar*ochial*is* de aysb*er*ton a festo San*c*ti Ioh*anni*s ante portam latina*m* anno
d*omi*ni mill*esi*mo Quingentesimo S*e*cun*do* vsq*ue* ad idem *festu*m anno d*omi*ni
5 mill*esi*mo Quingentesimo tercio

* * * *

[f. 37r]
Item for mendyng of Sirpell*ys* & paper & nayl*ys* ————— iij s ij d
Item p*ro* cere ———————————————— xxxj s j d
Item for grese for the bell*ys* and belle coler*ys* and for a
10 Schoffyll ———————————— ~~iiij d ob~~ ij s viij d ob
Item for makyng clene of the ameltor*ij* and mendyng of
the bell whele ———————————————— viij d
Item for mendyng of the ledde and pesyng of ropys ———— ij s vij d
Item for m*er*ciament*ys* gurdell*ys* & lacys for þ*e* vestiment*ys* — vj d
15 Item for helyngstonys lyme & sonde ———————— vj s ij d
Item for helyng ———————————————— vij s
Item for iiij rochett*ys*. ———————————— iij s x d
Item for mendyng of a bell claper ———————— ij s
Item for lathis & lathenayle ———————————— viij d ob
20 Item for mendyng of a pype of ledde w^t oute the towre ——— v s
Item for havyng downe of þ*e* belle ———————— xiiij d
Item for Sawd*er* helyng pynnys and yreworke ———— ij s iiij d
Item for crest*ys* ———————————————— xij d
Item for caryge of þ*e* bell to excet*er* & for ther labo*ur* and

25	coste that caryd —————————————————————	iiij s vj d
	Item for suspencion & turneys to the corte ———————	iij s iiij d
	Item for wex and makyng. —————————————————	vj s iiij d
	Item for francensense and mendyng of bokys ———————	iij s iiij d
	Item to will halewill for rente—————————————————	vj d
30	Item Ipayde to will Erle for makyng of the Cowntys ————	ij s iiij d
	Item Iohanni pridiaux pro scripcione ———————————	ix d
	Item for reparacion a pone howsys longyng to the churche ——	iij s xj d

Notes

Text

Part of the notes of Expenditure for each of three years. The text has been edited, with Latin words and phrases translated, in Alison Hanham (ed.), *Churchwardens' Accounts of Ashburton, 1479–1580*, Devon and Cornwall Record Society, New Series, Vol. 15 (1970), pp. 28–31. Translated extracts also appeared in a pamphlet [John H. Butcher], *The Parish of Ashburton [in] the 15th and 16th Centuries; as it appears from extracts from the Churchwardens' Accounts* (Yates & Alexander, London, 1870).

Manuscript

In word-final -*yng*, as in (A10) *trussyng*, the letter *g* is almost always extended by a slight hook, but there is no evidence that an additional *e* is intended. However, in (B24) *barre* the final *r* is extended by a hook which has been taken to indicate *e*, by analogy with the use of the same mark following *r* to indicate the ending of the Latin word (A11) *facturo*.

(A31) *Item Item* is a clear error of dittography.

Glossary

For detail on the terminology of church bells see Trevor S. Jennings, *Bellfounding* (Shire Album No. 212, Shire Publications, Princes Risborough, 1988, repr. 1992).

(A8)	*Schyppe*	boat-shaped container for incense
(A10)	*trussyng Gurdellys*	ropes for tightening bells on their stocks
(A10)	*spereschefte*	See note
(A12)	*caste*	plastered, (rough)cast
(A13)	*Bergyn*	=bargain, contract
(A21)	*rowcaste*	=rough-cast
(A22)	*Seffe*	=sieve
(A22 etc.)	*helyng* †	roofing
(A23)	*pergettyng*	plastering
(A23)	*churche howse*	building used for parish purposes such as church-ales
(A23)	*lathis*	=laths, lengths of wood to which roof-tiles are fixed
(A24)	*lathenaile*	nail(s) for fixing laths to batons
(A24)	*pynnys*	=pins, wooden pegs
(A25)	*ameltorijs*	See note
(A31)	*wenscote*	=wainscot, panelling

(A31)	*Belcolerys*	hanging-straps, baldricks
(A32)	*chetell*	=kettle, cauldron
(A34)	*belstocke*	block from which bell is hung
(A34)	*Sege*	=siege, throne (for bishop?)
(A35)	*yeate*	=gate (see note to (B30) *dormer*)
(A36 etc.)	*pesyng*	=piecing, splicing
(A36)	*ropis*	bell-ropes
(A37)	*Skynnys*	=skins, leather (for organ bellows)
(A38)	*Sirpellys*	=surplice (for clergy)
(A39)	*albys*	=albs, white linen robes (for altar-boys)
(A40)	*mason worke*	stone-work
(A42)	*cariage*	transport of goods
(B11)	*Schyndelstonys*	thin roofing-slates or tiles
(B11)	*ovys Bordys*	=eaves-boards, fascia-boards
(B15)	*gemeys*	=gemels, hinges
(B18)	*makyng*	moulding [candles]
(B21)	*dormer*	roof over dormer-window (see note)
(B22)	*crestys*	ridge-tiles
(B31)	*yreworke*	=iron-work
(B32)	*Ibofte*	=bought
(B36)	*drayng*	=drawing, transporting
(C10)	*Schoffyl*	=shovel
(C14)	*merciamentys*	?goods from the mercer (see note)
(C17)	*rochettys*	See note
(C20)	*w^t oute*	outside
(C22)	*Sawder*	=solder
(C26)	*suspencion*	?excommunication
(C26)	*turneys*	=attorneys
(C26)	*corte*	ecclesiastical court
(C30)	*Cowntys*	=accounts
(C32)	*longyng*	=belonging

Latin

(A1–5) *Heading*: The account of John Paty, Thomas Shabetor, John Cliff and Thomas Ascot, keepers of the goods of the store of the parishioners of the parish church of Ashburton, for one complete year from the Feastday of John at the Latin Gate in the year of our Lord 1500 to the same Feastday in the year of our Lord 1501.

(A7)	*pro facturo computi*	for making the account
(A8)	*pro emendacione*	for mending
(A8)	*de argento*	of silver
(A9)	*pro Sirpos*	for rushes
(A10)	*pro*	for
(A11)	*pro facturo ceri in diuersis temporum anni*	for moulding wax at various times of the year

(A12)	*in Solucione diuersis hominibus*	in payment to various men
(A18)	*apud*	at
(A18–19)	*contra eos de Bikenton hoc anno*	against the people of Bickington this year (see note)
(A43)	*domino willielmo austyn in nomine rewardi de computi*	to Sir William Austin as a reward on the account (see note)

(B1–5) *Heading*: As in previous year, but changed names of churchwardens and date 1501–1502.

(B8)	*pro orgonicis*	for the organ

(C1–5) *Heading*: As in previous two years, but changed names of churchwardens and date 1502–3.

French

(A8 and B38)	*le*	the

Explanatory notes

(A3) *The Feastday of St John at the Latin Gate* is 6th May.

(A10) *Spereschefte*: (=spearshaft) From its inclusion in the same entry as *trussyng Gurdellys*, probably some part or tool for the bells.

(A18) *contra*: Elsewhere in the accounts the Latin preposition meaning 'against, in opposition to' is used as Latin for *against* in other contemporary English senses such as 'in preparation for the arrival of', but the sense here is the simple one. The church at Bickington, three miles away, was a daughter church of St Andrew's at Ashburton, and was supposed to send an annual quota of 8s 4d to help maintain it. This was unpaid and in dispute at this time, although the statement of Income for 1500–1 records that Bickington did send 12d to help maintain the Ashburton bells.

(A25) *ameltorijs*: Hanham argues convincingly that this is an attempt at a plural form of *ambulatory*, normally meaning 'cloister' but here referring to the church aisles. However, the earliest example in OED is a century later than this text.

(A29) As in several of the entries which follow, the lack of punctuation and/or conjunctions obscures the fact that the items listed are in a co-ordinated series, 'For X, for Y, for Z'.

(A43) *Sir William Austin* is named with the courtesy-title regularly used at this time for clergy who were not University Graduates. He was the Curate, paid by the non-resident Vicar to deputise for him at the church, and also, as here, receiving payment from the churchwardens for extra services.

(B21) *dormer*: The porch on the North side of the church has an upper-storey or parvise, referred to later in the accounts as *le clerkes chumber*. Evidently at this period there was at least one dormer window set vertically into the sloping roof, and this would have its own small roof over it. The mention of this dormer as over the church *yeat* suggests that whenever the *yeat* is mentioned it is the gate into the North porch which is meant rather than an entrance gate to the church grounds.

(C14) *merciamentys*: Perhaps an ad hoc invented word to mean 'goods from the mercer', although the usual word for this is *mercery*. The known word *merciament* (a shortened form of *amerciament*) does not fit here, since it means 'amercement, fine', though there is an occurence of it in this sense in the accounts for 1551–2.

(C17) *rochettys*: The word, also spelled elsewhere with an *a*, could be *rochet* (a kind of surplice) or *ratchet* (some mechanism for the bells?). The latter is attractive, though the word is quoted in OED only from the late seventeenth century, but the former is more likely, since it frequently occurs alongside *surplice*. There remain difficulties: why a Parish church should want four rochets, normally worn by Bishops, and why four apparently cost less than two albs for altar-boys. However, it is possible that the cost is for mending rather than purchase.

(C31) *Iohanni pridiaux pro scripcione*: What he wrote is not specified, since the fee paid to William Erle for *makyng* the accounts normally means that he 'did' the accounts and wrote them out for the churchwardens. John Prideaux was himself a churchwarden in this year.

Background

The parish church of St Andrew at Ashburton, on the edge of Dartmoor, has an almost unbroken set of Churchwardens' accounts from 1479–1580.

The accounts for the earliest years are written in Latin, but by 1500 the Latin is giving place to English, though some entries are still in Latin, and others macaronic. The Latin is not always accurate, and Hanham suggests that it is sometimes influenced by the English to the extent of reflecting dialect usage, such as a Devon confusion of *beat* and *bait* explaining the phrase (in the accounts for 1541–2) *Castigacione vrcium* for 'bear baiting'.

The man who wrote out the accounts quoted here is known from his name appearing in A7, B7 and C30. He also wrote the accounts in the late 1480s, and himself served as churchwarden for the two-year period 1483–4, which suggests that he was a local man of standing and mature age. An entry under Income in 1503–4 includes mention of him as one of several parishioners who have purchased seats in the church, and his occupation is given: *Item pro vno Sege vendito willielmo Erle baker* _____ *viijᵈ*.

Topics for linguistic investigation

1. The spellings (A10) *Spereschefte*, (A19) *Bikenton*, (A21) *rowcaste*, (A27) *wexe*, (A32) *chetell*, (A35) *yeate*, (A38) *Sirpellys*, (B31) *yreworke*, (C22) *Sawder*, (C26) *turneys*, (C30) *cowntys*, (C32) *longyng*.
2. The relationship of the forms (A22) *Seffe*, (C10) *Schoffyll*, (A28) *plummer*, (B32) *Ibofte* to variants found in the accounts for other years: *zeve, schovyll* and *shule, blumbar, boȝgt* and *bowȝffte*.
3. The origin and survival into the Early Modern period of the initial vowel in (A28, B25 and C30) *Ipaide* and (B32) *Ibofte*.
4. The forms (B27 and 28) *nedᵗ* and *levᵗ*; (A21) *he*, (B14) *mason ys hyre*, (A39) *childer*.
5. The figurative use of existing words as a source for vocabulary-items relating to church bells.

Text 10

Thomas Darby: York [c.1520]

(Company of Merchant Adventurers of York Manuscript Estate and Tenancy
Papers 2)

[f. 1v] Iesu To the Ry3th Wors<ch>ypffull mast*er*ys & Compan*n*e off the
Trenitte Gylld

[f. 1r] Theys ar the gudd*is* that Thom*a*s Darby laytt tenand To the trinite gylde
hays left in the hows and off the grownnde gwylk he is nott A greyd wythe for

5   and also the grett rep*a*rac*i*on wylk the sayd thom*a*s mayd off thare sayd
tennamentt*is* off his awnne gudd*is* w^t owtt <a>ny penne A lowannis and also
the ferms wylk I hayff {payd} yow trewly

ffyrst I hayff payd 3ow for farme y^t I was yowre Tennand
the spays off xxxviij 3ers _____ iij$^{xx\ li}$ xvj^{li}

10 Also I mayd Rep*a*racions off the same rentt off my nawnne
gudd*is* wylk I had neu*er* A penne A lowyd for bott payd
my farme _____ ~~x^{ii} vj^{ii}~~ {xlvj^{li}}
Summa y^t 3^e hayff off me in farme w^t rep*a*racons is _____ vj^{xx} ij^{li}
Thes ar the gudd*is* that I hayff left be hynd me

15 It*em* the glasyng off the wyndows in the hall and parlor
Cost me _____ iij^{li} xiij^s iiij^d
It*em* the syllorryng and pallorryng off parlor_____ xxvj^s viij^d
It*em* for syttyng A lyght in parlor syde_____ x^s
It*em* for makyng off A chymnay w^t ij stows _____ xxvj^s viij^d

20 It*em* for A nownd in the butt*e*re w^t ij hawm*er*ys _____ x^s
It*em* for two hovyns in the kycchyn _____ xiij^s iiij^d
It*em* for A rang*is* w^t a chymnay in the kycchy*n*_____ xx^s
It*em* for A kowttyng hows w^t A Bay wyndow in the schop_____ xiij^s iiij^d
It*em* for the bynkk*is* in the hall w^t A dubyll hek I bowght
thame off nycholis beu*er*lay _____ x^s

25 Item A Par kays in the ware hows _____ x^s
It*em* A hows mayd w^t in the brew hows _____ xiij^s iiij^d
It*em* thre prevays mayd in the same hows whare ne*er* noyn*e*
was mayd a fore _____ xl^s

30 Also rasyng off the garthyng w^t y^e 3att*is* and payll*is* w^t s*er*tan
frutt threys cost me Redy mony_____ vj^{li} xiij^s iiij^d
Also y^e haue A pleg*is* off myne y^t is bett*er* than_____ iij^{li} vj^s viij^d
Summa here off theys p*a*rsill*is* is _____ xxiij^{li} vj^s viij^d

53

Summa to*talis* off the holl sum y^t 3^e haff off me ys _____ vij$^{xx\,li}$ v^{li} vj^s viij^d

35   gwylk sum*m* wolde by vj hals gud*is* howssis als ytt ys and 3^e A low me no more
      Bott v li wylk I thryst schall be ~~payde~~ prouyd ys nott done nother to gud Ryght
      nor Concyens/ Thare fore I p*ra*y yow latt me hayff syk A mend alls I schall haff
      no kaws To co*m*plane me to the kowrtt off Conya*n*s wylk I wyll be layth to do/
      y^t knaws god

Notes

Text

The text has not been edited before. It is mentioned briefly by D. M. Palliser, 'Civic
Mentality and the Environment in Tudor York', in *Northern History*, Vol. XVIII (Leeds,
1982), p. 97. See also David M. Smith, *A Guide to the Archives of the Company of
Merchant Adventurers of York*, Borthwick Texts and Calendars No. 16 (Borthwick
Institute of Historical Research, University of York, York, 1990).

Manuscript

A photograph of lines 8–26 from this document, together with a commentary, appears
as Plate II on pp. 38–9 above.

In (1) *Iesu*, the short form is *Ih̵u*, with the letter *h* being used Greek-style for *e*.

In (6) *any* the conjecturally restored vowel-letter is because there is a small hole in the
document.

Abbreviation makes some readings less than certain. In noun plurals such as (6)
tenamenttis and (11) *guddis* the mark of abbreviation has been expanded to *is* by analogy
with the full forms (35) *howssis* and (1) *masterys*. It is possible that (11) *neuer* and (28)
neer, (20) *buttere* and (32) *better* should similarly be expanded with *ir* or *yr*, but there is
no in-text warrant for this. The *is* abbreviation gives further problems in (22) *rangis* and
(32) *plegis*, where it produces suspect forms which the preceding indefinite articles
indicate to be singular.

Confusable letters cause some problems: The four minims transcribed as *nn* in (4)
grownnde etc. could be intended as *un*. Similarity between *t* and *c* and between *k* and *b*
means that in (23) *kowttyng* interpretation has to take into account the possible readings
kowccyng and *bowttyng*. The letters *e* and *o* are also extremely alike in this manuscript; it
is possible that (28) *noyne* is a more Northern *neyne*.

Glossary

The terms employed to describe the building-works which Darby has had carried out
are particularly difficult, since they are of the period and often local. For detail not in
OED or WRIGHT, see Glen L. Pride, *Glossary of Scottish Building,* 3rd Issue (Scottish Civic
Trust, Glasgow, 1989).

(4)	*gwylk*	which
(5)	*reparacion*	repairs
(5)	*thare*	those
(7)	*ferms*	rents

(10)	*my nawnne*	=my own
(17)	*syllorryng*	plastering (or perhaps timber-lining) the ceiling
(17)	*pallorryng*	See note
(18)	*lyght*	window
(19)	*stows*	=stoves
(20)	*nownd*	See note
(20)	*buttere*	=store room (for liquor)
(20)	*hawmerys*	cupboards
(24)	*bynkkis*	rack, cupboard
(24)	*hek*	door
(26)	*Par kays*	pair of door- (or window-) frames
(28)	*prevays*	=privies
(28)	*neer*	=ne'er, never
(30)	*rasyng*	digging over
(30)	*garthyng*	=garden
(30)	*payllis*	fence-stakes
(32)	*plegis*	=pledge, money given as security
(32)	*parsillis*	=parcels, individual items
(36)	*Bott*	than
(36)	*thryst*	=trust
(38)	*Conyans*	=?conscience (see note)
(38)	*layth*	=loath, reluctant

Proper name

(25)	*nycholis beuerlay*	Nicholas Beverley, York mercer and Guild-member

Explanatory notes

(17) *pallorryng*: Not an identifiable word in this form, but if the spelling confuses *l* and *r*, then there are several possibilities. Pride *Glossary* has *parraling* 'partition', or it could be a short-form of *apparelling* 'decorating, ornamenting'. OED also has *parel* 'chimney piece'. It is known that the Hall was panelled with wainscot in the Sixteenth Century.

(20) *nownd*: Possibly a spelling for *nowne* 'oven' (OED NOWNE), but the word *hovyns* is used in l. 21, and an oven in a buttery is extremely unlikely. Or perhaps for *mownd*, *mawnd* 'basket' (OED MAUND), but this seems out of place and unlikely in a list of major building-works. Most likely of all, as descriptive of joinery-work, a version of the word *muntin* 'upright between two panels' (OED MUNTIN and MONTANT).

(23) *kowttyng hows*: Probably 'counting-house', but the reading might be *kowccyng hows* 'cooking-house' (though unlikely in the shop, and predating OED citation of similar combinations), or even *bowttyng hows* 'bolting-house (where flour was sifted)' (OED BOLTING).

(38) *the kowrtt of Conyans*: Probably a figurative reference, the change in spelling from (37) *Concyens* being insignificant. But Wheatley (see below) suggests the interpretation 'the Court of Conveyance', in reference to some body (otherwise unrecorded) dealing with property etc.

Background

Thomas Darby's specification of his thirty eight years' occupancy of the property described here suggests that this expenses-claim was written c.1520, when Darby was in his sixties. He died in 1524, was Guild Master of the York mercers 1494–5, held civic office in the 1490s, and entered the Corpus Christi Guild in 1480, so may be presumed to have been born c.1455.

The Company of the Merchant Adventurers of York owned and leased out many properties in the city. This document clearly results from a dispute. The house is thought to have been in Goodramgate, York. See D. M. Palliser, *The Company of Merchant Adventurers of the City of York: a brief history of the gild* (Company of Merchant Adventurers, York, 1985) and Louisa Wheatley (Assistant Archivist, Merchant Adventurers' Hall), *Biographical Register of the York Mercers Guild 1420–1503* (unpublished).

Topics for linguistic investigation

1. Southern English equivalents at roughly the same period for (4) *hays*, (4) *gwylk* and (5) *wylk*, (6) *awnne*, (30) *ʒattis*, (35) *gudis*, (35) *hals* and *als*, (37) *syk*, (38) *layth*, (39) *knaws*.

2. Scottish equivalents at roughly the same period for (4) *gwylk* and (5) *wylk*, (11) *A lowyd*, (15) *hall*, (18) *lyght*, (28) *whare*, (32) *haue*, (32) *than*, (35) *hals*, (35) *more*.

3. The syntactic structure in (4) *gwylk he is nott a greyd wythe for*, (11) *neuer A penne*, (35) *vj hals gudis howssis als ytt ys*, (35–6) *no more Bott v li*, (38) *no kaws To complane me*, (39) *yᵗ knaws god*.

4. Survey other Accounts texts in regard to the construction (19) *for makyng off A chymnay*.

5. The vocabulary of building and furnishing.

Text 11

Household of Countess of Devon: Devon 1524

(Public Record Office Manuscript E36/223)

[f. 45v] Necessarys

Item for j qu*arter* of veluet to mynd my lad*ys grace* Curtell _____ ij^s viij^d

Item to my lad*ys grace* at poltimore for her offreng_____ xij^d

Item a yenst midsome^r for vij yeard*ys* of satyn for lyneng of

5   my lad*ys grace* slape p*ar*te the yeare vj^s_____ xlix^s

Item for vj yeard*ys* of satyn breg*ys* to the same p*er* the

    yeard ij^s iiij^d_____ xiij^s

Item for a yeard j qu*ar*t of tawny veluet xij^s viij^d the <y>eard_____ xv^s xj^d

Item for iiij brode yeard*ys* of black for my lad*ys grace* slape _____ xxij^s viij^d

10   Item for j elle of fyne holand _____ xxij^d

Item for ij brod yeard*ys* di*midia* of lyneng for my lad*ys*

    grace Curtell_____ ij^s xj^d

Item reward pd to Symo*n* plant by m^r co*m*ptroller whan

    that my yong ladye was bro3t*h* to bedd w^t chyld_____ xl^s

15   Item for a naylle of tawny veluet for my ladys *grace* sloppe _____ xv^d

Item to m^r hurtt*ys* for di*midia* dosyn glouys for my lad*ys grace*_____ xviij^d

Item for my ladys *grace* offry*n*g in die assumptcio*n*is

    beate marie _____ xx^d

[f. 46r] It*em* payd for my ladys *grace* offory*n*g apon th^e

20   assumption day off o^r lady _____ xx^d

Exspenc*ys* in p hu*n*tty*n*g It*em* rewardyd to þ^e kep*er* off

    marshod park whan my ladys *grace* was ther _____ liij^s iiij^d

Item to hys wyff {& her s*er*uatt*ys*} for mett & drynk &

    her labor _____ xiiij^s x^d

25   It*em* rewardyd to Iohn agawntt wher my lordys *grace* Lay

    by m^r Co*m*ptroller_____ xx^s

It*em* rewardyd to his do3ther & his s*er*ua*n*tts by

    m^r Co*m*ptrollers < ILLEGIBLE >_____ v^s viij^d

It*em* to a man for caryag off venson to Iohn agavnt þ^e wensday __ iiij^d

30   Item to Iohn a gavntt s*er*uatt for caryag off ale birell to colomb __ iiij^d

Item to a man for caryag off a pasty off redder fro Iohn agaunte

    to þ^e park & for caryag off þ^e pasty agen to Iohn agavntt*ys*_____ iij^d

Item payd to Trystra*m* hop*er* for caryag off venson_____ iiij^d

35
Item payd to Iohn peny for ij horsses caryag & for a gentyll
{for} a woma*n* to ryd apon w^t myladys *grace* ij days & for
fechyng of wyn to Iohn agawntt*ys* at ny3th————————————— xxij^d
Item to Rychard Lambpray to Iohn blakmor & to Richard ped
ech off them w^t a horsse to marshowd vale w^t caryag off ale———— xv^d
Item to Iohn Runky for ij horss w^t þ^e su*m*pter horsse and

40
hym selff————————————————————————— ij^s
Item ij horss*ys* for þ^e yowry ——————————————— xvj^d
Item for j horss for *propo*nser off T*r*istams bysn ——————— viij^d
[f. 46v] ~~Item to þ^e kyngys collectors the ij^d tir for my ladys~~
~~seruantys~~————————————————————————— xx^d

45
Item to m^r *com*ptroller for dyu*e*rs thyng bo3th for my ladys
& oþer charges as by a byll ————————————————— xviij^li
Item for j yerd off blak sati*n* to mend my lad*ys grace* ↀcurtell
at colcum ————————————————————————— vj^s viij^d
Item to m^r amner*er* for the almes————————————— iiij^li iiij^s

50
Item for x ell*ys* off lyn clot*h* for my ladys *grace* at xvj^d *p*er ell ——— xiij^s iiij^d
Item for vij ell*ys* off fyn clot*h* for my ladys *grace* at xxij^d a ell ——— xij^s x^d
Item for ij ell*ys* off lynclot*h* for my ladys *grace* ——————— ij^s ij^d
Item for d*imidia* dos*yn* glouys for my ladys *grace* —————— xviij^d
Item to Robert red off Tyu*e*rton for xij pare off hosyn for my

55
ladys *grace* by þ^e hole yere ——————————————— xxj^s

Notes

Text

Extract only. Various extracts were printed in J. S. Brewer, *Calendar of Letters and Papers, Foreign and Domestic, of the Reign of Henry VIII*, Vol. 4, Part I (1524–26) (HMSO, London, 1870), pp. 338–42, and the same version was also printed in articles by Mark Cann in *Western Antiquary*, Vol. III (Plymouth, 1883–4), pp. 68, 76–7, 79–80, 83, with an acknowledgement of an earlier appearance in *Weekly Mercury*, September 1883. The text is discussed in Margaret Westcott, 'Katherine Courtenay, Countess of Devon, 1479–1527' in Todd Gray, Margery Rowe and Audrey Erskine (eds), *Tudor and Stuart Devon* (University of Exeter Press, Exeter, 1992), pp. 13–38.

Manuscript

The legibility of most of the manuscript is much reduced by stains resulting from chemicals once used to render the document easier to read. The lines edited here are some of the few which are relatively free from discolouration, though l. 28 is illegible.

This extract is probably the work of two writers; the hand changes at l. 13, and so do certain spelling preferences.

The word-final abbreviation-symbol usually expanded as *ys* (as in (16) *ladys*) also occurs in (14) *bro3th* where, by analogy with (45) *bo3th*, it has been taken as standing for final *h*.

Money totalled at the foot of each page has been omitted by the editor.

Glossary

(2)	*quarter*	unit of measurement, quarter of a yard, 9 inches
(2)	*Curtell*	=kirtle, gown
(3)	*offreng*	charitable donation
(4)	*a yenst*	=against, in preparation for
(5)	*slape* (also (15) *sloppe*)	=slop, loose outer-garment
(6)	*satyn bregys*	Bruges satin
(6)	*to the same*	for the same [purpose]
(8)	*tawny*	brown
(9)	*brode yeardys*	See note
(10)	*elle*	unit of measurement, 45 inches
(10)	*holand*	linen (originally from Holland)
(11)	*dimidia*	(Latin) half
(13)	*reward*	extra payment
(13)	*comptroller*	household-official dealing with expenditure
(15)	*naylle*	measure of length for cloth, one sixteenth of a yard, $2\frac{1}{4}$ inches
(19–20)	*th^e assumption day off o^r lady*	Feast of the Assumption, 15 August
(23)	*mett*	=meat, food
(25)	*Iohn agawntt*	inn named after John of Gaunt
(26)	*Lay*	spent the night
(30)	*birell*	=barrel
(31)	*redder*	=red deer
(34)	*gentyll*	easily managed horse
(36)	*at nyȝth*	=at night, in the evening
(37)	*ped*	See note
(39)	*sumpter horsse*	baggage-horse
(41)	*yowry*	=ewery, store of silverware, table-linen etc.
(42)	*proponser*	See note
(42)	*bysn*	=business
(49)	*amnerer*	=almoner, household-official dealing with alms
(50)	*lyn*	linen
(54)	*hosyn*	stockings

Local placenames

(3)	*poltimore*	Poltimore, Devon (a property of the Bampfylde family)
(22)	*marshod park*	Marshwood Park Dorset
(38)	*marshowd vale*	Marshwood Vale, Dorset
(48, 30)	*colcum, colomb*	Colcombe Castle, Colyton, Devon (a Courtenay property)
(54)	*Tyuerton*	Tiverton, Devon

Explanatory notes

(9) *brode yeardys*: *broadcloth* was woven 2 yeards (72 inches) wide, so this is either '4 yards [of fabric] 2 yards in width', or *broadyard* is transferred to serve as a linear measurement of 2 yards, so '8 yards [of fabric]'.

(16) *m^r hurttys*: Westcott, *Katherine Courtenay*, identifies a Mr Hurst named as a tradesman elsewhere in the Accounts with William Hurst, who at this time was Mayor of Exeter. His standing could account for the use of *m^r*.

(17–18) *die assumptcionis beate marie*: the Latin name of the Feast Day is translated when the entry is repeated in the lines immediately following, after the start of a new page.

(37) *ped*: Probably a surname rather than a spelling of *paid*, but the syntax of the item is tangled.

(42) *proponser*: The word is clearly written but highly abbreviated, using conventional abbreviation-marks which produce the form as presented here. To read *purposes* is attractive, but unjustified. OED lists an adjective PROPENSE 'having an inclination [towards something]' and also a noun PURPENSE (later PREPENSE) 'to plan ahead, premeditate', but neither makes an appropriate agent-noun for this context.

Background

These household accounts run from Michaelmas (25 September) 1524 to Michaelmas 1525, and are kept by someone (or two people) in the Countess's household. There is no evidence as to whether he/they is/are of Devon birth.

Katherine Courtenay, Countess of Devon (1479–1527), was the sixth daughter of King Edward III and his queen Elizabeth Woodville. At the time of these accounts she was a widow, living on her Devon estates at Tiverton, Colyton and Broadclyst. Her son Henry had inherited the restored title of Earl of Devon which his father, Sir William Courtenay, had been deprived of by attainder because of suspected conspiracy against Henry VII. Katherine Courtney figures here as *my ladys grace*, and Henry Courtenay, 23 at this time, as (25) *my lordys grace*. It is probably his second wife who is mentioned in l. 14 as *my yong ladye*.

Topics for linguistic investigation

1. Differences in spelling-preferences that distinguish the writer of lines 1–12 from the writer of the remainder of the text.
2. The spellings (2) *mynd*, (3) *offreng*, (4) *a yenst*, (22) *marshod*, (25) *Iohn agawntt*, (29) *caryag*, (29) *wensday*, (41) *yowry*, (45) *bo3th*, (49) *amnerer*, (55) *hole*.
3. The inflexional morphology of (30) *gavntt*, (45) *thyng*, (54) *pare*, (54) *hosyn*.
4. The syntax of (5) *parte the yeare*, (13–14) *whan that my yong ladye* …, (29) *þe wensday*, (35–6) *for fechyng of wyn*.

Text 12

Churchwardens of Strood: Kent 1555

(British Library Manuscript Additional 36,937)

[f. 2r]   a° 1555.

The accumpt*is* mayd by Edward week*is* & Rog*er* branche chyrchwardons of
strood gevy*n* be ffor the pareche the xxiiij. day of may: & in the ffyrst & secu*n*d
year of the Reyng of kyng phylyp & qwen Mare:

                    *   *   *   *

5	[f. 2v] expenssis	
	It*em* payd to *sir* wyll*ia*m Dune ffor goyng to maidston on haullo thursday	ij^s
	It*em* payd ffor ow^r dyn*eris* at the vysytacyon	ij^s iiij^d
	It*em* gevyn to Ihon adams	xij^d
10	It*em* gevyn to Ihon greffen in his seknes	xij^d
	It*em* gevyn to okle in his syknes	xij^d
	It*em* payd to vmffray ffor a horsse hyd	xx^d
	It*em* paid ffor a payr of brechis to Ihon adams	ij^s ij^d
	It*em* to Ihon Danyell ffor makyng of ye bawdrek*is*	ij^s
15	It*em* paid to blayk ffor ye ees & tong*is* & a kee to ye vest*ere*	ij^s vj^d
	It*em* ffor ij tapars ffor the allt*er*	viij^d
	It*em* ffor a sholl	vj^d
	It*em* gevyn to Ihon greven	vj^d
	It*em* ffor Ryngyng apon *prossescyon* twsday	ij^d
20	It*em* paid ffor ow^r Dynn*er* at the vystacyo*n*	xx^d
	It*em* gevyn to mallt*is* wyff	iiij^d
	It*em* gevyn to ye pov*erte* att allowtyde in mony & bred	x^s
	It*em* payd for the pyk*is* to byllton	v^s
	It*em* paid for a pyn to ye pyx	ij^d
25	It*em* paid ffor ij^{li} of wax at *cristymes*	xvj^d
	It*em* ffor a pond of candell at *cristymes*	iiij^d
	It*em* gevyn in Allmos to the pur pepyll at *cristymes*	v^s
	It*em* gevyn to mallt ffor beryng atorche at *cristymes*	j^d
	It*em* gevyn to a pur chyld y^t lay in ye strett	iiij^d
30	It*em* paid to Ihon ffawden ffor wax & strykyng at hallowtyd	

cristymes & ester & ffor the paschall ——————— iiij^s x^d

Item paid to Roger branche ffor ij^{li} of wax ——————— xxij^d

Item paid to Ioon Danyell ffor washyng of the chyrche gear ——— xij^d

[f. 3r] Item gevyn in bred to ye pouerte apon gudffryday ————— vj^s

35 Item ffor watchyng of the sepulcar mett & drynk ——————— xx^d

Item gevyn to thomas pond {at ester} ——————— xij^d

Item gevyn to mother stook ——————— xij^d

Item to the chyrchwardons ffor ther paynes ——————— iiij^s

Item ffor the buk maykyng & Regesteryng ——————— xx^d

40 Summa totalis ——————— iij^{li} ij^s viij^d

* * * *

[f. 3v]   1555
The Invitory of the chyrche gudis
Item a chalis of sylver & gyltt
Item a cop of whytt Dameske
45 Item a whytt vestmentt w^t albe
Item iij surplecis & ~~a Rachett~~
Item yij towells
Item acrosse w^t the banner
Item a hersse clothe of sylk
50 Item ayalow clothe of sylke ffor ye hye all allter & another of dornix
Item atorge a basyn a lauer of puder
Item ij tapars of ye hye alter & a pascall
Item a sepulcar apresse achest w^t iij lokis & an old chest in ye vestre
Item a crysatour ij cruwettis asacryng bell apext for ye sacrament
55 Item a bybell ye paraphrasis of erasmus asaulter in latten a masse buke a manuell
aprosesseyoner ij salter bukis in ynglech & amanuell
Item ij alterclothis & on of diaper of ye gyft of mother bettis
Item iij banner staffis w^t clothis anold antyfoner a torche a holy watter stoke of
led iij coshyngis a corprex w^t ye clothe ~~a payr of sensars~~ a ladder apayr of sensars

Notes

Text

Extract only; the manuscript contains accounts from 1555 to 1763. The text has been edited in Henry R. Plomer (ed.), *The Churchwardens' Accounts of St. Nicholas, Strood*, Part I: 1555–1600, Part II: 1603–1662, Kent Records (Kent Archaeological Society), Vol. V (1927).

Manuscript

The *ne* in (38) *paynes* and the *ue* in (56) *amanuell* are hurriedly and indistinctly written, and could be challenged. In (55) *manuell* all letters are clear, but the *n* and *u* are identical.

The writer nearly always dots not only *i* but also *y*, except where it represents a consonant in *y*^e and *y*^t.

The final stroke of word-final *m* and *n* is always lengthened. Many other letters word-finally are followed by a light stroke which has been taken as empty, but occasionally a firmer line has been read as as an additional *e*, as in (3) *pareche*, (42) *chyrche*, (58) *torche*.

The item *cristymes* (25 etc.) is always written with a horizontal line above the last syllable, although no abbreviation is evident.

There is an error of dittography in (50) *all aller*.

Glossary

For detail on words relating to the church year, and vestments, vessels, books etc. see J. G. Davies, *A New Dictionary of Liturgy and Worship* (SCM Press, London, 1986).

(7)	*haullo thursday*	Ascension Day (see note)
(8)	*vysytacyon*	official visit by Bishop or Achdeacon
(14)	*bawdrekis*	=baldrics, from which clappers of church bells hang
(15)	*ees*	=eyes, eyelets (in baldrics)
(17)	*sholl*	=shovel?
(19)	*prossescyon twsday*	Tuesday of Rogation week (leading up to Ascension Day) when processions are held
(22 and 34)	*y*^e *poverte*	the poor
(22) *allowtyde* (and (30) *hallowtyd*)		Feast of All Saints, 1 November
(23)	*pykis*	See note
(30)	*strykyng*	moulding candles
(31 and 52)	*paschall*	large Easter Candle
(33)	*gear*	See note
(35)	*watching*	keeping vigil
(35)	*sepulcar*	=sepulchre, tomb (see note)
(35)	*mett*	=meat, food
(37 and 57)	*mother*	courtesy-title for elderly woman
(42)	*invitory*	inventory (see note)
(44)	*cop*	=cope
(46)	*rachett*	=rochet (a vestment)
(50)	*dornix*	silk/woollen fabric (see note)
(51)	*(a)torge*	(?)torch (see note)
(51)	*lauer*	=laver, ewer
(51)	*puder*	=pewter
(53)	*sepulcar*	See note to l. 35
(53)	*(a)presse*	cupboard
(54)	*crysatour*	=chrismator, chrismatory (container for consecrated oil)
(54)	*(a)sacryng bell*	consecration-bell, rung at elevation of Host
(54)	*(a)pext*	=pyx (box for keeping Host)
(55)	*(a)saulter* (and (56) *salter*)	=psalter, psalm-book
(55)	*manuell*	=manual, service-book for use of priest

(56)	*(a)prosesseyoner*	=processioner, book of prayers for use during processions
(57)	*diaper*	See note
(58)	*antyfoner*	=antiphoner, book for use in singing responses etc.
(58)	*stoke*	=stock, stoup or basin for holy water
(59)	*coshyngis*	=cushions (for books)
(59)	*corprex*	=corporas, corporal (see note)
(59)	*sensars*	=censers

Explanatory notes

(7) *haullo thursday*: The name 'Hallow-Thursday' was also used for Maundy Thursday in Holy Week (See OED THURSDAY), but the Accounts run May to April, so begin at Ascensiontide 1554 and end at Easter 1555. The final letter of the word *haullo* is doubtful; Plomer *Strood* reads *haulls*, an alternative form which is on record (see OED HALLOW n.).

(23) *the pykis to byllton*: Possibly =*picks* (i.e. tools) or *pikes* (i.e. weapons) or maybe *pyx*, though elsewhere in the text this is spelled more conventionally. Sent for repair to *byllton* (a place or a person?) or the reason for a payment to *byllton* (a person).

(33) *washyng of the chyrche gear*: *Gear* was frequently used in reference to church vestments, but presumably only certain items (e.g. surplices) were washable.

(35) *watching of the sepulcar*: The Easter Sepulchre, listed in the inventory l. 53. This was an elaborate structure, mainly of wood, set up in church on Maundy Thursday, and in it were placed consecrated Hosts for Good Friday and Easter-eve and the Cross used for Good Friday ceremonial Veneration. Candles were kept burning before it, so watchers were organised to check on the candles at intervals, especially during the night. A further possibility is that parishioners kept vigil throughout the period, so that refreshments were provided.

(42) *invitory*: Not merely an idiosyncratic spelling; OED records several instances of the form, though it labels it as 'corrupt'.

(50) *dornix*: A fabric often used for hangings and vestments. The name (see OED DORNICK) is an eponym based on the place of manufacture, Doornik (=Tournay) in Flanders, though an alternative spelling *dornock* sometimes led to mistaken attribution to Dornoch in Scotland.

(51) *atorge*: Possibly a torch, but the word is spelled more conventionally in l. 58, and the items listed alongside suggest that some third pewter vessel used at the altar is named here.

(55) *ye paraphrasis of erasmus*: Erasmus' Paraphrases on the Gospels. An injunction by Edward VI in 1547 ordered priests to buy it, to improve their understanding of Scripture.

(57) *diaper*: A white fabric with a self-coloured woven pattern. Medieval texts use it to refer to a rich fabric, but later it is applied to fine linen. See OED DIAPER.

(59) *a corprex w^t ye clothe*: The corporal is itself a cloth, kept in a corporal-case or burse when not in use. The inventory transfers *corprex* to refer to the complete item, i.e. 'a burse with the corporal'.

Background

Since these accounts are for the year 1554–55, they fall within the period of the return to Catholic practice under Queen Mary, following Protestant worship in the reign of King Edward VI. Of the items listed in the Inventory, especially the books, some probably date from former Catholic times, some from the Protestant era, and some from the new Catholic period.

Topics for linguistic investigation

1. The evidence relating to the pronunciation of consonants in the spellings (14) *bawdrekis*, (17) *sholl*, (19) *prossescyon*, (25) *cristymes*, (50) *hye*, and to that of vowels in the spellings (15) *ees*, (33) *chyrche*, (35) *mett*, (42) *gudis*, (44) *cop*, (50) *yallow*.
2. What can be learned from the variant spellings (10) *greffen* and (18) *greven*, (10) *seknes* and (11) *syknes*, (14) *makyng* and (39) *maykyng*, (22) *allowtyde* and (30) *hallowtyd*, (24) *pyx* and (54) *pext*, (31) *paschall* and (52) *pascall*.
3. The etymology of the names of objects used in church ceremonial.
4. *Damask* and *dornick*: Find out about eponyms from place-names at this period.

Text 13

Property in Appleby: Westmorland 1562
(Cumbria Record Office, Kendal, Manuscript WD/Ry, box 131)

Accordynge to y^{or} Lordshipp*es* Comm*a*ndme*n*t And Com*m*yscion we hayve
vewyt the ~~the~~ hovses of the vicarage of sanct*e* lavre off Appelbe not to so full A
valove ~~And~~ as we wold hayve doyne yf we had beyn sworne

5   fyrst for the Rep*a*racons of the wheyt barne & vj sparr*es* and ij fothers of
watlynge lackyn and none to {be} gotte*n* ther
It*em* for wryght worke/ watlyng/ thekyn/ and wavlynge the
sayd barne _____ vj^s
It*em* for thacke to be bovght to the sayme _____ vj^s viij^d

It*em* for the hayver barne And bygge barne/ xx sparr*es*/ ij fothers of watlyng
10   and wodd for ij dores & non ther to be gotte*n*
It*em* for the wryghtworke/ watlyng/ thekyn and wavlyng
& x days_____ v^s viij^d
It*em* for thake to be bovght to the sayd barnes _____ iiij^s

It*em* for the kylne whiche ys In decay And Clean goynedovne And no wodde
15   lefte bot v pec*es* of evell temer of no vaylov & the sayd kylne was of iiij Cuppell*es*
of temer/ and All the wodde ys lackyn for the sayd kylne and none theyr to be
gotten/ Wherefor we fynd yt must hayve for the byldy*n*g of the sayme Agayne/
iiij Cuppell*es* of new temer wth all other wodd*es* belo*n*gy*n*g therto and also iiij
fothers watly*n*g
20   It*em* for the wryght warke of the sayme kylne_____ xl^s
It*em* for watlyng/ thekyn/ And wavly*n*ge/ makyn/ the
kylnepot and for thake to be bovght to same _____ xxx^s

It*em* for the haybarne/ stabyll And Covhouse ys In suche decay that thay wyll
fall dovne the sayd hovse ys of vj Cuppell*es* of temer wherefor*e* the on half*e* of
25   the sayd greyt temer wylnot s*er*ue to the byldynge of the sayme therfor*e* yt must
hayve iij Cuppell*es* of new temer and all other wodd*es* therto belo*n*gynge wth v
fothers of watlynge And none ther to be gotte*n*
It*em* for the wryght warke of the sayd hovses_____ xxxiij^s iiij^d
It*em* for watlynge thekyn and wavlyng of the sayd hovses_____ x^s

66

30   Item for thake to be bovght to the sayme_____ vj^s viij^d

Item on buttery And on larder hovse Clear goyne Dovne therefore yt must have
ij Cuppell*es* off new temer and all other wodd*es* belo*n*gynge to the same and no
wod lefte bot iiij pec*es* y^t wyl do no s*er*ues
Item for the wryght warke of the sayd butt*ery*_____ xx^s
35   Item for watlyng thekyn And wavlynge_____ vj^s viij^d
Item for thake to be bovght to the sayme_____ iij^s iiij^d
Item thayr lak*es* wodd for x Dores the warkma*n*ship of
the sayme_____ x^s
Item for the havle for thake to be bovght to the sayme _____ iij^s iiij^d
40   Item for thekyn And mendyng Croslofte wavlles And
slaterwarke _____ iij^s viij^d
Item for slaytt to the sayme _____ < BLANK >

Item for the garner hovse yt lack*es* o*n* Rybbe on helynge o*n* wy*n*doy ij paer of
dov*r*e chek*es* And no wodd ther
45   Item for the wryghtwarke of the sayme iiij days _____ ij^s iiij^d
Item for thekyn watlyng And for thake to sayme_____ iiij^s viij^d

In Wytnesse of all the p*r*emiss*es* we hayve setto o^r seyll*es* And subscribed o^r
names the xxiiij day of October In an^o quarto Elezabeth Regine &c
forthermore be yt knowen that forsomoche as thar ys Corne and hay in the
50   forsayd barnes we Cannot p*er*fyetly know what Decay the sayd barnes ys in
whayr the sayd corne and hay sta*n*des

Thomas	Heugh	Antony	Iohn
Thereller	carluert	poullay	Calvert
	X	**X**	**X**

Notes

Text

The document has been edited and discussed by Blake Tyson, 'The Elizabethan
Farmstead at St Lawrence's Vicarage, Appleby', *Transactions of the Cumberland &
Westmorland Antiquarian & Archaeological Society*, Vol. XCIV (1994), Art. X, pp.
121–34.

Manuscript

In addition to a typical secretary *y* the writer uses another form, reminiscent of ʒ, where
the tail does not curve back to the right. They have not been distinguished in
transcription, since there appears to be no pattern of use, and the two forms occur in
repeats of the same item, thus (20) and (28) *wryght*, (6) and (29) *wavlynge*.
  The sign treated as an abbreviation-mark for a final *e* in some words is so minimal that

it could be challenged as a mere word-final hook. Thus (24) *wherefore*, (25) *therfore*, (44) *dovre*, and (2) *sancte*, (24) *halfe*.

In (25) *greyt* the reading is not clear, since the second letter (here read as *r*) is written over a letter with a descender, probably a *y*. Also unclear is (48) *&c.* The first signature (52–3) is virtually illegible, conjecturally transcribed here *Thomas Thereller*.

Of the signatures in lines 52–3 numbers 1, 2 and 3 are written in different hands, while number 4 appears to be in the same hand as the document. Since numbers 2, 3 and 4 also have marks, they are probably not holograph signatures.

Glossary

For building terms see Tyson, *Elizabethan Farmstead*, and Glen L. Pride, *Glossary of Scottish Building*, 3rd Issue (Scottish Civic Trust, Glasgow, 1989).

(2)	*vewyt*	=viewed, inspected
(2)	*hovses*	buildings
(2)	*full*	detailed
(3)	*valove* (and (15) *vaylov*)	=value, valuation
(3)	*sworne*	admitted to office by a formal oath
(4)	*Reparacons*	repairs
(4)	*sparres* †	rafters
(4)	*fothers*	cart-loads
(5)	*watlynge*	branches for wattle (see note)
(5)	*lackyn*	=lacking
(6)	*wryght worke* †	work done by a joiner or carpenter
(6)	*thekyn*	roofing (see note)
(8)	*thacke*	roofing-materials (see note)
(9)	*hayver* †	oats
(9)	*bygge* †	barley
(14)	*Clean*	utterly
(14)	*goynedovne*	=gone down, ruinous
(15)	*temer*	=timber
(15)	*Cuppelles*	=couples, pairs of beams (see note)
(22)	*kylnepot*	floor of kiln
(32)	*buttery*	store for food
(32)	*larder hovse*	store for food, especially meat
(39)	*havle*	=hall, principal room of house
(40)	*Croslofte* †	gallery across end of hall
(41)	*slaterwarke*	work done by a slater
(43)	*garner hovse*	granary, store for corn
(43)	*Rybbe* †	roof-timber, purlin
(43)	*helynge* †	roof
(43)	*wyndoy*	=window
(44)	*dovre chekes* †	uprights for doors
(47)	*premisses*	aforesaid statement
(47)	*setto*	=set to, affixed

(47)	*seylles*	=seals
(47)	*subscribed*	signed
(49)	*forsomuche as*	because

Local placenames

| (2) | *sancte lavre* | St Lawrence |
| (2) | *Appelbe* | Appleby, Westmorland |

Explanatory notes

(5) *watlynge*: wattle is usually interwoven branches or withies, forming the foundation for a plaster wall, but can also refer to branches supporting roof-thatch. Tyson, *Elizabethan Farmstead*, suggests the latter sense here, pointing out that in this area walls are normally of stone rather than wattle and plaster.

(6 and 8) *thekyn, thacke*: It is likely that the roofs were thatched, but the term also covers roofing of other materials (OED THACK).

(15) *Cuppelles*: pairs of beams forming roof trusses or, more likely, cruck-frames.

Background

St Lawrence Vicarage had attached to it a number of farm buildings, which were leased out by the owner of the living, at this time the Dean and Chapter of Carlisle.

This document is a survey by four assessors inspecting the various buildings, and estimating the cost of the work necessary to make good the delapidations they find. Their standing is not noted, but a later inspection (1582) was carried out by two carpenters and two *wallers*, and it is likely that this earlier group of inspectors was constituted in a similar way.

Topics for linguistic investigation

1. The use of vowel + *y* in the representation of vowels, and its implications in regard to vowel-length.
2. The evidence relating to the pronunciation of vowels in the spellings (5) *thekyn*, (10) *wodd*, (15) *temer*, (20) *warke*, (43) *wyndoy*.
3. The evidence relating to the pronunciation of consonants in the spellings (5) *lackyn*, (15) *temer*, (50) *perfyetly*.
4. The forms (2) *vewyt*, (17) *gotten*, (23) *ys*, (43) *lackes*, (50) ys, (51) *standes*.
5. Consult a dialect dictionary for the areas which at this time used (4) *sparres*, (6) *wryght*, (43) *Rybbe*, (44) *chekes* in the senses they have here.
6. *Hayver* and *bygge*: Investigate the use and etymology of local names for crops.

Text 14

For a Ship: Rye, Sussex 1589

(East Sussex Record Office Manuscript RYE 72/1)

[f. 1v] bought a pese of tymber to make the bote thaught &
for 2 knees _____ 20ᵈ

bought ovlld Saylldes to make stovding Saylles & tope armors ____ 35ˢ

bought 4 ores _____ 8ˢ

5   bought 30 fute of bord & 40 fovte of plancke _____ 4ˢ

payd to the coper for worcke_____ 24ˢ   6ᵈ

bought 3 yerdes of Lefont tavyta & a Skayne of Syllcke for the
trompeters _____ 6ˢ   4ᵈ

bought ellme plancke for to macke careges for the brase peses _____ 12ˢ

10   payd for the makyng of 3 Stockes _____ 10ˢ

bought canvys & whyt clothe to make carterreges for the gvners ____ 8ˢ

bought 10 ~~Sker~~ {Saker} & mynyon Slydyng Shote_____ 11ˢ   8ᵈ

bought 7 Saker Rovnd Shote wayng 32ˡⁱ _____ 2ˢ   8ᵈ

bovght 8 mynyon Shote _____ 12ᵈ

15   bought a tande hyde _____ 9ˢ   6ᵈ

bought Leders for 2 boge barell _____ 2ˢ   6ᵈ

bought 3 Seves for the povder & a Spaye _____ 16ᵈ

bought wode to macke tamkyns _____ 4ᵈ

bought 3 dosen of platers _____ 7ˢ 10ᵈ

20   bought 2 dosen & 2 dysses _____ 2ˢ   6ᵈ

bought 2 dosen trenchers _____ 3ᵈ

bought 6 tankerd_____ 3ˢ   6ᵈ

bought 2 cope dyshes & one dosen Spones _____ 12ᵈ

for a payer of beloves _____ 8ᵈ

25   payd for okman Expences for to go to tenterdon fayer & for the
brynging it home_____ 2ˢ   4ᵈ

[f. 2r] bought 6 hocshed to put in the befe _____ 10ˢ

bought 12 boshall of Salte_____ 24ˢ

for the carege of it_____ 8ᵈ

30   bought 16 copell < HOLE > at 14ᵈ the copull _____ 18ˢ   8ᵈ

bought for hamo< HOLE > 2 tonne & halfe &
one p< HOLE >_____ 18ˢ 10ᵈ

bought for <w>ater 2 tonne caske {& a hallfe} _____ 6ˢ   4ᵈ

70

	bought 2 flyches backen wayng 64^{li} at 2^d ⅟ the pond	13^s	4^d
35	payd to the porter for carege of 6 hocshed & one bonne of befe & for 2 tonne of water	3^s	8^d
	payd to a lyter to carye the bere a bord	2^s	
	payd to one to carye the buter & cheses		3^d
40	payd to grynland for caryng the erne ordenance A bord the Shype		12^d
	bought 6 bedones	6^s	
	bought threde to make the cartreg		6^d
	bought 74^{li} of buter at 4^d the pond	24^s	
	payd for the crockes		12^d
45	bought 6 dosen of Candells	21^s	
	payd for a lyter to carye the water & Stronge bere A bord		12^d
	bought 3 qartes of ovylle	5^s	
	for a botell to pute it in		8^d
	bought 4 galandes of mvster Sede	2^s	8^d
50	bought crockes for the gonners & Stuard	2^s	6^d
	bought 2 bolldes for the Stuard		10^d
	bought 6 galand vynger	4^s	
	bought Rvmlete to put the vynneger in		8^d
	payd to gryndland for caryng the brase ordenance & byfe A bord		12^d
55	bought of goodwyfe hellyerd a cetell	2^s	
	bought of thomas welles one barell of fyshe & 6 cupell code	31^s	
	bought of goodwyfe mylles a vyrkyn of buter	18^s	
	bought 12 cupell of code	20^s	
	bought 100 of dryde fyshe	14^s	
60	bought 11 boshall of pese	22^s	
	bought 3 hocshed to put in the pese	2^s	8^d

Notes

Text

Extract only. From the records of the Borough of Rye, Sussex. The complete text has been edited in Richard F. Dell (ed.), *Rye Shipping Records 1566–1590*, Sussex Record Society, Vol. LXIV (1966), pp. 45–9.

Manuscript

Money totalled at the foot of the page (after l. 26) has been omitted.

Glossary

For detail on ship's equipment see John Smith, *A Sea Grammar* (London, 1627), facsimile reprint in English Experience series (Amsterdam, 1968), and Peter Kemp (ed.), *The Oxford Companion to Ships and the Sea* (Oxford University Press, London,

1976 and Granada Publishing, St Albans, 1979). On gunnery see Michael Lewis, *Armada Guns* (Allen & Unwin, London, 1961).

(1)	*bote*	ship's boat
(1)	*thaught*	=thwart, seat across boat for rowers
(2)	*knees*	naturally-bent pieces of timber, in this case for supporting thwarts
(3)	*stovding Saylles*	=studding-sails, extra sails used in fair wind
(3)	*tope armors*	=top-armours, pieces of canvas to protect men up the mast during battle
(6)	*coper*	=cooper, cask-maker
(7)	*Lefont tavyta*	taffeta from the Levant
(7)	*Skayne*	=skein (see note)
(9)	*careges*	=carriages, wheeled stands
(9)	*peses*	=pieces, cannon
(10)	*Stockes*	gun-carriages
(12)	*Saker*	a kind of cannon
(12)	*mynyon*	another kind of cannon
(12)	*Slydyng Shote*	See note
(13)	*Rovnd Shote*	cannon balls
(16)	*Leders*	=leathers, probably carrying-straps
(16)	*boge barell*	=budge barrel, small portable powder-barrel made of metal
(17)	*Spaye*	?=spade
(18)	*tamkyns*	wooden stoppers or wads
(23)	*cope dyshes*	?cups
(27)	*hocshed*	=hogshead(s), large cask(s) (or measure of capacity)
(28)	*boshall*	=bushel, unit of measurement of capacity (8 gallons)
(34)	*flyches*	=flitches, sides (of bacon)
(35)	*bonne*	?=bone
(36)	*tonne*	=tun, large cask (or measure of capacity)
(37)	*lyter*	=lighter, barge loading goods
(39)	*erne*	=iron
(39)	*ordenance*	=ordnance, cannon
(41)	*bedones*	?=beddings, wooden blocks on which cannon rest
(44)	*crockes*	pots (or ?hooks)
(47)	*ovylle*	=oil
(49)	*galandes*	=gallons
(49)	*muster*	=mustard
(50)	*Stuard*	=steward, man in charge of stores and catering
(51)	*bolldes*	=bowls
(52)	*vynger*	=vinegar
(53)	*Rvmlete*	=runlet, cask
(55)	*goodwyfe*	courtesy title for middle-class woman
(55)	*cetell*	=kettle, cauldron
(57)	*vyrkyn*	=firkin, small cask (or measure of capacity)

Explanatory notes

(7) *A Skayne of Syllcke*: since skein always refers to a quantity of thread, this must be silk thread rather than silk fabric.

(12) *Slydyng Shote*: an unidentified type of shot, possibly an alternative name for one of the common types such as chain-shot or case-shot.

(25) *tenterdon fayer*: Fair at Tenterden, Kent, 8 miles inland from Rye.

(42) *threde to make the cartreg*: canvas cartridges needed stitching.

Background

The ship is the *William* of Rye, and she is being equipped for service against the Spanish Armada. All South coast towns were required to do this, and the town of Rye arranged to charter a local ship and see to its fitting out as a ship of war.

Topics for linguistic investigation

1. A survey of the area of origin of texts which have spellings such as (7) *tavyta* and (57) *vyrkyn*.
2. The significance of the alternative spellings used in this text for (1) *make*, (3) *Saylles*, (5) *fovte*, (11) *gvners*, (30) *copell*, (35) *befe*, (39) *grynland*, (42) *cartreg*, (53) *vynneger*, (61) *put*.
3. The evidence relating to the pronunciation of consonants in the spellings (1) *thaught*, (13) *wayng*, (16) *Leders*, (37) *lyter*, (49) *mvster*.
4. What system does the writer appear to be using in regard to when to put a plural inflexion on a plural noun?
5. Syntactic choice as shown in (9) *ellme plancke for to macke careges* and (42) *threde to make the cartreg*, (19) *3 dosen of plateres* and (21) *2 dosen trenchers*, (25–6) *for the brynging it home* and (39–40) *for caryng the erne ordenance A bord the Shype*, (53) *Rvmlete to put the vynneger in* and (61) *3 hocshed to put in the pese*.
6. The vocabulary of measurement.
7. The vocabulary of gunnery.

Text 15

Richard Warwick: ?Northamptonshire 1601

(British Library Manuscript Althorp A.31 Document in Bundle 28)

The r*igh*t worshipfull Ser Robart Spencer the 10ᵗʰ of November 1601
Inpr*im*es: for makinge towe strayt bodied
ashe colored satten gownes, for yoʳ tow eldest
daughters _____ xvj s

5   for canvas, stifininge and bent*es* _____ iiij s viij d

for fustion to line the bodies, and sleues and to border them ____ viij s

for towe elnes of white taffita to line vnder the cutt*es*_____ xvj s

for cuttinge and cacinge the satten _____ viij s viij d

for xiiij ounces of silver sprigg lace at vj s iiij d an ounce____ iiij l viij s iiij d

10   for an ounce and a halfe of silver parchement lace, to binde
the bodies at 5ˢ – 6ᵈ_____ viij s iij d

for an ounce of silver spangled tast*es* and plade lace, for
stomachers and collers _____ vj s viij d

for fower yard*es* of white cobweb Lawne to puffe the gadges

15   and sisees _____ v s

for sowinge silcke to bothe gownes _____ v s

for whalbones to the bodies _____ xx d

for tow pare of whalebone sleues _____ viij s

More for makinge three Carsie gownes for three of yoʳ

20   daughters _____ xx s

for canvas stiffninge and bent*es* _____ vj s

for lininge to the bodies and sleues and fustion to border
the skert _____ vj s viij d

for whale bone to the Bodies of all the three gownes _____ ij s iiij d

25   for lace to binde all there bodies and for sowinge silcke _____ iiij s

for eyght yard*es* of silver tinsele to line vnder the cut*es*,
at 2ˢ – 6ᵈ – yd _____ xx s

for cuttinge the bodies and sleues of them _____ iiij s

for silver stuffe to puffe the slishes _____ iiij s

30   for half an ounce of silver edginge to edge the stomachers
and collers _____ iiij s iiij d

for three pare of whalebone sleues _____ x s vj d

More for makinge tow petecot*es* of stript silck mockado,

	wth a silcke & silver bindinge lace _____	vj s
35	for v yard*es* of beas at 2^s – 6^d _____	xij s vi d
	for ribin, silck, and buckrome _____	xviij d
	for an ounce of bindinge lace _____	iiij s
	for white fustion to them _____	xvj d
	for thre pare of bodies _____	xiij s iiij d
40	for tow varthingales _____	x s
	The whole Some is _____	xv^{li} j^s ix^d

Recave this xiijth of novembar 1601 this xv^{li} j^s ix^d in full disc\<arg>e of all
accontes for the dah\<ters> of < ILLEGIBLE > Recaved it by the hand of of
william hee sketh & pay in full dicarge of al Reconigs By ✝ mee Richard warwick

Notes

Text

From the papers of the Spencer family of Althorp, near Northampton. The text has not
been edited before.

Manuscript

The account and the receipt at the end appear to be in the same hand, the looser spelling
of the receipt may be because it is written on-the-spot and more hurriedly. Haste also
explains the dittography in l. 43, where *of* is written at the end of a line and also at the
beginning of the next.

The letters *n* and *u* are not distinguished, but raise no problems except in (9 etc.)
ounces, which might be *onnces*. The letters *a* and *u* are also confusable. In (44) *Reconigs*
the minim-strokes might represent the equally deficient spelling *Recoings*; there is no
abbreviation-stroke for a missing *n*.

The text in lines 42–3 is badly rubbed away where the document has been folded.

Glossary

On fabrics and fashions, there is more detail than in OED in Janet Arnold (ed.), *Queen
Elizabeth's Wardrobe Unlock'd* (Maney, Leeds, 1988) and in C. W. and P. Cunnington,
Handbook of English Costume in the Sixteenth (Seventeenth) Century (Faber & Faber,
London, 1954 (1955)).

(2)	*strayt bodied*	with narrow tight-fitting bodice
(3)	*ashe colored*	light grey
(5)	*bentes*	stiffeners (see note)
(6)	*fustion*	coarse cotton fabric
(6)	*bodies*	bodices
(7)	*elnes*	=ell, measure of length, 45 inches
(7)	*cuttes*	ornamental slashes where under-fabric shows through
(8)	*cacinge*	=casing, lining
(9)	*sprigg*	with flower pattern

(9)	*lace*	braid for binding edges
(10)	*parchement*	See note
(12)	*tastes*	silk ribbon for binding edges (see note)
(12)	*plade*	=played, folded
(13)	*stomachers*	neckline-to-waist panels, intended to be seen through lacings of outer bodice
(14)	*cobweb Lawne*	very fine light linen fabric
(14)	*puffe*	decorate with ruched lightweight material
(14)	*gadges*	=gauges, gathers
(15)	*sisees*	=scissures, ornamental slashes
(19)	*Carsie*	=kersey, coarsish woollen fabric
(26)	*silver tinsele*	rich thin fabric with silver thread woven into it
(29)	*slishes*	slits, slashes
(33)	*petecotes*	=petticoats, richly decorated underskirts intended to be seen
(33)	*stript*	=striped
(33)	*silck mokado*	See note
(35)	*beas*	=bias, edging material diagonally cut
(36)	*buckrome*	=buckram, coarse gummed fabric for lining
(40)	*varthingales*	frameworks of whalebone hoops to spread out skirt

Explanatory notes

(5) *bentes*: possibly stiffeners of stiff hollow-stem grass (OED BENT n[1] 'reed'), but these were phased out by whalebone stiffeners before the end of the sixteenth century, so it is likely that either the old word has been retained for the new material or else this is OED BENT n[2] 'a piece bent into a curve'.

(10) *parchement lace*: some kind of braid, but experts are not sure what it was like. OED defines it as 'braid with a parchment core', but Arnold, *Wardrobe*, takes alternative spellings such as *passamaine* and *passament* to indicate that it was 'some kind of braid made by twisting threads in the hand'.

(12) *tastes*: Earliest example in OED TASTE n[2] is 1847, with the suggestion of an origin in US local use.

(33) *silck mockado*: OED cites other examples of this phrase to suggest that although *mockado* is generally a lower-price fabric, the name could also refer to a quality material.

(40) *varthingales*: The spelling cannot be taken as indication of an accent with voicing of initial [f] to [v], since in this word at this period spellings with *v* are as common as those with *f*, the word being borrowed from OF *verdugale*, from Spanish *verdugado*. However, English forms retaining this *v* usually retain the *d* also, instead of substituting *th*. See OED FARTHINGALE.

Background

Nothing is known about the tailor, identified in the receipt as Richard Warwick. Although the Spencer home was Althorp, Northamptonshire, the dresses may have been made locally or elsewhere, perhaps in London.

Sir Robert Spencer (1570–1627, and from 1603 1st Baron Spencer of Wormlington) of Althorp, Northamptonshire, had four sons and three daughters. In 1601 Mary was 13 years of age, Elizabeth 12 and Margaret 4. The cost of the dresses should be set against a later seventeenth-century comment that Sir Robert had 'the most money of any person in the kingdom'.

This receipted account is among a bundle of bills settled and expenditure incurred by his man William Hesketh (see l. 44).

Topics for linguistic investigation

1. Investigate the forms (6) *bodies*, (7) *elnes*, (18) *pare*.
2. Early Modern English vocabulary-expansion as exemplified by the verbs (6) *line*, (6) *border*, (8) *case*, (14) *puff*, (30) *edge* and by the nouns (7) *cut*, (29) *slish*, (44) *discharge*.
3. The derivational morphology of (5) *stifininge*, (13) *stomachers*, (14) *cobweb*, (14) *Lawne*, (16) *sowinge*, (17) *whalbones*, (19) *Carsie*, (33) *stript*, (33) *petecotes*.
4. The origins of Early Modern English names for fabrics and fashions.

Text 16

Joshua Baudon: West Looe, Cornwall 1655–56

(Cornwall Record Office Manuscript B/WLO/33)

[f. 1r] Mayor Ioshua Baudon
The 29th day of October <1656>
Account what I haue disborst <on the towne bu>snes as followith

	li	s	d
Octb Impr*i*mos for ye Iury	00	04	00
for 4 quart*es* and 1 puynt of sac<k> 18d *per* q<t>	00	06	09
Novb mor Layd out to one man an*d* his wiff an*d* Childron			
yt cam {from} Ierland	00	00	06
mor to 3 saymen yt Lost there ship	00	00	06
decemb 26 gaue to ffrancies willes when Hee went to bresto	00	10	00
28 gaue a french man	00	00	01
Ianury 12 pd for apare of shoes for mathew di*er* bee sids 8d of			
ye vse of Pip*er* Money	00	01	06
15 gaue to asayman that was taken by abrast man of war	00	00	02
22 pd to will Popham & Peter weskot for 3 month Rat	00	00	10
26 pd Iohn winter an*d*william goard for Caring			
away 2 barges of Roble from ye beach vnder ye Cay	00	04	00
26 gaue to apor sayman of London that Lost ther shep	00	00	03
Febrary 12 payd Hew gord ffor mendinge ye Cayes	00	11	00
14 pd will gord for bringinge 1 barge of stones	00	04	06
24 pd peator steevens when hee was prest {& went to			
cornell Rous p*ayd* ye gard18d}	00	02	06
March 8 pd the Hondred Bayly when hee warned mee to size	00	00	08
11 pd will Popham & Peetor weskot for 3 month Rat	00	00	10
13 pd will Cortize when hee went to st Iues	00	08	06
per spent about that busnes at Est Low	00	00	06
21 p*ayd* Iohn Hendey for Reedinge ye Lake	00	01	00
24 for my Charg for goinge to size an*d* Hors hier	00	10	06
<1>656 Apill :4th: pd Iohn Hendey for Clensinge the			
streete by denell Bath dore	00	00	06
17: pd apore man that came out of turkey	00	00	02
24 spent about towne Busnes	00	05	06
30: pd apor man that came from turkey	00	00	04

		li	s	d
	May :7: p^d to the Iewry	00	04	00
	:7: p^d for 1 quartt of sack	00	01	06
35	:26: p^d Thomas Dier for caringe apost Letter to foay	00	01	06
	:29: p^d m^r Axford and timothy mellow for Coping y^e			
	Charter	01	03	00
	mor spent vpon mr Axford to procurhim and att y^e			
	doing of it	00	01	06
40	Iuly 3: p^d to 4 french men that ware taken by adunkark	00	00	04
	4: for goinge to plimith to speke wth the price Ofiyers			
	about the sute	00	04	00
	15: p^d Iohn Hendey for mendinge the stille to Hanavore	00	00	04
	18: p^d to william Popham and Peator weskott for			
45	3 month Ratt	00	00	10
	22: p^d to Elizebeth Gerry for Lodginge ataken man &			
	{meat for} his soper	00	00	04
	23 spent about twone Busenes	00	00	08
	Agist :2: payd to the hondred Bayly 1^s: & spent vpon him 6^d	00	01	06
50	18: p^d spent when the Indentures ware made	00	01	02
	20: for my Expence to Bodmond & {22} horshier {3s 4d}	00	03	04
	26: for my horshier and Expenc for goinge to shilling			
	game	00	01	06
	30: gaue to 6 frenchmen wch ware taken	00	00	04
55	Sept 12: gaue to apore woman wch had 4 Children	00	00	03
	17: payd for sack {at ye Last Cortt}	00	00	09
	22 p^d to tow french men that ware taken	00	00	02
	29: p^d to apost that came to Pres ahors	00	00	06
	October :10: payd peeter weskott & will: Popham for 3 month			
60	Ratt.	00	00	10
	11 spent about the towne busnes	00	03	00
	12 gaue to aman of Coume that was taken att say	00	00	02
	14 p^d to ffrancies willes for Hirent of ponpark	00	05	00
	20: gaue to PLimoth men y^t war taken att 2 times	00	00	10
65	21: day to 3 men that ware taken	00	00	02
	22: day payd for maken CLeene the hall	00	00	02

[f. 1v]	Disborsm<ents>			
		li	s	d
	<O>ctober 24 ffor settinge in <good order> ye towne hall			
	wth Labr & neles	00	01	10
70	24 payd to m^r CLeme<nts f>or his <f>ees	00	10	00
	payd to william Cortize for goinge to penryn about			
	y^e solger	00	05	00
	<2>6 payd to Paskow gord & william gord for there fee	00	05	00
	p^d to y^e post	00	03	04

75   Leyd out to the spanyard as I will aproue in seuerall
           payments wch the day of themonth ssuted _____ 02 10   4
           mor p^d the sollger_____ 00 00   6

Notes

Text

Mayoral account from the Borough records of West Looe (West Looe Town Trust). Text extracts were printed in A. L. Browne (ed.), *Corporation Chronicles, being some account of the Ancient Corporations of East Looe and West Looe in the County of Cornwall* (John Smith, Plymouth, 1904), Chapter VI.

Manuscript

The word *and*, when not abbreviated to *&*, is often written by *an* followed by a looped-back flourish. That this probably represents a final *d* is apparent from full forms which occur, but the same sequence of *n* plus hook is also used in (28) *Hendey*, where, since the *d* is also present, it appears to be merely a form of *n*.

A special letter *p* is employed in the short-form *p^d*, and is used on its own, also for *payd*, in lines 21, 26, 59. The shape is that normally used for the abbreviation *per*, and in l. 5 it has that value.

Large *L* and *C*, as in (6) *Layd* and (6) *Children*, are perhaps word-initial forms rather than capitals; the *L* also occurs occasionally in initial clusters, as in (64) *PLimoth* contrasting with (41) *plimith*.

In (48) *twone* the spelling of the vowel may be intentional, or may be *ow* misordered by a slip of the pen; cf. (31) *towne*.

Reconstruction has been necessary where the leaf has been damaged, as in lines 3, where the space calls for several words, and 68, where two words appear to have been lost.

Glossary

(3)	*disborst*	=disbursed, paid out
(4)	*imprimos*	=imprimis, (Latin) word used to introduce the first item in a list
(4)	*Iury* (and (33) *Iewry*)	=Jury (for Borough Court)
(5)	*quartes*	liquid measures of 2 pints
(5)	*sack*	white wine
(12)	*Piper Money*	money for a piper (see note)
(13)	*taken*	captured (by a privateer seizing his ship)
(13)	*abrast man of war*	a warship from Brest, Brittany
(14)	*Rat*	=rate, charge
(15)	*Caring*	=carrying
(16)	*Cay*	=quay
(17)	*shep*	=ship
(20)	*prest*	=pressed, forcibly enlisted into army or navy

(21)	*cornell*	=colonel (see note)
(22)	*Hondred*	=hundred, sub-division of a county
(22)	*Bayly*	=Bailiff, chief officer
(22)	*warned mee*	gave me an official summons
(22)	*size*	=(the) assize(s)
(26)	*Reedinge*	?clearing reeds from (see note)
(35)	*(a)post Letter*	letter sent through the Post Office
(36)	*Coping*	=copying
(38)	*procurhim*	See note
(40)	*(a)dunkark*	privateer (not necessarily from Dunkirk)
(41)	*price Ofiyers*	=prize officers, officials controlling the sale of ships taken as prizes
(43)	*stille*	=stile
(47)	*meat*	food
(50)	*Indentures*	apprenticeship agreements
(58)	*(a)post*	rider carrying mail
(63)	*Hirent*	ground-rent
(77)	*solger*	=soldier

Local placenames

(24)	*st Iues*	St Ives
(25)	*Est Low*	East Looe
(35)	*foay*	Fowey
(41)	*plimith*	Plymouth
(43)	*Hanavore*	Hannafore
(51)	*Bodmond*	Bodmin
(52–3)	*shilling game*	Shillingham
(62)	*Coume*	Coombe
(63)	*ponpark*	Pound Park
(71)	*penryn*	Penryn

Explanatory notes

(9) *bresto*: The final letter might be an *e*, making the place Brest (Brittany) rather than Bristol, but Brest is spelled *brast* in l. 13, and Bristol seems a more likely destination.

(12) *Piper Money*: OED has PIPE-MONEY in this sense. Possibly the donation of shoes and music was for Dyer's wedding.

(17) *ther shep*: A switch from singular to plural.

(21) *cornell Rous*: *coronel* is a common variant for *colonel* at the period (see OED COLONEL). Colonel Anthony Rous of Halton, St Dominick, was a leading Cornish Parliamentarian, serving on the Cornwall County Committee, in 1653, 1654 and 1656 representing East and West Looe in Parliament, and sitting on the Council of State.

(26) *Reedinge the Lake*: This must refer to the pond of the local tide-mill, a Borough responsibility since they owned the mill and rented it to tenants; *Reedinge* must be the clearing of reeds and other vegetation, although OED does not record this sense. Despite

its linguistic attractiveness, Browne's reading *Late* (=Leat) is not justified.

(28) *1656*: January to March have been 1655, and the new year begins here.

(38) *procurhim*: Probably =*procure him* 'persuade him to do this job', but since the work is copying the town's Charter, this might be *parchment*, noting the cost of materials and appearing in a confused spelling with the *pro* symbol in error for *par*.

(46) *Elizebeth Gerry*: The Borough Court Records of West Looe at this time list her as a licensed Alehouse keeper.

(52–3) *shilling game*: Shillingham, near Looe, was a home of the Buller family, many generations of which were Free Burgesses of West Looe. Sir Richard Buller was Sheriff of Cornwall and General of the Parliamentary Forces in Cornwall.

(63) *Hirent of Ponpark*: The Borough rented Pound Park, which was Duchy of Cornwall land. The five-shilling annual rent had been in dispute some years before, the Crown claiming forty shillings, but the Borough had won.

(65 and 66) *day*: Probably an expansion of the date in each case. The entry in l. 66 then begins in the standard style with *payd*, but that in l. 65 is unusual in this account in beginning with *to* rather than *gaue to* or *payd to*.

(68) *ye towne hall*: During the Commonwealth period the ancient parish church on West Looe quay was secularised into a guildhall.

(70) *m^r CLements*: Thomas Clements was High Steward of West Looe.

Background

East Looe and West Looe, often at this period called by its old name of Portbighan, are small towns on either side of a river. At this time they were two separate Boroughs, each with its own Mayor, though Cromwell in 1653 allowed them only one shared Member of Parliament.

Joshua Baudon was Mayor of West Looe for the year from Michaelmas 1655. The use of first person forms in these accounts (3, 22, 27 etc.) suggests that he himself wrote these accounts, setting them out at the end of his year of office. Since he, unless it is another of the same name, served as Mayor again 1670–71 and 1675–76, he must have been relatively young at this time. His occupation is not on record, but an elder male relative, Thomas Baudon, who was also prominent in Borough affairs and who served as Mayor 1657–58, was an innkeeper in the town. The family continued to provide Mayors for West Looe until the late eighteenth century.

The number of charitable donations to destitute people landed at Looe and needing financial help after being *taken* is because privateering was common in the English Channel at this time, and capture by Barbary pirates was also frequent (30 and 32). When the victims were Frenchmen (54) it is more than likely that their ship had been taken by a Looe-based privateer. That the Borough claimed payment for at least one prize-ship captured by local men is evident from ll. 41–2.

Topics for linguistic investigation

1. To what extent does the evidence of other spellings in this text support the suggestion of pronunciation presented by the spelling (62) *say*?

2. The evidence relating to the pronunciation of vowels in the spellings (5) *puynt*, (16) *Cay*, (17) *shep*, (27) *hier*, (40) *adunkark*, (57) *tow*.
3. The evidence relating to the pronunciation of consonants in the spellings (9) *bresto*, (43) *Hanavore*, (51) *Bodmond*, (63) *Hirent*, (66) *maken*, (72) *solger*.
4. Why (23) *3 month Rat* and (29) *denell Bath dore*?
5. *A pore woman w*^{ch} *had 4 Children*: Survey other texts of the mid/late seventeenth century to check currency at this time of the relative pronoun *which* in relation to people.

Text 17

Churchwardens of Minchinhampton: Gloucestershire 1664

(Gloucester Record Office Manuscript P217 CW/2/1)

[p. 248] The true and Iust Accoumpt of ffrancis Manning and Mr Syddenham Payne Churchwardens ffor the yeare 1664

	l – s – d
Received of the Churchwardens of Rodburrow	00 – 06 – 08
Received of Charles wood ffor one acker of Land	00 – 02 – 00
Received of the parisheners	12 – 00 – 00

*   *   *   *

Payd as ffolloweth payd att visitation to the Register ffor	
penticost the boocke of artickles & oath and other ffees	00 – 07 – 00
payd our expences att visitation	00 – 05 – 00
payd 2 silk strings ffor Ionathan Harris his boy	00 – 00 – 07
payd Thomas Lord pro mending the Clock	00 – 01 – 00
payd the High Constables att the 4 quarter Sessions ffor the	
Kings bench and Marshalsy	02 – 12 – 00
payd ffor the destroying of varmins	00 – 08 – 04
payd ffor the Releife of pooreTravilers	00 – 08 – 09
payd for a silk string pro Iosiph Mayoes Childe	00 – 00 – 03
payd the Ringers pro Ringing the bels vppon the	
5th of November	00 – 01 – 06
payd for the Carridg of the bel wheeles from Ceciter	00 – 02 – 06
payd ffor the bel wheeles	01 – 10 – 00
payd ffor nayles & tape to Mrs Tooke	00 – 00 – 06
payd the Parrotor with the presentments	00 – 01 – 00
payd Thomas Gill pro 2 belropes & Carridg of them	00 – 06 – 00
payd Iohn Horrell ffor his ffyer & his work	00 – 03 – 06
payd ffor lead & soudder & his work to Mend the Leads	02 – 19 – 06
payd Edward Lord ffor one Iron to hang the Claper	00 – 01 – 03
payd Tho: Nelmes ffor beare ffor hiller boy being sick of	

the Pox _____	00 – 00 – 10
payd Richard for Mending the Church Ladder_____	00 – 00 – 04
30 payd the Parrator i booke ffor yᵉ ffast _____	00 – 01 – 00
payd ffor i brush to Cleane the Church_____	00 – 00 – 06
payd Iohn Horrell *pro* keeping the Clock _____	01 – 00 – 00
payd Iohn Horrell *pro* Ringing the 8 a Clock bell _____	00 – 15 – 00
payd Iohn Horrell ffor one dayes work _____	00 – 01 – 00

*   *   *   *

35   Payd ffor drawing out of the transcript and keeping of our
accoumpts and partchments _____ 00 – 05 – 06

*   *   *   *

[p. 249] Memerandom in the Yeare 1664
That I Iohn Manning of the p*ar*ish hath ereckted And bilded Won seat vpon
his own Cost And Charg for his wife and famely or Aney wothr persons As him
40   shall Plase ther Being and having The Anchent Rite And Titell to that seat This
seate standing And gooying to the Pillow that stand Neare vnto Peorch deoare
vpon the Lift hand As wee doe Com in and Soe Recheth from that Pillow {to
the} vant in that Allow this Consented And granted and Plased By the Church
warddons ~~si~~ {Mʳ} Sidnum Payn And frances Manning

45   {this seat was by yᵉ Cons<ent> of yᵉ Chansellor in Larged by Noah Perrers,
which place belongeth to yᵉ house where now Soloman Cook Leveth/}

Contributurs to this seat Laurens Sherar for his wife ~~And Iohn Bath for his wife~~
And Nathanell hearn for won person And Bethia {p*ar*rsly} widow for her sellfe
Hanah Hulins for her self

50   {ye widdow parslys seat aboue men*ci*oned: is Given to mary Casy by yᵉ widow
Skirte <   >}
Memorandum that the seate wheare Phillip Vezy Steven Wood and Thomas
Hayward doeth vsily sit in – Iohn Deane the sonn of Clotherboock deane was
att the charge to raise it hier putt a doore too it and other repayers – wheare
55   vppon a low and authorise {him} to haue two plases the on att the vpper end of
and in the saide seat. Wittnes my hand the 25 day of March in the yeare of oʳ
Lord 1672

per Syd*denham* Payne

Notes

Text

Extracts only. Short extracts 1555–1714 were edited by John Bruce (ed), 'Extracts from the Accounts of Churchwardens of Minchinhampton in the County of Gloucester' in *Archaeologia*, Vol. XXXV (1853), Item xxxii, pp. 409–452.

Manuscript

Pages 248 and 249 are recto and verso of one leaf. The Memo occupying page 249 is a compilation in a number of hands, the first (37–44) being an attempt at elaborate calligraphy. Additions and insertions were made at various times, noting changes in seating.

In line 51, the inserted section appears to have further letters or another word following *Skirte*, but the binding is too tight for it to be read.

In line 11 etc. the abbreviation for the Latin preposition *pro* is used in place of English *for*.

Glossary

(7)	*visitation*	official visit by Archdeacon
(7)	*Register*	diocesan Registrar
(8)	*penticost*	pentecost-money (see note)
(8)	*the boocke of artickles*	list of articles for preparing presentments (see note)
(8)	*oath*	copy of churchwardens' oath of office (see note)
(10)	*strings*	ribbons (see note)
(11)	*pro*	for (Latin)
(13)	*Kings Bench and Marshalsy*	London prisons (see note)
(14)	*varmins*	animals or birds declared to be pests (see note)
(19)	*Carridg*	=carriage, transport
(22)	*Parrotor*	=paritor, apparitor, summoning officer for eccelesiastical court
(22)	*presentments*	reports to diocese (see Texts 57 and 59 below)
(25)	*soudder*	=solder
(25)	*Leads*	lead roofing
(27)	*beare*	=bier
(30)	*ffast*	fast-day
(39)	*wothr*	=other
(40)	*Plase*	=place (see note)
(41)	*Pillow*	=pillar
(41)	*deoare*	=door
(43)	*vant*	=font
(45)	*Chansellor*	diocesan officer
(53–4)	*was att the charge*	bore the cost
(54)	*hier*	=higher
(58)	*per*	by (Latin)

Local placenames

(4)	*Rodburrow*	Rodborough, Stroud
(19)	*Ceciter*	Cirencester

Explanatory notes

(7–9) *visitation*: Visitations were made at Pentecost (Whitsun) and at Michaelmas, the Archdeacon and diocesan officials coming to a central point in the area, with churchwardens of all parishes attending, bringing with them payments, presentments, reports on their parish etc. See Introduction to Presentments, pp. 280–288 below. *Pentecost-money* was paid in the post-reformation period to the Cathedral of the Diocese, as the mother-church of the local parishes; in pre-Reformation times, when it was known as Peter's Pence, it was paid to Rome. The *Articles* were the list which comprised the questionnaire by which the churchwardens had to be guided in making their presentments (see below, page 280). The *Oath* is probably the oath of office to be used when the wardens were sworn in.

(10 and 16) *silk strings*: These are identified in later entries as *Strings for those that had the evill*; the skin-disease known as the King's Evil was thought to be cured by the royal touch in a ceremony used until the reign of Queen Anne. It included presentation of a coin hung on a white ribbon, and from these entries it appears that the parish either undertook to supply this or paid the appropriate fee.

(12–13) *the Kings Bench and Marshalsy*: Two London prisons. Churchwardens' duties at this time included handling the statutory parish payments.

(14) *varmins*: The payment of bounty-money to people bringing skins or heads to prove that pests had been killed was required of churchwardens from 1566. Vermin included moles, hedgehogs, foxes and otters, crows, magpies, bullfinches and kingfishers.

(17–18) *the 5th of November*: It was customary to ring church bells to mark the anniversary of King James I's escape from assassination in the 1605 Gunpowder Plot.

(40) The ambiguity of the spelling *plase* and the lack of punctuation increases the confusion in the syntax. It may mean 'any other persons whom he shall place' or 'any other persons, as shall be pleasing to him', and *ther* may finish this phrase or introduce the next.

(43) *Allow*: Possibly a spelling for *hallow*, so 'the font in that sacred place'. But the use in l. 55 of the verb *a low* (=allow) suggests that this may also be intended here, though the syntax is confused.

(53) *Clotherboock*: Name spelled *Clotterbooke* and *Clotterbuck* in accounts for other years.

Background

Minchinhampton is a small Cotswold town drawing prosperity at this period from the manufacture of cloth.

The careful record of seats for private use is characteristic of the period, when seating was much disputed and churchwardens were responsible for attempting to calm troubled waters.

Topics for linguistic investigation

1. The evidence relating to the pronunciation of vowels in the spellings (4) *Receaved*, (14) *varmins*, (24) *ffyer*, (38) *Won*, (40) *peorch deoare*, (42) *Lift*, (46) *leveth*, (54) *repayers*.
2. The evidence relating to the pronunciation of consonants in the spellings (39) *wothr*, (40) *Anchent*, (40) *Rite*, (43) *vant*, (54) *hier*.
3. The evidence of spelling in regard to the pronunciation of unstressed vowels.
4. The forms (14) *varmins*, (25) *Leads*, (38) *bilded*, (41) *stand*, (38) *hath*, (42) *Recheth*, (53) *doeth*.
5. The constructions (10) *Ionathan Harris his boy*, (23) *Carridg of them*, (35–6) *keeping of our accoumpts*, (46) *which place*, (53) *doeth ... sit*, (54) *wheare vppon*.
6. The use of the prepositions (6) *of*, (17) *vppon*, (27) *of*, (38) *vpon*, (41) *vnto*, (53) *in*, (54) *too*.

Depositions

Plate III

Plate III

Text 21B
Robert Wilson: Selkirk 1540

Scottish Record Office Manuscript TD84/153 f. 282v
Edited text 21B/1–10

Robert Vilsoune mareit of ye aigis of xxxvij ʒeiris dewly sworne in Iugisment
depones be his greit aycht yᵗ he vas vorkand in dauid mynto stair ane certain
ʒeir syne and he hard done strang say to dauid mynto yat scho had coft
ye auld caldroun fra ye gudman of edschaw for xiiij s or xv s and sperit at

5 hyme geif he had ony mony & scho said yat scho had no mor in hir purss
bot viij s iiij d and he ordinit hir to pass & borrow ye remayne and wⁱin ane
bony spaice ye gudman come riddand to ye stair fut & criet vpone dauid mynto &
Done strang & yai passit doun and I sat & saw yaim geif hyme mony one
his cloik Lap bot verily I kenne noᵗ how meikill mony scho & he deliuerit to hym

10 and be ye aycht yᵗ I haif maid I hard yaim aggreit be all yᵗ I culd
heir se & vnderstand

Characters: Use of ʒ in (1) ʒeiris. Use of y in (5) yat, (6) ye, (8) yai.
Allographs: Long and short s e.g. (2) stair and (2) vas. Characters u and v operating as allographs, (7) vpone dauid; final stroke of numeral realised as j, (4) xiiij.
Capitals: Not consistently used for proper names, (8) Done but (3) done. Use of capital form in (9) Lap.
Abbreviations: (6) wⁱin, (9) noᵗ, (10) yᵗ; (2) mynto and (9) hym, (1) Iugisment, (9) verily and deliuerit, (2) certain.
Punctuation: None.
Typical spellings: (4) edschaw and (5) scho; (2) greit, (9) cloik and (10) haif maid; (2) vas vorkand; (2) aycht; (4) auld; (4) caldroun and (8) doun; (7) gudman.
Problems of Interpetation: Does (5) geif begin with g or ʒ? Are (1) Vilsoune, (7) vpone and (8) doun intended to end in the same way? Does (9) noᵗ imply underlying nocht? Does the mark above (5) hyme and (6) remayne indicate omitted letters?

Introduction to Depositions

Depositions[1] are statements from court cases, where witnesses, or occasionally the accused person, give an account of what they saw, heard or did.

Much material of this kind is associated with criminal courts. These ranged from those at national level, such as Texts 22 and 23, to local borough courts, such as those of Southampton (Text 31), and throughout England annual Assizes and four-times-a-year Quarter Sessions (Text 30) were held at convenient towns within each county. American colonies established fairly parallel patterns (Texts 29 and 32). There were also church courts (Text 27), which dealt with immorality rather than crime, and these were also the place where requests for marital separation were heard (Text 24).

Other depositions come from special hearings of various kinds. Text 20, for example, records depositions given when a College in Leicester was being scrutinised by its Diocesan authorities in a special Visitation; Text 26 is from a Special Commission of the church court of the Diocese of Exeter, set up to handle a breach-of-promise case. Moreover, from the time of Henry VII to that of Charles I cases, usually involving an incident which led to riot or civil disturbance, might also be heard, following appeal, by the King's Court of Star Chamber (Texts 18 and 19).[2]

Depositions are spoken text, written down by a clerk. It is, however, dangerous to envisage the deponent in the witness-box giving evidence which a clerk takes down as the witness speaks. The regular procedure was for depositions to be made in advance and in private, and to be read aloud in court, the witness being present to confirm his or her evidence and to answer any questions that might arise. Nevertheless, occasional texts identify themselves as true witness-box statements, as with the depositions of the Wyards in Text 29, whose testimony is *taken in open Cort*.

Often it is clear from the text that the deposition is taken locally while the case is heard at some higher level, as in Text 28A, where the Lancashire boy's testimony is *taken at Padian*, that is Padiham, not far from his home. Sometimes the whole court is shifted to the relevant village; the special diocesan hearing for Gawen and Robarda Champernowne (Text 24) is on record as having been held in the local church at Staverton, rather than in Exeter. But secular courts were less accommodating; the Yorkshire witnesses in the Star Chamber case of Sir John Bulmer made their depositions locally at Gisburne (19/2 and 28), but probably had to go to London for the actual hearing. A dispute over common grazing rights in York in 1535 led to a disturbance which resulted in a Star Chamber case, and townspeople who were summoned to London were funded from cash raised for their Corpus Christi pageant-play.[3]

Even conceding a range of practice about when and where a deponent's story is being taken down, the modern reader is inevitably in the position of receiving the witness's words through the ears, head and hand of a clerk. It is virtually impossible to generalise as to who these clerks were, since there would be wide variation in training and experience. Major courts employed professionals, but a local Justice of the Peace might call on whatever member of his household or family was available, or even act as his own clerk. A great deal of linguistic interest in depositions lies in the tension between what appears on paper and what may be reconstructed as having been said by the deponent.

The underlying text of every deposition is a first-person narrative, on the lines of *Last Wednesday I was in the market-place and I saw so-and-so.* However, it is very rare indeed for the documents in which depositions are recorded to present them in this form. Standard practice is for the deposition to be changed to reported speech in the third person, *She says that on Wednesday she was in the market place and that she saw so-and-so.* Usually this is removed even further from the original spoken text by formal expansion to something like *This deponent says that on the Wednesday aforesaid she, this deponent, was in the market-place aforesaid and that she saw the said so-and-so.*

Among the depositions selected here, only a few are not altered in this way. The exceptions are the depositions of Henry Jeffrey (Text 25) and of John Remington (Text 32), and the series from Selkirk, Scotland (Text 21). Jeffrey's statement, although the heading describes it as *taken before* the Mayor and Recorder of the Cinque port of Rye, . could be a document that he himself has written out, and which the authorities are now accepting from him, rather than a spoken account written down by the Mayor's clerk. It owes nothing to legal formality,

> I stayde there in the hall settinge downe vpon the Settill of the longe table and they Reconynge vpon the litle table nexte the fyer (25/19–20).

Remington's deposition is introduced as indirect speech would be, but immediately launches into a record of direct speech,

> The depocishon of Iohn Reminton
> This deponant Testifieth that I herd Iohn Godfry saie to my father that if he drived the Cattell vp to the wods to winter then my ffather shod say and haue cas to repent that he did drive them vp and thes wordes he said in a great rage and Pashon and after this my father and I did drive vpe The cattell and I for the most part did tend them (32/1–6).

The unorthodoxy of presentation is almost certainly because this is a document from seventeenth-century Massachusetts. Some years previously, Massachusetts had ruled that

> all testimonjes shalbe presented in writinge to the Court, either attested before a magistrate, or (if the party be within ten mils of the Court) to be then attested in Court vppon oath.[4]

So every witness had to produce a written deposition to swear to, either by writing it out himself, or by finding someone willing to do it for him, and relying on the limited experience of whatever neighbour was to hand. It was unlikely that either the witness or the friend would be familiar with traditional deposition style. The text which results is particularly interesting in its failure to edit out the speaker's own morphology and syntax, possibly because the writer himself saw nothing in need of improvement,

> presently I locke vp in to the swamp and I se a crow come to wards me flying and pecht vpon a tre a gainst mee and she locke at me and the horse and doge ... then I begune to mistrust and thinke it was no crow and thought if it was not a crow it could not hurt my soule though it hurt my body and Horse and as I was a thinkeing thus to my selfe the hors I was vpon fell down vpon on sid in plain growne vpon my lege (32/10–17).

The Selkirk records are in a half-way situation, each of them partly converted to indirect speech, and then, after a few lines, switching to straight quotation,

> Robert Vilsoune mareit of ye aigis of xxxvij 3eiris dewly sworne in Iugisment depones be his greit aycht yᵗ he vas vorkand in dauid mynto stair ane certain 3eir syne and he hard done strang say [such-and-such] and wᵗin ane bony spaice ye gudman come riddand to ye stair fut & criet vpone dauid mynto & Done strang & yai passit doun and I sat & saw yaim geif hyme mony one his cloik Lap bot verily I kenne noᵗ how meikill mony scho & he deliuerit to hym and be ye aycht yᵗ I haif maid I hard yaim aggreit be all yᵗ I culd heir se & vnderstand (21B/1–10).

Large-scale exceptions such as these are rare, but even depositions employing the normal transference into reported speech do occasionally have moments where the normally buried first-person forms surface, sometimes for a clause or two,

> The foirsaid Thom mett hir be ye way healsit hir and said ... Sche ansuerit ... Bot Thom said ... And than was I sumthing blyther fra he tauld me yt my gudeman wald mend Than Thome Reid went away fra me in throw ye 3ard of monkcastell and I thoᵗ he gait in at ane naroware hoill of ye dyke nor onye erdlie man culd haif gane throw and swa I was sumthing fleit (23/11–25),

and sometimes in a single pronoun, albeit followed by a formal identifying phrase inserted by the clerk,

> the said sirʳ Iohn lighted. of his hors & threwe his hawke from hym. and there hadd Strykken to gidder. hadd not bene Thomas ffalconer Iohn Bayly & I the said christoffer maughenne which partyd theym (19/47–50).

Normally, however, the clerks' work is thorough, and it is not difficult to envisage that long practice would make the transposition into indirect speech a more or less automatic process. However, it must be asked to what extent the clerks, once this simple alteration was admitted and even expected, went further along the same road.

The use of a noun phrase of appropriate formulaic pattern instead of the simple pronoun which the witness almost certainly employed is one such development. Depositions vary a great deal in the degree to which they employ these, less use probably reflecting less formality in either the court or the individual clerk. Further, a careful clerk will be careful to employ the noun proper to the role of the speaker in the case,

> then this deponent went out of the Path (29/9–10),
> a Neighbour whom this Informer knoweth (28/23–4),
> vnder the woodstacke where this Examinate left it (30/15–16).

A clerk may also label others with a similarly precise noun, such as *the libellant Nicholas Trefry* (26/7). As an extension of the same process, when a witness speaks about another person by name, *Walter Baker* becomes *one Water baker* at first mention (18/4), and then *the Seyd water Baker* at subsequent mentions (18/6). This kind of change to witnesses' original depositions had become a convention as providing a way of ensuring that nothing ambiguous was put on record. A *he* pronoun left in a statement could often refer to anyone.

Further intrusions into what a witness said were made in order to ensure that the processes of law were properly observed. The way that so many depositions begin with information about the witness, which must have been derived from questions put to them, reflects the legal need to identify them before accepting their testimony. Sometimes the information may be relevant to the case, as where it is recorded that the witness to Bothwell's behaviour on the night of the explosion that killed Darnley was Bothwell's *seruitour* (22/1), or it may be important to the weight given to the statement, as where a text states that Hugo Rist, giving evidence in relation to the alleged adultery of the Lady of the manor, had lived there for sixteen years (24/1), but that, in another case, Tamaris Leonard, giving evidence about her neighbours, was an incomer who had lived in the village for only eight months (26/2). But more often it is totally irrelevant; Thomas Henderson's evidence in regard to the ill-treatment of cattle is independent of the fact that he is aged twenty and unmarried. To the present-day reader, of course, these details may well be of interest, since through them it may be possible to correlate the language of the deposition with the age, birthplace and social standing of the witness.

The intrusions by the clerk into the witnesses' depositions almost inevitably give many texts two levels of language. This is particularly interesting at those points where linguistic change was in progress, with traditional and newer features both in use, and where regional usage differed from London standard, and the most striking instance of this is in the morphology of the third person singular (indicative) of verbs. Most clerks tend to prefer the *-eth* ending, but the witnesses own language may favour *-s*, the originally Northern form, gaining currency everywhere during the Early Modern period.[5] In Text 19, the clerk introduces Thomas Falconer's evidence about events in early sixteenth-century Yorkshire by supplying, *The said Thomas Sayth that …* (19/7), but when Falconer remembers words he heard spoken, he recalls the question *lyes then thy handd in thy swerd to me* (19/24). In an early seventeenth-century text from Devon, forms such as *remembreth* and *knoweth* are attractive evidence of the continued use of *-eth* in the South-west at this date, until one realises that the context of the examples is *this deponent thinketh that shee the said Margery Stone was angrye* (27B/26–7) and *this* *deponent knoweth not* (27/29), so that both are the work of the clerk, supplying third person forms in place of the first person verbs which the witness herself must have used. The *-eth* inflexion may possibly be the form that the clerk himself would use in speech, but it is much more likely that they are conservative forms deemed suitable for the formal situation. A parallel doubt has to be applied to the evidence in regard to the syntactic structure of verb groups in negative constructions. An example such as *this deponent knoweth not* cannot be taken as indicative of negatives without *do*-support being used in the everyday English of the place and date to which the deposition belongs.

A further matter in which we have to attempt to reconstruct the hidden text of many depositions is where an apparent sustained statement is in fact produced by the clerk processing the replies to a number of questions posed to the witness. Many depositions must have been derived from questioning, but in many this can be gathered only from hints in the text. For example, in Text 20 John Wetwood's testimony reads like a sustained story. After twenty-three lines it closes with the formulaic attestation of truth, *& this he hard & saw* (20/14), but then adds a postscript, *but he saw noon of them handle neyther swerdis nor daggars* (20/14–15), which must surely be the witness's response to a question put to him after his main statement was finished.

More clearly, some clerks record both questions and replies, the questions being rephrased as indirect speech (third person forms replacing second person), and put into the passive so that the syntax stresses the person questioned rather than the unspecified questioner,

> beinge asked when & how often he lay wth her she sayth that he had to doe wth her three tymes before Christmas last and beinge asked whether the soldier that she formerly named did not ly wth her, she sayth that neyther he nor any other had to doe wth her but only the sayd Slan. And beinge asked whether she did not say that if she suffered others should suffer with her she denyeth that she sayd soe (31/36–42).

There is an equally clear second example where Elizabeth Dunlop responds to a series of questions,

> ITem sche being inquirit quhat kynd of man yis Thom reid was, declarit he was ane honest wele elderlie man gray bairdit and had ane gray coitt w[t] lumbart slevis of ye auld fassoun … ITem being interrogat, how and in quhat maner of place ye said Thome reid Come to her ansuerit as sche was gangand betuix hir awin hous and ye ȝard of monkcastell dryvand hir ky to ye pasture (23/1–3 and 7–9).

Many of the other texts may be similarly based, though the series of question and answer is not actually stated.

Where a witness replies to a question which is also recorded, vocabulary can be of interest. Sometimes the text makes it clear to whom the choice of words belongs. In the example above where the court questions Mary Gashe, the exchange runs,

> beinge asked whether the soldier that she formerly named did not ly wth her, she sayth that neyther he nor any other had to doe wth her but only the sayd Slan (31/38–40).

The question offers her the phrase *lie with*; she rejects it in favour of the less direct *have to do with*. However, where only a response disguised as a freely offered statement is on record, we cannot be sure whether the wording is the witness's own, or whether it was fed to them by an unrecorded question, or, indeed, whether all the words are from the interrogation, with the witness's *yea*, *aye* or *yes* being expanded to include the question. For example, in Text 30 Stephen Badcocke is on record as follows, *And he further saith that the said Sowe came directly from Tho: Wards house ward* (30/9–10). The final phrase, meaning 'from the direction of Thomas Ward's house', is of interest. But, assuming this is the reply to a question, was that question *Where did the sow come from?*, or was the phrase using *ward* supplied to him in the question *Did the sow come directly from Thomas Ward's house ward?*

While there are some cases where we can say with certainty that some of the language is that of the clerk rather than of the witness, and other cases where there is a degree of uncertainty, there is ample evidence that clerks in general carried out with scrupulous care their task of setting down what the deponent said. Details such as the inclusion of the switch from *lie with* to *have to do with* are particularly impressive, and another instance of the noting of synonyms occurs in Text 29,

> Then this depon[t]: made Answeare yo[u]: Lye for there hangs out yo[r]: Rogerry still ffor his yarde hang'd then out of his Breeches (29/62–3).

The clerk follows his witness, Eleanor Wyard, in employing the neutral word *yarde*, as she speaks to the court, but the more colloquial *Rogerry*, as she recalls the remark she made to the accused man at the time of the incident. Similar care with linguistic detail, this time in regard to second person pronoun and verb forms, is demonstrated in the same text where both husband and wife make their depositions. The husband is on record as saying that he said, *Villaine what are yo[u]: doeing heare*, but the wife says that he said, *O thou wicked Rogue what art thou doeing* (29/29–30 and 59–60).

Instances like this probably reflect a general meticulousness, though it is possible that a clerk took particular trouble when he noticed that witnesses were not in verbatim agreement, since it is not difficult to find examples. When two men give their accounts as to what they heard said by people loitering suspiciously near a friend in the stocks, one deponent heard a fairly plain conversation,

> the seid george dede leye his hand vpon his key whiche dede hang by his purse seying I thinke I cowde opun this lokk w[t] this key and than seid master hugh I thinke ye will nat/ than seid the seid george I trowe I am nat so madde (20B/20–23),

but the other heard an exchange full of lively exclamation and oath,

> the seid george villeris ... leide his hand vpon a litle keye which dede ange by his purse/ seying I holde xls that I cowde vndoo this lokke w[t] this keye./ and than seid this deponent by god I trowe that ye will nat/ and than seid the seid georg no by the roide ye shall nat fynde me so madde (20B/7–12).

The depositions, thanks to the clerks that wrote them down, reflect the different language-styles of different people.

It is for this reason that several of the texts quoted here show language that strongly suggests the kind of person the witness was. William Boston, in Text 18, is an early sixteenth-century churchman who revels in the drama supplied by Latin-based terms, such as *contencion, multytude, coniecture, countenaunce & gesture, innumerable, opprobryous,* and *moderatt and pacyffye.* In Text 30 Stephen Badcocke is a mid-seventeenth-century shoemaker with an even greater sense of the dramatic as he unfolds his part in a gruesome discovery,

> his heart gave him that there was some strange accident ... this Examinate being much troubled at what he sawe the day before, & seing the said sowe againe, & finding his heart to rise againe at it ... his heart smote him & he began to suspect that there was somewhat of Providence in the great distraction of the Cattle (30/6–20).

In contrast to the way in which the written text here allows self-portrayal by means of language, there is one case where it appears that the writer of the deposition is doing the very opposite, that he is attempting to write a text in language which the deponent himself almost certainly did not speak. This is the second deposition of Edmund Robinson (Text 28B), in which the boy confesses that his former deposition of witch-craft in rural Lancashire was untrue. The words attributed to him are that

> as he hopeth god will blesse him all that tale and story by him so told as aforesaid is false and feigned and hath no trueth att all in itt butt only as he hath harde tales and reportes made by women and such Lyke persons so he framed his tale out of his owne Invention and out of no other ground, for that there was never any suche thinge done or intended butt was a meere fiction of his owne (28B/19–24.

Despite the engaging beginning, appropriate to a simple and honest lad, the vocabulary of the remainder is patently unlikely, but the writer is taking care that the boy is not on record as admitting in so many words to a *lie,* presumably in an attempt to get him pardoned for his *invention* and *fiction* rather than prosecuted for perjury.

Occasionally non-standard lexical items are put on record, such as Robinson's *bullas* 'wild plums' (28A/8). These may sometimes be vocabulary familiar to, and indeed used by, a local clerk, certainly in the Scots texts, and probably where items such as *threpyd vpon* and *garthe* occur in the deposition, locally taken, of the two Yorkshiremen in Text 19. American items such as *swamp* in its American sense, and local tree names, are found in the texts from Virginia and Massachusetts (29 and 32).

Notes

1. The term Deposition is used in this section to cover what in fact is a range of types of statement. Sometimes the statements are from deponents, but others are from informants or examinants.

2. For a handy summary of procedures see Philippa White, *Quarter Sessions Records in the Hampshire Record Office* (Hampshire County Council, Winchester, 1991), and M. G. Smith, *The Records Generated by the Procedures of the Church Courts* (Devon Record Office, Exeter, 1989). For detail on Church courts see Anne Tarver, *Church Court Records: An Introduction for family and local historians* (Phillimore, Chichester, 1995).

3. Angelo Raine (ed.), *York Civic Records,* Vol. III, Yorkshire Archaeological Society Record Series No. CVI (1942), p. 172.
4. Decree of 1650; Nathaniel B. Shurtleff (ed.), *Records of the the Governor and Company of the Massachusetts Bay in New England,* Vol. III, 1644–57 (White, Boston, 1854 and reprint, AMS Press, New York, 1968), p. 211.
5. This example does not hold good in Scottish texts, where *-is* was the inflexion used by both clerks and witnesses.

Text 18

William Boston and others: Peterborough 1517
(Public Record Office Manuscript STAC/21/109)

Text A

[f. IIIr] The saying of Dane wyllyam Boston Sworne

The Seyd Dane wyllyam sayth thatt after {my lord of lyncoln and} the abbott
of the monastery of Peturburgh had spokyn w^t the Townysmen in ow^r lady
chappell he hard wordes of soo greatt contencion by one Water baker mynysterd
to Thomas Whetley seruant to the seyd abbott beyng in the chyrch thatt the
5 Seyd Dane wyllyam boston thought verely thatt the Seyd water Baker wold
haue vyolently strykyn the Seyd Thomas whetley in thatt holy place of god/ In
the exchewyng wherof the Seyd dane wyllyam Boston beyng a lyttull besydes
made greatt spead to the seyd Thomas whetley & toke hym w^t hym ffrom the
10 Company of the Seyd watur/ And thys doon the Seyd dane [f. IIIv] wyllyam
boston went to a certeygn Chamber callydd the Checker for thentent to pay
certeygn money & to solysett other matteres y^t he had thear to doo/ wher he
fownde a greatt multytude of peapull {of the towne amountyng} as he myght
conscyence coniecture to the Number of xl persoons or moo beyng in a great
15 marvelous furye and angre as ytt appearyd not onely by ther ~~con~~ countenaunce
& gesture butt also by ther Innumerable {onresonable} opprobryous wordes.
and w^t Cumpany the afforseyd dane wyllyam boston acordyng to good maner
& as tokyn of amytee profferyd theym to drynck for the Intent Sumwhat to
moderatt and pacyffye ther great ffurye butt they renouncyd ther proffer
20 Saying playnly they wold noon/ and perchaunce cometh by Thomas wheatley
to whom water baker seyd callyng hym knaue thatt & yf he cam w^{t}owte the yates
he Shuld haue hys head or Crown crackyd/ and Thomas wheteley sayd ayen
and yf he gave hym one strype he shulbe Suer of an other Strype/ Then Seyd
Robert Toche nay & yf ye goo to strypes ye shall haue strypes enough emongyst
25 yow and therw^{t}all the Seyd Dane wyllyam boston beyng in great fear went in
to the checker & iij men folowyng hym w^t whoom he had certeygn bysynes. &
shytt the doore to hym and then Robert Edward opunly w^t an hye exclamacion
& dyuers other dyd banne & curse the abbott of the monastery w^t many other
shamefull wordes. and emongyst all {~~other~~} petur Edward Seyd on to the
30 Company. hard ye nott/ Syrs how ffalsly he (referryng ytt to the abbott) made

a lying excuse saying y^t he myght nott ~~abyde~~ Stand & ffull Iudasly for yf ytt ~~hade~~
wer to oppres {or ondoie} a ~~s~~ poore man he wyll fynd the means to stand an
hoole afternoon/ to the whych petur dane wyllyam boston sayed beyng in the
Checker & the othur w^toute thatt ys vnmanerly spokyn and In especyall of yow
35   y^t ar or woldbe reputyd as a man of honestee thus to rayle vppon an honorable
~~prele~~ prelatt and specyally in thys the Kynges & hys monastery and in hys
absens to the whyche answerd the Seyd petur/ honorable/ nay he ys the dewle
the dewle dyuers tymes repetyng the Same and addyng thertoo butt and thow
thynck ytt nott well seyd cum thow fforth & amend ytt or the prowdest of yow
40   all/ Then the seyd dane wyllyam boston Sayd I am a relygyouse man & a prest
wherfor I may nott amend ytt as ye doo move me butt in the persoon of my
master I doo councell and alsoo monysshe yow to aduoyde hys howse or elles to
Seasse of yowr Raylyng for thys ys noo place of Iestyng/ butt to thys answerd
all they thatt they wolnott goo owte of the monastery for hym nor yett for hys
45   master

Text B

[f. XIIr] The Saiyng of sir Richard Sparke clerk which wold nott be sworn but
Seyd he hard it of a Man which was nott brought afor vs

Robert edward wyll spende all hys happe harlottys that he makys in a yer to the
valuer of twenty markys to helpe them w^tall

5   percyvall alys wyll performe that he promysyd

~~wyllyam rayner sayd yf they spede not well ther schall nother lorde ner monke~~
~~Loke owth of the gattys~~ {Memorandum it was prouyd afor vs this man was not
ther}

Henry tanner seys that he wyll not fayll them as Long as he has a peny

10   Crystofer alynson seyd that he wolde spende xx^th nobyllys and yf that wolde not
serve he hadde bowe and arowys

Rychard pantun seyd and I haue xx^thy ~~nobl~~ nobyllys and a good byll

Ihon new Ihon skolys Ihon sokelyng water mortun Robert clerke robert throp
sey they wyll do the best for them in worde and dede that they cane

15   wyllyam alyn wyll kyll and sley yf y^ey spede not well

Theys wordys they hadde the ij day of december at Ihon brymbull Howsse at
ny3th when they harde the Letter redde that woas send them fro London

Notes

Text

From the records of the Court of Star Chamber. The text has been edited in I. S. Leadam (ed.), *Select Cases before the King's Council in the Star Chamber*, Vol. II, Selden Society, Vol. XXV (1911), pp. 131–2 and 138. Extracts, conjecturally restored to first-person narrative, appear in James Sutherland (ed.), *The Oxford Book of English Talk* (Clarendon Press, Oxford, 1953 and later reprints), pp. 10–11.

Manuscript

Texts A and B are in totally different hands, except that the Text B title (lines 1–2) and inserted marginal note (lines 7–8) are in the Text A hand. Possibly Text B, which is a separate leaf, is a written 'saiyng' from Richard Sparke to which the title and note have been added by the clerk assembling the many documents in this case. The Text B hand is notable for its date in being italic in style, though it also has conservative use of the letter ʒ.

In line A17 the superscript-abbreviation w^t may stand, as elsewhere, for *with*, but perhaps represents *which*.

There is sometimes uncertainty concerning initial capitals in Text A: small and capital *w* are distinguished virtually by size alone. For the letter *s* there are two different shapes, one of which has been taken as a capital despite appearing randomly, as in (A22) *Shuld*.

Glossary

(A1)	*Dane*	master (courtesy title for priest)
(A4)	*contencion*	dispute
(A4)	*mynysterd*	addressed
(A8)	*exchewing*	avoidance
(A8)	*a lyttull besydes*	a short distance away
(A11)	*Checker*	Exchequer
(A12)	*solysett*	=solicit, attend to
(A14)	*conscyence*	honestly (reduced from *in conscience*)
(A17)	*maner*	manners
(A18)	*amytee*	friendship
(A18)	*profferyd*	offered
(A21)	*& yf*	if
(A21)	*w^{t}owte*	outside
(A21)	*yates*	=gates
(A22)	*ayen*	=again, in reply
(A23)	*strype*	blow
(A28)	*banne*	curse
(A31)	*Iudasly*	treacherously (like Judas Iscariot)
(A37)	*dewle*	=devil
(A38)	*and*	if
(A39)	*or*	before ('in the presence of')

(A40)	*relygyouse man*	man belonging to a religious order, monk
(A41)	*move*	urge
(A42)	*councell*	advise
(A42)	*monysshe*	admonish
(A42)	*aduoyde*	=avoid, leave
(B3)	*happe harlottys*	See note below
(B4)	*valuer*	=value
(B4)	*w'all*	with
(B10)	*nobyllys*	=nobles, gold coins
(B12)	*byll*	halberd
(B15)	*spede ... well*	succeed

Explanatory notes

(B3) *happe harlottys*: Hapharlots are coarse coverlets (OED HAPHARLOT). The compound word, like the contemporary *wraprascal* is an exocentric compound based on *hap* 'wrap' and *harlot* 'rogue (of either sex)'. Presumably the speaker is a weaver or producer of coverlets of this kind. The word was read by Leadam. *Select Cases*, as a phrase *harper and harlottys*, which he glosses as 'Irish coins and pointed boots (OED HARLOT)', suggesting that Edward is a shoemaker.

Background

Boston is called on for an eye-witness account of trouble at Peterborough arising from a dispute between town and Abbey concerning grazing-land. The case has been taken to the Star Chamber at the Abbot's request, since one of his men was injured. Richard Spark's evidence concerns various Peterborough citizens and their militant declarations in regard to the quarrel.

Topics for linguistic investigation

1. Evidence from spelling that Texts A and B are written by different clerks.
2. The evidence relating to pronunciation in the spellings (A4) *Water*, (A13) *peapull*, (A19) *ther*, (A21) *yates*, (A27) *shytt*, (A37) *dewle*.
3. The use of *thou* and *you* pronouns.
4. A comparison between the forms of 3rd person present indicative verb in the two Texts.
5. Different ways of reporting speech in Text B.
6. Boston's character as revealed by his choice of vocabulary.

Text 19

Thomas Falconer and Christopher Maughan: Yorkshire 1518

(Public Record Office Manuscript STAC 2/9)

[f. 176r] The deposecyon of Thom^as falconer seru^aunt to sir william Bulmer Sheryffe of yorkshire Examyned at Gisburn the furst day of Septembre In the xth yere of kyng herryy the viijth afore the lorde latymer & sir Iohn Norton knyght of the knowlege of a Ryott Supposyd to be done by sir Iohn Bulmer
5 knyght the viijth day of octobre In the vijth yere of o^r sayd Soueraigne lorde vpon christoffer Conyers of Pynchynthorppe

The said Thom^as Sayth that the said christoffer Came the said day of octobre to Northcote nere Gysburn & then & there desired sir Iohn Bulmer that he wold put one other in his Rowme to be Collector for there was oder that was more
10 able then he And the said sir Iohn Aunswerd yf that the lord latymer his cosyn sir Iames Strangeways and his ffader woldput In Ane other he shuld haue his ffurderaunce And the said christofer threpyd vpon the said sir Iohn that he myght doo it if he wold and he said that he hadd nothyng to doo but vnder his ffader./ And as they shuld haue departyd then said sir Iohn Bulmer to the said
15 christofer Cosyn ye haue summonyd my fader is ten^andys vnto yor courte And the said christoffer Aunswerd & sayd ẏ ȝey it was his Right And sir^r Iohn Bulmer said Ageyne he trowyd not it was his Right And he sayd it was his Right he was chefe lorde and he wolde speke in that and lett for noo man And sir^r Iohn Bulmer Askyd hym if he hadd Seen his Auncestorys Sewt his Auncesto^rs courte.
20 And he sayd Ageyn ȝey that hadd he done and that shuld he make proffe vpon/ And then said sir^r Iohn Bulmer he lyed and he said he lyed nott And then sir^r Iohn Bulmer shoke his handd at hym & Seyd go yor way. I wyll haue noght to do w^t you. And the furste worde that I the said Thom^as herdd after the said sir^r Iohn Bulmer. Sayd lyes then thy handd in thy swerd to me. And w^t that drewe
25 his Swerde & wold haue stryken the said christofer but I the said Thom^as lett hym.

*   *   *   *

witness christoffer mawghenne seruaunt vnto sir^r Iohn Bulmer. Swo^rne & Examinyenyd. At Gysburn Aforesaid. the day & yere Abouewritten Affore the said lorde latymer & sir Iohn Norton knyght

104

30   The said chr*ist*offer Sayth, that s*ir*ʳ Iohn Bulm*er* was hawkyng In A garthe
behynd Gisburn and then at the nedd*er* mylne. and could haue no game vnto
he came vnto A plac*e* callid North Cote. And there his hawk kild A pye. and
aft*er* the rewardyng of the hawke the said s*ir*ʳ Iohn Toke the hawke on h*y*s owne
handd and then & there came chr*ist*ofer Conyers & badd god Evyn to the said
35   s*ir*ʳ Iohn And the said s*ir*ʳ Iohn. Sayd good Evyn. Cosyn Conyers. then sayd the
said s*ir* chr*ist*offer s*ir*ʳ it is shewyd me. that ye haue mayd me A Collecto*r*. And
the said s*ir*ʳ Iohn sayd nay if ye bee one ye were mayd by bett*er* men then I. but
I cannot tell if ye be ~~one~~ or not And the said chr*ist*offer Sayd [f. 177r] ye haue
bene eu*er* Ageyn me. And all is for yone p*r*ior Sake Cosyn Sayd the forsaid s*ir*ʳ
40   Iohn ye may say as ye will. for So ye say that my ffader shuld Suett yo*r* courte.
And that was never seen that none of myn Auncesto*r*s Suttyd yo*r* Auncesto*r*s
courte. And he said by god*y*s blode that shuld they & w*t* that pullyd his swerde
Afore hym And the said s*ir*ʳ Iohn sawe that and said goo thy ways I will haue
nothynge At doo w*t* the. And then the said chr*ist*offer Came nere the said s*ir*ʳ
45   Iohn. And the said s*ir*ʳ Iohn pulled owt h*y*s swerde & gafe hym flatlyng*y*s in the
Nekk And then the said chr*ist*offer lighted w*t* his swerde drawene in his handd
toward*y*s the said s*ir*ʳ Iohn. & then the said s*ir*ʳ Iohn lighted. of his hors &
threwe his hawke from hym. and there hadd Strykken to gidd*er*. hadd not bene
Thom*a*s ffalconer Iohn Bayly & I the said chr*ist*offer maughenne which partyd
50   theym. And then the said chr*ist*offer ~~Conyers~~ Conyers was very hote. & the said
s*ir*ʳ Iohn. sayd Cosyn. goo yo*r* way. for I will haue no more. to do w*t* you. And
the said chr*ist*offer Sayd fye on yo*r* cosynnage I defye you. for I hadd rather dye
In my Right. And the said s*ir*ʳ Iohn Sayd. I will do you no wronge. And the said
chr*ist*offer folowid hym styll. defying hym. And ever as the said s*ir*ʳ Iohn wold
55   turne to hym. he wold Saye. kyll me And the said s*ir*ʳ Iohn wold Say. I will
neyther kyll the nor medle w*t* the. And thus the said chr*ist*offer folowyd vpon
the said {s*ir*ʳ} Iohn the spac*e* of three houndreth ffotes. And then the said
chr*ist*offer Turned Agayn. And so they dep*ar*tid. And the said chr*ist*offer Sayd
that he shuld goo & kyll the pryor of gisburn And w*t* that wentt his way./

Notes

Text

From the records of the Court of Star Chamber. The text has been edited in William
Brown (ed.), *Yorkshire Star Chamber Proceedings*, The Yorkshire Archaeological Society
Record Series, Vol. XLI (1908), pp. 69–70.

Manuscript

The character ꝟ is used twice in the word *ꝟey* 'yea' (16 and 20).
    There are some problems associated with the expansion of abbreviations:
    (16 etc.) The title *sir*ʳ is written with the abbreviation for vowel + *r* followed by
superscript *r*, but superscript *r* elsewhere probably indicates *ur*, (27) *swo*ʳ*ne*, (36)
*Collecto*ʳ, (51) *yo*ʳ.

Several words are written with a horizontal stroke over them which would normally indicate an omitted letter, probably *m* or *n*. But since there is one *m* or *n* already present, and no supporting evidence of spellings with doubled letters, the mark has been considered as empty, and ignored. Thus (31) *game*, (34) *came*, (37) *men*, (53) *wronge*. A similar empty mark is employed in (47) *Lighted*, (53) *Right*, (56) *neyther*, where it appears merely to consolidate a cluster of consonant-letters.

Sometimes the last stroke of a final *n* is looped back. Although it is possible that a further *e* is intended, this loop has been deemed to be empty. Thus (2) *Gisburn*, (21) *then*, (28) *Abouewritten*, (29) *Norton* (33) *on* etc. A similar convention used with final *u*, (51, 52) *you*, gives rise to slight doubt as to whether the final letter might be *w*.

After other letters, however, a very small curl added to a letter seems to be more than a flourish or an abbreviation, and has been transcribed as *e*. Thus (33) *hawke*, (40) *courte*, (44) *nothynge* etc.

The proper name (27 etc.) *christoffe*r is written with Greek *xp* for *chr*.

Glossary

(2)	*Examyned*	questioned
(4)	*Ryott*	attack
(9)	*Rowme*	place
(9)	*Collector*	parish officer collecting alms for the poor
(12)	*ffurderaunce*	advancement
(12)	*threpyd vpon* †	persistently asserted to
(16)	*Ʒey*	yea, yes
(17)	*trowyd*	believed
(18)	*lett*	stop (intransitive); in l. 25 transitive
(19)	*Sewt*	attend as tenant's obligation
(30)	*garthe* †	enclosed ground
(31)	*nedder*	=nether, lower
(31)	*mylne*	mill
(31)	*vnto*	until
(32)	*pye*	magpie
(33)	*rewardyng*	giving (hawk) a piece of the kill
(43)	*goo thy ways*	go away
(44)	*At doo* †	to do
(45)	*flatlyngys*	with the flat side
(46)	*lighted*	dismounted
(52)	*cosynnage*	(a) calling me cousin; and simultaneously (b) cheating
(56)	*medle*	fight

Background

Guisborough, known at this time as *Gisburn*, is a few miles from Middlesbrough in North Yorkshire. Its Priory was both prosperous and strongly supported locally. Nearby Pinchingthorpe had two manors, one of which was Priory property, held by Sir William Bulmer and his son Sir John, while the other was the property of Christopher Conyers.

The Bulmers and the Conyers were related by marriage. The dispute between Christopher Conyers and the Prior of Guisborough concerned land and enclosure-rights, and Conyers appealed to the Star Chamber following what he claimed was an unprovoked attack by Sir John Bulmer, championing the Prior. Bulmer servants are here giving their testimony as to what took place. Sir John Bulmer's support of Guisborough Priory led to his execution for his part in the Pilgrimage of Grace in 1537.

Topics for linguistic investigation

1. The relationship between punctuation and syntactic structure.
2. The use of 2nd person personal pronouns.
3. The underlying 1st person narrative.
4. Reasons for inverted order where subject follows verb.
5. Local features in the language.

Text 20

John Wetwood and others: Leicester 1525
(Lincolnshire Archives Manuscript Vj/8)

Text A

[f. 17r] d*ominu*s Ioha*nne*s Weatewod … Ad vjt^{um} he saith that vpon relique sonday at even song certayn off my ladies s*eruau*nt*is* stode in the porche at the quere door & the dean bad them goo bak & they stode still & then the dean called m*aster* dale & told hym off it & he made them goo bak/ & then imm*ediate*ly cam
5   moo other off my ladys s*eruau*nt*is* & he bad them goo bak sayng yt was no place for them & oon off them ansuerid & said my lord I will stand with yor leve/ and then the dean said nay I will gyve the noo leve here is noo place for the/ And then he said I will stand here and aske you noo leve & then my lord dean called this depone*n*t & m*aster* dale & went all to gidder to my lady then beyng in the
10   churche & the dean shued my lady the demeano^r off hir s*eruau*nt*is* & she said to hym ageyn/ looke well to yor awn s*eruau*nt*is* for they kepe noughty ruele and yor broy*er* s*eruau*nt*is* in the ~~for~~ ffyrth & forest ther can noo woman goo theyr for them but they wilbe busy with them and iff they vse yt they will be killed for yt and that shortely & this he hard & saw/ but he saw noon of them handle neyther
15   swerd*is* nor daggars/

*   *   *   *

[f. 34r] D*ominu*s Thom*a*s Hurderon … dixit q^d m*agister* Thom*a*s wigston dixit hec vel sim*i*lia v*er*ba/ Ies*u* that a man may not say hys prayers but {y^t} he must be thus spoken vnto/

Text B

[f. 76r] m*agister* Hugo Asseton m*agiste*r choristaru*m* iuratus et examinatus &c

Ad iiij^{tum} art*iculu*m dicit that he knowith nothing in that mat*er* but vnd*er* the forme folowyng./ he seith that George Villeris was at the house of this deponen*tis*/ and this deponent and he came in to the college/ and whan they
5   ware interid ~~in to~~ w^t in the yatt*is* the oon said to the other lette vs see Walls he is in the stokk*is* or other leike word*is* and soo they came in to the house wher he

satte in the stokk*is*/ and this deponent satte hym down on a form./ and the seid
george villeris went to the ende of the stokk*is* wher the lokke ded ange and toike
the loike in his hande/ and leide his hand vpon a litle keye which dede ange by
his purse/ seying I holde xls that I cowde vndoo this lokke w*t* this keye./ and
than seid this deponent by god I trowe that ye will nat/ and than seid the seid
georg no by the roide ye shall nat fynde me so madde./ et deponit q*d* di*c*tus
georgius p*r*otulit dicta verba ioco et non al*i*as nec intendebat sic facere et erat
p*r*es*e*ns et ista vidit et audiuit.

10

Thomas Wals iuratus et exa*m*i*n*atus sup*er* quarto Interragatorio

15

Ad iiij*tum* Int*er*rogator*io* dicit that he was in the stokk*is* but he seith that he neu*er*
harde ne knewe the word*is* conteyned in the first p*ar*te of the article/ et quo ad
georgiu*m* villeris dicit q*d* m*aster* hughe Asseton and the seid george came to this
deponent sittyng in the stokk*is* in the kicchyng w'in the porteris house and askid
hym as he dede./ and then the seid george ~~to~~ dede ~~h~~ leye his hand vpon his key
whiche dede hang by his purse seying I thinke I cowde opun this lokk w*t* this
key and than seid m*aster* hugh I thinke ye will nat/ than seid the seid george I
trowe I am nat so madde./ et dicit iste iuratus that he hard non other word*is* on
his conscience but thes befor reherside/ and this deponent seith that he seid to
the port*er* I pray you lette the stokk*is* stonde w'out for than I trust I shall {nat}
sitte long here/ and this deponent seith by the~~r~~ vertue of his oithe that he harde
noo thretyng*is* of brekyng of the stokk*is* of enny s*er*ua*u*nt belongyng to my lady
{ne yet enny other p*er*sone} Int*er*rogat*us* wherfor he seid that if the stok*is* war
w'out ~~I~~ {he} trust ~~I~~ {that he} shuld nat sitte long ther/ and he seith that then
yf he {hade} ben w'out his frynd*is* or sume other wold haue labourid for ~~me~~
hym and therfor he seid soo and for non other cause/ and also he thowght that
my lord george ~~we~~ wold cume that way and to haue hade co*m*passion of hym yf
he hade sitten w'out

20

25

30

Notes

Text

From the records of the Bishop of Lincoln's 1525 Visitation of Newarke College and
Hospital, Leicester. The text has been edited in A. Hamilton Thompson, *Visitations in
the Diocese of Lincoln 1517–1531*, Vol. III, Lincoln Record Society, Vol. 37 (1947), pp.
148 and 170 (Text A) and 222–3 (Text B).

Manuscript

Two corrections are of interest. In B26 the definite article has a crossed-through *r* at the
end. The original *ther* spelling might have been a slip of the pen, but perhaps it was a
Northern demonstrative, as in Scots *thir*. In B29–30 the alterations show the process of
converting 1st person narrative to the 3rd person.

Frequently the writer adds a backwards-turning flourish to final *m* or *n*. Since there is no evidence that this in intended as a mark of abbreviation, it has been ignored here. Thus (B7) *down*, (B7) *form*.

The abbreviation expanded to *master* in B18 and 22 has been expanded as *magister* in the Latin introduction.

In (A1) *relique* and (A3) *quere* the letter *q* is virtually identical with the letter *g*.

Glossary

(A1–2)	*relique sonday*	third Sunday after Midsummer
(A3)	*quere*	=choir
(A11)	*ageyn*	in reply
(A11)	*noughty*	wicked
(A11)	*ruele*	conduct, discipline
(A12)	*ffyrth*	wooded country (see note)
(A13)	*be busy with*	have sexual relations with
(A13)	*vse*	persist in doing
(B5)	*yattis*	=gates
(B10)	*holde*	bet
(B11)	*trowe*	assure
(B17)	*article*	formal question asked of witness
(B20)	*as*	how
(B24)	*reherside*	quoted
(B25)	*w'out*	outside
(B27)	*thretyngis*	threats

Latin

(A1) Master John Wetwood ... to the sixth (question)

(A16–17) Master Thomas Hurderon ... said that Master Thomas Wigston spoke these or similar words

(B1–2) Master Hugh Aston, Master of the Choristers, sworn and examined etc. In reply to the fourth question says

(B12–14) and he says that the said George uttered the said words as a joke and did not intend to do anything else, and he was present and saw and heard these things.

(B15–16) Thomas Walls sworn and examined regarding the fourth question. In reply to the fourth question he says

Explanatory notes

(A12) *ffyrth and forest*: a common formula, but Thompson, *Visitations*, identifies this as a specific topographical reference to Leicester Frith and Charnwood Forest.

Background

The Dean, Canons and other clergy and laity of Newarke College and Hospital, Leicester, were under scrutiny for general laxity and low morale, and more especially because there had been disputes between the College and the household of Lady Hungerford, who lived within the precincts. There was an Episcopal Visitation, in the course of which members of the College answered questions devised to discover whether there was any substance in the accusations that Lady Hungerford's men had made trouble by actions ranging from dumb insolence to scuffles.

Topics for linguistic investigation

1. Ways of spelling long vowels.
2. Spellings suggesting local pronunciations.
3. The difference between: (A8) *you* and (B11) *ye*; (A7) *noo* and (B23) *non*; (A4) *hym* and (B7) *hym*; (A7) *the* and *the*.
4. The grammar of insult in Text A.
5. The two witnesses' versions of the same conversation in Text B 7–12 and 20–23.

Text 21

John Lauder and others: Selkirk, Scotland 1540
(Scottish Record Office Manuscript TD84/153)

Text A

[f. 276v] That day Ihone of lauder admittit preif to ye said thomas be Iames
saltoun ye said Ihone devly sworne in presence of oʳ Iugis granttis hyme of ye
aigis of xlviij ȝeris depones be his gret aycht ȝat Iames saltoun chassit thome
Nycholl ky throu his medo in feriosite wᵗ ane kavil of ane tre as he vnderstud

5   and quhen he oʳ tuk yaim he straik yaim realy and quhen he coucht noᵗ ouer hy
yaim he slang ye porcioune of yat tre at yaim and I stud at my dur & saw this
and quhidde\<er> he did skayᵗ or noᵗ to his ky I ken noᵗ

*   *   *   *

[f. 278v] Thomas Hendersoun of ye aigis of xxᵗⁱ yeiris noᵗ mareit devly sworne
in Iugisment depones be his greit aycht yᵗ he kennit thom Nycholl skaᵗ anent ye

10   deid of twa ky ye tynsaill of ane kowes milk and ye deid of ane stirk I saw noᵗ
quhen Iames saltoune straik yʳ ky in ye medo for yan I vas one ye feld bot quhen
I come hayme Ihone of lauder stud one his awin midding at his dur and said to
me yᵗ Iames straik yaim evyll and kest ane Roung at yaim quhen he myᵗ noᵗ {our}
tak yaim I and Iok ȝoull slew ane of yʳ ky yʳeftir and I fand ȝousterit blud and

15   vorssum abone hir hudder The toyʳ kow vas put to vinterhoup to Ioke vatsoun
& yar scho deit and I sawe neuir bot hir skyne qˡᵏ vantit ane quarter of It I kennit
ye stirk deit & yat kow ȝeid ȝeild and ferder I ken noᵗ

That day Ihone of roull mareit of ye aigis of xxvj ȝeiris or yʳby devly sworne
depones be his aycht yᵗ he kennit thom nycholl skayᵗ verray weill bot he saw noᵗ

20   quhen ye ky war striking bot as Ihone of lauder schew to me I helpit thom
hendersoun to slay ane kow and I saw diuerss blay straikis one hir bak and hanch
banis wᵗ pairt of blud & vorssum and meikill ȝoustrit blud & vorssum betuex
hir hinder lygis abune hir hudder I kend ane stirke deid and ye kow ȝeid ȝeild
the third kow vas put to vynterhoup to Iok vatsoun I ken yᵗ is deid for I saw thre

25   quarteris of hir hid send hayme to thomas nychoill

112

Text B

[f. 282v] Robert Vilsoun*e* mareit of ye aig*is* of xxxvij ʒeir*is* dewly sworn*e* in
Iug*is*me*nt* depones be his gr*e*it aycht y*t* he vas vorkand in dauid my*n*to stair ane
c*er*tain ʒeir syne and he hard done strang say to dauid my*n*to yat scho had coft
ye auld caldroun fra ye gudma*n* of edschaw for xiiij s or xv s and sperit at hyme
5   geif he had ony mony & scho said yat scho had no mor in hir purss bot viij s iiij
d and he ordinit hir to pass & borrow ye remayne and w*t*in ane bony spaice ye
gudma*n* come riddand to ye stair fut & criet vpone dauid my*n*to & Done strang
& yai passit dou*n* and I sat & saw yaim geif hyme mony one his cloik Lap bot
v*er*ily I ken*n*e no*t* how meikill mony scho & he deliu*er*it to hy*m* and be ye aycht
10   y*t* I haif maid I hard yai*m* aggreit be all y*t* I culd heir se & vnderstand

Kait of burn*e* mareit of ye aig*is* of Lv ʒeir*is* devly sworn*e* in p*re*cence of ye
p*ro*vest bailʒeis & Inquis*itouris* depones be hir gr*e*it aycht y*t* done strang come
to borrowe iiij s at me to geif philp scot for ane auld caldroun*e* and I gat vp and
ran*e* eft to hyme and craiffit hyme iiij s y*t* I gaif his wyf & his doucht*ir* and
15   p*ro*mis*y*t hyme to strik one ye iiij ss in done strang hand*is* for ye said iiij ss y*t* I
craiffit hy*m* and he bad me craif ye iiij ss at yair*is* hand*is* y*t* I gaif my stuff to and
sa I lent hir iiij s and stud besid quhill scho & dauid deliu*er*it one his clok lap
xiiij s or ell*is* xv s for ane auld caldroun*e* at ye stair fut & he one horss bak

besse keyne relyk of vmquhill alane keyne devly sworn*e* in Iug*is*me*nt* of ye aig*is*
20   of Lvij ʒeir*is* depones be hir gr*e*it aycht y*t* scho hard done strang cum In to hir
husband alane and desirit to borrow miony & said y*t* scho had coft ane caldrou*n*
at ye gudma*n* of edschawe & scho behuffit to haif p*air*t of miony y*t* scho vantit
I saw my husband geif hir p*air*t and I lukit furcht at my vondok and saw philp
scot one horss bak & one his clok lap scho vas deliu*er*and hyme mony scho
25   ken*n*is no*t* ye nomor of ye miony I hard done say to alane y*t* scho behuffet to geif
hyme xv s for It

helyner down*e* Relict of vmqu*i*ll robert cheshol*m* wedo no*t* mareit deponis be
hir gr*e*it aycht devly sworn*e* in Iug*is*me*nt* and admittit sais y*t* philp scot callit
vponn hir to hauld ye briddill renʒe quhen done strang & dauid my*n*to var
30   deliu*er*and ye xiiij s or xv for held vp ane p*air*t of clok lap and done said to dauid
& me I tak vitness y*t* I haif pait ʒ*ow* and dauid geif It ca*n* no*t* be me*n*dit It is gud
brass and worcht ye sow*m* & yis I hard & sawe

Iok down*e* devly sworn*e* depones y*t* he ken*n*it y*t* done strang & dauid my*n*to coft
ye auld caldrou*n* fra ye gudma*n* of edschawe bot he ken*n*it no*t* ye v*er*ray priss &
35   I ke*n* It was pait for

Notes

Text

From the records of the Burgh Court at Selkirk, Scotland, case of *Nycholl* v. *Saltoun* (Text A) and case of *Mynto* v. *Scot* (Text B). The text has been edited in J. Imrie, T. I. Rae and W. D. Ritchie (eds), *The Burgh Court Book of Selkirk*, Part I: 1503–1545, Scottish Record Society, Vol. 89 (1960), pp. 223, 225, and 230–31.

Manuscript

A photograph of lines B1–10 from this document, together with a commentary, appears as Plate III on pp. 90–91 above.

There are some problems associated with abbreviations. Horizontal strokes similar to marks of abbreviation but above letters written with minims have been considered as empty. Thus (A4) *saltoun*, (A15) *vatsoun*, (B29) *vponn*, (A12) *hayme*.

Note that distinctive Scots (A15) *abone* depends on a distinction between *n* and *u* which is virtually lacking in this hand. In (A23) *abune* is more certain.

Glossary

(A1)	*preif* †	=proof, witness
(A1)	*be*	=by, in regard to
(A3)	*depones*	testifies
(A3)	*gret aycht*	solemn oath
(A4)	*ky*	=cows
(A4)	*feriosite*	fury
(A4)	*kavil* †	piece (of wood)
(A5)	*straik yaim realy*	actually struck them
(A5)	*coucht*	=could
(A5)	*ouer hy* †	overtake
(A7)	*skay′* †	harm
(A9)	*kennit … ska′* †	knew … to be guilty of doing harm
(A16)	*anent* †	in respect of
(A10)	*deid*	=death
(A10)	*tynsaill* †	loss
(A10)	*stirk* †	heifer or young bullock
(A11)	*on ye feld*	out of town
(A12)	*midding*	refuse-heap
(A13)	*Roung*	=rung, cudgel, large branch
(A14)	*ȝousterit* †	festering (OED YOUSTER)
(A15)	*vorssum* †	pus (OED WORSUM)
(A15, 23)	*abone, abune* †	above
(A15)	*The toy′*	=the (that) above
(A15)	*vinterhoup*	name of a farm, ?Winterhope
(A16)	*vantit*	=wanted, lacked
(A17)	*ȝeid ȝeild* †	went dry

(A21)	*straikis*	=strokes, marks left by blows
(B2)	*stair*	staircase
(B2–3)	*ane certain ʒeir syne* †	exactly a year ago
(B3)	*coft* †	bought
(B4)	*sperit (at)* †	asked (of)
(B6)	*ordinit*	ordered, told
(B6)	*pass*	go
(B6)	*remayne*	unpaid balance, remainder
(B6)	*bony space* †	good while
(B7)	*criet vpone*	shouted for
(B12)	*provest* †	=Provost (equivalent of English Mayor)
(B12)	*bailʒeis* †	=Bailies (equivalent of English Aldermen)
(B12)	*Inquisitouris*	investigating officials
(B14)	*eft*	back
(B14)	*craiffit*	asked (ditransitive verb)
(B15)	*strik one*	settle for
(B19)	*relyk* †	widow
(B19)	*vmquhill* †	deceased, late
(B22, 7)	*gudman* †	owner or tenant
(B22)	*behuffit*	=behoved, needed
(B23)	*furcht*	=forth, out
(B23)	*vondok*	=window
(B29)	*briddill renʒe*	=bridle rein
(B31)	*geif*	=if

Background

In Text B the case is about disputed ownership. If the huge cauldron was not, in fact, paid for, then it is the property of the heir of the man from whom Minto and his wife claim they bought it.

Topics for linguistic investigation

1. Spelling preferences differing from those of Southern English, but not marking differences in pronunciation.
2. Spellings indicating local pronunciation.
3. Differences from a Southern English text in the inflexional morphology of verbs.
4. The morphology and syntax of: (A3–4) *thome Nycholl ky*, (A7) *I ken no'*, (A20) *quhen ye ky war striking*, (B16) *yairis handis y¹ I gaiff my stuff to*, (B22) *scho behuffit to haif.*
5. Words used in Southern English, but with a different meaning in Scots.
6. The etymology of words special to Scots.

Text 22

William Powrie: Perth, Scotland 1567
(British Library Manuscript Cotton Caligula C.I)

[f. 327r] Williame powry borne in Kinfawnis *se*ruito*ur* to the erle boithuile
deponis ... that Iohnne hepburne of boltoun at ten ho*uris* at evin com*m*andit
the deponar and patrik wilsoun to tak vp ane carage of two males the ane ane
tronk and the vyer ane ledderin maill qlk*is* war liand in the said neyer h<all>

5   Qlk*is* the deponar and the said pat*ri*k put on and charget vponn twa hor<s> of
my lordis the ane being his sowme horse and cariit the same to the ʒet of the
enteres of the blak freris And yar laid the same doun quh<air> the erle bothuile
accum*p*aniit w^t Robart ormestoun and Paris callit fre<nch> paris and vythers
twa qlk*is* hed cloik*is* about yair faces met the saidis deponar and Patrik wilsoun

10   And yat ʒoung tallo the laird of ormest<oun> and Iohnne hepburne of boltoun
wes awaittand vponn the deponar and Pa<trik> wilsoun w^tin the said ʒet And
yat yair the saidis thre p*er*sonis w^tin the saide <ʒet> Ressauit the saidis twa
charges qlk*is* the deponar knew yan to be pulder Be<caus> the same wes in
sindrie polk*is* w^tin the said*is* maill and tronk and the dep<onent> and ye said

15   Pat*ri*k wilsoun helpit yame in w^t the saim and the powder <beand> takin fra
yaime the said Iohnne hepburne of boltoun send this deponar for candell and
yat he coft sex half pen*n*y candill fra geordie burnis wy<f> in ye kowgait and
deliuerit to the said Iohnne. And yat the said*is* p*er*sonis Ressavaris of the powder
hed ane bowel w^t yame w^t ane litill licht cand<ell> And als the said*is* p*er*sonis

20   w^tin the said ʒet oppin*n*it the tronk and maill and <tuik> out the polk*is* w^t the
powder And **X** euery ane of yame tuke ane vponn <his> bak or vnder his arme
and cariit the saim away to the bak wall of th<e> ʒaird that is nixt the treis And
yane the said Laird of ormestoun Iohnne hepburne of boltoun and ʒoung tallo
Ressauit the pewder fra yame A<nd> wald suffer the deponar and his m*ar*row

25   to pas na forder And quhen the deponar and his marrow come bak agane to the
said frer ʒet the twa ho<rs> that cariit the said*is* tronk and maill war awaʒ And
yat yai cariit th<e> s*ame*n tronk and maill agane to the abbay And as yei come
vp the blakf<rer> wynd the quenis grace wes gangand befoir yaime w^t ly^t
torches A<nd> that ye deponar and his marrow being c*um* in to the said erlis

30   ludgeing <in> the abbey thai tariit y^r ane ho*ur* or mair and yan ye said erle come
And immediatlie take of his clay^tis that wes on him v*idelicet* ane pair of bla<k>
weluet hoiss traissit w^t siluer and ane dowblet of satin of the s*ame*n m<aner>
and put on ane vyer pair of blak hoiss and ane dowblet of Canwa<s> And take

his syde Ryding cloik about him And inco*n*tine*n*t Past furt<h> accompaniit
with frenche Paris the deponar georde dalgleis And p<atrik> wilsoun And
come doun the turnepyke and endlang the ~~wall~~ kirkw<all> of the quenis gardin
qll yai come to the bak of the cun3ehouss And vp the bak of the cun3ehouss and
the bak of the stabillis qll yai co<m> to the can*n*ogait And deponis that as yai
~~b~~ come by the 3et of the [f. 327v] quenis south gardin The twa sentynallis that
stude at the 3et that gangis to the vter cloiss spierit at yame quha Is yat? And
yai ansu*e*rit frennd*is* The sentynallis sperit quhat frend*is* And yai ansu*e*rit my
Lord boithuillis s*er*uandis ITem deponis that yai come vp the can*n*ogait and to
the nether bow And findand the bow stekit Patrik wilsoun cryit to Iohnne
galloway and bad him oppin the port to s*er*uandis of my lord boithuellis Quha
come and oppin*n*it the port And yai enterit and 3eid vp abone bassyntynis houss
on ye south side of the gait And knokit at ane stair and callit for the Laird of
ormestoun and Robert ormestoun and nane ansu*e*rit yame And yan yai slippit
doun ane cloiss beneth the frer wynd and come to the 3et at the ~~f~~ blakfreris And
enterit in at yat 3et And 3eid quhill yai come to the bak wall and dyke quhair
the deponar and patrik wilsoun Left the vyeris p*er*sonis befoir expr*e*mit w^t the
pewder as said Is And yair the erle boithuile Past in over the dyke And bad the
deponar patrik wilsoun and geordy dalgleis tary still yair qll he come bakwart
to yaime And forder deponis that yai tariit y^r half ane ho*ur* and hard neuir din
of ony thing Qll at Last my Lord accu*m*paniit w^t 3oung tallo & Iohnne hepburne
of boltoun come to the deponar and vy*er*is twa p*er*sonis being w^t him And evin
as my lord and thir twa come to the deponar and his marrowis at the dyke Thai
herd the crak and yai past awa3 togidder out at the frer 3et and sinderit quhen
yai come to the kowgait And p*art* vp the blakfrer wyend and sum vp the cloiss
qlk Is vnder the cardinallis well And met no^t qll yai come to the narrow of the
bow And 3eid doun ane cloiss on the northside of ye gait to haif loppin the wall
of leith wynd and y^r my lord tho^t it ouer heich and come agane abak to the port
And causit cry vponn Iohnne galloway and said yai war s*er*uand*is* of my Lord
boithuell*is* And Iohnne galloway Raiss and Leit yame furth and syne yai Past
doun sanct marie wynd and doun the bak3ard*is* of the can*n*ogait and to the said
erlis ludgeing And as yai Past by the quenis gardin befoirspe*c*ifiit the s*a*m*e*n
sentynallis sperit at yame quha yai war And yai ansu*e*rit yai war s*er*uand*is* of my
Lord boithuilis And als sperit quhat crak yat was And yai ansu*e*rit yai knew no^t
And the sentynallis bad yame gif yai war seruandis of my Lord boithuellis gang
y^r way/ My lord come in to his ludgeing and Imediatlie callit for ane drink and
tuke of his clay^t*is* inco*n*tine*n*t and 3eid to his bed and tariit in his bed about half
ane ho*ur* qll mast*er* george hakket come to the 3et and knokt and desu*i*rit to be
in at my Lord and quhen he come in he apperit to be in ane gret effray And wes
blak as ony pik and no^t ane word to speak My lord inquirit quhat Is the mater
ma*n* And he ansu*e*rit the kingis houss Is blawn vp And I trow the king be slane

(line numbers in margin: 35, 40, 45, 50, 55, 60, 65, 70)

Notes

Text

From the documents concerning the murder of Lord Darnley, husband of Mary Queen of Scots. The text has been edited in R. Pitcairn, *Criminal Trials in Scotland 1478–1644*, Vol. I, Part 2, Bannatyne Club (Edinburgh, 1833), p. 493.

Manuscript

The cross in l. 35 has been inserted to mark an important point in the narrative.

Horizontal strokes (which would normally indicate an abbreviation) over *-oun* have been treated as empty, since identical spellings without the stroke also occur, and none with any additional letter.

Because of the confusability of *n* and *u*, the Scots spelling (45) *abone* could be Southern English *aboue*.

Glossary

(1)	*seruitour*	servant
(2)	*deponis*	testifies
(3)	*deponar* †	witness
(3)	*carage*	load
(3)	*males*	bags
(4)	*ledderin*	made of leather
(4)	*neyer*	=nether, lower
(5)	*charget*	loaded
(6)	*sowme horse* †	pack horse
(6)	*ʒet*	=gate
(7)	*enteres*	entrance
(7)	*black freres*	=black friars, i.e. Dominican friary
(13)	*charges*	loads
(13)	*pulder*	=(gun)powder
(14)	*sindrie*	individual
(14)	*polkis* †	small bags
(17)	*coft* †	bought
(24)	*suffer*	allow
(24)	*marrow* †	mate
(31)	*clayᵗis*	=clothes
(32)	*hoiss*	=hose, breeches
(32)	*traissit*	ornamented with lines
(33)	*Canwa<s>*	=canvas, thick coarse material
(34)	*syde cloik*	long cloak
(34)	*incontinent*	immediately
(36)	*endlang* †	along
(37)	*qll* (short for *quhill*)	until
(37)	*cunʒehouss*	mint

(40)	*gangis* †	goes
(40)	*cloiss* †	=close, passage
(40)	*speirit* †	asked
(43)	*bow* †	arched gateway
(43)	*stekit* †	shut
(45)	*port*	gate
(45)	*ʒeid*	went (preterite of *ga*)
(46)	*stair*	house opening off a staircase
(49)	*dyke*	wall
(50)	*expremit* †	expressed, mentioned
(57)	*crak*	explosion
(57)	*sinderit*	separated
(60)	*loppin* †	jumped
(63)	*syne* †	then
(72)	*effray* †	fright
(73)	*pik*	=pitch
(74)	*trow*	believe

Background

The murder of Henry Darnley, husband of Mary Queen of Scots, at Kirk o'Field, Edinburgh has never been fully solved. The evidence of Lord Bothwell's servants, such as Powrie, implicated their master and perhaps the Queen too. This manuscript was filed by the English authorities at the time, as part of their dossier concerning the Scottish Queen. While Bothwell went free, Powrie and others were executed. Powrie's place of birth, Kinfauns, is near Perth.

Topics for linguistic investigation

1. The use of the letters ʒ and *y*.
2. The full forms represented by words written abbreviated or with superscript letters.
3. A survey of other texts to check the use of question marks like that in l. 40.
4. Spellings which reflect local pronunciation.
5. The forms: (4) *qlkis*, (11) *wes*, (14) *saidis*, (25) *come*, (40) *gangis*, (43) *findand*, (45) *ʒeid*, (60) *loppin*, (63) *boithuellis*.
6. The use of the progressive construction.
7. Local words which have survived into present–day Scots.

Text 23

Elizabeth Dunlop: Ayrshire, Scotland 1576
(Scottish Record Office Manuscript JC 2/1)

[f. 15r] ITem sche being inquirit quhat kynd of man yis Thom reid was, declarit
he was ane honest wele elderlie man gray bairdit and had ane gray coitt wᵗ
lumbart slevis of ye auld fassoun ane pair of gray brekis and quhyte schankis
gartanit abone ye kne ane blak bonet on his heid cloiss behind and plane befoir
5   wᵗ silkin laissis drawin throw ye lippis yairof and ane quhyte wand in his hand
etc

ITem being interrogat, how and in quhat maner of place ye said Thome reid
Come to her ansuerit as sche was gangand betuix hir awin hous and ye ȝard of
monkcastell dryvand hir ky to ye pasture and makand hevye sair dule wᵗ hir self
10   gretand verrie fast for hir kow yᵗ was deid hir husband and chyld yᵗ wer lyand
seik in ye land ill and sche new rissine out of gissune/ The foirsaid Thom mett
hir be ye way healsit hir and said gude day Bessie and sche said god speid ȝow
gudemann etc
[f. 15v] Sancta marie said he Bessie Quhy makis thow sa grit dule and sair
15   greting for onye wardlie thing/ Sche ansuerit allace haif I noᵗ grit caus to mak
grit dule ffor oʳ gere is trakit and my husband is on ye point of deid, and ane
Babie of my awin will noᵗ leve and my self at ane waik point/ haif I noᵗ gude
caus thann to haif ane sair hart Bot Thom said Bessie Thow hes crabit god and
askit sum thing yow suld noᵗ haif done And yairfoir I counsell ye to mend to him
20   for I tell the Thy barne sall die and ye seik kow or yow cum hame/ Thy twa
scheip sall de to/ Bot thy husband sall mend and be als haill and feir as euir he
was/ And than was I sumthing blyther fra he tauld me yt my gudeman wald
mend Than Thome Reid went away fra me in throw ye ȝard of monkcastell and
I thoᵗ he gait in at ane naroware hoill of ye dyke nor onye erdlie man culd haif
25   ~~done~~ gane throw and swa I was sumthing fleit This was ye first tyme yat Thom
and Bessie forgadderit etc

ITem ye Third tyme he apperit to hir as sche was gangand betuix hir awin hous
and ye thorne of damwstarnok Quair he tareit ane gude quhyle wᵗ hir and sperit
at hir gif sche wald noᵗ trow in him Sche said sche wald trow in ony bodye did
30   hir gude and Thom promeist hir bayᵗ geir houss and ky and vyer graith gif sche
wald denye hir christindom and ye faith sche tuke at ye funt stane Quairvnto

sche ansuerit That gif sche suld be Revin at horis taillis sche suld neuir do yat/
Bot promeist to be leill and trew to him in onye thing sche culd do and forder
he was sumthing angrie w^t hir yat wald no^t grant to yat qlk he spak etc

35   ITem ye ferd tyme he apperit in hir awin hous to hir about ye xij hour of ye day
Quair yair was sittand thre tailȝeouris and hir awin gudeman and he tuke hir
apperoun and led hir to ye dure w^t him and sche followit and ȝeid vp w^t him to
ye kill end quair he forbaid hir to speik or feir for onye thing sche hard or saw/
And quhen yaj had gane ane lytle pece fordwerd Sche saw twelf persounes aucht

40   wemenn and foir menn The men wer cled in gentilmennis clething/ and ye
wemenn had all plaiddis round about yame and wer verrie semelie to se and
Thom was w^t yame and demandit gif sche knew ony of yame Ansuerit Nane
except Thom/ demandit quhat yaj said to hir/ ansuerit yaj baid hir sit doun and
said welcum besse and forder sche being ane lytill space fra yame Cryit besse

45   will thow go w^t ws. Bot sche ansuerit no^t·Becaus Thom had forbiddin hir And
forder declarit yt sche knew not quhat purpois yaj had amangis yame/ Onlie
sche saw yair lippis move/ And w^{t}in ane schort space yaj pairtit all away And
ane hiddeous vglie sowche of wind followit yame And sche lay seik q^{ll} thom
come agane bak fra yame etc

50   ITem sche being demandit gif sche sperit at Thom quhat persounes yaj war
{he} ansuerit yat yaj war ye gude wychtis yat wynnit in ye court of elfame Quha
come yair to desyre hir to ga w^t yame and forder Thom desyrit hir to do ye sam
Quha ansuerit Sche saw na proffeit [f. 16r] To gang yaj kynd of gaittis vnles sche
kend quhairfor. Thom said Seis thow no^t me bay^t meit worth and claith worth

55   and gude aneuch lyke in persoun and suld mak hir far better nor euir sche was.
Sche ansuerit yat sche duelt w^t hir awin husband and bairnis and culd no^t leif
yame And swa Thom began to be verrie crabit w^t hir and said gif swa sche tho^t
sche wald get lytill gude of him etc

Notes

Text

Extract from the Trial for Witchcraft of Elizabeth (Bessie) Dunlop, in the records of
the High Court of Justiciary, Book of Adjournal 1576–1584. The text has been edited
in R. Pitcairn, *Criminal Trials in Scotland 1478–1644*, Vol. I, Part 2, Bannatyne Club
(Edinburgh, 1833), pp. 49–58.

Manuscript

Since the account of the first meeting with Tom Reid is followed immediately by the
narrative of the third meeting, it is possible that some piece of the deposition is missing
between lines 26 and 27.

In l. 51 the pronoun *he* has been inserted presumably to clarify the subject in a
construction which from usage elsewhere, e.g. in l. 8, would imply the subject *she*. In the

expansion of abbreviations all omission-marks for nasals have been taken to be significant, but they may be intended as empty, in (40) *gentilmennis*, (41) *wemenn* etc.

The Scots spellings (46) *amangis* and (52) *ga* depend on a distinction between *a* and *o* which is not totally clear in either case. A similar lack of clear distinction between *n* and *u* means that it would not be impossible to read (4) *abone* as *aboue*. The three minims supplying the *m* in (51) *elfame* (equated with *elf-hame*, see note below) might well be read as *ni*, giving *elfanie*.

Glossary

(2)	*wele*	fairly
(3)	*lumbart* †	lombardy-style, ?made of black material (DOST LOMBARD, OED LUMBARDYNE)
(3)	*fassoun*	=fashion, style
(3)	*brekis*	=breeches
(3)	*schankis*	stockings
(4)	*gartanit* †	gartered (DOST GARTAN n.)
(4)	*abone* †	above
(4)	*bonet*	hat
(4)	*cloiss*	close-fitting
(5)	*wand*	rod (of office), or ?magic wand
(9)	*dule*	lamentation
(10)	*gretand* †	weeping
(11)	*land ill* †	See note
(11)	*gissune* †	childbed (CSD JIZZEN; not in OED)
(12)	*healsit* †	greeted
(15)	*wardlie*	of this world, earthly
(16)	*gere*	possessions
(16)	*trakit* †	?dwindled away (see note)
(18)	*crabit*	angered
(19)	*mend*	make amends; (21) get better
(20)	*barne* †	child
(20)	*or* †	before
(21)	*haill*	recovered
(21)	*feir*	sound
(22)	*fra*	after
(22)	*gudeman* †	husband; (13) form of address
(24)	*gait*	?got (preterite of GET), or ?went (=*ȝeid*)
(24)	*dyke*	wall
(24)	*nor*	than
(24)	*erdlie*	earthly, human
(25)	*fleit* †	frightened
(26)	*forgadderit*	met
(28)	*tareit*	=tarried, lingered
(28)	*sperit* †	asked

(30)	*graith* †	possessions, wealth
(31)	*christendom*	baptism
(31)	*funt stane*	font (stone)
(32)	*revin*	torn apart
(34)	*grant to*	agree to
(35)	*ferd*	fourth
(37)	*ʒeid*	went (preterite of *go/ga*)
(38)	*kill end*	place where kiln is
(41)	*plaiddis* †	=plaids
(46)	*purpois*	discourse, conversation
(48)	*sowche* †	blast
(51)	*gude wychtis*	good people
(51)	*elfame*	See note
(53)	*gang* †	go
(53)	*gaittis* †	ways
(54)	*meit worth* †	well-fed
(54)	*claith worth* †	well-clothed
(55)	*aneuch*	=enough
(55)	*gude lyke* †	handsome

Local placenames

| (11) | *monkcastell* | Monk Castle |
| (28) | *damwstarnok* | Damusternock |

Explanatory notes

(11) *ye land ill*: Not in OED; DOST identifies as name of some unspecified violent disease, or perhaps 'epidemic'; Pitcairn, *Criminal Trials*, suggests 'famine'.

(16) *trakit*: Not in OED; CSD has TRAIK 'be ailing, pine and die' but with animate subjects, while the subject here is *gear* 'possessions'. Pitcairn, *Criminal Trials*, suggests 'dwindle(d) away'.

(51) *elfame*: Not in OED; DOST has only this example; Pitcairn, *Criminal Trials*, suggests 'home of the elves', assuming a form *elf-hame*. The reading is difficult (see Manuscript above), but the alternative *elfanie* is equally unsupported by other texts, although DOST cites a 1583 use of ELPHYNE.

Background

Bessie Dunlop is described in the text as coming from *Lyne*. That this is Linn, just south of Dalry, Ayrshire, is confirmed by her mention of nearby Monk Castle, and of Damusternock, about 12 miles further south. There are further Ayrshire references elsewhere in the text. The document also names her husband, *Andro Jak*. Her narrative of meeting Tom Reid just after having had a baby does not necessarily mean that she is still a young woman at the time of her deposition, since this ranges back over several years.

She is accused of witchcraft on the basis of claiming to foretell the future, cure illness and find lost items. The questions about Tom Reid, her replies to which are recorded here, are put because she attributes all her knowledge to him, and that he appears to be some kind of agent for the Devil, especially since she says he told her that he was killed thirty years earlier at the Battle of Pinkie.

The document has a contemporary marginal note that she was found guilty, and burned.

Topics for linguistic investigation

1. Distinguish between (12) *ȝow*, (18) *thow*, (19) *yow*, (19) *ye*, (20) *the*, (20) *ye*.
2. Spellings that suggest local pronunciation.
3. The functions of the forms: (14) *makis*, (20) *cum*, (15) *greting*, (9) *ky*, (53) *yaj*, (45) *will*.
4. Prepositions and their use.
5. Linguistic differences between the dialoque quoted and Dunlop's own narrative.
6. To what extent Scots words can be said to cluster in certain semantic areas.

Text 24

Hugh Rist: Dartington, Devon 1582
(Devon Record Office Manuscript Chanter 861)

[f. 4v] Hugo Rist de Dartengton vbi moram traxit per xvj annos etatis xxx^{ta} annorum et vltra testis admissus &c partes litigantes per decem annos bene novit vt dicit

[f. 5r] Ad primum et secundum articulos deponit & dicit That within the space
5   of these three yeres last past, Gatchell having departed from Dartngton wth this deponentes master, m^r Gawin Champernowne to Exeter to the assises or sessions hath retourned home agayne the same night he went fourth and comme to dartington house about midnight and hath called this deponent lieng vnder the gate in the litle Lodge to lett him in. And this deponent hath risen oute of his
10 bedd and Lett him in, and this deponent marvayling that he retournd so sone asked him what the cause was of his soden retourne, and he aunswered That he had occasion to fetch writings and then fourthwth asked of this deponent How he might winne to my Ladies chamber and this deponent would bidd him go thether him self, but he would not be so content but would needs haue this
15 deponent goo thether with him/ And when Gatchell knocked at the chamber dore, and that it was knowen that Gatchell was there the chamber dore was opened streight waye, and Gatchell and this deponent went both in the chamber and the sayd Gatchell went to the bed side betwene to the Courteyne and the bed where the sayd Ladie Laye, and then this deponent went to his
20 chamber agayne, and Left the sayd Gatchell there, and before this deponent was past downe over the stayres he heard the chamber dore made fast and the sayd Gatchell before his going into the chamber ~~ded~~ desired this deponent of all Love that he would not tell his the sayd Gatchells wife of his retourne home agayne, and aboute two or three of the clocke the same morninge would take
25 his horse and ride to exeter agayne and would tell this deponent That he would be at exeter before his master was vpp. And further That it is not only one tyme That Gatchell hath vsed the sayd fashions, but that he hath donne the like three ~~of~~ or foure tymes [f. 5v] within these three yeres, but he this deponent did not goe in with Gatchell to the chamber but only one tyme but did bring him either
30 to the dore or somme part of the waye vt dicit et aliter nescit deponere vt dicit/.

Ad tertium articulum deponit et dicit That aboute two yeres and a half agonne

35

40

45

50

55

as he now remembreth Iohn Gatchell aforsayd and this deponent went to Iohn
Towpes in the church towne of Staverton to breakefast and in the way as they
went this deponent went vnto Gatchell my Ladye meaning the sayd Ladie
Robarda is much in your mowth I thincke you doe somwhat with her that you
ought not to doe And the sayd Gatchell at the first sayd noe there is no such
thinge, No sayd this dep*one*nt, Howe chaunce then the dores be opened vnto
you whensoeuer you comme, I cannot beleve but there is somme matter
betwene you, well sayd Gatchell to this deponent you are one, that I dare trust,
and {dare} putt my Life in yor handes, and I will tell you more than I will tell
anie bodie, but if you bewraye me I am vtterlie vndonne, q^d this dep*one*nt I
warrant you I will never bewraye you Then sayd Gatchell in deed the truthe is
I haue occupied my Ladie meaning the sayd Ladie Robarda, and I canne have
my pleasure of her whensoever I will If my m*aste*r be oute of the waye, but it
was Long before I could gett her good will. I thinck sayd he it was all most a xij
monthe before I could winne her but now all is well inoughe she is at my
com*m*aundeme*n*t and now the boye is borne it is the better, and it is no matter
what becometh of my m*aste*r for he will never doe nether thee nor me good so
Long as he livethe and I am sure of it if he should die and if my Ladie had five
thowsond poundes I should have all; and I praye the sayd he to this dep*one*nt
keep my councell and thou shalt haue a newe payre of hose of me and a new
doblet, and my Ladies gentle{wo}man mistris marie hath had as good as a fortie
poundes of me to keep my counsell, and she shall haue fortie and fortie poundes
more if she will herafter keep my counsell as she hath donne before vt dicit et
al*ite*r nescit deponere vt dicit/

Notes

Text

From the book of witnesses' depositions relating to cases heard at the Consistory Court
of the Diocese of Exeter 1582–85; case of *Champernowne* v. *Champernowne*. The text has
not been edited before.

Manuscript

Final *f* in (11) *of*, (14) *self*, (31) *half*, (49) *if* etc. is written with a flourish which has been
treated as empty. but which might denote a second *f*.

The superscript-abbreviation *m^r* serves both for title and full lexical item, so has been
transcribed accordingly, thus the two occurences in (6) *this deponentes master, m^r Gawin
Champernowne*.

Glossary

(8)	*lieng*	having a sleeping place
(10)	*marvayling*	being surprised
(12)	*fourthwth*	immediately

(13)	*winne*	find his way
(14)	*would needs*	was determined to
(27)	*fashions*	actions
(31)	*agonne*	ago
(33)	*church towne*	place with church serving several hamlets
(34)	*went*	said (see note)
(35)	*much in your mowth*	mentioned constantly in your conversation
(38)	*cannot ... but*	am forced to
(41)	*bewraye*	expose
(41)	*undonne*	ruined
(41)	*q^d*	=quod, said
(42)	*warrant*	assure
(43)	*occupied*	had sexual relations with
(45)	*good will*	consent
(45–6)	*xij monthe*	=twelvemonth, year
(47)	*no matter*	of no consequence
(51)	*keep my councell*	keep my secret

Latin

Lines 1–3: Hugh Rist of Dartington where he has been employed for sixteen years, thirty years of age and more, admitted as witness under oath, has known the parties in the case well for ten years, as he says.

Line 4: To the first and second questions listed he testifies and says ...

Lines 30 and 54–5: so he says and he knows of nothing else to testify to, so he says.

Explanatory notes

(34) *went*: the sense is clearly 'said'; OED has examples, from the 18th Century onwards, of the verb *go* in reference only to inanimates emitting sudden noise (e.g. *the bell goes clang*).

Background

The case was for 'separation from bed and board' (divorce permitting re-marriage not being available in the sixteenth century) between Sir Gawen Champernowne of Dartington and his wife Lady Roberda, on the grounds of her adultery. Witnesses gave their evidence at the church in Staverton near the manor of Dartington, Totnes.

Roberda Champernowne was the daughter of the Count de Montgomery, a Frenchman and leading Huguenot, and Gawen Champernowne was the son of a well-known and influential Devon man. This high-society scandal generated other documents that have survived, such as letters from Lady Roberda's family deploring her husband's cruelty. The couple were in their twenties at the time of the suit, which is said to have resulted in a separation being granted. However, of their eleven children, six were born previous to the separation and five after.

Topics for linguistic investigation

1. The use of 2nd person forms of the personal pronoun.
2. The difference between: (37) *be*, (39) *are*, (44) *be*, (46) *is*.
3. The distribution and significance of *shall* and *will*.
4. How auxiliary verbs are used to indicate habitual action.
5. How PDE would express the following: (21) *was past downe*, (47) *is borne*, (29) *did bring*, (36) *doe*.
6. A comparison between the vocabulary of sexuality in this text and that in Text 6E.

Text 25

Henry Jeffry: Rye, Sussex 1582

(East Sussex Record Office Manuscript RYE 47/25, Part II, Item 1)

The deposic*i*one of henry Ieffry of Rye aged xxviijth or ther about*es* being
sworne vppon the holy Evangelist the xijth of Maye A° R*egine* Elizabeth &c
xxiij°. taken before Mr Robert Iacson maior of Rye ffraunc*is* harys Iurat &
will*ia*m Appleton Recorder ther

5 Beinge in Towne I take it betwene Bartillmewe tyde and mychellmas and as I
Remem*b*er not longe after Bartillmewe in Ann° 1579. I came in as I was
accustomyd to doe one mornynge about ix or x of the clocke in the mornynge
to se howe my brother {Thomas Colbrane ~~& my~~} and Sister did, And hearinge
my brother somwhate hott in wordes wth one in his hall I stepte in and founde

10 hym and In° duncke Tayli*or* on Reconynge at whiche instaunte they were in
cont*r*oversye aboute the p*r*ice of Grograyne and veluit whiche the saide duncke
had boughte for hym at london as I after p*er*ceyvid for assone as my brother
sawe me he vsed thies wordes, well saide heare is he whoe soulde the Grograyne
for me and so callinge me vnto hym manyfestyd the matter vnto me desyringe

15 me to speake the trothe not onlye for howe muche I soulde the Grog*r*ayne but
also whate I thoughte bothe the Grog*r*ayne and veluit was woorthe because
duncke saide the Grog*r*ayne coste v s the yerde or vpwardes And in truthe it
was soulde for iij s the yearde and yett verye deare of that p*r*ice:/ By whiche
occasyon I stayde there in the hall settinge downe vpon the Settill of the longe

20 table and they Reconynge vpon the litle table nexte the fyer in tyme they grewe
~~it~~ to arguement in Reconynge of a som*m*e as I Remem*b*er aboute xxiij^{li} ode
monye the iuste som I cannot Remem*b*er wherof all was payde & Rebatid
savinge a Trifle I knowe not iustely howe muche but somwhate my brother
Restid in his dett And so went vnto his Cubborde vsinge thies wordes I would

25 haue sworne that he had Restyd in my dett from whence he broughte a Bagge
of monye begyininge to tell it oute vpon the table And he standing Ready to
Receyve his Reste, And then I went oute into the Kitchyn to my Sister And after
alitle space and other talk betwene them I know not whate they came bothe into
the entry and p*ar*tyd frindly, and p*r*esently after my brother and I goinge downe

30 to the strand together he vsed thies wordes to me by the way sayinge he woulde
have layde a greate wager duncke had byn in his dett but eu*er*ye man made hym
pay what they listyd, mary I care not sayd he for I am gladd all is even betwene
vs for I wyll never have any suche Reconynge to make wyth hym nor any other
whilst I lyve god wyllinge

35   *per* me henry Ieffry

129

Notes

Text

Among the records of the Borough of Rye, Sussex. The text has not been edited before.

Manuscript

Possibly the witness's own holograph, which would explain the unusual use of 1st person narrative. Although there is no clear difference of hand, the more formal heading (lines 1–4) and the signature (l. 35) are in ink of a different colour from that of the main text.

The abbreviation-symbol normally taken as denoting *er*, (31) *euerye*, also appears in (11 etc.) *Grograyne* and (18) *price*. It has been expanded in these words as simple *r*, but it could be argued that here too *er* is intended, recording an intrusive unstressed vowel.

A stroke over the *m* in (10) *hym* has been taken as empty, rather than indicating a second *m*, on the basis of *hym* spellings elsewhere in the text.

Glossary

(2)	*Evangelist*	Gospel book
(3)	*Iurat* †	municipal officer, especially of Cinque Ports
(5)	*Bartillmewe tyde*	period around Feast of St Bartholomew, 24 August
(5)	*mychellmas*	Feast of St Michael, 29 September
(10)	*Reconynge*	settling accounts
(11)	*Grograyne*	silk and wool fabric
(21–2)	*xxiij^{li} ode monye*	a shilling or so over £23
(22)	*Rebatid*	deducted
(26)	*tell*	count
(27)	*his Reste*	the balance due to him
(30)	*strand*	quay
(32)	*listyd*	liked

Topics for linguistic investigation

1. The evidence relating to pronunciation in the spellings (5) *Bartillmewe*, (11) *veluit*, (13) *thies*, (13) *heare*, (17) *yerde*, (24) *dett*, (29) *frindly*.
2. The use of constructions involving present participles.
3. The changes a contemporary clerk would have made if this deposition had been recorded in the usual form.
4. A survey of the use of *I know not* and *I care not* in other texts.
5. How many sentences are there in this text?

Text 26

Tamaris Leonard: Cornwall 1596

(Devon Record Office Manuscript Chanter 11038/16/1)

[f. 11r] Tomiris Leonarde of S<t> Mynver vxor will*e*mi Leonarde verbi dei
p*r*edicatoris vbi mora*m* traxit p*er* spatiu*m* octo mensiu*m* seu circiter etat*is* xix^tem
annoru*m* seu eo circiter lib*e*re condicionis vt dicit deponit et dicit … that on
friday last past was fortnight shee this deponent kept the said M^ris Aishe
5   companye as shee had donne at diu*er*se other tymes before and saith that they
walkinge together in the fieldes at St Saviors stile nere Padstowe mett wth the
libellant Nicholas Trefry who accompanied them vnto Mr Richard Prideaux his
garden where they founde him & his wife to whome they all made request that
they wolde come vnto the said libellant*es* howse to eate Creame and strawberries
10   wherevnto they aunswered wth a very good will. and after a litle tyme the said
Richard Prideaux and his [f. 12r] wife, this deponent, M^ris Aishe, and the said
Mr Trefry <were> all together in the howse of the saide Trefry betweene the
hour <of iij> and iiij^our of the clock in the after noone of the same day syttin<g>
at the table in the hall of the house wherein the said Nicholas <then &> now
15   dwelleth in Padstowe havinge reisons & Creame & strawberi<es> them vppon
the table the said Nicholas Trefry tooke a hande of <the said> reisons oute of
the dishe and offred them vnto tharticulate M^ris Eliz<a>beth Aishe who
refused them sayinge shee loved no reisons vnto whom the said Trefry
aunswered sayinge Then I pray yow give me one good reason: Yow knowe that
20   I have borne yow good will a longe tyme and nowe I pray yow lett me knowe yor
minde eyther to denie me or ells t<o> yelde to mee to whome shee aunswered
Truly Mr Trefry I knowe well yow have borne me good will a longe tyme & so
have I vnto yow likewise but I knowe my friendes will never give their consentes
but yett nevertheles I love yow aswell as eu*er* I loved Mr Aishe. Why then said
25   the said Trefry I pray yow make an ende of yt and having her hande in his hande
Mr Richarde Prideaux took them by the hand*es* sayinge Nowe cosen Aishe yf
yow minde to have him to be yor husban<d> & to forsake all others nowe speake
heere are none but yor friendes & th<ey> that wish yow both well and then shee
aunswered Yea truly. Th<en> the said Nicholas Trefry holdinge her by the
30   hande Said vnto the said M^ris Aishe I give yow my fayth and troth to be yor
husbande to whome the said M^ris Aishe aunswered and I likewise give yow my
consent therevnto and then they kyssed together and the said Trefry tooke of a
ringe from his finger & put yt vppon the forefinger of the said M^ris Aishe sayinge

131

35   vnto her nowe yow are my wife before God aswell as yf yt were donne in the
Churche To whome the said M^{ris} Aishe aunswered yea trewly.

Notes

Text

From the papers of a Special Commission of the Consistory Court of the Diocese of
Exeter, case of *Trefry* v. *Aishe*. No edition of the text has been printed before, but there
is a manuscript edition on pp. 176–81 of C. Henderson, *Cornish Manuscripts: Cornish
Historical Material gathered from the Records of the Bishop and Chapter of Exeter*, Vol. X,
compiled c.1924 and preserved in the Courtney Library, The Royal Institution of
Cornwall, Truro. Henderson's version is drawn on in a re-telling of the case in A. L.
Rowse, *Tudor Cornwall* (Jonathan Cape, London, 1941), p. 443.

Manuscript

Gaps in the text from l. 20 onwards result from wear at the edge of the leaf. Most can be
readily filled, but there is some doubt in l. 26 where the following word *them* argues a
missing preposition such as *before*.

There is no distinction between the letters *u* and *n*, giving rise to problems where *nn*
or *un* my be equally read. In (5) *donne* and (8) *founde* there is little to dispute, but (10 etc.)
aunswered could be challenged.

Glossary

(4)	*friday last past was fortnight*	a fortnight before last Friday
(7)	*libellant*	person who instituted the suit (see note)
(10)	*wth a very good will*	A reply equivalent to PDE 'we'd be delighted to'
(17)	*tharticulate*	the said (see note)
(26)	*cosen*	=cousin, a term for any fairly near relative (she is sister to his sister-in-law)
(27)	*minde*	intend

Latin

(1–3) Tamaris Leonard, wife of William Leonard, Preacher of the word of God, of St
Mynver, where she has lived for a period of eight months or thereabouts, nineteen years
of age or thereabouts, of free condition, as she says, testifies and says

Explanatory notes

(7) *libellant*: OED identifies this as a term used in ecclesiastical courts, but cites no
example before 1726.

(17) *tharticulate*: (=the articulate) the sense is probably generalised to 'aforementioned
in this case, said', since the word is used in this way in Text 27 below, another document
from the same Diocese. But OED gives sense as 'charged with the offence in this case',
which could be its meaning here, since it refers to Elizabeth Aishe.

(18–19) For other real-life puns see Texts 19 and 51.

Background

The people in this case are Cornish gentry, the families of Treffry and Prideaux being prominent in the history of the county. Elizabeth Aishe is a well-to-do widow, now under the wing of the Prideaux family because her sister is married to John Prideaux. The Richard Prideaux in this text, who is also called as a further deponent in the case, is probably John's younger brother. It is because John Prideaux and others are against the marriage between Elizabeth Aishe and Nicholas Treffry, seen as a fortune-hunter, that she is apprehensive about committing herself and, in fact, changes her mind the day after the events described here. Tamaris Leonard, the curate's young wife, is an incomer to Cornwall, and states that she was born at Romsey, Hampshire.

The case is unusual in that it is the man who is claiming to have been jilted. It is being dealt with by a special hearing for the Diocese of Exeter, within which Cornwall falls at this time. St Minver is close to Padstow, on the North Cornish coast, and the depositions are taken at Bodmin.

Topics for linguistic investigation

1. Why the pun on 'reason' and 'raisin' is of interest to historians of seventeenth-century pronunciation.
2. A comparison between the 2nd person personal pronoun forms in this text and those in some others.
3. Ways in which subordinate clauses are linked to make sentences.
4. The extent to which the exchange of vows between Trefry and Aishe may be identified as either formal or colloquial.

Text 27

Margaret Rewallyn and Jacob Fisher: Ottery St Mary, Devon 1614–15

(Devon Record Office Manuscript Chanter 867)

Text A (1614)

[f. 17r] Margareta Rewallyn de Awtrey S^{ca} maria vbi mora*m* fecit *per* xij annos fere annos aetatis sue sue xliij annoru*m* aut eo circiter test*is* admiss*us* &c. Iuratus &c deponit *pro*vt sequitur

* * * *

Ad 2 et 3 ar*ticu*los Libelli deponit et dicit That about fortnight before
5   Mydsom*er* last past as shee remembreth Et al*iter* recolit tempus this deponent
being at ~~William Cominges~~ the howse wherein w^m Cominge ar*ticu*late then &
now dwelleth, in the parishe of Chidley ~~did~~ was demaunded by the saide
Com*minges* wife how {~~did~~} all the people of Ottrey s^t Mary did stand in health
and this deponent aunswered they weare all well excepting henry Walkers wife
10   meaning the ar*ticu*late Elizabeth Walker but shee quoth this deponent is sicke,
why what sicknes hath shee demaunded the saide william Cominge, I know not
aunswered this deponent except it be the sicknes which is an ague that many
had within the said *pa*rishe for shee is quothe this deponent broken out about
the mouth. Noe, it is the pox, is {it} not? (replyed the saide william Coming)
15   that the saide Elizabeth Walker hath? noe verily aunswered this deponent, I doe
not thinke it ~~was~~ {is} the pox for I had ~~the Like~~ An ague this yeere my self and
did breake out about the mouth & face as shee doth nowe

Text B (1615)

[f. 103r] Iacob*us* ffisher al*ias* Tylman de otterye Ste Marie et sepe remanens
ap*u*d Loopitt sutor vestiu*m*, dicit se habitasse ap*u*d otterye fere per decem annos
vlt elaps*us* {etatis 25 annorum} test*is* admiss*us* &c partes Litigantes ♭ v*idelicet*
Margeria*m* Stone et dorothea Tottle bene novit vt dicit./

* * * *

5   [f. 103v] Ad secu*ndu*m ar*ticu*lum deponit et dicit That betweene Michaelmas
~~and~~ and Alhallontyde Last past, he this dep*onen*t being a Taylor did work in the

134

house of the husbande of the ar*ticu*late Margery Stone situate in the parrishe of
Looppitt ar*ticu*late and then and there the s*a*id Margerye tolde this dep*onen*t
That she did heere That Thomas ffollett was to playe with Margaret Crispen

10   al*ias* Stephens (meaninge the articulate Margaret Stephens) and that he did
putt his hand vppon the frenche bodyes, and that heerevppon the s*a*id Margaret
asked the s*a*id Thomas (meaninge the ar*ticu*late Thomas ffollett) whether he
were abasshed, and that vpon this speeche he catched her by the wrans nest,
and plucked awaye som*m*e of the hayre and wrapped it vp in a paper & shewed

15   it in one George Lanes house in Loopitt, Wherevnto this dep*onen*t replied
sayeinge M*ist*ris Stone I doe thinke it is not true, then the ar*ticu*late dorothey
Tottle who is daughter in Lawe to the s*a*id Margar~~et~~{ye} Stone, ~~sayde~~ beinge
then and there pr*e*sent, sayde That it was true, addeinge further these Word*es*
vi*delice*t, for wee have tolde ~~th~~ Tom ffollett (meaninge the fores*a*id Thomas

20   ffollett) heereof to his face and he did never deny it, but ~~sayde~~ {hee had} made
answere sayeing That although he had catched some of the hayre, yet hee lefte
the ~~ness~~ {nest} behynde, Then quoth this dep*onen*t ~~replyed~~ vnto the fores*a*id
Margerye Stone, I will tell her [f. 104r] what y*u* saye, whye doe quoth the s*a*id
Margar~~et~~{ye} I care not, addeing also these word*es* vi*delice*t, That was the

25   matter whie shee (meaneing the fores*a*id Margaret Stephens) was angrye with
Iohn, because he woulde not clawe her by the arse, and this dep*onen*t thinketh
that shee the s*a*id Margery Stone was angrye and mali{ti}ouslye bent against
the s*a*id Margaret Stephens, but wheth*er* she did beare any malice or anger
against the s*a*id Thomas ffollett this dep*onen*t knoweth not, but all the pr*e*misses

30   are true

Notes

Text

From the book of witnesses' depositions relating to cases heard at the Consistory Court
of the Diocese of Exeter 1613–1619, case of *Walker* v. *Cummings* (Text A) and case of
Follett v. *Stone and Tottle* (Text B). The text printed here has not been edited before. For
other material from the same source see Text 5 above.

Manuscript

In the Latin at the beginning of Text A (A2) the word *sue* is repeated by mistake, and in
A5 an essential *non* is almost certainly omitted.

   In Text B the clerk twice (l. B17 and 24) writes *Margaret* when he should have written
Margerye. When he realises and corrects his error it is typical of the orthographic
latitude of the period that he can score out the *et* and insert *ye* without feeling the need
to change *ar* to *er*.

   Verbal corrections in Text A suggest a clerk with a tendency to write down the
witness's words verbatim, but to refashion them immediately into legally acceptable
formality and precision: (A6–7) *at William Cominges* deleted and replaced by *at the howse
wherein w*^m* Cominge articulate then & now dwelleth.* (A7–8) *[she] was demaunded ... how*

did all the people of Ottrey s^t Mary changed to *[she] was demaunded … how all the people of Ottrey s^t Mary did stand in health.*

Glossary

(A5)	*last past*	last
(A6)	*articulate*	said (see note to Text 26 above)
(A7)	*demaunded*	asked
(A12)	*ague*	fever
(A13)	*broken out*	come out in sores
(A14)	*the pox*	syphilis (or possibly small-pox)
(B5)	*Michaelmas*	Feast of St Michael, 29 September
(B6)	*Alhallontyde*	Feast of All Saints, 1 November
(B9)	*to playe*	engaged in a (sexual) frolic
(B11)	*french bodyes*	(under) bodice
(B13)	*abasshed*	ashamed
(B13)	*wrans nest*	pubic hair
(B19–20)	*tolde … heereof* †	took … to task about it
(B26)	*clawe by the arse*	flatter, butter up (see note)
(B29)	*premisses*	foregoing statements

Latin

(A1–4) Margaret Rewallyn of Ottery St Mary where she has made her home for almost 12 years, 43 years of age or (or) thereabouts, admitted as a witness etc. Sworn etc. testifies as follows … To the 2nd and 3rd articles of the accusation she testifies and says
(A5) And otherwise does [not] recall the date
(B1–5) Jacob Fisher alias Tylman, tailor of Ottery St Mary and often staying at Loopit, says that he has lived at Ottery for almost ten years past, 25 years of age, admitted as a witness etc. knows well the parties in dispute, that is Margery Stone and Dorothy Tottle … To the second article he testifies and says

Local placenames

(A1)	*Awtrey S^{ca} maria* (also (A8) *Ottrey s^t Mary*)	Ottery St Mary, nr. Honiton
(A4)	*Chidley*	Chudleigh
(B2)	*Loopitt*	Luppitt

Explanatory notes

(B26) *clawe by the arse*: a more robust version of OED (under CLAW) *claw by the back* (also *by the sleeve*).

Topics for linguistic investigation

1. The roles played by various marks of punctuation.
2. The usefulness of: (A5) *remembreth*, (A7) *dwelleth*, (A11) *hath*, (A17) *doth*, (B26) *thinketh*, (B29) *knoweth* as evidence for seventeenth–century usage.

3. The functions of the verb forms: (A10) *quoth*, (A12) *be*, (B7) *situate*, (B13) *were*, (B13) *catched*.
4. The difference bewteen the quoted speech is Text A and the narrative around it.
5. The difference in syntax between (A15–16) *I doe not thinke it is the pox* and (B16) *I doe thinke it is not true.*

Text 28

Edmund Robinson: Pendle, Lancashire 1634

(British Library Manuscript Harley 6854 (Text A) and Public Record Office
Manuscript SP 16/271 (Text B))

Text A

[f. 22r] The Examination of Edward Robinson sonne of Edmond Robinson of
Pendle Forrest Mason taken at Padian before Richard Shuttleworth and Iohn
Starkey Esquires two of his Maties Iustices of the peace wthin the Countie of
Lancaster the 10th day of Februarie Anno d*omi*ni 1633

5   Who informeth vpon oath beinge examined touchinge the grete meetinge of
the Witches in Pendle, saith: That vpon All Saint*es* day last past, Hee this
Informer beinge wth one Henrie Parker a neere doore-neighbour to him in
Wheateley, who desired the said Parker to give him leave to get some Bullas, w^{ch}
hee did, in wch tyme of gettinge Bullas hee sawe two Grey hound*es* vi*delicet* a
10   blacke and a browne one come runninge over [f. 22v] the next feild towards
him, Hee verilie thinketh the one to bee Mr Butters and the other to bee M^r
Robinsons, the said Mr Butter and Mr Robinson then haveinge such like And
the said Greyhound*es* came and fawned on him, they haveinge about their
neck*es* either of them a Coller, to either of wch Collers was tyed a stringe, wch
15   Collers as this Informer affirmeth did shine like gold, and hee thinkinge that
some, either of Mr Butters or Mr Robinsons familie should have followed them,
but seeinge noe bodie to followe them, hee tooke the said Greyhound*es*
thinkinge to hunte wth them, and presentlie a Hare did rise verie neere before
him, at the sight whereof he cryed Loo, loo, loo, but the dogg*es* would {not}
20   runn, wherevpon hee beinge verie angrie tooke them, and wth [f. 23r] the
string*es* that were at theire Collers tyed either of them to a litle bush at the next
hedge, and wth a rodd that hee had in his hand hee beate them, and in stead of
the blacke Greyhound one Dickensons wife stood vpp a Neighbour whom this
Informer knoweth, and in stead of the browne Greyhound a litle Boy whom this
25   Informer knoweth not at wch sight this Informer beinge afrayd, endeavoured to
runn awaie, but beinge staied by the woeman vi*delicet* Dickensons wife, shee put
her hand into her pocket and pulled forth a peece of silver much like to a fayre
shillinge, and offered to give him it to hold his tongue, and not to tell, wch hee
refused, sayinge, nay thou art a witch wherevpon shee put her hand into her
30   pocket againe, and pulled out a [f. 23v] thinge like unto a bridle that gingled,

138

wch shee put on the litle Boyes head, wch stood vpp in the browne Greyhound*es* stead, wherevpon the said Boy stood vpp a White horse. Then ym*m*ediatlie the said dickensons wife tooke this Informer before her vpon the said horse, and carried him to a newe howse called Horstons, beinge a quarter of a myle off,

35   whether when they were come, there were diverse p*er*sons about the doore, and hee sawe diverse others com*m*inge rydeinge on horses of severall colours toward*es* the said howse, wch tyed theire horses to a hedge neere to the said howse to the number of sixtie or thereabout*es* as this Informer thinketh, where they had a fyre and meate roastinge, and some other meate stirringe in the said

40   howse, whereof a younge woeman whom this Informer knoweth not, gave [f. 24r] him flesh and bread vpon a trencher, and drinke in a glasse, wch after the first tast, hee refused, and would have noe more, and said it was nought, and p*re*sentlie after, seeinge diverse others of the said Companie, goinge to a Barne, neere adioyninge, hee followed after, and then hee sawe six of them kneelinge,

45   and pullinge all six severall ropes, wch were fastned or tyed to the topp of the howse, at or wth wch pullinge there came in this Informers sight flesh smoakeinge, butter in lumpes, and milke as it were flyinge from the said ropes, all wch fell into ~~the said~~ {six} basons wch were placed vnder the said ropes, and after that these six had done, there came other six, wch did soe likewise, and

50   dureinge all the tyme of their soe pullinge, they made such fowle [f. 24v] faces that they feared this Informer, soe as hee was gladd to steale out and runn home

Text B

[f. 119r] The Examinac*i*on of Edmond Robinson of the p*a*rishe of Newchurch in the County of Lancaster (aged Tenne yeares or theraboute) ~~examined~~ taken before George Longe esq^r one of his Ma*iesties* Iustices of peace of the County of Midd*lesex* by Comaundem*ent* of the Right ho*nora*ble Sir ffrauncis

5   windebank knight one of his Ma*iesties* Principall Secretaries the xth daye of Iuly 1634

This Exam*ina*t saieth that whereas he told his ffather and mother and the Iustices of peace and the Iudges of Assizes of the County of Lancaster and divers other p*er*sons, of divers thinges Conce*r*ninge the fyndinge of twoe

10   greyhoundes wth Collers and Leashes and the startinge of a hare, and that the said greyhoundes did refuse to ronne att that hare, and that he this exam*ina*t did tye those greyhound*es* to a Bushe, and did beate them, and that therevpon the one of them did presently assume the shape of a woman and the other of a boye and that the woman did offer this exam*ina*t xij d to saye nothinge and that

15   she putt a bridle in the boyes mouthe and the boye became a white horse and tooke vp this exam*ina*t, and carryed him on his backe to a place called horestanes in Pendle fforrest, where he saw he sawe a nomber of lx p*er*sons gathered togeither who did there ~~eate and drinke~~ give this exam*ina*t meate, &c/ he nowe saieth that as he hopeth god will blesse him all that tale and story by

20   him so told as aforesaid is false and feigned and hath no trueth att all in itt butt
only as he hath harde tales and reportes made by women and such Lyke *persons*
so he framed his tale out of his owne Invention and out of no other ground, for
that there was never any suche thinge done or intended butt was a meere fiction
of his owne wch when he had once told and that his tale had gotten Credytt he
25   still *per*sisted in att vntill he came to the kinge his Cocheman att Richemond to
whome he declared theis in wise as he nowe setts downe wch is the trueth and
nothinge els/

[f. 119v] He sayeth that the reason why he so Invented the said tale was for that
his mother havinge brought him vp to spynne wooll and also vsed him to fetch
30   home her kyne, he was appointed {one tyme} to fetch home her kyne butt did
not do itt, but went to play wth other Children. And beinge come {home} and
fearinge Least his father or mother wold beate him for neglectinge to bringe
home the kyne, he made this tale for an excuse and for no other ende or
purpose/

Notes

Text

Since the Robinson case was much publicised in its own time there are various
contemporary manuscripts, and documents were printed in John Webster, *The
Displaying of Supposed Witchcraft* (London, 1677). The manuscripts and later printed
accounts are listed with a discussion of the case in Wallace Notestein, *A History of
Witchcraft in England from 1558 to 1718* (Oxford University Press, London, 1911),
Chapter VII. For a more recent consideration, see the Introduction to Laird Howard
Barber, *An Edition of the Late Lancashire Witches by Thomas Heywood and Richard Brome*
(PhD Thesis, University of Michigan, published by Garland Publishing, New York and
London, 1979). Robinson's confession (here Text B) is summarised in John Bruce,
Calendar of State Papers, Domestic Series, of the Reign of Charles I 1634–1635 (HMSO,
London, 1864), p. 141.

Manuscript

In B17 there is a clear dittography error, *he saw he sawe*.
In B17 the placename *horestanes* has a spelling in keeping with the Lancashire setting,
but since *a* and *o* are written very alike, it might be challenged, especially in the light of
(A34) *Horstons*.

Glossary

(A6)	*All Saintes day*	1 November
(A7)	*doore-neighbour* †	next-door neighbour
(A8)	*Bullas* †	wild plums
(A19)	*Loo*	cry urging dog to chase
(A26)	*staied*	stopped (transitive vb)

(A35)	*whether*	=whither
(A41)	*trencher*	plate
(B10)	*startinge*	running into the open
(B30)	*kyne*	cows

Local placenames

(A1)	*Pendle Forrest*	Pendle Forest
(A2)	*Padian*	Padiham
(A8)	*Wheateley*	Wheatley Lane
(A34)	*Horstons* (and (B17) *horestanes*)	The Hoarstones
(B1)	*Newchurch*	Newchurch in Pendle

Background

The events recorded here took place twenty years after a notorious witchcraft case centred on the same area of Pendle Forest. The boy's witch story, and his subsequent confession that it had all been made up was received as sensational, though the recantation was ignored by many who preferred his original vivid tale, including the playwrights Heywood and Broome (for an edition of their play *The Late Lancashire Witches* see notes on Text). The Robinson they portray only slightly resembles the lad in these documents, but it is interesting that the play gives prominence to the two words *bullace* (which seems to have been in widespread dialect use) and *jingled* (which does not appear to be special, unless possibly in Robinson's pronunciation), as if they caught the public's attention at the time.

In Text B, Robinson admits that his story of what he imagines a witches' sabbath to be like is based on gossip, *reportes made by women and such Lyke persons*. It is engaging that the feature which has most impressed the boy is the abundance of food and drink.

Topics for linguistic investigation

1. Spelling as evidence that Texts A and B are not written by the same clerk. Does any feature reflect the different areas where the depositions were taken down?
2. The forms (A5) *informeth*, (A29) *thou*, (A29) *art*, (B24) *gotten*, (B26) *whome*, (B26) *setts*, (B30) *kyne*.
3. How the subject-matter of Text B makes its syntax different from that of Text A.
4. How the clerk of Text B refers to Robinson, and why.
5. The use of participial constructions.
6. The credibility of the texts as records of the speech of a child.

Text 29

Robert and Eleanor Wyard: Virginia 1644

(Circuit Court of Northampton, Eastville, Virginia; Manuscript: Accomack
County Court Records, Orders, Deeds, Wills, etc. No. 2 1640–45)

[f. 200r] Att A Co^{rte} houlden at Northampton the 28th: of Iuly An^o: 1644/
Present/ Argoll Yardley Esqre:

M^r: Abedience Robins   M^r: Edward Douglas
Capt William Stone   M^r: Edward Scarburgh

5   The examinacion of Roberte Wyard taken in open Co^{rt}:

This deponent saith That at or about the second day of Iuly 1644 this deponent
haueing Layne at the house of m^r: Seaverne with his wife goeing homeward
about sixe or seaven of the Clocke in the morning at the entring into the woods
this depon^t: espyed a fellow out of the path standing wth: a Calfe. then this
10   deponent went out of the Path and tooke a Pochery tree betweene this depon^t:
and him to see what hee was a doeing, being come wthin twenty pases or
thereabouts this depon^t: saw him the sayde ffellow wch was Nathaniell Moore
(whoe liued at m^r: Seaverns Buggering of the [f. 200v] Calfe w^{ch}: was Tyed to a
smale tree w^{ch}: stood cloase to a greate Tree soe that hee was sidewise to this
15   depon^t: to this depon^t: whoe saw him Buggering the sayde Calfe ffower or ffiue
tymes in his Accion hee the sd Nathaniell had the Calfe by the Tayle and his
yard thrusting into the Calfe seuerall tymes, wipeing his ffingers on the Calfes
side and wiped the Calfes breech wth: his hand & wipeing his hand on ye Calfes
side, Then this deponent becked to his wife w^{ch}: stood behinde this depon^t: &
20   shewed her the ffellow saying looke doe yo^u see what yonder ffellow is doeing
shee answeared whoe is it? and this deponent sayde it is yor man Nathaniell,
then shee sayde what a Villaine hee is, This deponent and his wife stood
lookeing on the sd Nathaniell continueing in his Buggering the Calfe wth: the
aforesd Accions from thence this depon^t: went wth: in ffiue pases to a Locust
25   tree wth: this depon^{ts} wife And the sd Nathaniell still continued in his Accion of
Buggering the Calfe after this depon^t had stayed there a while hee this depon^t
went slaunting into the Path hard by him, and hee turneing his head about saw
this depon^t: and his wife wherevpon hee left offe & turn'd about the Calfe
haueing not had tyme to put vpp his yard, Then this depon^t: sayde; Villaine
30   what are yo^u: doeing heare, hee made answeare nothing Resting the Calfe what
should I doe Then this depon^t sayde yo^u: villaine yo^u: lye yo^u: are Buggering the
Calfe hee Answeared yo^u: lye, then this depon^{ts}: wife sayde yo^u Lye for wee stood
lookeing on yo^u: Then this depon^t: told him the sd Nathaniell Villaine yo^u: haue

done ynough to bee hang'd hee Replyed dooe yor: worst I care not what yo^u:
35　cann doe, Where vpon this depon^{ts} wife willed this depon^t: to take notice of the
Calfe soe this deponent turned about & looked on the Calfe w^{ch}: was a little
Black Calfe vnderhalu'd on the Right eare Then hee the sd Nathaniell vntyed
the Calfe & came leadeing the Calfe and bidd this depon^t stand by and lett the
Calfe come by, soe this depon^t went part of his way homeward & turn'd Back
40　agayne & went to the owner of the Calfe M^r: Conaway and Brought him to the
plase & shewed him where Moore had done the Act./

Robert X Wyard
his　　　marke:/

Capt *per* Hump Price deput Clarke in aperta Curia

45　[f. 201r] The deposicion of Ellino^r Wyard taken in open Co^{rt}:

This depon^t: sayth That at or about the second of Iuly 1644 this deponent
comeing wth: her husband Robert Wyard from the house of M^r: Seaverne and
comeing over a style by M^r: Seaverns entring into the woods this deponents
husband sayde dost thou see what yonder fellow is a doeing soe this deponent
50　went a Little out of the Path & steep't behynde a tree soe this deponent stood
there And her husband drewe neerer to a fellow w^{ch}: was Buggering a Calfe as
did seeme to this depon^t: at her entrance over the style soe after this depon^t:
husband had taken a full veiw of the sayde ffellow, hee becked to this depon^t: to
come vpp soe this depon^t come vpp to her husband and sayde O Lord whoe is
55　it hee answeare<d> it is yor: man Nathaniell wherevpon this deponent & her
husb: went vpp close to him soe neere that hee might haue stroock him wth: his
stick where the sd Nathaniell stood Buggering the Calfe houlding the Calfe by
the tayle {a}Crosse~ing~ the path soe the sd Nathaniell Espied this depon^t & her
husband step't beside the Calfe, wherevpon this depon^{ts}. husband sayde O thou
60　wicked Rogue what art thou doeing hee Replyed Resting wth the Calfe Noe sd
this depon^{ts} husband thou art Buggering the Calfe hee the sd Nathaniell
Replyed noe yo^u: Lye, Then this depon^t: made Answeare yo^u: Lye for there
hangs out yor: Rogerry still ffor his yarde hang'd then out of his Breeche<s>
wherevpon hee the sd Nathaniell took thend of his shirt & a shakeing it sayde
65　Looke here where is it, wth that this depon^{ts}: husband sayde thou hast done that
w^{ch}: thou must hang ffor hee Replyed saying doe yor worst wherevpon this
deponent & her husband went a little waye off where this depon^t willed
her husband to take notice of the Calfe w^{ch}: hee accordingly did soe the sd
Nathaniell vntyed the Calfe biding vs stand out of the way & lett the Calfe come
70　by And further sayth not./

Ellino^r X Wyard
her marke

Capt *per* Hump Price deput Clarke in aperta Curia

Notes

Text

From the records of the County Court of Accomack-Northampton, Virginia, USA. The text has been edited in Susie M. Ames (ed.), *County Court Records of Accomack-Northampton, Virginia 1640–1645*, Virginia Historical Society Documents, Vol. 10 (University Press of Virginia, Charlottesville, 1973), pp. 371–3.

Manuscript

In (55) *answeare*<*d*> and (63) *Breeche*<*s*> letters appear to have been lost at the edge of the leaf, but a case for both words as they stand might be argued.

The writer sets a colon after most superscript-abbreviations. This has been retained here.

In ll. 14–15 the words *to this depon':* have been written twice.

Glossary

(1)	*houlden*	held
(5)	*examinacion*	questioning, interrogation
(7)	*Layne*	stayed the night
(8)	*entring*	entrance
(10)	*Pochery tree* †	North American tree (not in OED, but Webster has POCHOTE tree)
(17)	*yard*	penis
(18)	*breech*	hinder parts
(19)	*becked*	beckoned
(24–5)	*locust tree* †	North American flowering tree
(27)	*slaunting*	taking an oblique line
(35)	*willed*	told, urged
(37)	*underhalu'd* †	with a piece clipped out (cf. WRIGHT, HALVE vb. used in English Lake District)
(63)	*Rogerry*	penis

Latin

(44 and 73) Taken down in open Court by Humphrey Price, Deputy Clerk.

Explanatory notes

(30–31) *what should I doe*: Equivalent of PDE *What are you implying that I am doing?* See OED SHALL Section 15.

Background

Very few of the earliest colonists who went to Virginia survived, so that the true period of settlement was the late 1620s and 1630s. In 1644, therefore, the Wyards and the 'man', Nathaniel, are almost certainly first-generation Virginians, born and brought up in some part of England and bringing their language with them, but adding to it lexical items for new things encountered in the New World.

Topics for linguistic investigation

1. The use of apostrophes.
2. The verb forms: (1) *houlden*, (7) *layne*, (34) *hang'd*, (38) *bidd*, (54) *come*, (62) *Lye*, (63) *hang'd*.
3. A survey of texts to see how often, where, when and by whom an *a* is used before a present participle.
4. Syntactic alternatives that could have been used instead of participial constructions in lines 7–9.
5. How the two witnesses differ in recalling what was said at the time of the incident.
6. Find out more about names used by early settlers for American flora and fauna.

Text 30

Stephen Badcocke: Essex 1645

(Essex Record Office, Manuscript Q/SBa 2/57 Item 9)

[f. 3r] Stephen Badcocke of great Warley Shoemaker sworne saith That not long after Christmas last This Examinate being vpon Warley Common, sawe the Cowes there pushing & overthrowing one th'other wth. greate violence & roaringe, & this Examinate going to parte them, sawe a sowe coming from amongst them wth. a peece of flesh in her mouth, not like any carryon or the flesh of any beast, & that he conceived he discerned small ribbs vpon it, & his heart gave him that there was some strange accident in regard the sowe was greedy in devouring it & the cattle making soe vnusuall & vnheard of a noyse whereof the like had never beene seene before, nor since. And he further saith that the said Sowe came directly from Tho: Wards house ward; And that the next morning after (this Examinate being much troubled at what he sawe the day before, & seing the said sowe againe, & finding his heart to rise againe at it) he was induced to followe the said sowe to see whither she would lead him to the place from whence she had the flesh the day before, & the said sowe went round about Wards house, & in through [f. 3v] the forre doore & soe vnder the woodstacke where this Examinate left it being vnwilling to goe into his neighbours yard. And this Examinate saith that he had not heard at that tyme that W^m. ffuller was missing nor till aboute a weeke after, & then hearing of it his heart smote him & he began to suspect that there was somewhat of Providence in the great distraction of the Cattle & the flesh wch. the sowe brought abroad And further saith that he hath heard Goody Penny (who lives neere the said Ward) say that aboute the tyme that the rumour began in the Countrey (that W^m. ffuller was made away) she sawe early two or 3. mornings a very great thicke smoake come out of the chimney of the said Thomas Wardes house, wth. a very vgley & noysome stinke whereat her heart did rise very much, & she began to have some suspition of the said W^m. ffuller's making away. And he saith that Iohn Reeve his Iourneyman sawe the sowe downe vnder the Cowes & the Cowes vpon her & goring her. And that one Goody Hadgley living thereaboutes sawe likewise the flesh in the Sowes mouth./

I: Mathews.

Notes

Text

From Essex Quarter Session records. The text has not been edited before.

Manuscript

Abbreviations with superscript letters are followed by a full-stop. This has been edited out where the word has been expanded to full form, (2) *Examinate*, (22) *rumour*, (17) *neighbours* (where it is a colon that is used), but retained where the word and its short form are familiar through frequent occurence elsewhere, e.g. (3) wth. etc.

Glossary

(7)	*gave*	told
(7)	*in regard*	because
(10)	*from ... ward*	from
(19)	*smote*	pained
(20)	*distraction*	madness
(21)	*abroad*	out of doors
(21)	*Goody*	title for lower-class married woman
(23)	*Countrey*	district
(23)	*made away*	murdered
(25)	*vgley*	offensive (to the smell)
(25)	*noysome*	evil-smelling
(25)	*rise*	stir with indignation

Background

The case in which this witness is testifying concerned the disappearance of a child-apprentice, local rumours suggesting that he had been murdered by his master, Thomas Ward, and the body concealed where it had been dug up by the sow. Great Warley is in the South-west corner of Essex, near Romford.

Topics for linguistic investigation

1. The use of brackets and of apostrophes.
2. The circumstances producing the verb forms: (17) *saith*, (21) *hath*, (21) *lives*.
3. The use of participial constructions.
4. The use of co-ordinated clauses.
5. The syntax of (6–9) *his heart ... nor since.*
6. Detailed analysis of how and why the language of the text suggests what Badcocke is like.

Text 31

Mary Gash: Southampton 1649
(Southampton City Archives Office Manuscript SC9/3/12)

[f. 18r] The Examinacion of Mary Gashe of the towne and County of
Southampton single woman taken the day & yeare aforesayd before the Iustices
aforesayd.

Who confesseth that vpon wednesday morninge [f. 18v] last {about 8 of clocke}
5   she was deliuered of a child in ~~the~~ the dwellinge house of Mr Henry Pitt her
master and beinge asked whoe was present wth her when she was deliuered, and
whether the sayd Child was livinge or not when it was borne sayth that her sayd
Child had noe life at all in it when it was borne, and she sayth that there was
noe body present with her when she was deliuered ~~th~~ of the sayd child, and
10   beinge asked whoe begat her wth child she sayth that one Edward Henshman a
souldier, ~~a~~ was father of the {sayd} Child, and that he had to doe wth her first
in her master Higgens his house after euery body of the house was gone to bed
in the night tyme ~~a little before Easter~~ about Shrovetyde last as she now
remembreth but the certen tyme she cannot tell, and afterwards about Easter
15   last he had to doe wth her this examinate agayne, and she sayth that presently
after she was deliuered of her sayd Child mistris Anne Levett this examinates
mistrisses kinswoman looked into the roome where she was and the child was
then layd vpon the ground in a Cloth vnder the table by this examinate, and,
there it lay all that day from eight of clock in the morninge ~~in~~ till ~~sixe~~ about sixe
20   of clock at night, and then she this examinate tooke the sayd child and put it into
~~the her master~~ the house of office in the sayd cloth; And beinge further asked
whether she did not feele her child stirre or move within her body before she
was deliuered she sayth that she did never feel the sayd child stirre or move in
her body, but she sayth that about twoe dayes before she was deliuered she had
25   a desire to a rotten peare wch then layd in her mistresses Chamber window
[f. 19r] but doubtinge her mistresses displeasure she did forbeare to eat him
although she had some longinge thervnto

the marke of
Mary **X** Gash

*   *   *   *

30   [f. 20r] The further examinacion of Mary Gash of the sayd Towne & County
        taken before Iames Capelin Esqʳ ~~May~~ Maior Peter Legay and Roberte Wroth
        Aldermen Iustices etc the 30ᵗʰ day of August 1649.

        whoe beinge advised and admonished to speake only truth, and then asked
        whoe was the father of her child she sayth that Willyam Slan the servant of
35   [f. 20v] Mʳ Willyam Higgens was the only father of her child and that he the
        sayd Slan, and none but he had carnall knowledge of her, and ~~she~~ beinge asked
        when & how often he lay wᵗʰ her she sayth that he had {to} doe to wᵗʰ her ~~twoe~~
        ~~or~~ three tymes before Christmas last and beinge asked whether the soldier that
        she formerly named did not ly wᵗʰ her, she sayth that neyther he nor ~~any~~ any
40   other had to doe wᵗʰ her but only the sayd Slan. And beinge asked whether she
        did not say that ~~others~~ if she suffered others should suffer with her she denyeth
        that she sayd soe, but she sayth that she did say that the ~~fa~~ true father of the
        Child should know it as well as she, and if there were any sufferinge for him he
        should suffer as well as she./ and beinge further asked whether her child had
45   life at the birth she sayth that the sayd Child had noe life in it at the tyme of her
        deliuery which was about eight of Clock in the morninge in a little dark buttery
        next to the kitchen
                Iames Capelin Maior   the marke of
                Peter Legay   Mary X Gash
50   Peter Seale
                Robert Wroth

Notes

Text

From the Southampton Borough records. The text, together with other documents
in the case, has been edited by S. D. Thomson (ed.), *The Book of Examinations and
Depositions Before the Mayor and Justices of Southampton 1648–1663*, Southampton
Records Series, Vol. 37 (1994), pp. 26–9.

Manuscript

The various changes made by deletion and insertion are of interest in that they are
clearly done at the time of writing, as in l. 13 where *a little before Easter* is corrected to
about Shrovetyde last as she now remembreth but the certeyn tyme she cannot tell. Other
corrections eliminate dittography, while in l. 31 the clerk changes the spelling of a word.
    The writer uses either full or abbreviated forms for *master* and *mistress*. In the case
of *master* there appears to be a distinction between the title (abbreviated in l. 5) and the
full word (l. 6), and this distinction has been preserved here. But the shortened *mʳⁱˢ* used
in lines 16 and 17 has been expanded since, like the full form in l. 25 it is not a title.

Glossary

(1)	*Examinacion*	questioning, interrogation
(10)	*begat*	got (with child)
(11)	*had to doe wth*	had sexual relations with
(13)	*Shrovetyde*	Shrove Tuesday, the day before Lent, forty working-days before Easter
(15)	*presently*	immediately
(21)	*house of office*	privy
(26)	*doubtinge*	fearing
(46)	*buttery*	pantry

Explanatory notes

(26) and (43) *him*: In l. 26 it seems likely that this is the clerk's attempt to set down a conventional spelling for the pronoun form actually used, which was probably [ən] 'it/him'. If the same analysis is offered for l. 43 *for him*, the phrase means 'on account of it/him (i.e. the baby)'.

Background

The case against Mary Gash hinges on the traditional legal argument that concealing one's pregnancy indicates an intention to murder the baby.

Topics for linguistic investigation

1. Analysis of the kinds of changes made within the manuscript.
2. The distinction between (19) *lay* and (25) *layd*.
3. The constructions: (10) *whoe begat her wth child*, (12) *her master Higgens his house*, (12) *after euery body of the house was gone to bed*, (19) *eight of clocke*, (26–7) *she did forbeare to eat him although she had some longinge thervnto*.
4. A reconstruction of the original forms of the questions put to Gash.
5. What factors determine which of the various terms for sexual relations is employed?

Text 32

John Remington: Massachusetts 1665

(Massachusetts State Archives, Judicial Archives, Suffolk Files Collection,
Manuscript #725 <14th file paper>)

[f. 725r] The depocishon of Iohn Reminton

This deponant Testifieth that I herd Iohn Godfry saie to my father that if he
drived the Cattell vp to the wods to winter then my ffather shod say and haue
cas to repent that he did drive them vp and thes word*es* ~~the~~ said *in* a great rage
and Pashon and aft<er> this my father and I <di>d drive vpe the cattell and I
for the most part did tend them: and a bout the midell of desember last as I was
a coming ho<m>e from the cattell a bout a Mille from them: then the Hors I
rid on begun ~~the~~ to start and snort and the dog that was with me begun to whine
and cry and it still I mad a shift to sit on the ho<r>se still for a matter of a
quarter of a mill and then I smelt a swe<et> smill like seder and presently I
locke vp in to the swamp and I se a crow come to wards me flying and pecht
vpon a tre a gainst mee and she locke at me and the horse and doge and it had
a veary great and quicke Ie and it had a veary great bill and then the Sd crow
flew of that tre to a nother after mee then I begune to mistrust and thinke it was
no crow and thought if it was not a crow it could not hurt my soule though it
hurt my body and Horse and as I was a thinkeing thus to my selfe the hors I was
vpon fell down <v>pon on sid in plain growne vpon my lege and as sone as
I a<   > the Horse was fallen then the crowe came and flewe Round me
severall times as if she would lite <vp>on mee but she ~~should~~ did not Tuche
me then the hors ris and went a bout fower Rod and then stod still and I lay on
the growne still and was <not> abell to follow hime for the Present then when
I came {~~to my selfe~~} a litell <la>tter to my selfe I mad a shift to cripe on my
hand*es* and ~~mmmmmm~~ {knes} the hors and the crowe screc<h>d and mad a
noise like a catt and the hollowing of a man then I gott vp on the hors and went
on ~~the~~ (then the crowe a peared to me somtimes a great Crow and somtimes like
a littell burd and soe continved with mee a bout a Mill and a halfe furder and
she flewe vpon the doge and bete hime to the last all this whill after I fell withe
the hors I was tacken veary sicke and thought I should haue died tell such time
the crow left me and then the doge mad on me and rejoyest very much after the
crow left vs: and then the Second day fowling I being at home Iohn Godfry cam
to my fathers hous in a great Rage and aske of me how I did and I toulld hime
prety well only I was lame withe the hors falling on me too days befor then said

Godfry every Cockating boy must rid I vnhorst on boy tother day I will vnhors
the shortly {to} if the Rid*es* my Hors then said I I am not abell to carre vettel*es*
35   vpon my back then said godfry tis a sorre hors cannot carre his ow prove<n>dar
then said Godfry to me Iohn if the hads ben a man as the wast a boy the had*es*
died on the spott whar the gott the fall the<n> said my Mother to godfry howe
canest the tell that thar ~~was~~ {is} no<ne> but god can tell that ~~now~~ and except
the be more then a ordnary man t<he> canest not tell that then {sd} godfry bed
40   my mother hould ~~thy~~ {her} tungue he kn<ew> what he sed better then she and
said I say a gen had he bine <a man> as he was a boy he had di{e}d on the spote
whare he fell

Notes

Text

From the Court Files of Suffolk County, Massachusetts, USA. The text has been edited
in John F. Cronin (ed.), *Records of the Court of Assistants of the Colony of the Massachusetts
Bay 1630–1692*, Vol. III (The County of Suffolk, Boston, 1928, reprinted AMS Press,
New York, 1973), pp. 160–61.

Manuscript

A central vertical crease and damage at the right hand edge of the leaf make for some
gaps. In most cases the text can be conjecturally restored.

In (30) *Second* the *S* is written as a correction on top of an earlier *m* (perhaps the start
of *monday*). The correction from *thy* to *her* in l. 40 shifts Godfry's words into indirect
speech. In l. 23 the deleted word is illegible.

Although final *d* and *e* are very like each other, they are distinct in (17) *growne* 'ground'
and (18) *Round*.

Glossary

Note: Familiar words are often obscured by spelling, especially (10) *seder* (=cedar), (17)
growne (=ground), (30) *fowling* (=following), (35) *carre* (=carry).

(9)	*still*	stopped (?pret. vb.)
(11)	*swamp* †	See note
(11)	*pecht*	=pitched, alighted
(12)	*a gainst*	facing
(17)	*plaine growne*	open ground
(20)	*Rod*	a measure of length, about 5 metres
(24)	*hollowing*	shouting
(29)	*mad on*	See note
(33)	*Cockating*	saucy, cocky
(34)	*vetteles*	=victuals, (human) provisions
(35)	*provendar*	(animal) fodder

Explanatory notes

(11) *swamp*: Possibly an English dialect word, but contemporary comments cite it as an Americanism in regard to its meaning, which in American usage is not 'boggy land' but 'low-lying uncultivatable land with trees and bushes'.

(29) *mad on*: The context suggests the meaning 'came to' or perhaps 'fawned on'. Although OED records from this period combinations of *make* with *to/for/off*, it has *make on* only as (intransitive) 'hasten' or (transitive) 'light (a fire)'.

Background

By this date it is quite likely that this young deponent was a second-generation settler, born and brought up in Massachusetts.

The Massachusetts authorities legislated that depositions must be presented in writing (see above, Introduction to Depositions, p. 93) so that this document is possibly written by an amateur helper with fewer language skills than the more usual English professional clerk.

Topics for linguistic investigation

1. The evidence relating to pronunciation in the spellings (5) *Pashon*, (10) *smill*, (17) *growne*, (19) *lite*, (22) *cripe*, (34) *vetteles*, (35) *ow*, (40) *tungue*.
2. The vowels in the preterites of strong verbs.
3. Second person personal pronouns and verb forms.
4. The auxiliary verbs in: (2) *shod say*, (18) *was fallen*, (19) *would lite*, (33) *will vnhors*, (41) *had ... bine*, (41) *had died*.
5. Defining a 'Sentence' in this text.
6. An analysis of what it is that gives this deposition a colloquial feel.

Journals

Plate IV

Plate IV

Text 33
Henry Machyn: London 1557

British Library Manuscript Cotton Vitellius F.V f. 74r
Edited text 33/64–72

The xxix day of Iune was sent peters day was a smalle
ffare keft in sant margatt cherche yerde as wolle & odur small
thyng*es* as tornars & odur & ye sam day was a godly a
prossessyon ye wyche my lord abbott whent w^t ys myter
5   & ys crossear & a grett number of copes of cloth
of gold & ye wergers & mony worshephull gentyll men
& women at westmynster whent a prossessessyon

The sam day at after non was ye ij y{e}ere myne
of good m*aster* < BLANK > lewyn yrmonger & at ys durge was
10   all ye leverey ye ffurst m*aster* altherman drap*er* & aft*er* to her plasse
& they had a kake & a bone a pesse be syd ye p*ary*che & all comers
& wyne he nowgh for all comers

Characters: Use of *y* in (3) *ye*, but cf. (1) *The*.
Allographs: Two forms of *r*, long-tailed variety in (1) *peters*, (2) *ffare*, (2) *yerde* etc. Long
and short forms of *s*, e.g. *was sent*. System for *u* and *v* not confirmed, since *w* used initially
in (6) *wergers*, and in view of (10) *leverey*. Final stroke in numeral realised as *j*, (8) *ij*.
Capitals: Used to begin each entry, but not elsewhere, even for proper names.
Abbreviations: (3) *y^e*, (4) *w^t*. (3) *thynges*; (10) *draper* and *after*; (11) *paryche*. Extreme
abbreviation in (9) and (10) *master*.
Deliberate gap: In line 9 Machyn must have meant to insert the missing first name
when he could discover or remember it, but never did.
Typical spellings: (4) *wyche* and (4) *whent*; (4) *ys* and (12) *he nowgh*; (6) *wergers*; (8)
myne.
Problems of interpretation: (2) *keft* is perhaps a spelling for 'kept'; if the reading is
really *kest*, some form of 'cast' is suggested, but is this any more satisfactory? Can we
consider the spelling (7) *prossessessyon* as a slip of the pen, in view of (4) *prossessyon*?

Introduction to Journals

Journals commit to paper the events of a day. They are private documents, aiming at no reader other than oneself at some future time, looking back to review past events and experiences.

Journal writing was not uncommon in the sixteenth century, and flourished in the seventeenth,[1] especially with the growth of self-awareness and spiritual introspection. The genre does not have hard and fast boundaries in respect of subject-matter; since each writer sets down those things which he or she considers have made the day notable, journals vary as widely as the people who write them. On Friday 19 August 1664 Roger Lowe records the transactions of Lancashire village life,

> 19 fridaij I borowed a horse and went to Humphrey Burscoes in Lowton for to buij hony and wax of his sisters but theij ware too hard for me (35/42–3),

while Samuel Pepys closes the entry for the same day with news of international affairs,

> The news of the Emperour's victory over the Turkes is by some doubted, but by most confessed to be very small (though great) of what was talked; which was 80000[d] men to be killed and taken of the Turkes side.[2]

Some journals set out to record a particular type of occurrence. In 1686 the Bishop of Chester kept a journal which, while mentioning domestic matters briefly, always included detailed records of people, decisions, promises and correspondence arising from his Diocesan work,

> [December] 6. I wrote to my cousin Peter Whalley of making my cousin P. Haddon curate of Wigan, at £40 per ann. and the perquisites of a reader, and cousin P. Whalley apparitor general, and to Mr. Holmes, to whom I sent an offer of Patrick Brompton for £80, and a dispensation for non-residence of Daniel Pinner, rector of Deane in Cumberland, because he was in a consumption; to H. Bulstrode and Jo. Ashton, Peter Haddon, Mr. Pemberton. I took the oaths at the Quarter Sessions in Chester, which were adjourned to this day for that purpose. I discharged Mr. Peake from attending the cure of Wigan any longer than till Christmas, becaue he is vicar of Bowden. The governor, recorder, Sir Thomas Grosvenor, and Dr. Angel, dined with me.[3]

The degree to which journal writers have had personal involvement in those things

158

recorded also varies, and ranges through things experienced – things witnessed – things heard of. Roger Lowe (Text 35) concentrates on his own experience, Henry Machyn (Text 33) and Thomas Rugge (Text 34) record things seen and heard of. The writer of Text 36 mixes all three levels. Other writers describe things witnessed, but add their own reaction to what they have seen. Thus while Thomas Rugge vividly depicts Charles II's triumphal entry into London at his restoration, John Evelyn, after his equivalent account, adds,

> I stood in the strand, & beheld it, & blessd God: And all this without one drop of bloud, & by that very army, which rebell'd against him: but it was the Lords doing.[4]

A journal can also be the place where thoughts rather than events are set down,

> 20 Aug I am now 27 years old, Lord teach me now to number my days that I may apply my heart unto true wisdom, let the time past suffice to have followed the vain devices and desires of my own wicked heart and grant that henceforth I walk in newness of life to thy praise and glory and to my own salvation.[5]

In many journals personal comment, meditation and prayer arise from chronicling a day. This is commonest where a journal is kept as a devotional exercise with the specific aim of tracking spiritual experience,

> March ye fift. I did receave a great dell of mercy from the Lord in regard of that terrible fall I had in my daughter Harcourt's chamber, – when the stoole I lent on, first fayld me, and gave me a blowe crose my navell, which in some respects might have prooved very preiudisiall to me, if the Goodnes of the Lord my God had not prevented. – the Lord help me to remember his goodness, and to be thankfull all the dayes of my life for it.[6]

Roger Lowe, who, though devout, is not writing a spiritual diary, often closes an entry with a meditation,

> I was verij much troubled in my thoughts bij reason of Dr Naylors and mine falling out but Especially my greefe was because of my greatt love to Emma which by reason of my longe time could not be perfected but god is alsufficiant trust in yᵉ lord o my soule and thou shalt see the event of all to gods glory and thy comfort in yᵉ end (35/66–70).

This kind of addition to an account of the day's events arises naturally where a journal is being written at the end of a day, with no knowledge of what the next day will bring.
   Occasionally a text shows that the day-by-day system is not being rigidly adhered to. When the writer of Text 36 records the exceptionally hard winter of 1683–4 he must be writing in retrospect,

> Octʳ 25, 1683 ues also a great storme of snow And continued a great Frost from yᵉ end of Novʳ till Feb: 1684, The River of Thames at London was frozen yis uinter so yᵗ Coaths & boothes uere yʳon for a moneth or 6 uekes (36/29–31),

and the status of the December entries immediately following is therefore rendered doubtful; he is either writing well after the events, or copying notes made at the time.

A similar problem about time is apparent in Evelyn, when he writes, ostensibly on 13 March 1661,

> This after noone his highnesse Prince Rupert shewed me with his owne hands the new way of Graving call'd Mezzo Tinto, which afterwards I by his permission publish'd in my Historie of Chalcographie, which set so many artists on Worke, that they soone arived to that perfection it is since come, emulating the tenderest miniature.[7]

Not every journal entry can be automatically assumed to have been written on the day claimed.

An area of doubt more important to an examination of the language has also to be considered where journal entries describe current events. The entries are probably original, but there is also the possibility that the language in which the news-items are recorded is copied verbatim from elsewhere. In the related genre of Chronicle, where the important events of each year are set out, the use of derivative material is common, as one Chronicler copied the work of another. For example, a Chronicle from Kings Lynn records major events of the year 1516,

> In this yere was sant stevens flud: such a frost ensued that men wth carts myght pass betwyne westmynster and lambethe ... In this yer on may day w[ch] is called the yle may day was there an insurrection in london of yonge persons agaynst alyans of the wch divers were put to execution and the resudewe cam to Westmynster wth halters about ther neks and were pardoned.[8]

Much of this wording is taken directly from that of the Continuation of Fabyan's *Chronicle*,

> This yere was suche a frost, that all menne with cartes might passe bytwene Westminster & Lambeth. One Maye euin, this mayre his yere, the begynnyng of the .ix. yere of y[e] kyng, was an insurreccion of yong persones against alienes, of the whiche diuerse were putte to execucion, and the resydewe came to Westminster with halters about their neckes, & were pardoned.[9]

Moreover, in a journal written to please oneself copying into one's own book some interesting item from some contemporary news-sheet (of which there were a number[10] in the seventeenth century) is entirely within the jurisdiction of the writer, and there is no reader to make a charge of plagiarism. So when Thomas Rugge writes about the accidental shooting of Mr Fenn (Text 34A), or the execution of the woman who murdered her illegitimate baby (Text 34B) we cannot be entirely sure that the language is not derivative. Unless a specific source can be identified, internal consistency of language within a journal is the only authentication of originality. However, the doubt must still remain, even where the day's news is something heard from an acquaintance. In one day's entry, Rugge describes a boating accident (Text 34D), and he names the informant from whom he has heard about it, *I had this story of the boyes brother who was drownd*. But although this confirms that there is no written source, there is no certainty that phrases such as *had a minde to* have not been picked up from the way the informant told the story. It is for this reason that those texts and portions of texts which are totally personal, recording what the writer himself has done during the day, are particularly valuable.

Who were the people who kept journals? The only essential factors were literacy, which in turn demanded some degree of education, and self-awareness. Inevitably, many journals were kept by men of the professional class, clergy, lawyers, doctors. The un-identified writer of Text 36 was almost certainly a notary. Where a woman[11] kept a journal, she was invariably upper class. For the linguist, as well as for the social historian, the most interesting journals are those kept by members of the middle class, educated enough to be able to produce a relatively fluent story and to write it down, but not so literate as to conceal from the modern reader their own kind of English.

The journal of Henry Machyn (Text 33) has for many years[12] been for historical linguists an acknowledged source of information on the pronunciation of London English of the mid-sixteenth century. He was a London tradesman, involved in the provision of funeral trappings, so with a professional interest in the London pageantry he so often witnesses and describes. A century later, and virtually unnoticed as yet by linguists, Roger Lowe (Text 35), apprentice-shopkeeper and much-sought-after literate and numerate villager in a small community, writes in English which provides us with much of interest in regard to the Lancashire dialect of the seventeenth century. Thomas Rugge (Text 34) is another Londoner, a mid-seventeenth-century master barber. The higher social standing of the Edinburgh man who wrote Text 36 would, if he were English, produce a fairly bland and standard written language, but since he is a Scot his journal is of interest in its indications of the degree to which his language retains or has lost traditional Scots features.

In a journal, there is no publisher to iron out local or non-standard or idiosyncratic linguistic features, nor is the writer at pains to persuade, impress or dazzle any reader but himself. Sometimes self-awareness may spur him on; Roger Lowe is delighted to congratulate himself on the witty way he has played with words during the day,

> saturdaij Constables of Hadocke and Goleborne came to have me write theire presentmts for assizes and when I had done I writt poore is provided highwaijes repaired these querijs answerd and clarke vnrewarded att which they laughed most heartily (35/44–7),

but journals are usually places where writers can be themselves, or at least the selves they imagine themselves to be.

Since they are writing for no-one but themselves, writers of journals often use language in ways which arise from this. One general stylistic feature is the economy of allusiveness in referring to people, places and circumstances familiar to the writer, which he has no need to explain. Roger Lowe can write *I went to dockelane to see Raph this morneing* (35/65) without further specification.

Since it has to serve only the writer, and to remind him of the day when he looks back at the entry at some later date the syntax of journals is also characterised by what it leaves out. Some writers dispense with the normal elements which bind parts of a sentence together. The journal of landowner Henry Townshend has entries such as *My stable pluckt downe* and *The swine houses tyled*,[13] and Pepys' writing constantly has entries such as *Up; and all the morning in my chamber*.[14] Even where verbs are not omitted, omission of the *I* subject is particularly common practice in many journals. It is interesting, however, that in the four journals included here there is only one instance of syntactic reduction,

Edin^r ye 13 & 14 Nov^r, 1684, at Leith uynd foot wth W:H: incognito (36/64).

A similar feature of journal syntax is where a writer begins an entry with a mention of the day's weather, usually because it is important to his situation. This is customarily done without verbs,

A blustring cold day, and the evening very wet,[15]
This mornyng faire calme wether or rather a Littell wind n° w. erly./ but calme most parte of night.[16]

The use of patterns such as these is, of course, self-imposed. That they are not universally employed, being absent, for example, in the journal of Roger Lowe, suggests a possible correlation with linguistic sophistication.

Writers of journals often impose syntactic patterns on themselves, habitually framing their entries in some chosen way. In very many of his journal entries Henry Machyn (Text 33) sets himself as standard format the arrangement date + verb group with *be* + subject,

The xxx day of may was a goly maygam in fanch chyrche strett (33/47)
The v day of Iunj was bered in sant peters in chepe master tylworth (33/51).

This inversion after an initial adverbial is an option available at the period, but Machyn uses it more often than not, although he is not totally committed to it in every entry. Other writers have their own preferences, such as constantly using the present tense,

Thursday 1 May Mrs Leky bring me a letter from my wife. Sir Ralph Ashton desire to gett the Bishop advise for him. I get it. Mr West propose his son to Mr Bish and me.[17]

Not only is the writer of a journal free to have syntactic preferences, but, writing for himself, he has no need to disentangle syntactic complexities he lands himself in. Thomas Rugge, for example, has trouble with subordinate clauses in,

then [followed] a Regiment of horse swords drawne as was all that day thet had swords their (= *'there'*) had them drawne/ for the deffence of his majesty (34E/3–5),

and Roger Lowe writes,

I came my way and came to the window that Emm Potter laij in chamber (35/34–5),

while William Machyn tacks his clauses together as each occurs to him,

The xxvij day of may at after none was a woman grett w^t chyld was slayn gohyng in ffynsbere ffeld w^t her hosband w^t a narow shott in ye neke ye wyche she was a puterer wyff (33/38–40).

It is in their use of syntax like this that the writers of journals present us with written language pretty close to what we expect of spoken English.

Many journals also share with spoken English an unsophisticated use of co-ordination rather than subordination in the telling of a story. The elements of Machyn's narrative are typically joined with ubiquitous *and*,

> The xxxj day of Ianuary my lord tresorer lord of myssrul cam to my lord mare & bad my lord to dener & ther cam a grett cumpane of my lord tresorer men w^t portesans & a grett mene of musysyonars & dysse gyssyd and w^t trumpetes & drumes & w^t ys conssellers & dyver odur offesers & ther was a dulvyll shutyng of fyre & won was lyke deth w^t a dart in hand (33/13–17).

The morphology of journals is characterised by the use of 1st and 3rd person pronouns and verbs, but the absence of 2nd person forms. Since no-one is being addressed, the range of syntactic structures is also reduced by an absence of questions and imperatives. Exceptions occur where a writer 'talks to' himself, as in Lowe's

> trust in ye lord o my soule and thou shalt see the event of all to gods glory and thy comfort in ye end (35/69–70),

but here Lowe's words are, as in many of the meditations and prayers included in journals, coloured by the language of the Bible, even if they are not specific quotations. So that his use here of *thou shalt* and *thy* does not necessarily demonstrate that he himself used *thou* forms in ordinary conversation.

Notes

1. The terms 'Journal' and 'Diary' are almost interchangeable, but the former (usually *Diurnall*) is the common contemporary word, and avoids the ambiguity of the use of 'Diary' in the present century, where the term can also be applied to an engagement-book. For a discussion of the genre, see Alan MacFarlane, *The Life of Ralph Josselin* (Cambridge University Press, Cambridge, 1970), Chapter I (pp. 3–11), 'Diary-Keeping in seventeenth-century England'. For an extensive bibliography, see George Watson (ed.), *The New Cambridge Bibliography of English Literature* (Cambridge University Press, Cambridge, 1974), Vol. I (600–1660), Section 6.II, Letters, diaries, autobiographies and biographies, Cols. 2259–64.
2. Robert Latham and William Matthews (eds), *The Diary of Samuel Pepys* (Bell & Sons, London, 1971), Vol. V, p. 247.
3. Joseph Hunter (ed.), *The Diary of Dr. Thomas Cartwright, Bishop of Chester*, Camden Society, Vol. 22 (1843), p. 16.
4. E. S. De Beer (ed.), *The Diary of John Evelyn* (Clarendon Press, Oxford, 1955), Vol. III, p. 246.
5. The Revd Thomas Naish 1696; Doreen Slater (ed.), *The Diary of Thomas Naish*, Wiltshire Archaeological and Natural History Society Records Branch, Vol. 20 (1965), p. 37.
6. Sir Simon Harcourt 1661; Edward William Harcourt (ed.), *The Harcourt Papers* (James Parker (for private circulation), Oxford, 1885), Vol. I, p. 195.

7. De Beer, *Evelyn*, Vol. III, p. 274.

8. Ralph Flenley (ed.), *Six Town Chronicles of England* (Clarendon Press, Oxford, 1911), p. 192.

9. Henry Ellis (ed.), *The New Chronicles of England and France ... including the different continuations* (Rivington, London, 1811), p. 696.

10. For a brief account, see Mrs. Herbert Richardson, *The Old English Newspaper*, The English Association Pamphlet No. 86 (December 1933).

11. For example, Lady Margaret Hoby and Lady Anne Clifford.

12. Machyn's dialect phonology as suggested by his spelling was examined in some detail in Henry Cecil Wyld, *A History of Modern Colloquial English* (Basil Blackwell, Oxford, 1920 and later editions), pp. 141–7.

13. J. W. W .Bund (ed.), *Diary of Henry Townshend of Elmley Lovett 1640–1663*, Worcestershire Historical Society, Vol. 37 (1915), p. 1.

14. Latham and Matthews, *Pepys*, Vol. V, p. 131 .

15. Charles E. Long (ed.), *Diary of the Marches of the Royal Army during the Great Civil War; kept by Richard Symonds*, Camden Society, Vol. 74 (1859), p. 55.

16. Journal of Richard Cocks 1615; British Library Manuscript Additional 31,300 f. 48r. In Edward Maunde Thompson (ed.), *Diary of Richard Cocks*, Hakluyt Society Series I, Vol. 66 (1883); the notes on weather are not transcribed.

17. John Harington 1651; Margaret F. Stieg (ed.), *The Diary of John Harington, MP 1646–53*, Somerset Record Society, Vol. 74 (1977), p. 66.

Text 33

Henry Machyn: London 1556–7
(British Library Manuscript Cotton Vitellius F.V)

[f. 65r] The xx day of Ianuary at grenwyche pa<rke gate y^e> quen grace
pensyonars dyd mustur ... & be twyn ij or iij of ye cloke thay cam downe &
mustered a for ye que<n> grace a ffor ye parke gatt for ther stod ye quene grace
on he & my lord cardenall & my lord admerall & my lord montyguw & dyuers

5 odur lord*es* & lades & so a ffor ye pensyoners rod many gentyll men on genet*es*
& lyght horsses butt spesyall ther rod on gentyll man ys nam ys m*aster*
< BLANK > a pon ye lest mulle thatt evere I say & so thay rod to & fro a for y^e
qwyne & ther cam a tumbler playd mony prate ffett*es* a for ye quen & my lord
cardenall y^t her grace dyd layke hartely & so her grace dyd thanke them all ffor

10 ther payne & so aft*er* they p*a*rtyd ffor ther wher of ye pesyonars l & mo besyd
ther men of armes & ther wher of pepull of me*n* & vome*n* a boyff x m pepull
& mo

*　*　*　*

[f. 65v] The xxxj day of Ianuary my lord tresorer lord of myssrul cam to my lord
mare & bad my lord to dener & ther cam a grett cumpane of my lord tresorer

15 men w^t portesans & a grett mene of musysyonars & dysse gyssyd and w^t
trumpet*es* & drumes & w^t ys conssellers & dyver odur offesers & ther was a
dulvyll shutyng of fyre & won was lyke deth w^t a dart in hand

*　*　*　*

[f. 68r] The xxiij day of marche was a com*m*ondeme*nt* cam y^t ye kyng & ye quene
wold ryd fram ye towre warff thrughe london w^t ye nobuls of ye raym<e> boyth

20 lord*es* & lades & at ye towre warff my lord mayre {mett} ther gracys boyth &
thrugh london my master*es* ye altherme*n* & ye shreyff*es* & all ye crafft*es* of
london in ther leuer*es* & ther standyng*es* set vp of evere craft of tymbur & y^e
strett ~~mmmmmmmmmmmmm~~ & ye trumpett*es* blohyng w^t odur enstrementt*es*
w^t grett joye & plesur & grett shutyng of gones at ye towre & ye wayt*es* plahyng

25 of saint peters led*es* in chepe & my lord mayre bare ye septer a for ye kyng & y^e
quen

*　*　*　*

[f. 70v] The ffurst day of may was creatyd at whytt hall {m*aster*} perse ye yerle of northumberland w^t viij harold*es* & a dosen of trumpeters thrugh ye quen chambur & thrugh ye hall & a for hym my lord of penbroke & my lord

30   montyguw & then my lord of arundell & my lord of rutland & hym sey<lf> whent in ye myd*es* all in cremesun weluett in th<e> parlement robes & whyt a hatt off veluett & a cro<wne> of gold on ys hed.

It the sam day a bouet non ther wher serten spaneard*es* ffowyth at ye cowrt gate a gaynst one spaneard & one of them ffrust ~~in~~ {him} thrugh w^t ys raper & ded

35   contenent & ij of ye spaneard*es* y^t kyld hym was browt in to ye cowrt by on of ye gard & he deleu*er*d them to ye knyght marshall seruand*es* to haue them ye marshellsay

*   *   *   *

[f. 71v] The xxvij day of may at after none was a woman grett w^t chyld ~~s~~ was slayn gohyng in ffynsbere ffeld w^t her hosband w^t a narow shott in ye neke y^e

40   wyche she was a puterer wyff

*   *   *   *

[f. 72r] The xxv day of may was raynyd at westmynster one a ffrenche man y^t was taken in skarborow when y^t thomas stafford was taken w^t ys adherent*es* & cast to dee & so cared to ye towre a gayne

The sam day was hangyd at tyburne xvij on was a nold woman of lx yere the

45   trongyest cut purs of a voman y^t has ben herd off & a lad a cut purs ffor ye tyme he be gane well

*   *   *   *

[f. 72v] The xxx day of may was a goly maygam in fanc<h> chyrche strett w^t drumes & gunes & pykes & ix wordes dyd ryd & thay had speches evereman & ye mo<ris> dansse & ye sauden & a elevantt w^t ye castyll & ye sauden <&> yonge

50   morens w^t targattes & darttes & ye lord & ye lade of y^{<e>} maye

The v day of Iunj was bered in sant peters in chep<e> m*aster* tylworth goldsmyth w^t mony mornars & w^t ij why<te> branchys & xij stayf*es* torchys & ye xij pore me*n* had gow<nes> of mantyll ffrysse & iiij grett tapurs & ys mas was keft<e> on wyssunmonday & aft*er* ther was a grett dener

*   *   *   *

55   [f. 73r] The x day of Iune ye kyng & ye quen toke ther Iorney toward hamtun

cowrte for to hunt & to kyll a grett hartt w^t serten of {y^e consell} & so y^e
howswold tared at ye whytt hall tyll ye saterday ffolowhyng they cam a gay<ne>
to whytt hall

60   The xvj day of Iunij my yong duke of norffoke rod a brod & at stamfford hyll
my lord havyng a dage hangyng on ys sadyll bow & by mysse ffortune dyd shutt
yt & yt on of ys men y^t ryd a ffor & so by mysse fforten ys ~~dyd fflyng~~ horsse dyd
fflyng & so he hangyd by on of ys sterope & so thatt ye horsse knokyd ys brayns
owtt w^t fflyngyng owtt w^t ys leges

*   *   *   *

[f. 74r] The xxix day of Iune was sent peters day was a smalle ffare keft in sant
65   margatt cherche yerde as wolle & odur small thyng*es* as tornars & odur & ye sam
day was a godly a prossessyon ye wyche my lord abbott whent w^t ys myter & ys
crossear & a grett nomber of copes of cloth of gold & ye wergers & mony
worshephull gentyll men & women at westmynster whent a prossessessyon

The sam day at after non was ye ij y{e}ere myne of good m*aster* < BLANK >
70   lewyn yrṁonger & at ys durge was all ye leverey ye ffurst m*aster* altherman
drap*er* & aft*er* to her plasse & they had a kake & a bone a pesse be syd ye p*ar*yche
& all comers & wyne he nowgh for all comers

Notes

Text

Extracts only. The text has been edited in John Gugh Nichols (ed.), *The Diary of Henry
Machyn, Citizen and Merchant-Taylor of London, from AD1550 to AD1563*, Camden
Society Original Series, Vol. 42 (1848). Machyn's language is examined in Henry C.
Wyld, *A History of Modern Colloquial English* (Basil Blackwell, Oxford, 1920 and later
editions), pp. 141–7.

Manuscript

A photograph of lines 64–72 from this document, together with a commentary, appear
as Plate IV on pp. 156–7 above.

As its British Library shelf-mark suggests, this manuscript was once owned by Sir
Robert Cotton (1570–1631). The manuscript suffered badly in the fire by which the
Cottonian collection was damaged in 1731, the top half of all leaves being badly scorched
away at the edges. To get readable stretches of text extracts from the lower halves of
leaves have been selected, though even here some letters at the ends of lines have been
lost and are conjecturally restored here. The restored *h* in (47) *fanch chyrche* is the
reading in Nichols, *Machyn*.

In the phrase (44–5) *the trongyest cut purs of a voman*, the word *of* is written on a small fragment torn from this leaf (f. 72r) and stuck on the next one (f. 73r) where it obscures the second half of the word conjecturally restored as (57) *a gayne*.

The blanks for names in lines 7 and 69 are left by the diarist.

The deleted text, probably three or four words, in l. 23 is illegible.

In transcription, lower-case *d* has been used throughout, even though in some instances it might be intended as a capital, since the text very rarely uses capitals except at the beginning of each day's entry.

Double *f* has been transcribed as such.

In (11) *m* 'thousand' the writer employs the same abbreviation (*m* with a looped-round tail) as he uses, with different signification, in (6) *master*.

In the word (45) *y^e* the superscript letter is indistinct and could be *s*, making *ys* 'his', but nowhere else does Machyn make the second letter of this word a superscript one.

Glossary

Note: Machyn's spelling conceals many familiar words, thus (16) *ys* 'his', (17) *dulvyll* 'devil', (27) *yerle* 'earl', (31) *whyt* 'with', (33) *ffowyth* 'fought', (54) *kefte* 'kept', (71) *bone* 'bun', (72) *he nowgh* 'enough' etc. Single lexical items written as two words can also confuse, (3) *a for*, (15) *dyyse gyssyd* etc. Beware of possessive constructions with no possessive inflexion evident, (3) *y^e quen grace*, (13) *my lord tresorer lord of myssrul*, (40) *a puterer wyff* etc.

(3)	*a for*	before, in front of
(5)	*genetes*	=jennets, small Spanish horses
(7)	*lest*	=least, smallest
(8)	*tumbler*	acrobat
(8)	*prate*	=pretty, skilful
(8)	*ffettes*	tricks
(9)	*layke*	?laugh (see note)
(10)	*payne*	pains, trouble taken
(10)	*l*	roman numeral for 50
(11)	*a boyff*	=above, more than
(11)	*x m*	roman numerals for 10,000
(13)	*lord of myssrul*	master of Christmas revels
(14)	*bad*	invited
(15)	*portesans*	=partisans, halberds
(15)	*mene*	=meinie, retinue
(15)	*musysyonars*	musicians
(21)	*craffies*	trade guilds
(22)	*leueres*	=liveries, ceremonial costumes (but cf. l. 70)
(22)	*standynges*	standards
(24)	*waytes*	municipal wind-band
(25)	*ledes*	lead roof
(35)	*contenent*	(reduced form of *incontinent*) immediately
(40)	*puterer*	pewter-smith
(41)	*raynyd*	=arraigned, brought to trial

(43)	*cast*	condemned
(45)	*trongyest*	?=strongest, most thorough-going
(45)	*cut purs*	=cutpurse, pickpocket
(47)	*goly*	See note
(48)	*ix wordes*	=the Nine Worthies (see note)
(49)	*sauden*	sultan
(50)	*morens*	moors
(50)	*targattes*	small round shields
(52)	*stayfes torchys*	tall thick ceremonial candles
(53)	*mantyll ffrysse*	=mantle frieze, cloak-weight woolen cloth
(53)	*tapurs*	ceremonial candles
(60)	*dage*	hand-gun
(62)	*fflyng*	kick
(65)	*tornars*	wood-turners
(69)	*ij yeere myne*	second anniversary of funeral
(70)	*durge*	requiem mass
(70)	*leverey*	members of livery company, guild (but cf. l. 22)

Local placenames

For London in the early sixteenth century, see Mary D. Lobel (ed.), *The British Atlas of Historic Towns*, Vol. III, *The City of London From Prehistoric Times to c.1520* (Oxford University Press, Oxford, 1989, and 1991 reprint).

(1)	*grenwyche parke*	Greenwich Park, surrounding Greenwich Palace, 3 miles downriver from London
(19)	*ye towre warff*	Tower Wharf, quay by Tower of London
(25 and 51)	*saint peters in chepe*	St Peter Westcheap, Cheapside
(27, 57, 58)	*whytt hall*	Palace of Whitehall, Westminster
(33)	*ye cowrt gate*	?Not an actual placename
(37)	*marshellsay*	Marshalsea prison, Southwark, on south side of Thames
(39)	*ffynsbere ffeld*	Finsbury Fields, open space used for archery, to north of City
(41 and 68)	*westmynster*	Westminster
(43)	*ye towre*	Tower of London, prison as well as Palace
(44)	*tyburne*	Tyburn, place of execution outside both London and Westminster, near present-day Marble Arch
(47)	*fanch chyrche strett*	Fenchurch Street
(55–6)	*hamtum cowrte*	Hampton Court Palace, about 13 miles upriver from London
(59)	*stamfford hyll*	Stamford Hill, about 4 miles north of London
(64–5)	*sant margatt*	Church of St Margaret, New Fish Street, near London Bridge

Explanatory notes

(1), (18) etc. The Queen at this time is Queen Mary I, married to King Philip of Spain.

(9) *layke*: Most probably a spelling for 'laugh'. There is a verb *lake* 'amuse oneself', but this appears in Northern dialects only.

(47) *goly*: probably =jolly; but there is the possibility of an error for *godly*, an adjective Machyn uses freqently in reference to (ecclesiastical) pageantry, as in l. 66.

(48) *ix words*: The Nine Worthies, nine men famed in Biblical, Classical and Medieval story, provided a popular theme for pageants, as reflected in Shakespeare's *Love's Labour's Lost*.

(71) *her plasse*: If this is 'their place', that is the Drapers' Hall, the conservative 3rd person plural possessive form *her* is of interest.

Background

Machyn is known only through this journal. Nichols, *Machyn*, uses the text to identify him as a Londoner, of the parish of Trinity the Little, by Queenhithe, a tradesman who supplied the trappings necessary for funerals. In his journal he noted down those local events which interested him, particularly the spectacles which provided lavish street theatre in his time. Wyld, *Colloquial English*, describes him as 'a priceless guide to the lower type of London English of his day'.

Topics for linguistic investigation

1. Evidence for the progress of the Great Vowel Shift supplied by the spellings (8) *qwyne* and (17) *shutyng*.
2. The evidence relating to the pronunciation of consonants in the pairs (17) *dulvyll* and (19) *rayme*; (45) *voman* and (67) *wergers*; (23) *blohyng* and (61 (2nd occurrence)) *yt*; (31) *whent* and (40) *wyche*.
3. The extent to which spellings suggest that all unstressed vowels are reduced to [ə].
4. The evidence relating to pronunciation in the spellings (4) *he*, (14) *dener*, (20) *boyth*, (21) *shreyffes*, (27) *yerle*, (33) *ffowyth*, (34) *ffrust*, (35) *browt*, (49) *elevantt*, (54) *wyssunmonday*, (70) *yrmonger*.
5. A comparison between the evidence on sixteenth-century London English offered by this text and that provided by Text 62.
6. Re-write a short passage (e.g. lines 6–12, 38–40 or 64–8) using present-day syntax. What kind of syntactic changes are involved?

Text 34

Thomas Rugge: London 1659–60

(British Library Manuscript Additional 10,116)

Extract A

[f. 52v] Ian 59 28 the twenty eight theire ware 3 or 4 Gentlemen drin<king> att
the deuill tauern by temple barre on^e of the them called m^r fenn a Lawer and
one of the Company had a pockett pistolle a bout him and hee beeing disired
by one of the Company how a pistoll might be charged on a sudden wch was don

5   and haueing primed and Cocked in puting the pistoll into his pockett the Cock
tooke hold in one of the Ribones that be longed to his breeches and it dicharged
and shot m^r fenn who was standinge by the fier, into the should and brest and
made a great hole that a child might put in its hand into the wound hee spake
only hold mee hold mee made 2 or 3 groanes and died in the place, the persons

10 ware all Aprehended brought befor a magistrate and caried to prison and their
kept for a little space but all quite for that it was a mischai*n*ch

Extract B

[f. 53v] Ian 59 31 This day a man and a woeman ware executed at tiborn<e>
the man for killinge a bayliffe the woeman wch had a bastard child borne of hir
she to shunn the shame of <it> shee put her infant aliue into an earthren pott
and Couered it ouer with Cold watter and put a paper one ye top of the pot and

5   sent it to the Bake house which<e> pot was put into the ouen the heet of the
ouen warm<ed> the watter an*d* the child reviued an*d* the child reviued an*d* it
Cryed the baker took out the pott an*d* took out the Child an*d* it liued 2 houers
the baker made a very Close search and the party was found and
Apreh<ended> an*d* att Sessions Condemned an*d* suffred att tyborne for this

10 fact

Extract C

[f. 81r] Alderman Bunce A person who for loue of his ma^{tie} was banishe*d* wth
D^r drake and Capt: titius, concerning that buissness of m^r loue the minister,
who After wards was beheaded on tower hill vnpon the score of his Ma^{ti} this
Alderman Bunce att his first Apearence in the Royall Exchange his freinds came

171

5   so fast a bout him for Ioy hee was yitt aliue, that he was constrained to absent
him selfe to refresh him selfe hee beeing weary with speaking to his frinds & a
quantances/

Extract D

[f. 81v] in this month a marchants ship that was bound for sea, lying att Graues
ende and the officers in number sixtee<n> had a minde to see their wiues and
frinds in London beeing in a longe boate and the theames beeinge very Rouffe
14 of them was drownd and tow for the present saued a boye that stood vpon
5   the keele of the longe boat out of which the men was Cast out of a payer of oares
Came by and one of the oares put forth his hand to pull the boye into his boate
the boy pulled so hard that both man and boy was drownd I had this story of
the boyes brother who was drownd,

Extract E

[f. 99v] his Majesty Rode betwene the duke of york and the duke of Gloucester
and after followed a troop bear headed wth whit Coulours, then the Generals life
Guard then a troop of Gentilmen wth Skie coulors fringed wth gold then a
Regiment of horse swords drawne as was all that day thet had swords their) had
5   them drawne/ for the deffence of his majesty such shouting as the oldest man
a liue neuer heard the like/ fiue Regiments followed last of all except a troope
of gentilmen of the best qualitie Red Coulors fringed wth gold in seuerall places
strowinge of flowers by yonge maidens Rich Carpes and Cussions and mantles
in windows in the strond and many flower potts w^t all sorts of flower as at that
10   time of the yeare would aforde this beeing done all things that might express
Ioy the Ioy was that night ended wth almost att eury doore wth bonfieres in
westminster a very great fiere made and on the top of the fier they put old oliuer
Cromwell and his wife in Sables (theire pictures lifely made like them in life
which was burnt in the fire and stats armes the which did not want Supplys of
15   monys to buy beere to [f. 100r] cheer ther hearts vp in such a free will offringe
as any may Iudge vpon such an occatioun, and the might after this in St
martains lane neere new street end a person, that al a longe in those our dayes
of the late protectour hee was a Zeoure to hide the kings frinds as ministers and
others (made a bonefiere by his gate which was made by the best Arttise in
20   London for their were fier works so Artefuishall that seuerall fiugers att the
flying into the Aire they were to be seene Charles the second/ the kings Armes)
wth out the side of the house and a lion a lion at the foote of the kings Armes
beeing placed ther a hogshead of Claritt wine rane very plentifull to all that
Could take it in ther hatts or Cups or glases and seue^all Medele of his majesty
25   pictuers was throwne out att Mr Iohn Adlers windows, for Any that Could
Citch, then few days aftar his majesty was in england his ma^tie Conferred the
honour of knight hood vpon this sd Adlear, the whole Charge that Mr Iohn

Adler/ was att was vauled at 100^l and 500^l and thus much for the 29 and 30 of may 1660:

Notes

Text

Extracts only. The text has been edited by William L. Sachse (ed.), *The Diurnal of Thomas Rugg 1659–1661*, Camden Society, 3rd Series, Vol. 91 (1961).

Manuscript

Some conjectural restoration has been necessary where tight binding makes letters at the right-hand end of lines on verso pages impossible to read.

Each manuscript page has a heading relating to the principal anecdote related there, thus f. 52v has the header *M^r ffenn killed by a mischance*. These have been omitted here. The reference to year and month in A1 and B1 has been placed within the text, but in the original it is written in the margin.

The text contains some less usual abbreviation, thus (B6 etc.) *and* written as *an* with a looped final stroke, and (E1) *betwene*, (E9) *windows*, where instead of abbreviation by omission of the nasal-letter, it is the vowel-letter which is omitted.

It is possible that the words (A7) *should*, (E8) *Carpes* are intended as shortened forms, but there is no confirmation of this from punctuation or mark of abbreviation.

In (E20) *fiugers* 'figures', the word is first written *fugers*, then an *i* has been added in different ink, but without deletion of the *u*.

In (E16) *might* there is a clear error for *night*.

Glossary

(A7)	*should*	=shoulder
(A11)	*quite*	=quit, released
(A11)	*mischainch*	=mischance, accident
(B3)	*shunn*	evade
(B3)	*earthren*	made of clay
(B8)	*Close*	detailed
(B8)	*party*	person responsible
(C3)	*unpon the score of*	for the sake of
(D3)	*longe boate*	ship's boat
(D5)	*payre of oares*	boat rowed by two men
(D6)	*oares*	rowers
(E2)	*Coulours*	standards
(E3)	*Skie*	sky-blue
(E8)	*Carpes*	=carpets
(E8)	*mantles*	cloaks
(E10)	*aforde*	supply
(E13)	*Sables*	See note
(E13)	*lifely*	to the life

(E14)	*stats armes*	See note
(E14)	*want*	lack
(E18)	*Zeoure*	See note
(E20)	*Artefuishall*	=artificial, skilfully contrived
(E23)	*hogshead*	large cask
(E28)	*vauled*	=valued
(E28)	*100¹ and 500¹*	£100 and £500

Explanatory notes

(E13) *in Sables*: ?wearing black clothes (in mourning for defeat). It is tempting to suggest that *Tables* 'painted on boards' is intended, but the manuscript has a clear initial *S*.

(E14) *stats armes*: the national arms which had been used instead of the Royal Arms during the Commonwealth period. As well as the flags of England, Ireland and Scotland it included Cromwell's personal arms in the centre.

(E18) *a Zeoure*: a Biblical name, Zoar (Isaiah 15: 5), used here as if a person, but in fact a place of refuge.

Background

Rugge was a Master Barber working in London. His Diurnall (his own title) contains many entries on current political events, with the text of speeches, parliamentary enactments and so on. As well as derivative material, he writes his own account of local happenings, sometimes, as in Extract D, citing the source of his anecdotes. His eye-witness account of King Charles II's triumphal entry into London at the Restoration is parallelled (but with less local colour) in the more famous diaries of Samuel Pepys and John Evelyn.

Topics for linguistic investigation

1. The evidence relating to pronunciation in the spellings: (B7) *houers*, (C6) *frinds*, (D3) *Rouffe*, (E2) *bear*, (E8) *strowinge*, (E8) *Cussions*, (E19) *Arttise*, (E20) *fier*, (E20) *Artefuishall*, (E26) *Citch*.
2. Reasons for using *was* instead of *ware*.
3. The syntactic function of (B3) *shee*, (C5) *him*, (E18) *hee*, (E21) *they*.
4. Why does Rugge have problems with prepositions in (A8) *a greate hole that a child might put in its hand into the wound*, (D5) *the longe boat out of which the men was Cast out of*, (E11) *the Ioy was that night ended wᵗʰ almost att euery doore wᵗʰ bonfieres*?
5. Disentangle the structures in (E3–5) *then a Regiment of horse swords drawne as was all that day thet had swords their) had them drawne/ for the deffence of his majesty* and (E9–10) *and many flower potts wᵗ all sorts of flower as at that time of the yeare would aforde*
6. A comparison with present-day English in the choice of preposition in (A3) *a bout*, (A4) *on*, (D7) *of*, (E8) *of*, (E23) *to*.

Text 35

Roger Lowe: Ashton-in-Makerfield, Lancashire 1664
(Wigan Archives Service Manuscript D/DZ A.58)

[f 22r] August 1664.

8 mundaij being Ashton wakes att this time I had a most ardent Effection to
Emm Potter and she was in compeny att Tankerfeilds with Henry Kenion and
it greeved me very much Henry Low came to me and would have me go to
Tankerfeilds spend 2d so we went to the next chamber to that they ware in att

5 last they came by vs and I movd Emm to stay to drinke with me which she did
but would not stay with me neither there nor no where els would not come to
me tho she said she would and I was in avery sad eflicted Estate and all by reason
of her

10 wedensday Emma went to bringe one pegg lightfoote tords home and I went

10 after her and we spoke to each other and Ellin Harrison came vnto vs and tooke
vs and was in a great rage against Emma and this was matter of great greife of
harte vnto me but my trust is in god who will helpe in trouble tho the storme
be now yet I ha<ve> hopes I shall see a calme this is my hopes and till then Ile
waite one god

15 14 lords daij I went to neawtown and heard Mr Blakeburne and he enioind old
William Hasleden and I to come to Rothwells which we did and had 2 pintes of
wine which he would have paijd for but I would not suffer it after I came home
I went to Elizebeth Rosbothom and I spoke my mind to her concerneinge
Emma which I could not doe without teares and she did pitie my state I was

20 very discomforted

15 mundaij the sun began to shine for Elizebeth Rosbothom had told Ellin my
greefe and she pities my condition so as she resolved she would never act against
me [f. 22v] so I went to John Rosbothoms and staijd awhile and both Ellin and
Emma came down and Ellin went her way and Emma and I went into chamber

25 and there we professed each other<s> loves to each other so I was abundantly
satisfied within my selfe and I promisd this night to come see her in her chamber
god will arise and show pitie to his distressed servent

175

16 old Mr Woods came to town and was all night att William Hasledens and
they would have had me to sup*er* but Mr Woods ingagd me to come to be with

30   hime I was this afternoone with Willia*m* Chadocke and Thomas Heijes casting
vp their accounts and aft*er* I had done with them I came to shop and shutt it vp
and went to Willia*m* Hasledens they ware att praij*er* aft*er* pray*er* M*r* Woods
discourse was concerneinge wars and troubles that he and old Willia*m* had
beene in togath*er* so att far in night I came my way and came to the window that

35   Emm Pott*er* laij in chamb*er* and I would gladly have come in but she durst not
let me in but she rise vp to the window and we kisd and so I went to bed

17 att night I went to Docke lane to get Raph Hasleden to go for me to Leigh
to fetch goods he was not att home but I spoke to Sarah and bought 2 li of wax

18th thursdaij this morneinge we went with Cart and wat*er*s ware vp att
40   Penington bridge we gat *our* comodities into Cart and so parted Leigh & came
well home

19 fridaij I borowed a horse and went to Humphrey Burscoes in Lowton for to
buij hony and wax of his sist*er*s but theij ware too hard for me

saturdaij Constables of Hadocke and Goleborne came to have me write theire
45   p*re*sentmts for assizes and when I had done I writt poore is p*ro*vided highwaijes
repaired these querijs answ*er*d and clarke vnrewarded att which they laughed
most heartily

22 mundaij I was desired bij Gawth*er* Tayler wife to ride before Eles her
daught*er* to the funerall of Lucie Taylor of Sankey Hall and I left my Mrs
50   occasions att ashton to answ*er* their expectation went to Sankey Hall came
againe with buryinge to winwicke and whiles drinkeinge was I gat Emm*a* into
a place above where we talked about some things and in this while Eles Taylor
like an vnworthy women [f. 23r] went and tooke anoth*er* to ride before her so
that when I came to take horse there was none for me I was highly p*er*plex<ed>
55   yet bore it very patiently Iohn Moodij and I came home to gath*er* and as we ware
comeinge Iohn Pott*er* and Emm*a* behind hime ov*er*tooke vs and he askd me
what I would give hime att Neawton I promisd hime a q*t* of Ale and att Neawton
he light and we staijd and ~~receivd~~ ware very merij Anon dicke Naylor comes
and falls a quarrellinge with me in so much as we fell to it but Iohn Pott*er*
60   vindicated mij cause nobly and poor Emm*a* stickd close to me so they gatt dicke
awaij with adeale of shame to his p*ar*t so we all came to gather home and William
Sixsmith would needs have John Moodij and I ride be hind hime which we did
and so ridd into towne but it was night I tooke John Pott*er* into Alehouse and
spent 6d on hime

65   26 frideij I went to dockelane to see Raph this morneing who had receivd a hurt

by a fall of a horse as he was goeinge to assizes I was verij much troubled in my
thoughts bij reason of Dr Naylors and mine falling out but Especially my greefe
was bec*ause* of my greatt love to Emm*a* which by reason of my longe time could
not be p*er*fected but god is alsufficient trust in y*e* lord o my soule and thou shalt
70   see the event of all to gods glory and thy comfort in y*e* end

28 lords daij I went to Leigh my Mr was gone to assizes att noone I was very
disconsolate but I went to Iohn chadockes house and I mett with Iohn Hindley
we went hee and I to top of steeple and Discoursed of form*er* daijes and
passages past & gone there was burijd one Sand*er* Sixes who had his necke
75   broken in rideinge between dean Church and bent when we ware come from
top of steeple Iohn chadocke was seekeing vs so we went altogather to Ale house
and spent Each of vs 1d so parted att night I came home to Ashton and went
see Raph Hasleden and parted and came to bed

Notes

Text

Extract only. Excerpts from the Diary were printed in 'Local Gleanings' articles in *The
Manchester Courier*, and subsequently in *The Leigh Chronicle* in 1876, with a collected
form published by the newspaper in 1877, edited by 'J. B.'. This has been reprinted
with an introduction by Ian Winstanley (ed.), *The Diary of Roger Lowe of Ashton in
Makerfield, Lancashire 1663–1678* (Picks Publishing, Ashton-in-Makerfield, 1994).

Manuscript

There are some problems of legibility because of ink showing through from the other
side of the leaf.

Many words have a stroke over an *m* or *n*, which has been taken as empty rather than
indicative of omission of a further *m* or *n*. Thus (9) *home*, (13) *calme*, (37) *lane*, (21) *sun*,
(58) *Anon* etc.

The expansion of the name of Lowe's beloved presents problems, as it appears only
as *Emm*, occasionally without any mark of abbreviation, but generally with a stroke over
the second *m*. This form has been expanded to *Emma*, but there is no confirmation for
a full spelling.

The paragraphing used here, whereby each day's record begins on a fresh line, is an
editorial addition; Lowe's text runs on continuously.

Glossary

(1)	*wakes* †	annual holiday
(2)	*in company with*	keeping company with
(5)	*movd*	urged
(10)	*tooke*	caught
(15)	*enioind*	=enjoined, made

(18)	*suffer*	permit
(20)	*discomforted*	disheartened
(30–31)	*casting vp*	adding up, doing (accounts)
(34)	*so att* †	so that
(34)	*came my way*	left
(38)	*li*	pounds (Latin abbreviation)
(40)	*comodities*	goods
(45)	*done*	finished
(48)	*ride before (X)*	ride with (X) on pillion
(49)	*Mrs*	mistress, (female) employer
(50)	*occasions*	business
(52)	*above*	upstairs
(58)	*light*	dismounted
(62)	*would needs*	was determined to
(68)	*time*	period of apprenticeship
(74)	*passages*	events
(75)	*bent*	heath

Local placenames

(1)	*Ashton*	Ashton-in-Makerfield
(15)	*neawtown*	Newton-le-Willows
(37)	*Leigh*	Leigh
(40)	*Penington*	Pennington
(42)	*Lowton*	Lowton St Mary's
(44)	*Hadocke*	Haydock
(44)	*Goleborne*	Golborne
(49)	*Sankey*	Sankey
(51)	*winwicke*	Winwick

House or farm names

(2) *Tankerfeilds*; (16) *Rothwells*; (65) *dockelane*.

Background

Roger Lowe lived at Ashton-in-Makerfield, near Wigan, and was serving a long apprenticeship to a shopkeeper who, living in nearby Leigh, left Lowe to manage the shop. His date of birth is not known, but he seems to be a fairly young man at the time of writing this Journal. It gives a blow-by-blow account of Lowe's life in the village community, time spent in the ale-house and discussing religion, and his pursuit of Emma Potter, together with his own feelings about himself. His literacy and numeracy, combined with his evident popularity, made him much sought-after as a friend to hand when any official writing or reckoning needed to be done, and he records his writing of wills, letters, accounts and presentments for his fellow-villagers.

Topics for linguistic investigation

1. The extent to which Lowe's text is disadvantaged by its total lack of punctuation.
2. The forms and tenses of the verbs in lines 58–64.
3. The seventeenth-century use of compressed pronoun + auxiliary forms such as (13) *Ile*.
4. Are the following constructions in general use in the seventeenth century?: (6) *neither there nor no where els*, (34) *so att … I came*, (73) *we went … to top of steeple*, (75) *when we ware come*, (77–8) *I … went see Raph Hasleden*.
5. Local features in Lowe's language.
6. Lowe's use of special language in religious comment and meditation.

Text 36

A Notary: Edinburgh 1682–4
(Edinburgh University Manuscript Laing I/327/9a)

[f. 1v] Edin^r ye 18 day of May 1682 being Thursday Dyed Adam Bothwell of a high Malign Feaver in 6 dayes sickness betwix 9 & 10 houres of ye day in my Chamber & bed

5

10

15

Edin^r upon Weddensday ye 28 of June 1682 Mr Ninian Patersone Minister at Libbertoun-Kirk being accused by ye Heretors of his paroch befor ye Bp: & Presbytery of Edin^r for his dabauched life and prophan conversacioun as blasphemy curseing breaking ye Lords day calumniating ye Ordinar brethren & parochiners [f. 2r] Drunkness & stricking his servants & oyers &c He appelled from y^m to ye Primat Dr Burett who did remitt ye same againe to his ordinary & brethren Who yen did proceed to call ye uitnesses to make faith in communi forma He did again Appell to Kings Maj: as supream Head of ye Church To which it was ansuered That altho yey had take ye Test Yet his Maj: power did not reach y^t far to medle With ye power of ye Keys and intrinsick Government of ye Church which yey denayed to be in ye Kings prerogative And fand befor ye halfe of ye uitnesses had deponed yat ye whole Lybell was more y^n sufficiently proven And yrfor did depose ye sd Mr Ninian Patersone ab officio et beneficio, and ordain'd ye same to be published ye nixt sunday at Libbertoun Kirk to declair ye same vacand: which ues don by M^r Al: Malcolm minister in E^{dr} conforme to ye sd order.

20

25

Edin^r ffryday ye 26 Ianry 1683 at 12 a cloak at night Wm Morisone of Prestoungrang his eldest sone & child ues born And vpon ye next day Saturday ye 27 at 7 a cloak at night in y^r own Lodging in Peebles uynd Baptized by ye name of Alexander, his Guidsr being Goodfayer by Mr Geo: Trotter Minister of ye Tron Churche Witnesses Sr Wm Bennet of Grubbet, Sr Pat: Murruy Deucher Henry Trotter of Mortonhall Cragintynie Dean younger Mr Wm Monipenny Advoca<t> & me &c

Ed^r Sunday 20 May 1683 In Colledge Kirk I toke ye Sacramente y^r.

[f. 2v] Edin^r Sepr 25 & 26, 1683, uere stormy dayes wth great snow

180

30 Octr 25, 1683 ues also a great storme of snow And continued a great Frost from ye end of Novr till Feb: 1684, The River of Thames at London was frozen yis uinter so y^t Coaths & boothes uere y^{r}on for a moneth or 6 uek*es*.

Edin^r in our own house Moonday ye Tenth day of December 1683 my sister Ionet Dyed of a spoted Feaver on ye 15 day of her sickness at 9 a cloak in ye Morning in ye 31 year of her Age vnmaread And ues lyed yat night in ye Tron
35 Church at 9 a cloak ~~at nig~~ And ye nixt day 11th D^{er} burried in ye Gray-fryers Church yard near Trotters Tomb

D^{er} 26, 1683 This night at 11 a cloak y^r ues a ffire att Ed^r in ye north side of ye street opposit to ye Cross.

This week also Ioseph Ionstou*n* of Hiltou*n* ues murdered by Mr Wm Home
40 brother to ye El of Home at ye Hirsell in ye Merse

Edin 3d March 1684 in ye Upper Pareliament house Sir Wm Sharp < LEFT UNFINISHED >

[f. 3r] Edin^r 30 April 1684 In in Mr Geo: Bannerman Advocat his house in Niddriewynd I ues uitnes to ye marrige of George Anderson mer*chan*t &
45 Barbara Tailz*fer* performed by mr Ro^b Bannerman Minister at Neutou*n* Aled^r Bosuell also uitnes

Edin^r 7 May 1684 being Weddensday a Publique ffast for ye bad weay^r being such a storme as non doe remember of ye like

Edin^r 2^d July {1684} I did se ane Eclyps of ye sun at little after two in ye after-
50 noon ye sun being half obscured and continued till past yre houres

Edin 10 Iuly, 1684 The El of Pearth as Chancellour & Marq. Queensbury as Thesaurer uere recevd wth a very great concourse of people of all sort*es*

Libberton Kirk Sunday ye 3^d of Augt 1684 I toke ye Sacrament by Mr Ro^b Farquair.

55 Edin^r 15 day of Augt 1684 yat morning betwixt 1 & 2 in ye Morning I receivd 2 uoonds in ye street by an vnknown persone on on ye shoulder & ye oy^r in ye left breast Giving no offence

St Andrew 22 Augt 84 y^t night betwixt 10 & 11 dyed D^r Al: Burnet ye ArchB*isho*p a good man

60 Kirkcaldie Fryday ye 3^d of Octo^r 84 Iohn Trotter sett sail at ye Road y^r for France

Mortonhall Moonday 27 Octo[r] 84 at night being a great Frost and storme of snow I did sie great Lightning & heard Thunder

Edin 31 Oct[r] I ues on y[e] Norr Loch and many ues y[r]on 3 dayes before bearing.

[f. 3v] Edin[r] y[e] 13 & 14 Nov[r], 1684, at Leith uynd foot w[th] W:H: incognito.

Notes

Text

Extract only. The text is printed in *Report on the Laing Manuscripts preserved in the University of Edinburgh*, Vol. I (Historical Manuscripts Commission, HMSO, London, 1914), pp. 424–7.

Manuscript

Throughout the text the letter here interpreted as initial, and sometimes medial, *y* (for *th*) could, in fact, be a hasty *th*. That the same letter-shape is followed sometimes by a superscript letter, as in (13) *y[t]*, and sometimes not, as in (34) *yat*, does not help.

The initial *u* in (28) *uere*, (37) *ues*, (46) *uitnes* etc. could be argued to be *w*.

The writer leaves the entry at the foot of f. 2v unfinished (l. 42). The spelling (9) *Burett* is his error for *Burnett* (as in l. 58). The second *in* in l. 43 is either a dittography error or an *m*, an undeleted false start for the *M[r]* that follows.

Glossary

Note: The use of the letter *y* sometimes obscures familiar words: (8) *oyers*, (10) *yen*, (23) *Goodfayer*, (30) *yis*, (47) *weay[r]*, (50) *yre* etc. (though on *y* see note under Manuscript above).

(2)	*Malign*	very contagious
(5)	*Heretors* †	property owners (see note)
(5)	*paroch*	=parish
(6)	*Presbytery* †	local eccelesiastical court
(6)	*conversacioun*	behaviour
(7)	*Ordinar* (also (9) *ordinary*)	Bishop
(7)	*brethren*	fellow-clergy
(8)	*appelld*	=appealed
(9)	*Primat*	Archbishop
(10)	*make faith*	affirm, testify
(12)	*take y[e] Test*	subscribed to the Test Act (see note)
(13)	*power of the Keys*	disciplinary power (see note)
(13)	*intrinsick*	internal
(14)	*prerogative*	(royal) right of direct authority
(15)	*deponed* †	testified
(19)	*conforme to* †	in accordance with
(22)	*uynd* †	lane (in street name)

(23)	*guidsr* †	grandfather (OED GOODSIRE)
(31)	*Coaths*	=coaches
(33)	*spoted Feaver*	fever characterized by spots, ?meningitis
(52)	*Thesaurer* †	Treasurer
(52)	*concourse*	crowd
(63)	*Norr*	=North (in place-name)
(63)	*bearing*	thick enough to skate on

Latin

(10–11)	*in communi forma*	formally
(16)	*ab officio et beneficio*	from his holy orders and his parochial appointment

Explanatory notes

(5) *ye Heretors of his paroch*: Owners of land and property, with financial and administrative responsibility for local and church affairs and property.

(12) *altho yey had take ye Test*: Signing the 1673 Test Act acknowledged the Church of England (at this time also in Scotland) and therefore the authority of the King as Head of the Church. Later in the year the writer records his own Taking of the Test as a prerequisite for his admission as a Notary.

(13) *ye power of the Keys*: Ecclesiastical authority to impose discipline, the phrase derived from Matthew 16:19.

(64) *W:H*: Possibly William Hume (39–40).

Background

The writer is not known, though the Diary tells us his occupation and his strong ties with the Liberton/Mortonhall area on the fringe of Edinburgh, and with certain families. The reference to his sister's burial in Greyfriars churchyard (1. 35–6) fails to lead to a surname, for although there is a contemporary register of burials, the list for December 1683–March 1684 is missing from it. The Journal consists of only five small leaves, with entries 1682–5, recording local and national events alongside personal and family matters.

Topics for linguistic investigation

1. The equivalents in earlier Scots texts of: (10) *proceed*, (12) *which*, (12) *take*, (13) *not*, (15) *whole*, (22) *night*, (23) *being*, (28) *snow*, (29) *great*, (45) *Tailzfer*, (45) *performed*, (48) *such*, (58) *dyed*, (64) *foot*.
2. The pairs: (5) *Libbertoun* and (53) *Libberton*, (12) *was* and (21) *ues*, (21) *next* and (35) *nixt*, (23) *Guidsr* and (59) *good*, (47) *a* and (49) *ane*.
3. Can any correlation be established between subject-matter and the use of Scots linguistic features?
4. Evidence in this text that the late seventeenth century was a period when soon-to-be-lost and recently developed syntax were both available.

Letters

Plate V

Plate V

Text 37
William Godolphin: Cornwall [1532]

Public Record Office Manuscript SP1/70 f. 113r
Edited text 37/3–14

My devte wᵗ dev reuerens yn my most vmbyll wysse don plesyȝth
hyt yowr maysterschyppe to onderstond that I Recevyd yowr gentyll
and lovyng letter to me derectyd datyd the ffurste day off Iune by
yowr sseruaunt herry the tenour ther off was to have ij proper ffelowes
5   ffor the ffett off wrastelyng I have send to yowr maysterschyppe ij off
my hovsold seruauntys whyche yowr seruaunt herry dyd very well know
that yn thes partes thay wer takyn ffor the beste and the suryste ffor that
ffett yowr maysterschyppe may truste them ffor ther truthe I wilbe bovnd
yn as moche as I am worthe ther ynglysse ys not perffett I covdnot
10   macke no fferder seerche to try any better then thos the tyme was so
schorte as your seruaunt herry can aserten yow but yn Contenent a
pone the syȝth off yowr letter y cavsyd wrastelyng gamys to be made
to the entent I wolde have the beste yff hyt wolde plesse yow

Characters: Use of ȝ in (1) *plesyȝth* and (12) *syȝth* (but not in (11) *yow*).
Allographs: Two forms of *r*, the tailed variety in (1) *reuerens*, but see (4) *herry* and (6) *herry*. Long and short *s*, (7) *suryste*, (4) *was*. Characters *u* and *v* not consistently used, (1) *reuerens* and (1) *vmbyll*, but also (5) *have* and (12) *cavsyd*. Final character in numerals realised as *j*, (4) *ij*, and initial *I* in (3) *Iune*.
Capitals: Distinctive capital C in (11) *yn Contenent*.
Abbreviations: No use of superscript forms here. Abbreviation entirely by marks: (2) *maysterschyppe*, (2) *onderstond* and (3) *letter*; (4) *proper* and (9) *perffett*; (6) *seruauntys*; (11) *yn Contenent*.
Punctuation: None.
Typical spellings: (11) *schorte*; (3) *derectyd*, (5) *wrastelyng*, (7) *takyn*, (9) *ys*.
Problems of interpretation: Why does the sequence *-ȝth* have a line above it? In (6 etc.) *seruauntys* do the two minims make an *n* (with abbreviation omitting *u*) or a *u* (with *n* omitted)?

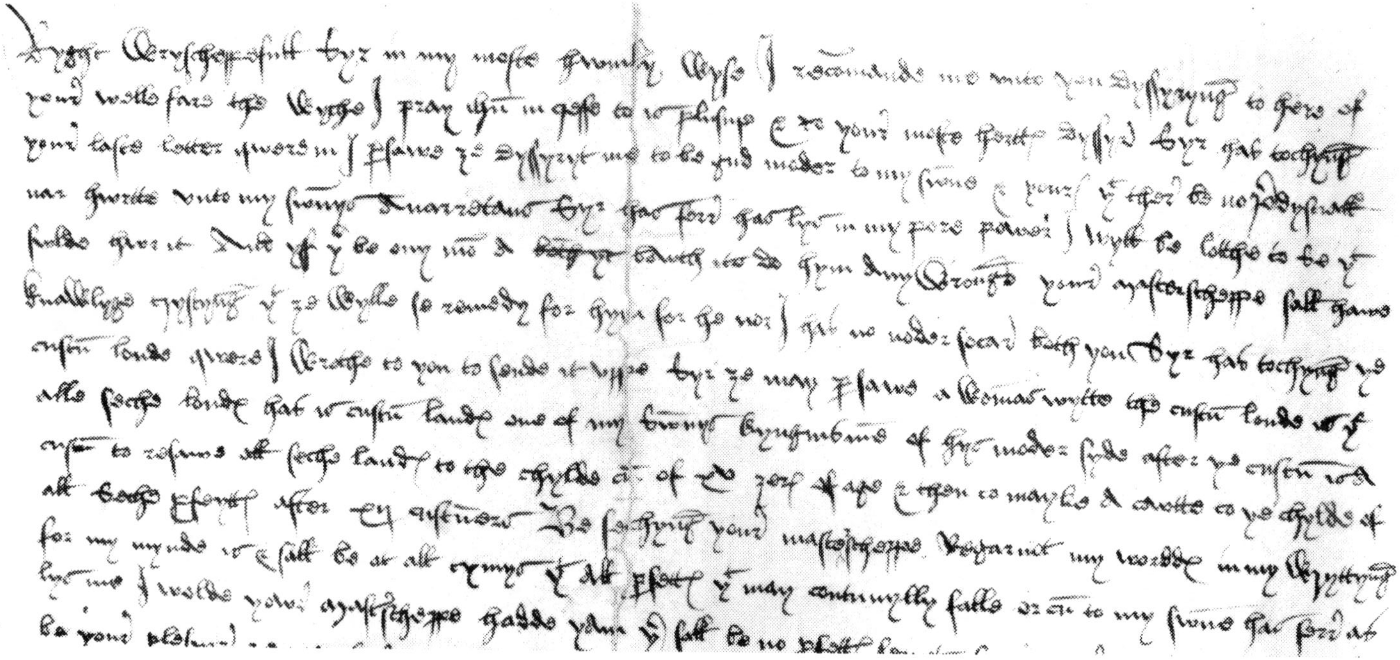

Plate VI

Plate VI

Text 46
Alice Radcliffe; Lancashire [1524]

Lancashire Record Office Manuscript DDKE/HMC2 f. 1r
Edited text 46/3–18

Ryght Wryscheppefull Syr in my moste hwmly Wyse I recom̄mande me vnto you Dyssyrynge to here of
youre welle fare the Wyche I pray iesu in cresse to is plusure & to youre moste herttys Dyssyre Syr has tochynge
youre laste letter qwere in I p*ersawe* ȝe Dyssyryt me to be gud moder to my swn̄e & yourys yᵗ there be no p*re*dysciall
nar hwrtte vnto my swn̄nys Anarretans Syʳ has ferre has lys in my pore power I wyll be lotthe to Se yᵗ
swlde hwr it And yff yer be ony mon A ~~both yt~~ bowth to do hym Any Wronge youre masterscheppe sall hawe
knawlyge trystynge yᵗ ȝe Wylle se remedy for hym for he nor I has no noder socare both you Syr has tochynge yᵉ
custum londe qwere I Wrothe to you to sende it vppe Syr ȝe may p*ersawe* a Womans wytte the custum londe is yᵗ
alle seche londys has is custum landys one of my Swn̄nys kynginsmen of hys moder syde after yᵉ custum is A
custum to resawe all seche landys to the chylde cum of xv ȝerys of age & then to mayke A cowtte to ye chylde of
all Seche p*ro*feyttys after xij custum*er*s Be sechynge youre maste{r}scheppe Regarn̄ot my worddys in my Wryttynge
for my mynde is & sall be at all tymys yᵗ all p*ro*feyttys yᵗ may contunylly falle or cum to my swn̄ne has ferre as

5

10

Characters: Use of ȝ in (9) ȝerys, (3) ȝe (but (7) you). Use of y in (3) yᵗ.
Allographs: Two forms of r, the long-tailed variety in (2) in cresse, (6) trystynge. Long and short s, (3) laste, (6) se, (2) has. Characters u and v possibly used as allographs, but evidence here only from (4) vnto, (7) vppe, as w used in (5) hawe. Final letter of numerals realised as j, (10) xij, and initial i in (2) iesu.
Capitals: Some capitals clearly distinguished from lower case, (10) Be sechynge, (10) Regarn̄ot, but others uncertain (see below).
Abbreviations: (3) yᵗ, also perhaps (4) Syʳ but nothing omitted here. (2) herttys, (8) londys; (5) mon and (7) custum; (5) yer; contrasting abbreviations in (3) p*ersawe*, (3) p*re*dysciall and (10) p*ro*feyttys; traditional abbreviation in (2) iesu.
Punctuation: None.
Typical spellings: (1) hwmly; (3) qwere; (3) gud; (5) sall hawe; (7) londe; (2) has and is.
Problems of interpretation: Uncertainty about capitals, W, D and A. Is an additional –e really being signalled at end of words such as (1) Dyssyrynge?

Introduction to Letters

In 1624 William Paston was away from home, a young student at the University of Cambridge. After his mother had received letters from him she wrote back,

> I doe Like that thow doest inditt thy owne letters thy selfe. for thow weart wont to know how to speake to me. and euen so wold I haue the wright. (48A/10–12).

Like any parent, she wants to 'hear' her son in his letters home. For most people in the sixteenth and seventeenth centuries, letters are substitute speech, a means of communication when the other person is absent. Certainly some writers[1] attempt to develop their letters into a high-style art-form, but the results can be grotesque,

> Acordyng to my dewte coacted, I am (causeys consideryd) to geue yow notycyon of certyn synystrall matters, contrary to oʳ realme of Ynglond, specyally a ʒenst our most armipotentt, perprudentt, circumspecte, dyscrete, and gracyose Soueryng Lord the Kyng.[2]

Like dialogue, letters can be in any mood. Anne Clifton (Text 44) writes to her brother in reproachful anger; Florence Smith (Text 49) makes relaxed jokes to her husband. Moreover, just as conversations can deal with any topic under the sun, so can letters. Some of the letters edited here are about family, others are about business. William Fawnte (Text 39) wants to buy bear-cubs; Elizabeth Betts (Text 45) passes on a medicinal recipe; Ames Steynings (Text 42) is in dire straits at the Siege of Maastricht and begs for financial help; Kate Ashley (Text 47), in prison, protests her innocence; William Godolphin (Text 37) offers to send Cornish wrestlers to Court. The language used in each letter is, naturally, affected by its subject. From Steynings, for example, we have interesting contemporary military vocabulary; in Betts' letter the syntax and punctuation change radically when the recipe is carefully written out. The letter from James Stewart (Text 43), imprisoned for politico-religious activity, is a patchwork of texts from the Bible; Robert Newman (Text 41) tells the story of an assize-judge's treatment of a jury, and quotes some of what was said in court. Sometimes a letter is written without any major topic, but simply to keep contact during absence, and to keep the receiver in touch with all the little things that he or she is missing by being away. While actor Edward Alleyn was on tour, he asked his wife to write to him, and when she was obviously at a loss to know what to say, he offered some suggestions of what he would like to hear from her,

190

mouse you send me no newes of any thinges you should send of yor domestycall matters such things as happens at home as how yor distilled watter proves or this or that or any thing what you will … you send me not word of my garden but next tym you will[3]

The relationship between writer and addressee is, as in spoken dialogue, infinitely variable, and the language of address reflects this. Within the family, easy relationship terms are used, such as *my good childd* (48B/3), *loueinge vncle & Aunt* (42/6) and *dier biely* ('brother') (43/21). A wife begins a letter to her husband with *My Deare Hart* (49B/4). Between aquaintances titles and surnames are employed, *m^r Allin* (39A/3), and *my good Mastresse Cokworthy* (45/2). Where the letter is to a social superior, *yor masterschepe* (38B/3) and *Sir* (38B/4) appear to characterise this, but these terms of address present interesting problems of interpretation. When old Nicholas Glossope petitions Thomas Cromwell, stateman and Privy Councillor, for his support for an increased pension or a place in an almshouse, *yor masterschepe* appears straightforward. But when the same phrase is used (37/4) by William Godolphin, a distinguished gentleman later knighted by Henry VIII, we have to consider whether it may be an early-sixteenth-century courtesy rather than a mark of social inferiority. There is a similar case with two other letters, that of Anne Clifton to her brother (Text 44) and that of Alice Radcliffe to a family friend (Text 46). Clifton starts her letter with *Ryght wyrchypfull brodyre*, then goes on to call him *syr* several times. Is this because of their relative ages? or because of her sex? or is she choosing formal courtesy-terms deliberately because she is so angry with him? The comparable use by Radcliffe of *Ryght Wryscheppe full Syr* and *Syr* suggests courtesy alone, especially when, like Godolphin to Cromwell, she also employs *youre masterscheppe* (46/9).

The selection of second person pronoun between letter-writer and addressee is always worth examining. Non-family relationships are served by *you* forms; within the family, both *thou* and *you* forms appear. it is interesting that in 1518 Clifton, having the choice, keeps to *ʒe* and *ʒow* for her brother. Stewart (Text 43) also has *yow* for his brother, but by 1684 he had virtually no option of *thou*. In 1624 Katherine Paston calls her young son *thou*,

> I pray god blesse the farwell sweet harte to thy owne selfe:/ thy most louinge Mother Katherine Paston (48B/18–19)

Elizabeth Smyth did the same when her son Tom was at University,

> Thus dear Tom with my harty prayers to God to bless thee, now and ever I rest, Thy most loveing Mother Eliza: Smyth[4]

but when, as Elizabeth Gorges, she writes to him when he is an adult she modifies her pronouns,

> Thus prayeing god to blese you with yours I rest
> Your euer loueing mother Eilizabeth Gorges (50A/11–14).

Tom Smyth's wife, on the other hand, writes to him as *thou* with only occasional *you* forms,

I must now bid the godnight ... yet If thou wart in the bed I should kepe my eyes open
I still looke for the this day senight acording to your promies
thine Flo Smyth (49A/10–14).

It is evident from the many verbal parallels within the texts that people were aware of 'right' ways of starting and finishing a letter. So marked is this that when we find a letter that does not share the conventions, such as that of Kate Ashley (Text 47), we have to account for the difference. Several writers set at or very near the beginning of their letter an otherwise unattached past-participle phrase such as,

My dewty done to yor masterschepe (38B/3)
my humble seruice remembered vnto you (42/6)
mey Loue remembered (39/3).

In the first half of the sixtenth century a number of letters open with,

I hartyly recowmawnd me vn to ʒow (44/3)
I Recommande me vnto you in myn herty wyse (45/2–3)
in my moste hwmly Wyse I recommande me vnto you (46/3–4),

and it is interesting to find one letter that indicates the conventionality of the phrase by writing

I lowly Recomend me vnto yowre goodnes &c (38A/3).

Present-day conventions appear by the seventeenth century, such as,

Deere Tom I am glad to heare thou art well (49A/2–3).

Letter writers frequently end with a blessing,

god ... euer have yow yn hys blessyd keppyng w^t longe lyffe and prosperyte (37/20–21)
desiering god to Blesse you in all your Prosedinge (41/35–6)
I pray iesu to preserue you to youre hertys dyssyre (46/40),

and some begin with one,

the Lords blessinge be euermor vpon the (48/2).

The close of a letter can also be signalled with a phrase such as,

Thus biding you harely fare well I end (39A/21),

and the signature is generally preceded by a descriptive phrase,

Youre Pore kinesman ... to Commande in ani thinge I may (41/37–9)
You^r Louing frend to ves (=*use*) (39B/9)
your loweing brodr to dath (43/41–2)
yor owin trewe lover ('friend') (45/40).

Finally, it is at the end of the letter that place and date of writing are usually mentioned,

wrytyn at my powr howsse the xiijth day off Iune (37/21–2)

from my hous at Foston this ix of Nouembar (39B/7–8)
Wryttyn A wynmerly the vij day of October (46/41–2)
Hinton this Ash wensday (49A/15).

Although topics can vary, the conventions of letter-writing also make certain types of comment likely, such as thanks for letters received and comments on news sent in them, and the mention of friends to whom good wishes are sent or from whom greetings are passed on. Common too are comments from the writer about his or her own letter, particularly interesting when the language is under examination. Often they comment that the letter is being written hurriedly,

I am so strayted of time as I can not tary Longer to talke w^t the now (48A/14)
I woll not tary the post no longer … Scrybeled in gret hast in the Mary Rose at Plymouth, half our after 11 at night[5]

If this marks genuine haste the texts may reflect it. Also frequent are self-deprecating comments about one's style or, even more often, handwriting. Sometimes haste is offered as a reason,

I humbly intreate you favorably to accept these rude lines, for I want time either to write or compose them in a more comely forme.
The bearer stayed the writing thereof, which is the cause of my rusticke scriblinge and inditinge.[6]

Mary Queen of Scots, who grew up in France and normally used French, learned to speak, read and write English when she returned to Scotland at the age of nineteen. What she claims to be her first letter in English, written seven years later, includes the plea,

excus my iuel vreitin for y neuuer vsed it afor, and am hestet.[7]

General Tam Dalyell excuses his writing on the grounds that he does not normally write his own letters, but is forced to by considerations of security,

I feir your Lordship sal not be able to Maik sense of my skriblen yet durs I not Imploie an other pen.[8]

In the Early Modern period two groups of people had their letters written for them. Those who employed a secretary because of their rank or extensive correspondence arising from work, but who were capable of writing for themselves if they so wished, and those who lacked the necessary literate skills, so got someone else to do it for them. An illiterate person who needed to send a letter might go to a professional, or find a friend or relative to help. When Joan Alleyn 'wrote' to her husband, her letters were, in fact, written by Alleyn's business-partner Phillip Henslowe, who had married Joan's mother. Roger Lowe (the writer of Text 35) records in his journal that he wrote letters for neighbours,

Ann Greinsworth sent for me … I writt a lettr for her to her brothers then in London.[9]

> Richard Naylor ... was very sad concerninge Elizabeth Seddon acteings to him
> wished me to compose a lettr to her in his name which I did.[10]

He also had problems when he was accused of having added things he was not instructed
to,

> I was much troubled about a business that befell about writeing a letter for Ellin
> Ashton to her son Charles. She related that I writt to have her sonne come down that
> she knew not of which was a false lye.[11]

A Southampton court case of 1652 concerns a man who, accused of writing abuse when
a woman asked him to write a letter in affectionate terms to her sailor husband, admitted
that he had done it deliberately,

> and being asked why he wrote such scurrilous language in the sayd lettre, he sayth that
> the sayd Alice Mitchell bad him write what he this examinate thought fitt & that he
> wrote scurrilous language in the sayd lettre, because the husband of the sayd Alice
> Mitchell had formerly threatend to kill him.[12]

Assuming that most amanuenses were, in fact, trying to do their work honestly, there
remains the question of the extent to which a non-holograph letter is informative about
the language of the sender. Lowe says he is asked to *compose* a love-letter for Richard
Naylor. If that letter had survived, it would be virtually impossible to assign with certainty any element of the language to Naylor, We would not even know by which of the
two men a *Dear heart* or a *the Lord bless and keep you* had been supplied. Obviously, the
spelling of a letter is that of the person who actually puts it on paper. The vocabulary,
syntax and morphology are all uncertain. Sometimes, however, documents have survived which give us clues; the two letters from Nicholas Glossope (Text 38) are a case
in point. Glossope is an old man in humble circumstances, who probably never learned
to write. Moreover, he is almost blind, so that he would not be able to write even if he
knew how to. The two letters from him to Thomas Cromwell are in different hands, and
each is signed in a hand that matches that of its text. Not only are the two hands unlike,
but the letters have totally different orthography and spelling. They must be the work
of two different amanuenses. But they both deal with the same topic and they have very
striking similarities of wording and phrasing, which cannot come from anyone but
Glossope himself. It appears that there are two writers here, each of whom writes down
in detail what he hears the old man say.

The other texts in this section have been selected as examples of what seem to be
holograph documents, in which all features of the language can be attributed to the
sender. It is for this reason that letters are prime documents for addressing the question
of whether at this perod there are differences between the language of men and women.
The texts below have been grouped with this in mind.

Holograph letters are particularly interesting in the information they offer about non-
standard usage, such as the Northern pronunciation suggested in the letters of Clifton
(Text 44) and Radcliffe (Text 46), the East Anglian morphology of Paston (Text 48) and
the spellings of less educated writers of lower social status such as Taster (Text 40) and

Newman (Text 41). Information about the perception of word-boundaries may be found in several letters, and the definition of a sentence as a syntactic unit is an issue in very many.

Someone writing a letter is forced to make all the running in structuring his or her work. No listener asks questions or makes encouraging responses. There is no conversational approach to a topic, other than that which the letter-writer provides. After formal preliminaries, letters have to advance their own theme. Newman launches his with,

> This is to sertifi your Worshipe Conserning The biusnes at our sies ('assize') (41/7–8)

after which he begins to describe it. Taster begins by explaining that he wants support against victimisation,

> I Iohn. taster you^r poore vmble petissener desiriringe your worshipes all. to stande my goode ffrinde in the way of righte (40/1–2)

and then starts his tale. Clifton makes her two main points at the outset by stating that she is writing

> besechyng ʒow to be gud brodyre to me and hayffyng gret maruell of ʒowr vnkyndnes (44/4–5)

and her letter then gives more detail. Fawnte introduces his offer of a bull for sale by establishing what has led him to write to Alleyn,

> I vnderstoode bey a man which came with too Beares from the gardeyne that you haue a deseyre to beyh one of mey Boles (39/3–5).

Letters are usually on one side of a single sheet. At this period no envelopes are used; the letter is folded small, and directions for its delivery written on the outside, formed by the otherwise blank verso side of the sheet. In the texts collected here this endorsement is transcribed before the letter itself, because of the information it provides about the addressee. The small size of letters, combined with the ephemeral nature of most of the material, make it surprising that so many have survived from the Early Modern period. Many, indeed, are lost. Those that we have owe their survival to the receivers rather than the senders. Sometimes we can guess that a letter was kept for a purpose, such as Betts' letter with the medicinal recipe (Text 45). In other cases the person receiving the letter kept business files, Alleyn, for example, with his bull and bear-baiting business (Text 37). Gentry families tended to keep papers of all kinds; John Willoughby, to whom Steynings letter was sent (Text 42) kept his nephew's letter, together with a note of his reply, and when his daughter married into the Trevelyan family, the documents joined their family papers, kept at their family home until they were given into the care of the local county record office. Alleyn's papers are preserved in the College of God's Gift at Dulwich, which he founded. Letters to local officials were filed in Borough records, where they remain, usually at the local record office. Letters sent to state officials, such as Thomas Cromwell, even when they were on personal matters, became state papers, and were therefore preserved in what is now Her Majesty's Public Record Office. Occasionally, letters survive which were never delivered. Among the texts below, the letter from Stewart (Text 43) is filed, with others from him, among the Public Records of Scotland. Since the writer was a political prisoner at the time of writing, they were presumably confiscated. In 1623 a young man who had gone to Virginia wrote home to his parents, going into great detail about the hard and dangerous life he and the other colonists were leading.[13] His letter, together with those of other settlers, was intercepted, as the English authorities wanted to check on the kind of stories which were coming out of Virginia at a time when many were claiming that it was wonderfully successful colony. The outcome for the sender, as with so many of these letters, we do not know.

Notes

1. For an extensive list of texts and discussions of the genre see George Watson (ed.), *The New Cambridge Bibliography of English Literature* (Cambridge University Press, Cambridge, 1974), Vol. I, Section 6.II, 'Letters, diaries, autobiographies and biographies', and Vol. II, Section 5.VI, 'Letters, diaries, autobiographies and memoirs'.
2. Andrew Boord to Thomas Cromwell c.1530; Sir Henry Ellis, *Original Letters Illustrative of English History*, Third Series, Vol. II (Richard Bentley, London, 1846), p. 298.
3. Dulwich College Manuscript, Alleyn Papers I, Item 11.
4. Joseph H. Bettey, *Calendar of the Correspondence of the Smyth Family of Ashton Court 1548–1642*, Bristol Record Society Publications, Vol. XXXV (1982), p. 58.
5. Thomas Howard 1513; Alfred Spont (ed.), *Letters and Papers Relating to the War with France 1512–1513*, Navy Records Society, Vol. X (1897), pp. 160–61.
6. Both from Nehemiah Wharton 1642; Sir Henry Ellis (ed.), 'Letters from a Subaltern Officer in the Earl of Essex's Army, written in the Summer & Autumn of 1642' in *Archaeologia* XXXV (1853), Item xxiv, pp. 310–34.
7. Mary to Sir Francis Knollys 1568; Sir Henry Ellis, *Original Letters Illustrative of English History*, Second Series (Harding & Lepard, London, 1827), Vol. I, p. 253.
8. To the Earl of Lauderdale, September 1666; Edinburgh University Manuscript, Laing I. 139.
9. Journal entry for 17 May 1664; Ian Winstanley (ed.), *The Diary of Roger Lowe* (Picks Publishing, Ashton-in-Makerfield, 1994), p. 28.
10. Journal entry for 1 December 1663; *ibid.*, p. 20.
11. Journal entry for 5 February 1663; *ibid.*, p. 2.
12. S. D. Thomson (ed.), *The Book of Examinations and Depositions before the Mayor and Justices of Southampton 1648–1663*, Southampton Records Series, Vol. 37 (1994), p. 131.
13. Susan Myra Kingsbury (ed.), *The Records of the Virginia Company of London* (Government Printing Office, Washington D.C., 1906–1935), Vol. IV, pp. 58–9 and 62.

Text 37

William Godolphin: Helston, Cornwall [1532]
(Public Record Office Manuscript SP1/70)

[f. 113v] To the worscheypphull Mayst*er* Thomas Cromwell one off the Kyng*ys*
moste honerabyll Covnsell be thys delyv*er*yd

[f. 113r] My devte w^t dev reuerens yn my most vmbyll wysse don plesy3th hyt
yowr mayst*er*schyppe to ond*er*stond that I Recevyd yowr gentyll and lovyng
5   lett*er* to me derectyd datyd the ffurste day off Iune by yowr ss*er*uau*n*t herry the
teno*ur* ther off was to have ij p*r*oper ffelowes ffor the ffett off wrastelyng I have
send to yowr mayst*er*schyppe ij off my hovsold s*er*uaunt*ys* whych*e* yowr
s*er*uau*n*t herry dyd very well know that yn thes p*ar*tes thay wer takyn ffor the
beste and the suryste ffor that ffett yowr mayst*er*schyppe may truste them ffor
10   ther truthe I wilbe bovnd yn as moche as I am worthe ther ynglysse ys not
p*er*ffett I covdnot macke no fferder seerche to try any bett*er* then thos the tyme
was so schorte as your s*er*uaunt herry can as*er*ten yow but yn Co*n*tenent a pone
the sy3th off yowr lett*er* y cavsyd wrastelyng gamys to be made to the entent I
wolde have the beste yff hyt wolde plesse yow to avertes the kyng ys good g*r*ace
15   yff he com*m*avnde me by hys lett*er* or oder wysse to s*er*ve hym yn thys Iernay
I wilbrynge w^t me vj or viijth ther schalbe no bett*er* off ther bygnes com*m*e
owte off that p*ar*tes and at my com*m*yng vppe yowr mayst*er*schyppe schalle
see them all try~~dyd~~ by ffor any man see them doo any ffett and yff ye lycke any
off them bett*er* then thys ij ye schalhave yowr plesu*r* yn thys and yn all that ever
20   I can doo w{h}ylle I leve god wyllyng how eu*er* have yow yn hys blessyd
keppyng w^t longe lyffe and prosperyte wrytyn at my p*o*wr howsse the xiijth day
off Iune

yowrs to hys lytyll power
will*i*am Godolphyn

Notes

Text

An extract from this letter is printed in James Gairdner, *Letters and Papers, Foreign and Domestic, of the Reign of Henry VIII*, Vol. 5 (HMSO, London, 1880), p. 493. It was edited by Sir Henry Ellis (ed.), *Original Letters Illustrative of English History*, Third Series, Vol. II (Richard Bentley, London, 1846), pp. 217–19.

Manuscript

A photograph of lines 3–14 from this document, together with a commentary, appear as Plate V on pp. 186–7 above.

Final *-e* is sometimes reduced to a semi-superscript curl, as in (3) *devte*, (13) *made* etc. A different finishing-stroke added to final *-d* or *-g* is treated as empty, thus (4) *onderstond*, (4) *lovyng*.

Both occurences of the sequence *ȝth*, in (3) *plesyȝth* and (13) *syȝth*, have a line above, possibly noting them as a trigraph for a single sound.

In (18) *tryd̶y̶d* the writer crosses out a first (and a second?) attempt.

Glossary

(2)	*Covnsell*	Privy Council
(6)	*tenour*	gist
(6)	*fett*	=feat
(6)	*proper*	excellent
(12)	*aserten*	=ascertain, tell
(12)	*yn Contenent*	immediately
(14)	*avertes*	=advertise, inform
(15)	*Iernay*	=journey
(16)	*bygnes*	size
(20)	*how*	=who

Background

Undated, but after 1531, when Thomas Cromwell became a member of the Privy Council, and prior to his further preferments, such as Chancellor of the Exchequer (1533), Lord Privy Seal (1536), and Knight of the Garter (1537). Cromwell was executed in 1540.

Sir William Godolphin (c.1490–1570) was a gentleman whose home was at Godolphin, near Helston in the extreme West of Cornwall. He had a distinguished civic and military record, receiving his knighthood in 1544 after the Siege of Boulogne.

His Cornish wrestlers' imperfect command of English is because their first language is Cornish. For an account of the use of the Cornish language in the Early Modern period see Martyn F. Wakelin, *Language and History in Cornwall* (Leicester University Press, Leicester, 1975), especially pp. 88–96.

Topics for linguistic investigation

1. The spellings (3) *vmbyll*, (6) *wrastelyng*, (10) *ynglesse* (11) *perffytt*, (11) *macke*, (14) *avertes*, (20) *how*.
2. A survey of other texts that have *hyt* for 'it'.
3. The distinction between *ye* and *yow*.
4. The form, function and spelling of (3) *plesyȝth*.
5. The syntax of lines 6–9 *I have send … that ffett*.
6. Find out more about the use of the Cornish language at this period.

Text 38

Nicholas Glossope: Banbury, Oxfordshire 1533
(Public Record Office Manuscript SP 1/77)

Text A

[f. 77v] To my Ryght worshyppfull my synlular good master cromell

[f. 77r] Ie*s*u 1533 to master cromell
My dute Remembered I lowly Reco*mend* me vnto yowre good*ne*s &c Sur I sende
yow xij banbery chesses tone hallfe softe & the thother hallfe hard where of I
5   wolde to god they ware w^t xx thowsand pounde vnto yowre mastershyppe Sur
yt ys so that I am of age ammost iiij^{xx} yere I am Inpotent & lame of the gowte
& the crampe w^t sore paynes & wone of my yes ys gone de claro & the other very
feble & nowht Sur I be seke yow In all myte Ie*s*us name that yow woll hellpe me
iiij nobles more of my masters the taylers for I haue iiij nobles payd me eu*ery*
10   yere I thanke yowre mastershyppe & them or ell*es* ij nobles more In a yere to
make evene xls & wolld hellpe me well toward my lyvyn to be ther bedman w^t
a chamber & iiij quart*ers* of coles In a yere a monste the bedmen Sur I haue a
fetherbeed w^t a boullster for master wyll*i*am wellyfed sone that ys at cambreg
at yowre mastershype fyndeng wyll*i*am Sur my mystres yowre mother was my
15   avntte thomas allkokes wyffe of werkworth In the peke was my godmother &
my aunte bothe where for I beshe yowre mastershypp that yowre mastershyp
wyll loke vp on my byll at the Instances of owre blessed lady of svmshon as
shortly as may be & senddyng vn to master hubbulthorne for he wyll sarue
yowre commaundeme{n}tt w^t the master of the feloshypp of my masters the
20   tayllers they to wyll do yowre commaundement w^t {my} m*aster*s the wardyngs

Thus blyssed sentt ~~John~~ þ bapptysse haue yow In kepyng nyght & day amen.

                Be yowre True beedman
                Nycollas. Glossoppe

Text B

[f. 78v] To the right worshipfull and my singuler good mastar m*aster* cromwell
be this lett*er* deliu*er*ed.

199

[f. 78r] My dewty done to yor mast*er*schepe I hartely co*m*mend me vnto yor
goodnesse &c. Sir I dwell with my good lord of lincoln and he is my spetiall good

5   lord I thancke hym for my lord of northfolke sake and my lord of wilshier and
my lord wyndshore thes iij noble men put me to my lord of lincoln, the wiche
I ame Bownd to pray for spetially for my lord of wilshier. Sir sence I was w^t yor
~~mast*er*schepe~~ at yor howse afore Symon day and Iude at the same tyme whan
my lord came frome Banbury, I was neu*er* able to go furth of the howse sence y^t

10   tyme for I ame soo sore pained with gowte and crampe y^t it co*m*pelles me to kepe
my chair for I haue lost one of my eys & I ame lame that I cane not goo. and
therfor s*ir* in the honor of the assumtion of o^r lady co*n*tenew my good master
and vnto the masteres of the Taleres and all the wardanes, yow and they haue
gyven me iiij nobles in the ȝere and it is truly paed god thancke yor

15   mastarschepe. Sir I be sech yow get me iiij nobles more or elles ij nobles and a
cham*er* in the Taleres hall with the bede men and bede women and iiij quarters
of coles in a yere. Sir I will be sech my lord of northfolkes grace thanck yow for
me & my lord off whilshier and my wyndshore, wher apon I ame as trwe a bede
man to yor mastarschepe as any poore man that leues as knowith o^r lord god who

20   haue yow in hys keping eu*er* more. Amen Sir I ame of age allmoost iiij score
yere.

By yor s*er*ua*u*nt nicolis glossope
se^ruant to my lord of lincoln.

Notes

Text

These letters are summarized in James Gairdner, *Letters and Papers, Foreign and
Domestic, of the Reign of Henry VIII*, Vol. 6 (HMSO, London, 1882), pp. 311–12. Text A
was edited by Sir Henry Ellis (ed.), *Original Letters Illustrative of English History*, Third
Series, Vol. II (Richard Bentley, London, 1846), pp. 237–8.

Manuscript

Texts A and B are written in different hands, and in each case the signature is in the same
hand as the text. Because of his age and poor sight, both stressed in his letters, it seems
most probable that neither document is a holograph, but that both are written at his
dictation, using the writing habits and spelling preferences of each amanuensis.

Text A has some problem abbreviations: In (A11) *lyvyn* the final letter has a swirled-
back form which might indicate an abbreviation from *ng*, but since (A12) *bedmen* and
(A17) *svmshon* both have the same elaboration of final *-n*, it has been treated as empty,
and so presents an interesting present participle form. In (A12) *quarters* the expansion
has been made on the basis of a parallel plural in B16, but a case for *quarter*, or even
quartes, could be made. In the traditional abbreviated spellings for (A2) *Iesu* and (A8)
Iesus the manuscript uses the letter *h* Greek-style for *e*.

In (A5) *w^t* must represent 'worth', though used elsewhere (7 etc.) for 'with'

In (A4) *the thother* a line-break between the two words makes it uncertain whether this is a dittographical error, or whether the writer perceives *thother* as a word which may be preceded by a definite article.

Text B has a number of instances of final -*n* and -*m* written with a final stroke extended below the line and curled back. This has been treated as empty, as in (B4) *lincoln*, (B5) *hym*, (B8) *whan*.

Glossary

(A1, B1)	*synlular, singuler*	See note
(A1)	*good mastar* (and B4–5 *good lord*)	patron, benefactor
(A4)	*chesses*	=cheeses
(A5)	*your mastershyppe*	polite form of address to a superior
(A6)	*iiij*ˣˣ (and B20 *iiij score*)	eighty (4 × 20)
(A6)	*Inpotent*	weak
(A7)	*de claro*	(Latin) blind
(A8)	*nowht*	bad
(A8)	*be seke* (and A16 *beshe*)	=beseech
(A9)	*nobles*	gold coins worth 6s 8d
(A11)	*bedman*	beadsman, pensioner living in almshouse
(A12)	*quarters*	measures of weight, the fourth part of a hundred-weight, 28 lb.
(A14)	*at yowre masterschype fyndeng*	at your cost
(A17)	*loke vp on*	regard favourably
(A17)	*byll*	(letter of) request
(A17)	*Instances*	urgent entreaties
(A17)	*svmshon*	=Assumption
(A19)	*feloshypp*	Guild
(A20)	*wardyngs*	=wardens (of almshouse)
(A21)	*baptysse*	=Baptist
(B8)	*Symon day and Iude*	Feast Day of Saints Simon and Jude, 28 October
(B13)	*Taleres*	=Tailors

Placenames

(A4)	*banbery*	Banbury, Oxfordshire
(A13)	*cambreg*	Cambridge
(A15)	*werkworth In the peke*	Wirksworth, on edge of Derbyshire Peak District
(B4)	*lincoln*	Lincoln; *my good lord of lincoln* Bishop of Lincoln
(B5)	*northfolke*	Norfolk
(B5 and B18)	*wilshier, whilshier*	Wiltshire
(B6)	*wyndshore*	Windsor

Explanatory notes

(A1) *synlular good master* (and B1 *singuler*): When *good master* or *good lord* is used with the sense of 'patron, benefactor', it is often preceded by adjectives such as *syngular* or its synonym *spetiall* (B4). See OED SINGULAR.

(A22) *yowre True beedman*: Many letters of the period, especially those to superiors, close with 'your bead(s)man', a phrase signifying 'I will pray for you', based on an almshouse pensioner's duty, indicated in the etymology of the word, to pray for his benefactors. Glossope revitalises the formula, since he hopes to have quarters in an almshouse.

Background

Nicholas Glossope's stated age of 80 sets his birth in 1453.

Glossope's claim (A14–16) to a family link with Thomas Cromwell is ambiguous. It is possible that he is referring to two aunts, one who is Cromwell's mother, and another whose name Cromwell will recognise. Nothing is known of Cromwell's mother, but on the basis of this, the only known reference to her, biographers have suggested that his father, Walter Cromwell, married Glossope's sister. But the letter does not suggest that Glossope and Thomas Cromwell are first cousins. A more remote family connection might exist if we read Glossope as saying that Thomas Cromwell's mother, before (in her thirties) she married Walter Cromwell was first (in her teens) married to an uncle of his, Thomas Allcock of Derbyshire, standing godmother to him in 1453 as a young aunt-by-marriage. If the Baptism was in Derbyshire, then Glossope was presumably born there, although he now appears to be writing from Banbury, Oxfordshire.

The terms on which Glossope stands with Thomas Cromwell include some knowledge of his other dependant relatives. William Wellyfed (A13) was the student-age son of Cromwell's sister Elizabeth, who married William Wellyfed senior. Cromwell also paid for another Wellyfed child, his niece Alice, to be placed in a gentlewoman's household, and he made generous provision for the Wellyfed family, *my poor kinsfolk*, in his will.

Glossope's claims to extensive patronage from various members of the nobility might arise from a lifetime's employment as a tailor. His description of himself as *dwell[ing] with my good lord of lincoln* might relate to the fact that the lordship of the town of Banbury was in the possession of the Bishop of Lincoln, who therefore had a house there, and who was a benefactor of the almshouses which Glossope describes.

Glossope's requests to Thomas Cromwell were moderately successful, as we know from an associated letter (*L. & P. H. VIII*, Vol. VI, Item 698) from Cromwell to the Merchant Tailors, which also supplies more explanation: Cromwell writes that Glossope's existing annuity of 4 nobles was granted by the Tailors at the request of the Archbishop of Canterbury, and that the Tailors are now proposing to withdraw it on the death of the Archbishop (William Warham, died 1532). He asks the Tailors to continue the annuity under his own patronage, and to increase it by 2 nobles.

There was in Banbury the Hospital of St John the Baptist, where a dozen old people lived. It may not be accidental that Glossope's first letter to Cromwell ends (A21) with a reference to the patron saint of this foundation.

Who (A18) *master hubbulthorne* was is unknown.

Topics for linguistic investigation

1. The evidence for pronunciation provided by a comparison between the following spellings in Text A and their equivalents in Text B: (A1) *synlular*, (A1) *cromell*, (A3) *Sur*, (A6) *ammost*, (A7) *wone*, (A7) *yes*, (A11) *lyvyn*, (A8) *be seke* and (A16) *beshe*, (A17) *svmshon*, (A20) *wardyngs*.

2. The evidence provided by the two texts as to the extent to which an amanuensis reproduced the grammatical and verbal style of the person for whom he was writing.

3. The syntax of lines A8–12 *Sur I be seke ... a monste the bedmen* and of lines A14–20 *Sur my mystres yowre mother ... the wardyngs*.

4. The language of deferential address and the relative social status of writer and recipient, especially as shown here and in the letter of Sir William Godolphin (Text 39).

Text 39

William Fawnte: Leicestershire [c.1600]
(Dulwich College Manuscript Alleyn Papers II)

Text A

[Item 38; f. 83v] To mey Verey Louing frend mr Allin at the Palles Gardin at
London giue thes

[f. 83r] m^r Allin mey Loue remembered I vnderstoode bey a man which came
with too Beares from the gardeyne that you haue a deseyre to beyh one of mey
Boles. I haue three westerne boles at this teyme but I haue had verey ell loock
with them for one of them hath lost his horne to the queyck that I think hee will
neuer bee to feyght a gayne that is mey ould star of the west hee was a very esey
bol and mey Bol Bevis hee hath lost one of his eyes but I think if you had him
hee would do you more hurt then good for I protest I think hee would ether
throo vp your dodges in to the loftes oreles ding out theare braynes a genst the
grates so that I think hee is not for your turne. besydes I esteme him verey hey
for my Lord of Rutlandes man bad mee for him xx marckes. I haue a bol which
came out of the west which standes mee in twentey nobles if you so did leyck
him you shall haue him of my faith hee is a marvilous good Boole and coning
and well shapte and but fore eyre ould feine com leine and shuch a on as I think
you haue had but fev shuch fo^r I a seure you that I hould him as good a doble
bole as that which you had on mee last a singgle. and one that I haue played
therty or forrtey coursses be fore he hath bene tacken from the stacke with the
best dodges whiche halfe a dosen kneyghtes had if you send a man vnto mee hee
shall see aney of mey boles playe and you shall haue aney of them <of> reson
if the will pleseure you: Thus biding you hareley fare well I end

> Yours Louing ffrend.
> William. ffawnt

Text B

[Item 40; f. 85v] To my vere Louing frend Mr Allin at the Palis gardin giue thes

[f. 85r] m^r Allin I forgot to talcke with you when I was in london of the beare
which you sayde you had got and I did loock of it but it was a shee cob so my

5   Desire is that you would send me by this carie^r a hee cob and shuch a one as you
think will ~~b~~ mack a great beare and I will send you you^r mony for him by the
next carie^r. and I will be redeye to do you any kyndnes which leyes in mee to do
and so I ~~tacke my~~ bid you fare well from my hous at Foston this ix of ~~yyo~~
Nouembar.

> You^r Louing frend to ves
> William. ffawnte

Notes

Text

Among the Alleyn Papers. Text A was edited by J. P. Collier (ed.), *The Alleyn Papers*
(Shakespeare Society, London, 1843), pp. 31–2, and by George F. Warner in *Catalogue
of the Manuscripts and Muniments of Alleyn's College of God's Gift at Dulwich* (Longmans
Green & Co., London, 1881), p. 82.

Manuscript

No date, but at a time when Alleyn's bear and bull baiting business was well established,
and probably before Fawnte was knighted in 1603.

The marks interpreted here as full-stops within text A are not fully convincing, but
appear to be intended as punctuation.

In A20 text is lost because of a hole; the conjecturally restored preposition might be
in rather than *of*.

Glossary

(A10)	*dodges*	=dogs
(A10)	*loftes*	galleries
(A10)	*oreles*	=or else
(A10)	*ding out*	dash out
(A11)	*grates*	?railings
(A11)	*for your turne*	suited to your needs
(A12)	*man*	servant, employee
(A12)	*bad*	offered, bid
(A12)	*marckes*	monetary unit of 13s 4d
(A13)	*standes mee in*	cost(s) me
(A13)	*nobles*	gold coins worth 6s 8d
(A15)	*eyre ould feine com leine*	See note
(A16 and 17)	*doble (singgle) bole*	bull baited by two dogs at once (by one dog)
(A17)	*on*	from
(A18)	*coursses*	bouts
(A18)	*stacke*	=stake
(A21)	*the*	=they
(A21)	*pleseure*	please

(A21)	*harely*	=heartily
(B3)	*loock of*	look at
(B4)	*carie'*	=carrier, conveyer of letters and goods
(B9)	*ves*	=use (see note)

Explanatory notes

(A7) *star of the west*: The bull is named after the Evening Star, possibly also with a reference to its area of origin.

(A12) *my Lord of Rutlandes man*: Rutland (where the Duke of Rutland had a seat) adjoins the East of Leicestershire.

(A15) *but fore eyre ould feine com leine*: Probably the first four words =*but for our old*, but no satisfactory interpretation has been found for the phrase; Warner, *Catalogue*, points to a parallel phrase in a poem of 1618:

> I found a host, that might lead a host of men,
> Exceeding fat, yet named *Lean* and *Fen*.

(B9) *You' Louing frend to ves*: cf. letters which are signed with 'yours to command'.

Background

William Fawnte (c.1575–1639) was a gentleman, a member of the Faunt family of Foston, a few miles south of Leicester, and evidently engaged in the breeding of bulls and bears. He may be presumed to have been wealthy, since he was knighted (with forty-seven others, mostly from Lincolnshire and Leicestershire) at Belvoir Castle in 1603 as James I made his way south through Leicestershire to take up the English Crown, granting many knighthoods in return for large fees.

The letters were written to Edward Alleyn (1566–1626), actor, theatrical entrepreneur and founder of Dulwich College. With his father-in-law Philip Henslowe he ran a popular and lucrative bear and bull baiting business at Paris (often called 'Palace') Garden, Bankside, London, and eventually (1604) they secured the appointment of Masters of the Royal Game of Bears, Bulls and Mastiff Dogs. Vol. II of the Alleyn Papers at Dulwich College is a collection of Alleyn's correspondence 1598–1626 arising from this work.

Topics for linguistic investigation

1. Words where Fawnte uses the spelling *ey* (e.g. (A5) *teyme*) and their value in charting the progress of the Great Vowel Shift.
2. Ways of spelling other vowels.
3. The grammatical function of (A3) *remembered*, (A6) *that*, (A7) *feyght*, (A8) *hee*, (A13) *did*, (A14) *marvilous*.
4. The use of the prepositions (A3) *bey*, (A13) *in*, (A14) *of*, (A17) *on*, (B2) *with*, (B2) *of*, (B3) *of*.

Text 40

John Taster: Kent 1609

(Centre for Kentish Studies Manuscript QM/SB 830)

[f. 1r] Vnto you^r right worsupples all I Iohn. taster you^r poore vmble petissener
desiriringe you^r worshipes all. to stande my goode ffrinde in the way of righte
for the vicker of goodm*er*sham is agreate enimye of myne for at the tyme of my
mariage hemaried me soe fore as aightene pence woulde goe and then he stayed
5   and would not mary me tell he had ayghteene pence more and soe ever since he
hath Continued and seate all the parrishe againste me and soe muche as it hath
vndon me that iame not able to keepe my wiffe and my children and he would
not Crissen my child when it was borne and sette It from church and would not
Crissen it and then ibeinge soe troubled wente to Master Archdeacon and he
10   dide omite hime to crissen it the nixte Lordes daye and presente lye the childe
being sicke and like to dye my wife seante for him to crissen it and he refuseth
to come but seant his debytye be cause he was compeled to do it there fore he
hath savght all the meanes that he myght to vndo me and the strumpet hath
confesed before the Iustice that Iohn taster hath Layne wth her thre times and
15   the furst time was about the be ginninge of the greate ffroste aforthe nighte or
thre weakes after at the moste was the second time before Last Crismas was
Twelmunte ase she saythe nowe the third tyme was indrayinge of Thissell
hempe that he laye wth her in the ~~ha~~ hempe as she sayth wch was the last
batlematyde and then the Iustice dide demand of her wheather he gave her any
20   ffittes be twene thes tymes and she answered no and then he demanded whether
he gave her any mony and she answeared I thripence and then she answeared
he gave her threpence in hemsted carvet and then he de manded to knowe
whether he ever asked her wheather she weare wth child and then she answeared
no by her one confesion before the Iustice wee cancounte but ayghte and
25   Twenty weakes Master varnam conffessed be fore mistris brodnix that the
strumpet had line wth another but it was twelmunt agoo Last Crismas but ~~the~~
Master varnam willnot be knowe howe it is and this hardelye he deales with
mee./

Notes

Text

From Quarter Sessions papers (1606–1610) of Maidstone Borough Records. The text
has not been edited before.

Manuscript

(2) *desiriringe* is probably an instance of dittography.

Glossary

(1)	*worsupples*	=worshipfuls (see note)
(1)	*petissener*	=petitioner
(4)	*stayed*	stopped
(6)	*and soe muche as*	=insomuch as
(7)	*vndon*	ruined
(10)	*Lordes daye*	Sunday
(11)	*like*	likely
(14)	*Iustice*	Justice of the Peace
(16–17)	*Last Crismas was Twelmunte*	the Christmas before last (*twelmunte* =twelve-month, year)
(17)	*drayinge*	=drawing, harvesting
(17–18)	*Thissell hempe* †	See note
(19)	*batlemetyde*	=Bartholemewtide, Feast Day of St Bartholemew, 14 August
(19)	*demand*	ask
(20)	*ffittes*	sexual encounters (see note)
(21)	*I*	=aye, yes
(24)	*one*	=own
(26)	*line*	=lain
(27)	*be knowe*	acknowledge

Local placenames

(3)	*goodmersham*	Godmersham, between Canterbury and Ashford
(22)	*hemsted carvet*	Not identified

Explanatory notes

(1) *you' right worsupples*: wording considered appropriate for addressing the magistrates at the Quarter Sessions.

(9–10) *he dide omite hime to crissen it*: probably 'he [the vicar] neglected to christen it' with unusual use of a reflexive, though one would expect the clause to be introduced by *but* rather than *and*. But it is possible that Taster is confusing *omit* and *oblige*, and that he means 'he [the Archdeacon] made him [the Vicar] christen it'.

(17–18) *Thissell hempe*: Taster is almost certainly trying to put into writing the common name *fimble hemp*. Hemp was cultivated for its fibres, from which coarse hempen cloth could be woven. The sex of the male and female plants was confused, resulting in the male plants being termed *fimble* (i.e. female) *hemp* and the female plants *carl hemp*. They were gathered at different times, fimble hemp being reaped in July/August. See OED FIMBLE and HEMP.

(20) *ffittes*: This sense not clarified in OED, but for its colloquial use see Chaucer, *Wife of Bath's Tale*, Prologue l. 42.

Background

The reason why Taster and the Vicar of Godmersham are totally at odds is not established, though Taster's avoidance of 'Sunday' in favour of *Lordes day* could reflect militant Puritanism. Since the complaint about refusal to baptize was taken, as appropriate, to the Archdeacon, it is interesting that the continued altercation has now shifted from the Church court to the secular authorities at the Maidstone Quarter Sessions.

Topics for linguistic investigation

1. The evidence relating to the pronunciation of consonants in the spellings (1) *vmble*, (6) *and*, (8) *Crissen*, (17) *Twelmunte*, (19) *batlematyde*, (25) *varnam*.
2. The evidence relating to the pronunciation of vowls in the spellings (5) *tell*, (10) *nixte*, (15) *furst*, (16) *weakes*, (17) *drayinge*, (22) *thripence*, (24) *one*, (27) *this*.
3. The writer's perception of what constitutes a word, as exemplified by (4) *hemaried*, (7) *iame*, (9) *ibeinge*, (17) *indrayinge*, (24) *cancounte* and by (15) *be ginninge*, (15) *aforthe nighte*, (22) *de manded*, (25) *be fore*, (27) *be knowe*.
4. The sentence as a syntactic unit in this letter.
5. Compare Taster's way of dating past events with those used in other texts.

Text 41

Robert Newman: Newport-Pagnell, Buckinghamshire 1617

(Dulwich College Manuscript Alleyn Papers III, Item 75)

[f. 102v] To Mr Edward Allyen Esquier Dwelling in dullige deliuer This with spede

This letter most be deliuered to on m^r Willyam laton nere the Eex Change at the signe of the maydenhead and sent to dullidge to the aforesaid

5   [f. 101r] Sallutertation in the lord most louing and kinde m^r Allyen & Mistris
     Allyen with all vmbell Thanckes for my good Cheare and your grete Paynes &
     loue shoued vnto vs This is to sertifi your Worshipe Conserning The biusnes
     at our sies That my Lorde Cheife Gestis sat on the Geayle deliuerri and thankes
     be to god wee had good suckces in our besnes as wee Coulde wishe or desier wee
10   giue god thankes And to sertifi your worshipe More at large our besynes was
     the first that was Called vpon thare and when the Charge was giuen before the
     grante Iuri went our Conceler moued our Case and desiered that my lord and
     the Iuri Cho{u}lde heare our witnes Excamened be fore the wente and so the
     ware then my lorde sayd vnto the Iuri the case is playne goo forth so the went
15   and stayed away a grete whill and my lord sente for them and when the Cam in
     the sayde the Could not agree then my lord was anggry with them and sayd
     what Corrupt felloues are yee is not the mater playne in nought I will finde yee
     all and mack you anser it in the ster Chamber then on of the Contrari side sayd
     my lorde wee are a lenne of vs finde it and tene stand ag out then my lorde sayde
20   Call them ouer that I may Tacke thare names that are so Corrupt then sayd the
     forman this Cock was Euer hellen to be a honist man vntill this myshap befell
     and that my brother was a hout quarellsom fello then my lord Rise vp & sayde
     Thou art a palt{ri} Corrupt fello thy selfe get the of of the Iuri and let the next
     be for man so the wente forth and brought in willfull murther and then olde
25   Cock and his other sones Cried forth for marci vnto vs & set all thare frendes
     and ours vnto vs to desier vs by all meanes that wee wolde be pleased and the
     wolde thinck & ackknollig thare selles euer beholding vnto vs for his life if wee
     wolde Cese theare and not proceequit the lawe ani further & so vppon som
     Considderatio wee dide yellde/ And for the Constabell he was Commited at the
30   exeamennation of The witnes and lay at the Ieler house vntill the marro and
     then hee was finde at Twenti Nobles thus had wee Comfort in our heui bisnes

thankes be to god and to youre furtherance in all our prosedinge/ & I wolde
haue Com vp to Certifi youre worshipe but that I ame not yet prouided ase I
wolde bee thare fore I ame boulde to troubbell you with these fewe lines vntill
35   I Com vnto you No more vnto you at this tim but desiering god to Blesse you
in all your Prosedinge; from Newporte the 27 of Iuly 1617

> Youre Pore kinesman Robert
> Newman to Commande <in>
> ani thinge I <may>

40   My father Allyen & my mother & my brother Archbould & my brther Edward
Allyen with all vmbell ~~Commendacion~~ {Thanckes} vnto your worship

Notes

Text

Among the Alleyn Papers. Most of the text appears in George F. Warner, *Catalogue of
the Manuscripts and Muniments of Alleyn's College of God's Gift at Dulwich* (Longmans
Green & Co., London, 1881), pp. 105–6.

Manuscript

Lines 38 and 39 have conjectural restoration because of a hole in the manuscript.

In view of Newman's spelling there are no grounds for regarding (3) *Eex Change* or
(40) *brther* as slips of the pen, though they may be.

In line 31 the writer presumably started to writs *stand against*, but changed his mind.

Glossary

(3)	*the Eex Change*	the Royal Exchange, London
(3–4)	*at the signe of*	at an inn named
(6)	*good Cheare*	encouragement
(6)	*Paynes*	exertions
(8)	*sies*	=assize
(8)	*Geayle deliuerri*	Gaol delivery (see note)
(10)	*More at large*	in greater detail
(12)	*grante Iuri*	Grand Jury (see note)
(12)	*Conceler*	counsellor-at-law
(12)	*moued*	=moved, pleaded
(17)	*in nought*	=enough
(17)	*finde*	=fine
(19)	*a lenne*	=eleven
(19)	*finde it*	declare a crime has been committed
(19)	*stand out*	refuse to agree
(20)	*Call them ouer*	read out their names
(21)	*hellen*	past participle of *hold* 'consider'

(24)	*for man*	=foreman (of jury)
(27)	*beholding*	=beholden, indebted
(28)	*proceequit the lawe*	(= prosecute) take legal proceedings
(29)	*for*	as for
(30)	*marro*	=morrow, next day
(31)	*Nobles*	gold coins worth 6s 8d.
(33)	*prouided*	ready
(40)	*father*	father-in-law
(40)	*brother*	brother-in-law

Placenames

| (1) | *dullige* | Dulwich, Greater London |
| (36) | *Newporte* | Newport Pagnell, Buckinghamshire |

Explanatory notes

Legal procedures and terminology

Serious or complex legal cases were heard at **Assizes** (as opposed to Quarter Sessions). **Justices** were sent in pairs on circuits covering the country, assizes at Aylesbury, County town of Buckinghamshire, being part of the Midland Circuit. If *my Lorde Cheife Gestis* means 'the Lord Chief Justice' it is not explained why he himself is on circuit here. But Warner, *Catalogue*, suggests that this is Sir Henry Montague, Justice of the King's Bench, or else Sir Henry Hobart, Chief Justice of the Common Pleas. Parties would be advised and represented in Court by a **Councillor-at-Law**.

Assizes were the occasion of **Gaol Delivery**, that is clearing the county gaol of prisoners by bringing them to trial. A **Grand Jury**, which could have up to 23 members, was a jury of enquiry, not of trial. It examined whether there were sufficient grounds for a bill of indictment, and if at least 12 of the jurymen found this to be the case, a criminal trial would take place, with a Petty (i.e. trial) Jury to decide guilt or innocence. A Grand Jury might also be called to examine whether a verdict reached by a Petty Jury in a criminal trial was a false or corrupt one.

It is unclear from Newman's letter which function this Grand Jury is carrying out. It appears that the case concerns a brawl between someone called Cock and Newman's brother, resulting in the brother's death. One would therefore expect proceedings to have begun with the local Coroner and a Coroner's Jury. When this Grand Jury declares (under pressure) that there is a case of wilful murder to be answered, this could be reversing an earlier decision from a lesser court, and it clearly involves the attachment of blame to a corrupt Constable. A criminal trial (of Cock) should follow, but the decision whether or not to proceed with this seems, strangely, to rest with the Newman family, as relatives of the murdered man.

The threat (18) to bring a **Star Chamber** case against the jurors is because the Court of Star Chamber dealt with jurors' contempt of court. On Assizes at this period see the Introductory Volume of J. S. Cockburn, *Calendar of Assize Records: Home Circuit Indictments Elizabeth I and James I* (HMSO, London, 1985), especially Chapter V.

(13) *the*: Pronoun 'they', either referring to he Jury 'they were [made to hear the witness]' or to witnesses 'they were [examined]', in which case *witnes* represents a plural form.

Background

On Edward Alleyn, see notes to Text 39. Alleyn was by this time over fifty, a man of substance and standing, living on his Manor at Dulwich.

Robert Newman presents himself to Alleyn as a *pore kinesman*. Edward Alleyn's family came from Buckinghamshire, his father, Edward Alleyn senior, moving to London from Willen, and having two brothers, Thomas and William. Grandson to one of these brothers was another Edward Alleyn, a glover in Newport Pagnell, and Robert Newman married his daughter. He is therefore only a fairly distant relative to the actor, and also is two generations on, being son-in-law to Alleyn's cousin's son. However, family links have evidently been maintained, and Newman's letter is bringing Alleyn up to date in regard to a situation he has already shown concern over. In lines 40–41 Newman passes on the thanks of his in-laws. There is a further letter, dated 1623/4, from Newman to Alleyn, again mentioning his father-in-law (Warner, *Catalogue*, Book III, Item 95).

Topics for linguistic investigation

1. Put present–day punctuation into lines 15–24. Are there any problems?
2. Grammatical arguments for distinguishing the look-alike words in (2) *on* and (8) *on*; (11) *thare* and (27) *thare*, (17) *finde* and (31) *finde*, (23) *get the of of the Iuri*; (23 first instance) *the* and (23 second instance) *the*.
3. The evidence relating to pronunciation in the spellings (1) *Allyen*, (6) *vmbell*, (8) *sies*, (8) *Geayle*, (9 and 10) *bes(y)nes*, (17) *in nought*, (17) *finde*, (19) *a lenne*, (27) *selles*, (26) *desier*.
4. The forms (17) *yee*, (21) *hellen*, (22) *Rise*, (27) *thare selles*, (30) *Ieler*.
5. The syntax of (20) *that I may Tacke thare names that are so Corrupt*; (26–8) *to desier ... Cease theare*; (31) *thus had wee Comfort in our heui bisnes*; (33) *but that I ame not yet prouided*.
6. The use of *thou* and *you* personal pronouns.

Text 42

Ames Steynings: Somerset (Maastricht) 1632
(Somerset Record Office Manuscript DD WO 54/1/65)

[f. 2v] To the wor*ship*f*u*ll his Lovinge vncle m*r* Iohn Willoughby of Peehembury
Esq giue these I pray you in Devon nere Hunnington

Leaue this letter in London to bee deliu*er*ed to Exon Carrier att the signe of the
Starr in Bread Street to be left with m*r* moses Sarell of Hunnington att the signe

5   of the Angell to bee deliu*er*ed as a boue saide

[f. 1r] Loueinge vncle & Aunt my humble seruice remembred vnto you, with
many thackes for your extraordinary kindnesses towards vs, these are to certifye
you of our healths as yet wee haue passed throught a great many miseries both
by sea & Land since wee Left England and are now in great want for Lacke of

10   victualls all things are att such a dearth in o*r* Leager that the states meanes is
not able to find vs halfe the weeke, had not I brought with mee some money out
of Garisson for the which I was glad to Lumber my Trucke {w*th*} my apparell,
I had not wroten vnto you att this time, it was never knowen to the olddest that
now Liues in our army such Lamentable dearth for all things many a gentleman

15   which never tooke spad in there hands are now constraned to worke in the
Trenches and venter there Liues in the mouth of the cannon only for meanes
to keepe them from staruinge and besides haue spent all that ever they could
make, & many of them haue Lost there Liues if wee gett not masestreet the
sooner the prince of Orenge will haue but a smale Army for wee haue Lost many

20   of o*r* Commande{rs} & soldiers allready wee are soe stronge intrinch befor the
towne that the enimy is not able to beat vs out except his power {bee} invincible,
there is Late{ly} come downe to the army an enimy who is tiled magna de
sancta crusia who thinckes to releeue the towne with 15 thousand foot and
horse, wee haue had hard duety of it ever since and the prince him selfe is euery

25   night ridinge about the army, the enimy hath Lost many of his people all ready
and many wee haue taken prisoners and is not yeat instinch the prince is very
busye with him and keepes him dooinge night & day & the towne likewise the
greatest mischiufe that the enimy hath done vs is the stoppage of o*r* prouision
w*ch* wee hope will not be Longe wee haue taken twoo townes allready from the

30   king <of> sp{a}ine vandula and rowmount with the Lost of a feu men, there
was but one man of note Lost and that graue Earnest a braue Commaunder &

214

cosen to the Prince whose sonne hath now his place those townes wch are taken and now beseeched are in Luke Land wher<e> they haue been quiett this 50th yeeres it is a goodly Country for corne & fruit but now much spoiled by vs and

35 the enimy who hath Lately new forces com to releeue {him} both of foot & horse to the number of 15 thousand more and they haue giuen out a brauado that they will reliue the Rower before the will depart they are far stronger in horse then wee are had not wee ben instrinch it would haue been a bloudy day for vs befor this time wee doe vndermine day and night to worke vnder the walls

40 and wee are com within a stones cast of them it is a stronge towne & the walls are of stone and of a great hith and strong not to be scalled, wee haue Lost more men before it allready then there {were} at the taken in the Buse wee haue been this 8 weekes before it to the greefe of many a thousand soildier who haue endured a ~~great~~ great {deale} of misery, for wee by day and night in o^r armes

45 and can hardly haue two howers rest in fower and twenty if the king of spaine doe Lost this towne wch is Called masestreete wch now wee doe begeager then may the kinge of Swaden easily Come into fflanders wth his army good vncle it is a great deale of misery that a soildier doth endure besides dange<r> every minight of his Life if one man or two should endure alone & not thousands

50 there would be noe wares I and my sonn haue o^r share with the rest, wherefor I be seech you good vncle to send vs over fower or fiue pounds wth all the convenience you may for the redeeminge of our Truckes wch are now in Lumber with our Clothes wch wee shall Loose if you send not vnto vs, and then wee are quite vndone

Notes

Text

Extract only. Among the papers of the Trevelyan family. The text was edited by Sir Walter Calverley Trevelyan and Sir Charles Edward Trevelyan (eds), *Trevelyan Papers*, Part III, Camden Society, Original Series, Vol. 105 (1872), pp. 180–85.

Manuscript

The spellings (7) *thackes* and (12 and 52) *Trucke* are strange, but are almost certainly intentional; they do not result from an invisible or omitted abbreviation-stroke for *n*, since none such are used elsewhere.

In (22) *Lately* the inserted {*ly*} might be to improve the form, but appears to replace an earlier ending covered by a blot.

The conjectural restorations in lines 30, 33 and 48 are because of letters lost at the edge of the page.

Glossary

(3)	*carrier*	carter transporting goods and mail
(3 and 4)	*att the signe of …*	at the inn called …
(7)	*certifye*	inform

(10)	*victualls*	food supplies
(10)	*dearth*	scarcity
(10)	*Leager*	camp (of besieging force)
(10)	*the states*	the Government of the Netherlands
(11)	*find*	provide food for
(12)	*Lumber*	pawn (vb) (see note)
(12)	*Trucke*	=trunk (see note)
(15)	*constraned*	forced
(16)	*venter*	=venture, risk
(19)	*but*	only
(20)	*intrinch* (also (26) *instinch* and (38) *instrinch*) entrenched	
(21)	*except*	unless
(22)	*is tiled*	=is styled, named
(23)	*thinckes*	intends
(30)	*Lost*	=loss
(31)	*graue*	Count
(33)	*beseeched*	=besieged
(34)	*spoiled*	despoiled
(36)	*brauado*	boast (see note)
(37)	*the*	=they
(39)	*vndermine*	dig under the walls
(42)	*taken in*	=taking in, capturing
(43)	*before*	in front of, besieging
(46)	*Lost*	=lose
(46)	*begeager*	=beleaguer, besiege
(50)	*wares*	=wars
(52)	*Lumber*	pawn (n.)
(54)	*quite*	totally
(54)	*vndone*	ruined

Placenames

In Devon:

(1)	*Peehembury*	Payehembury
(2)	*Hunnington*	Honiton
(3)	*Exon*	Exeter (abbreviation)

In the Low Countries:

(18)	*masestreet*	Maastricht
(30)	*vandula*	Venlo
(30)	*rowmount*	Roermond
(33)	*Luke Land*	Luik (Liège) territory
(37)	*the Rower*	the Ruhr
(42)	*the Buse*	Bois-le-Duc

People

(19)	*the prince of Orenge*	Prince Frederick Henry, Stadtholder of Orange, and commander of the besieging army
(22–3)	*magna de sancta crusia*	The Marquis of Santa Cruz, commanding a relief force to support the besieged Spaniards
(31)	*graue Earnest*	Count Earnest of Nassau

Explanatory notes

(7–8) *These are to certifye you*: A frequent introductory phrase in letters, and usually, as here, with plural pronoun and verb.

(12) *Lumber*: OED quotes seventeenth-century examples of *lumber* (from earlier *lombard*) as a noun (see line 52 below), but as a verb from 1812 only.

(12 and 52) *Trucke*: In view of the context and of the parallel spelling (7) *thackes* 'thanks', this is almost certainly 'trunk', rather than the alternative reading 'truck, goods for sale'.

(33) *50ᵗʰ*: The addition of the superscript *th* is inaccurate but not uncommon.

(36) *brauado*: Although OED records the phrase *to giue a brauado* 'to offer battle by making a display' the context does not suggest that this is intended here.

Background

Religious and political discord in mainland Europe led to fighting in both the sixteenth and seventeenth centuries, and many Englishmen went to take part. The Siege of Maastricht was an action in the final stages of the Dutch War of Independence against Spanish rule. The Dutch army besieging the town included five regiments of English volunteers and three of Scots. Steynings and his son were in the regiment commanded by Lord Vere.

Maastricht was of strategic importance, as were the other towns mentioned here, as controlling the Maas valley (see lines 45–7), and it had been had been in Spanish hands since 1579 (see line 33), when it had been captured and many townspeople massacred.

The contemporary published report, *A Iournall, Of the taking in of Venlo, Roermont, Strale, the memorable Seige of Mastricht, the Towne & Castle of Limburch vnder the able and wise Conduct of his Excie the Prince of Orange, Anno 1632 … Compiled together by Capt. Henry Hexham quartermaster to the Regiment of the Lord Generall Vere* (Delft, 1633), gives a day-by-day log of the siege and presents a picture of an arduous and dangerous action. It is striking that although the near-starvation of the besieging force, which Steynings' letter stresses, is never stated, yet mention is made each time supplies are successfully brought in or captured.

Ames Steynings dated his letter 10 July 1631, but the year was 1632.

Ames Steynings was the son of Robert Steynings, Vicar of Broadclyst, Devon, 1589–1631, and third son of Philip Steynings of Holnicott, Somerset. John Willougby married Roberts sister (Ames' aunt). From other parts of the letter we learn that Steynings had a younger son being cared for by the Willoughbies while he and his elder son were in the Netherlands. From other letters it is clear that John Willoughby was much relied on by all his relatives for support and practical help. A note by him at the end of this letter records that he responded to this particular plea by sending money.

Topics for linguistic investigation

1. Information about pronunciation to be derived from the spellings (2) *Hunnington*, (8) *throught*, (16) *venter*, (30) *Lost*, (33) *beseeched*, (37) *reliue*, (41) *hith*, (42) *taken*, (49) *minight*.
2. The forms (10) *is*, (13) *had*, (13) *wroten*, (17) *them*, (20) *stronge*, (20) *intrinch*, (21) *bee*, (23–4) *foot and horse*, (25) *hath* alongside (27) *keepes*.
3. The constructions (11) *halfe the weeke*, (43) *this 8 weekes*, (43) *many a thousand soildier*, (45) *fower and twenty*, (49) *one man or two*.
4. How possible is it to define the circumstances in which the writer employs *do-support*?
5. Re-write lines 11–19 (*had not I ... a smale Army*) in present-day syntax, and discuss the changes involved.
6. The correlation between source-languages and dates of borrowing in items of vocabulary which relate to military matters.

Text 43

James Stewart: Scotland 1684

(Scottish Record Office Manuscript PC12/9A, Item 60)

[f. 1v] for Iohn Stort Thess

[f. 1r] ffor may very dier and lowieng broder hopien in the lord from may swiet
prieson & Ern pelies Edr tolboth the :5: deay of aGowst 1684

Dier broder I aknoleg may falt in not sendien yow a lien er now bot I sel seow
5   yow the reson grfor I did forbier I hef met w^t many tostiens in the fornies as
efer apowr theng met w^t gch is awondre to all yt sies & hers of the desponsesion
bot it meay be it be onknon to yow and many mo of owr dier friends bot the
weay I sell mek knon to you so yt if ye hef ocesion ye meay let it be knon to odrs
for it is of Great nesery yt so we meay not pot wrong mesconstrokesions upon
10   the nobell Cas & Gloriows cros & weays of dieliens of owr lord Iesows Chriest
gch it was no small comfort to mie to her of the nobell comendesion ye pot on
his cros bien yet not Com to the fornies: & sowr I am if Efery her of may hed
cowld send bak acomendesion of him & his swiet Cros & weys & dieliens of him
owt of the fornies to yow or any of his powr falowrs this deay it is may deowty:
15   now may dier biely I thenk it meay be no smal\<l\> Comfort to yow or any yt is
mekien yowr desayr redi\<r\> to choys afleckesions w^t the pepll of God yn to
InGoy the plesors of sien for aseson & reder to be ador keper in heawen yn to
dwall in the tent*es* of sien to her of his powr & weys of dielien w^t mie apowr
theng gch the liek was nefer hard nor sien her tofor in thes land w^t any the lieks
20   of mie bot not onto os not onto os I seay not onto os bot onto him be all Glory
& Ewerlastien pres: now dier biely the metr and to let yow wot gt is may minien
I hef ben :3: tiems befor as they called ym the lords of Iwestesery till aresefed
the sentens of death & I was owned of the lord so as they war pot to confowsieon
conser\<n\>ien powr mie yt they wost not gt to dow w^t mie thes thy sead in may
25   own herien: so they tok yt weay & Gef to mie reprayfell on after anodr & yn
they caled in :22: wotneses aGenst mie & may comperenc befor ym sowd aben
on the :4: deay of aGowst thes sam sead month & now they hef Gefen anoder
:8: deays deliey so it being all of the lord & notheng in mie or any hand I hef
{in} it I desayr yrfor to be at sobmesion gch is not esiey to atien to Glory to him
30   yt hes keped mie be his word & trowths as ~~le~~ from felien derekely in any theng
Glory to him yr is all yt the beliefr want*es* is in him & hie now in owr deay meks

[f. 1v] Owt yt word I woll mek the fowlies ons to confownd the weays now dier
biely I am no mor werien of his swiet cros yn the ferst day I com in to may pelies
Glory to him it is him self yt meks it so nor nefer lowt the thoughts of it entr in

35   may mind now I sell seay nomor at present bot desayrs yow & all to be seriows
& mek Good ws of presios tiem & proper for sorer trayles as ye sie yr dely
abowndin & oyt Gres meay mor sowper abownd now dier biely I recomend you
to him the lord Iehowah the God of eserall who can & woll cery his pepll throw
fayr & watr to aland yt flowth w^t melk & hony gr the Glory of God & his son

40   Iesows christ & the melody of enGls & the sonGs of mosies & & the lam & the
speriets of Gost men med parfiet seseth not fer well in the lord so I rest yowr
lowieng brodr to dath

may lowf to yow
and Robert Goodien
45   and Peter Erd peter desayrs two liens from yo{w} and marGret forst
and tomes wod tho onknon to yow
also all owr lowff to margret forest
and espesly mien
and if tiem pormet I woll wriet to yow at anoder ocesion

50   Yr was som of owr friends sent to sie and was seped & after they hef reculed
bak pedrick waker to preson for his lief be all aperens

Notes

Text

The text was edited in Henry Paton (ed.), *The Register of the Privy Council of Scotland,*
Third Series, Vol. IX (1684), (HMSO, Edinburgh, 1924), pp. 269–70.

Manuscript

For the use of capital and lower-case *g* see notes below.

Although the writer consistently uses superscript *t* in *w^t*, other short forms do not
have superscript letters, thus *ym, yn, yr, yt* for them, *than, thair, them, that,* and *gch,
gr, gt* for *quhich, quhair, quhat.* Without the use of superscript (4 etc.) *not* is identical
with the Southern English form, whereas in other Scots texts *no^t* is a short-form for
nocht.

Letters conjectured as having been cut off at the edge of the page have been restored
in (15) *redir* and (24) *consernien,* but both restorations could be challenged.

Glossary
Familiar words obscured by spelling

(3)	*Ern*	=iron
(3)	*pelies*	=palace
(4)	*seow*	=show

(5)	*tostiens*	=testings
(10)	*dieliens*	=dealings
(13)	*sowr*	=sure
(17)	*sien*	=sin
(17)	*reder*	=rather
(22)	*Iwestesery*	=Justiciary (see note)
(22)	*aresefed*	=I received
(26)	*sowd aben*	=s(h)ould have been
(29)	*atien*	=attain
(30)	*felien*	=failing
(32)	*fowlies*	=foolish
(32)	*weays*	=wise
(33)	*werien*	=wearying
(34)	*lowt*	=let
(36)	*proper*	=prepare
(37)	*oyt*	=O that
(38)	*eserall*	=Israel
(41)	*Gost*	=just
(41)	*seseth*	=ceaseth

Other items

(3)	*Edr tolboth †*	Edinburgh gaol
(5)	*grfor*	=quhairfor, why
(5)	*did forbier*	=did forbear, did not do so
(6)	*desponsesion*	=dispensation, happening specially sent by God
(9)	*nesery*	=necessary (n.), necessity
(15)	*biely †*	=billy, brother
(17)	*for aseson*	=for a season, for a while
(19)	*her tofor*	=heretofore, before now
(21)	*metr*	=matter, main topic
(23)	*owned*	acknowledged as accepted
(24)	*wost*	knew
(25)	*reprayfell*	=reprieval, a reprieve
(26)	*comperenc †*	=compearance, appearance in court
(29)	*at sobmesion*	content to submit to God's will
(31–2)	*meks Owt*	accomplishes, fulfils
(41)	*rest*	remain
(50)	*seped*	=scaped, escaped
(50)	*reculed †*	taken

Explanatory notes

(3) *aGowst*: This strange use of a capital *g* occurs several times here. To represent the consonant [g] (or [dʒ] in (40) *enGls*) the writer uses the capital both initially, as in (9) *Great*, and medially, as here and even in (40) *sonGs*. Lower-case *g* is reserved for word–

final position, as in (6) *theng* and present-participles such as (2) *lowieng* (though frequent spellings with *-ien* suggest that the [g] has been lost). When used word-initially here, lower-case *g* is employed instead of the *q* which appears in other Scots texts, where it is a short way of writing the sequence *quh* + whatever vowel is appropriate to the word. Thus (5) *grfor* instead of *q'for* or *quhairfor*, and (21) *gt* instead of *q'* or *quhat*. The form (6 etc.) *gch* (for *quich*) is a Scots-English hybrid.

(22) *the lords of Iwestesery*: Judges of the Court of Justiciary, the supreme criminal court of Scotland.

Biblical quotations and echoes

References below, in the 1611 spelling, are to the 1611 Authorised Version of the Bible (reprint, Oxford University Press, London, 1911).

(5)   Isaiah 48:10: *Behold, I haue refined thee ... I haue chosen thee in the fornace of affliction.*

(12)   Luke 12:7: *the very haires of your head*

(16–17)   Hebrews 11:25: *Chusing rather to suffer affliction with the people of God, then to enjoy the pleasures of sinne for a season.*

(17–18)   Psalm 84:10: *I had rather be a dore keeper in the house of my God, then to dwell in the tents of wickednesse.*

(20)   Psalm 115:1: *Not vnto vs, O Lord, not vnto vs, but vnto thy name giue glory.*

(23)   Psalm 70:2: *Let them be ... put to confusion, that desire my hurt.*

(29–31)   Jude:24–5: *Now vnto him that is able to keepe you from falling ... To the only wise God our Sauiour, be glory.*

(32)   1 Corinthians 1:27: *But God hath chosen the foolish things of the world, to confound the wise.*

(37)   Romans 5:20: *but where sinne abounded, grace did much more abound.* Note that many writers of the period have *superabound* here; see OED SUPERABOUND.

(38–9)   Psalm 66:12: *we went through fire, and through water: but thou broughtest vs out into a wealthy place.*

(39)   Joshua 5:6: *a land that floweth with milke and honie.*

(40)   Revelation 15:3: *And they sing the song of Moses the seruant of God, and the song of the Lambe.*

(41)   Hebrews 12:22–3: *But ye are come...to an innumerable company of Angels ... and to the spirits of just men made perfect.*

Background

The writer is clearly a Covenanter, probably one of the religio-political extremists known as Cameronians. Adherence to Covenanting doctrines led not only to refusal to take the required oath of allegiance to the King, but to terrorist activity, bringing arrest, imprisonment, questioning under torture, trial and sentence. The years 1684–88 in Scotland have been named 'the Killing Times' because of the number of executions, although most Covenanters who persisted in defying the authorities were not sentenced to death, but to transportation.

Assuming that this unsigned letter is not a totally fictional piece of covenanting propaganda, the writer may be conjecturally identified by his address to *Iohn Stort* (?=Stewart) as his *Dier brother* and *dier biely*, although a wider readership of 'brothers' in religion is very likely envisaged. Many Covenanters named Stewart figure in the records, and *The Register of the Privy Council of Scotland* includes a number of letters from an Archibald Stewart (of Lesmahagow), but he was executed in Glasgow in March 1684. A more likely candidate is James Stewart, who wrote letters to his *Loving bilies and sisters* from prisons in Glasgow, Stirling and Edinburgh throughout 1684, and received a sentence of banishment to *his Majesties Plantationes in America*. His letters bear a strong stylistic resemblance to this one, and also mention close links with the Forrest family (see lines 45 and 47–8). The records say he comes from Allanton, a few miles from Wishaw, Lanarkshire.

The fact that this letter, as well as those signed by James and by Archibald Stewart, is now among State Papers suggests that it failed to reach its destination but was intercepted. However, the manuscripts may be the confiscated originals or copies taken (with extreme care preserving the wild spelling) and filed. Some documents are endorsed with the word *transcribed*, but this remains ambiguous.

Robert Goodwin/Gooding (l. 44) and Margaret Forrest were also sentenced to be transported. Patrick Walker (l. 51) was sentenced to transportation, but the sentence was rescinded and in the 1720s, living in Edinburgh, he published *Six Saints of the Covenant*, a series of descriptions of covenanting 'martyrs', including an Archibald Stewart who was executed in Edinburgh in 1681. For a short account of Scottish Covenanters, see Thorbjörn Campbell, *Standing Witnesses: A Guide to the Scottish Covenanters and their Memorials* (Saltire Society, Edinburgh, 1996), especially pp. 1–25.

Topics for linguistic investigation

1. Problems in reconstructing pronunciation which are posed by the range of words in which the vowel is spelled *ie*.
2. The evidence relating to the pronunciation of vowels in the spellings (6) *theng*, (12) *may*, (14) *deay*, (14) *falowrs*, (18) *dwall*, (21) *pres*, and relating to consonants in the spellings (2) *lowieng*, (2) *hopien*, (12) *Efery*, (30) *derekely*, (41) *parfiet*, (51) *waker*.
3. Reasons for the morphological differences between the members of the pairs (9) *is* and (20) *be*, (21) *wot* and (24) *wost*, (29) *desayr* and (35) *desayrs*, (31) *wantes* and (49) *pormet*, (39) *flowth* and (45) *desayrs*, (4) *sel* and (49) *woll*.
4. The syntax of (19–20) *any the lieks of mie*, (24) *they wost not*, (32) *I woll mek the fowlies ons to confownd the weays*, (50) *Yr was som of owr friends sent to sie and was seped*.
5. Some problems in determining sentence-structures and sentence-boundaries in this text.
6. In what kinds of ways is the language Scots?
7. Consult OED on the post-1500 use of *super-* to make new words.

Text 44

Anne Clifton: Westmorland [1518]

(British Library Manuscript Additional 48,965)

[f. 26v] To my ryght wrychypfull brod*y*re s*y*r harre ~~eh~~ clyfforthe be thy byll byll
delyu*y*ryd *in* haste

[f. 26r] Ryght wyrchypfull brod*y*re I hartyly recowmawnd me vn to ʒow
besechyng ʒow to be gud brod*y*re to me and hayffyng gret maruell of ʒowr
5 vnkyndnes y*t* ʒ*e* wold not be here ʒowr selfe at thys tyme nor nowne for ʒow for
her hays bene all my husband*y*s hukkyll*y*s & brod*y*re And I hayd nobody to
speke In all my caws*y*s bot my selfe And my husband*y*s {frend*y*s} thynk*y*s y*t* my
frend*y*s ys vnkynd or ell*y*s yay sete lytyll p*r*ice by me y*t* yay wold nowne of yame
be here at thys tyme and eu*y*re ge*n*tylwoman mygh*t* hayfe t*r*ustyd to he{l}pe of
10 hyre {brod*y*r} I went I mygh*t* hayfe t*r*ustyd to ʒowr helpe & I knawe no thyng
y*t* ʒ*e* hayfe downe at london ~~as ʒyt~~ for me In all my matt*y*rys as ʒyt And y*t* hayfe
I grette maruell of seyng y*t* ʒ*e* hare daly at london for thorow t*r*ustyng of ʒowr
lab*y*re I ame lyeke to be pute bothe fro hodsoke & clifton for thorow t*r*ustyng
opon ʒow y*t* ʒ*e* wold hayffe bene gude brod*y*r & frende to me as ʒowr p*r*omes
15 was I ned not to hayffe rydyne nor gone {to lo*n*don} for no matt*y*rys as bot
thynkyng y*t* ʒ*e* wolde hayfe spokyn y*e* beste ~~y*t*~~ for In my matt*y*rys as well as for
ʒowr awn And y*t* ʒ*e* wolde hayfe mayd A supplicac*i*on And hayffe put yt vpe to
my lord cardinall In my name And y*t* hayd bene beste for me In my mynd and
I went ʒ*e* wolde hayfe spokyn to mast*y*r sufyer And tyll hayffe bene gude frende
20 for me And to hayffe spokyn to my lorde cardinall for me and yf ʒ*e* hayd done
so I wold hayff t*r*ustyd to hayffe hayd A answere or now and s*y*r ʒ*e* knawe y*t* yt
ys halfe A ʒere sene my husband dep*a*rtyd {wo Ie*su* p*a*rdon} And as ʒyt hays
{knaw} now*n* a*n*swere And her I ly & kepys hows to my grete coste & charge
and my vnkyll doctore schowys me I mu*n* pay for all man*y*re of thyng y*t* I hayfe
25 takyng sene my husband dep*a*rtyd And y*t* ame not Abyll for to do ffor y*e* knaw
howe I was lefte *in* grete trobyll & besenes & lytyll to helpe my selfe w*t* all y*er*for
s*y*r I went y*t* ʒ*e* wold hayffe spede my matt*y*rys mor schortly y*t* I mygh*t* hayffe
hayd su*m*e thyng to hayffe t*r*ustyd to And s*y*r bot yf ʒ*e* wyll be gud brod*y*re to
me & speke for me bett*y*r þ*en* y*e* hayffe don ʒyt I knaw no frenchype nor no
30 frende to t*r*uste to bot for to cowme vpe my selfe y*e* nexte terme & lab*y*re for my
selfe y*e* beste þ*t* I cane and {yet} ame I lytyll be holdyn to ʒow & to my syst*y*r
And I cane hayff no bet*y*r fauore at ʒowr hand*y*s bot to lab*y*r for my selffe and

y*er*for s*y*r beseche ȝow {to send me word} by y*ᵉ* berer her of qwat ȝ*ᵉ* cane do for
me In al my matt*yr*ys And s*y*r I pra*y*e ȝow þ*ᵗ* ȝ*ᵉ* & my brod*y*r {fyȝtwyll} & my

35 syst*y*r wyll speke to gyd*y*re & take ȝowr beste co*n*sell & vyce qwat ȝ*ᵉ* cane do for
me also ȝ*ᵉ* hayffe letyn clefton be lab*y*ryd forthe of my hand*y*s for I knaw hyme
þ*ᵗ* hays a grawnt of hyt y*er*for I thynke gret vnkynnes i*n* ȝow y*ᵗ* ȝ*ᵉ* hayffe letyn
ben lab*y*rd for me no mor at thys tyme bot Ie*s*u pre*s*er*ue* ȝow wrytyn y*ᵉ* sexte
{day} of marche

40   By ȝowr loffyng syst*y*r
                                     Ane clifton

Notes

Text

The letter has been edited by A. G. Dickens (ed.), *Clifford Letters of the Sixteenth
Century*, Surtees Society, Vol. 172 (for 1957) (1962), pp. 93–4.

Manuscript

The writer often adds a stroke at the end of final *d*, *t*, *g* and *ll*. This has been treated as
empty, since many of the same words also appear without the stroke, although there are
some instances of a further *e* being added.

The ampersand & sometimes has a stroke above it; this too has been treated as empty.

There is a clear error of dittography in (1) *byll byll*; in the same line *thy* is probably a
mistake for *thys*.

Glossary

(4)	*maruell*	astonishment
(6)	*hukkyllys*	=uncles
(6)	*brodyre*	=brothers (see note)
(8)	*set lytyll price by me*	do not value me
(10)	*went*	thought (pret. of *ween*)
(11)	*downe*	=done
(12)	*hare*	=are
(18)	*mynd*	opinion
(19)	*sufyer*	=surveyor (of crown lands)
(19)	*tyll* †	to
(21)	*or* †	before
(22)	*sene* †	since
(24)	*mun* †	must
(25)	*takyng*	=taken
(26)	*besenes*	anxiety
(26)	*w'ᵗ all*	with
(27)	*spede*	brought to a successful conclusion
(27)	*schortly*	quickly

(28)	*bot yf*	unless
(31)	*be holdyn*	=beholden, under obligation (because of help given)
(35)	*to gydyre*	=together
(35)	*vyce*	=advice
(36)	*labyryd forthe of*	?torn out of, wrested from

Placenames

| (13) | *hodsoke* | Hodsock, Nottinghamshire |
| (13) | *clifton* | Clifton, Westmorland |

Explanatory notes

(6) *brodyre*: The preceding phrase and the history of the morphology of *brother*, especially in the North, suggest that this is a plural form.

(13) *hodsocke & clifton*: Family estates.

(18) *my lord cardinall*: Cardinal Wolsey, at this time Archbishop of York, Papal legate, Lord Chancellor and the King's chief Minister.

(24) *my vnkyll doctore*: Dickens, *Clifford Letters*, identifies him as canon lawyer Dr Gamaliel Clifton, uncle to Anne's late husband.

(34–5) *my broder fy3twyll and my systyr*: Anne was the fifth of seven children from her father's first marriage.

Background

Anne Clifton (née Clifford) was born c.1493, so about twenty at this time. She was of a noble Westmorland family, the daughter of Henry 10th Lord Clifford (c.1453–1523). She married Robert Clifton, his death in 1517 (see line 22) leaving her a young widow. Since her late husband's family stopped her drawing income from her husband's estate, she was in considerable financial difficulty (lines 24–6). For help in establishing her rights she looked to her eldest brother, to whom this angry and reproachful letter is addressed. During his father's lifetime he was styled Sir Harry Clifford, but later Henry 11th Lord Clifford, 1st Earl of Cumberland and 11th Baron of Westmorland. Anne's hopes were evidently based on her brother's high standing at Henry VIII's court and his contacts there (lines 19–20).

Topics for linguistic investigation

1. The use of the characters *y*, *3*, *þ* and *th*.
2. The use of the following spellings in texts of roughly the same date from (a) the North of England, (b) the South of England, (c) Scotland: (1) *ryght*, (10) *hayfe*, (10) *knawe*, (13) *bothe*, (13) *fro*, (14) *gude*, (17) *awn*, (22) *wo*, (27) *schortly*, (33) *qwat*, (38) *mor*.
3. The function of the verb-forms (1) *be*, (6) *hays*, (8) *ys*, (8) *sete*, (11) *hayfe*, (11) *hayfe*, (12) *hare*, (22) *pardon*, (22) *hays*, (23) *ly*, (23) *kepys*, (24) *schowys*, (37) *hays*, (38) *preserue*.
4. The use of inverted order in (6) *her hays bene all my husbandys hukkyllys & brodyre*, (11–12) *y' hayfe I grette maruell of*, (31) *yet ame I lytyll be holdyn to 3ow*.

5. The grammar of negation in (8–9) *yay wold nowne of yame be here at thys tyme*, (15) *I ned not to hayffe rydyne nor gone to london for no mattyrys*, (22–3) *And as ʒyt hays knaw nown answere*, (29–30) *I knaw no frenchype nor no frende to truste to.*

6. A comparison with Southern and Northern texts of similar date in regard to the items (19) *tyll*, (21) *or*, (22) *sene*, (24) *mun*.

Text 45

Elizabeth Betts: ?Devon (London) [1522]
(Somerset Record Office Manuscript DD WO 54/1/6)

[f. 1v] To my good mastresse Cokworthy At Ernescomb in devonshere

[f. 1r] My good mastresse Cokworthy I Recommande me vnto you in myn herty
wyse and soo thanke you for yoʳ gret kyndnesse shewn vnto me and myn namely
vnto my doughter Modwen/ She Recommandeth her vnto you in her lowly
maner/ And I pray you thinke not me foryetfull in þᵗ I haue not sent vnto you
5   or this tyme/ ffor certeinly I thought vpon you neverthelatter/ And I haue
spokyn wᵗ a cunnynge phesicyan And I haue shewed hym all your diseasys/
And asmoche as I cowde youre complexyon And he ~~desired~~ {said} þᵗ he wold
See the parsone. And I said he cowde not ye were so ~~fe~~ fferre owte of this cuntre.
10   ffor I said vnto hym. þᵗ and ye were here yoʳ selfe ye cowde shew hym no more
of yoʳ grevys than I hadde don/ wherin I prayd hym. to shewe me some
Remedye And he was not willed soo to doo/ but he wold a made hit ~~hi~~ wᵗ his
owin handys/ And I felt wele þᵗ ye shuld abeen never þᵉ nere/ by his owin
wordys/ ffor it ys athynge þᵗ must be vsyd/ And then wᵗ fayre entrete And
15   sondry tymys comyng to hym/ I gaffe hym a pleasyr for teche me the medecyn
and to See hym make hit/ because I woldbe parfit in hit which medecyn he gaffe
a marvelous prayse for yoʳ disease/ To make you to have that ye haue wantyd
many yerys/

Take. a good handfull of ffemetery/ halfe ~~and~~ an handfull of mugwort/ And
20   halfe an handfull of ysop/ And pounde hem all to gyder in A morter/ And
strayn owte the Iewse. Then take alytell lesse of clene Rennyng Watyr/ than ys
the Iewse And put the Iewse and the Watʳ to gyder/ over the ffyre and boyle
hem tyll it {be} somewhat consumyd/ And then take it from the ffyre till it be
colde/ Then put thertoo eyther Sugar or clarefyed hony/ at yoʳ owyn pleasyr/.
25   Then take the whitys of vj eggys or more after the quⁿntite of the lycoʳ And
Swynge hem wele. Then haue all yoʳ medecyn cold as it ys/ into a panne And
then put thise whitys of Eggys a highe vpon. And then set þᵉ panne vpon þᵉ
ffyre and boyle it softly And when it ys Rysen on highe lyke a scome/ and lyke
a Cake/ then take that scome of wᵗ a Spone/ but beware þᵗ ye stere it not afore
30   the scome be takyn off ~~in n~~. And then take it fro the ffyre And strayne it And
Soo ye shall haue a fayre Syruppe of hit/

228

And vse it furst at morne/ colde/ And warme at evyn at eu*er*y tyme ix sponfull/ And thus when yo*^r* siruppe ys spent/ make you newe/ ~~It ys~~ And soo vse it tyll ye haue cause to leve it/

35 I sende you a payre of p*ar*dou*n* bed*ys* of a Chart*er*house called Beauvale. The p*ar*don ys iiij*^{xx}* dayes for eu*er*y word of the pat*er* nost*er*. the Aue. And the crede/ my husband Recom*m*andeth hym to mast*er* Cokworthy {and to you} and so doo I And to mastresse Avyse and to all yo*^r* household At London on Sent Kat*er*ine day

40 yo*^r* owin trewe lover Elisabeth Bett*ys*

[f. 1v] Mastresse I p*ra*y you when ye See mastresse vawtard that ye wol say I Recom*m*ande me vnto her And hertly thanke her as my husbond dothe of the {the} good {chere} þ*^t* mast*er* vawtard and she made vs/ I dare not be so bolde. To desire mast*er* pollard or his clerk this brenger to cary any more tokyns/ And

45 to mastress*e* Chichestr*e* I p*ra*y you that I be Recom*m*anded

Notes

Text

Among the papers of the Trevelyan family. The text was edited by Sir Walter Calverley Trevelyan and Sir Charles Edward Trevelyan (eds), *Trevelyan Papers*, Part III, Camden Society, Original Series, Vol. 105 (1872), pp. 12–13.

Manuscript

The letter *n* in final position is nearly always given a looped-back final stroke. This has been treated as empty.

The numerals in lines 32 and 36 are preceded by a small character which seems merely to introduce them. It has been edited out.

In l. 43 the repeat of *the* has been inserted by mistake.

Glossary

(6)	*or* †	before
(6)	*neverthelatter*	nevertheless
(7)	*cunnynge*	learned, skillful
(8)	*complexyon*	physical and mental make-up
(9)	*parsone*	=person
(10)	*and*	if
(11)	*grevys*	=griefs, problems
(13)	*never þe nere*	no nearer to your goal
(14)	*vsyd*	employed habitually (see note)
(14)	*entrete*	=entreaty, ?negotiation (see note)
(15)	*sondry*	several
(15)	*pleasyr*	=?pleaser or ?pleasure, ?tip

(17)	*wantyd*	lacked
(23)	*somewhat*	partially
(23)	*consumyd*	reduced[by evaporation]
(26)	*Swynge*	beat
(26)	*haue*	put
(27)	*a high vpon*	heaped on top
(28)	*softly*	gently
(29)	*of*	=off
(35)	*a payre of pardoun bedys*	See note
(40)	*lover*	friend, well-wisher
(44)	*this brenger*	bearer of this [letter]

Placename

(1)	*Ernescomb*	Yarnscombe, Devon

Explanatory notes

(14) *fayre entrete*: OED records *entreaty* only from (and mostly later than) this period, but senses range from 'handling, management' and 'negotiation' to 'supplication', any of which might be the meaning here.

(14) *it ys athynge þᵗ must be vsyd*: since the medicine is to be taken twice daily for an indefinite period, Betts insists that she cannot merely accept a small quantity made up by the doctor himself, but that she must ensure a supply by knowing how it is made

(15) *pleasyr*: The confused syntax here adds to the uncertainty of meaning. Perhaps she gave him a small payment, or perhaps she means that she ingratiated herelf with him so that he was pleased to help her. OED is unhelpful here.

(19–20) *ffemetry … mugwort … yssop*: fumitory, mugwort and hyssop, three plants commonly used in herbal remedies.

(35) *a payre of pardoun bedys*: a set of rosary beads blessed so that the user receives an indulgence (pardon) when the prescribed prayers are said, in this case the Our Father, Hail Mary and Creed.

(35) *a charterhouse called Beauvale*: Carthusian priory of Beauvale, Nottinghamshire.

(38–9) *Sent Katerine day*: Feast day of St Catherine of Alexandria, 25 November.

(44) *master pollard or his clerk*: Pollard is identified by Trevelyan and Trevelyan, *Trevelyan Papers*, as a London lawyer of Devonshire origin. Presumably it is the clerk who is acting as carrier for the letter.

Background

Nothing is known about Elizabeth Betts, though the letter is written from London (l. 38) and she mentions her husband and daughter. The content of the letter and the terms on which she and her family evidently stand in relation to the Cockworthy family and their (unidentified) Devon neighbours suggest that she is either a friend and former Devon neighbour, or that she perhaps has been employed as gentlewoman in the Cockworthy household.

The recipient is the wife of Nicholas Cockworthy, gentleman, of Yarnscombe, near

Barnstaple in North Devon. The letter must be before the marriage of their daughter Avyse since she appears (l. 38) still to be living at home. It is through Avyse's marriage to John Trevelyan of Nettlecombe, Somerset, that the letter, presumably preserved for the sake of the recipe, is among the Trevelyan Papers.

Topics for linguistic investigation

1. The use of the letter *þ*.
2. The evidence relating to pronunciation in the spellings (1) *devonshere*, (2) *mastresse*, (5) *foryetfull*, (9) *fferre*, (12) *a*, (16) *parfit*, (20) *ysop*, (21) *Rennyng*, (22) *to gyder*, (27) *thise*, (29) *stere*, (44) *brenger*.
3. The forms (3) *me*, (3) *myn*, (12) *hit*, (20) *hem*, (29) *ye*, (33) *you*.
4. The syntax of (5) *thinke not me foryetfull*, (16–17) *which medecyn he gaffe a marvelous prayse*, (17–18) *that ye have wantyd many yerys*, (21–2) *alytell lesse of clene Rennyng Watyr/ than ys the Iewse*.
5. Ways in which the language of the recipe is different from that of the rest of the letter.
6. The meaning and use of *wold* (=would).
7. The use of the prepositions (6) *vpon*, (9) *owte of*, (16) *in*, (25) *after*, (35) *of*.

Text 46

Alice Radcliffe: Winmarleigh, Lancashire [1524]
(Lancashire Record Office Manuscript DDKE/HMC2)

[f. 1v] To my Ryght wryscheppe full mast*er* syr Androw wynd*ys* hawr*e* be t be thys delyu*eryt*

[f. 1r] Ryght Wryscheppefull Syr in my moste hwmly Wyse I recom*m*ande me
vnto you Dyssyryng*e* to here of your*e* welle fare the Wyche I pray ie*s*u in cresse
5   to is plusure & to your*e* moste hertt*ys* Dyssyr*e* Syr has tochyng*e* your*e* laste
letter qwere in I p*er*sawe 3e Dyssyryt me to be gud moder to my swn*n*e & your*ys*
y*t* ther*e* be no p*re*dysciall nar hwrtte vnto my swn*n*ys Anarretans Sy*r* has ferr*e*
has lys in my pore power I wyll be lotthe to Se y*t* swlde hwr it And yff y*er* be
ony mo*n* A ~~both yt~~ bowth to do hym Any Wrong*e* your*e* masterscheppe sall
10   hawe knawlyge trystyng*e* y*t* 3e Wylle se remedy for hym for he nor I has no
noder socar*e* both you Syr has tochyng*e* y*e* custu*m* londe qwere I Wrothe to you
to sende it vppe Syr 3e may p*er*sawe a Woma*n*s wytte the custu*m* londe is y*t* alle
seche lond*ys* has is custum land*ys* one of my Swn*n*ys kynginsme*n* of hys moder
syde after y*e* custu*m* is A custu*m* to resawe all seche land*ys* to the chylde cu*m* of
15   xv 3er*ys* of age & then to mayke A cowtte to ye chylde of all Seche p*ro*feytt*ys*
after xij custu*m*ers Be sechyng*e* your*e* maste{r}scheppe Regarnot my wordd*ys*
in my Wryttyng*e* for my mynde is & sall be at all tymys y*t* all p*ro*fett*ys* y*t* may
contunylly falle or cu*m* to my swn*n*e has ferr*e* as lys me I wolde yowr*e*
Mast*er*scheppe hadde yAm y*er* sall be no p*ro*fett*ys* senyt from your*e*
20   Mast*er*scheppe Syr yff it be your*e* pleswr*e* 3e may sende in to the cu*n*tre And
then 3e may knawe of the custu*m* & the trawthe in all thy*n*gys Syr I p*er*sawe be
your*e* lett*er* 3e dysyre me to sende Wordde to your*e* Mast*er*scheppe of Seche
Artikyll*ys* has is in your*e* Wryttyng*e* y*e* Wyche 3e sende to me by my serwande
Thomas Iakesu*n* syr your*e* Wryttyng*e* come nott At me tell after the nateuite of
25   your*e* lade y*e* laste past Syr qwer*e* has 3e Wrotte to me thowchyng my swn*n*e
And my dogthter y*t* I swlde be contente w*t* thone ofyame Syr I wolde ~~be ga~~ to
god my doghtt*er* wolde be co*n*selde by me & hwr frynd*ys* Wyche thyng*ys* it wer*e*
& swlde be to hwr cu*m*furthe & howr*es* in tyme cu*m*hyng be sechyng*e* your*e*
Mast*er*scheppe to take no dysplesur*e* w*t* me for my doghtt*er* is of renabull hage
30   to gyf a nonswarre for hwr selfe And sche is not of gud mynde to leffe the
cu*n*ttre Syr y*er*fore I beseche you to be gud Mast*er* to my swn*n*e has long has he
is in your*e* keppyng for he has no noder fader both yow to soker hym Syr I wolde

232

be seche you gyff any mo*n* cu*m* to dyssyre the pore ten*n*ens the wech be long*ys*
vnto my swn*n*e to hawe thyam I be seche you lett nomo*n* hawe thyam both yame
35   y* ʒe hawe ponttit for it wolde be grett hwr to yame Syr qwer*e* ʒe com*m*ande it
me to speke w* my lorde steward or ell*ys* w* syr Re*chard* sachewerell ya cu*m* nott
throhe loncaschyre how be it I am boune be your*e* pwrr*e* bedde womo*n* y* it wold
plesse you to speke to seche me*n* for me in my sun*n*ys Ryght Syr I wolde dyssyr*e*
to be gud master to the berrer her*e* of wech is a por*e* tenent y* be long*ys* vnto my
40   sun*n*e And I p*r*ay ie*s*u to p*r*eserue you to your*e* hert*ys* dyssyr*e* Wryttyn A
wynm*er*ley the vij day of Octob*er*

By your*e* powr*e* bedde womo*n*
Alys Radclyff

Notes

Text

Among the family papers of Lord Kenyon. The letter has been edited by W. J. Hardy
(ed.), *Historical Manuscripts Commission, Fourteenth Report, Appendix Part IV: The
Manuscripts of Lord Kenyon* (HMSO, London, 1894), p. 32, and there is a reprint of this
in A. K. Hudson (ed.), *English Letter Writers* (Wheaton, Exeter, 1951), pp. 61–3.

Manuscript

A photograph of lines 3–18 from this document, together with a commentary, appears
as Plate VI on pp. 188–9 above.

A long-tailed form of *r* is used as well as a short one, but the distinction has been edited
out in transcription.

There is sometimes difficulty in determining whether an initial letter is a capital or
not, especially in regard to *d* where it depends on size alone, and with *a*, where a clear
capital form is used for the indefinite article and even medially in (19) *yAm*.

In (26) *dogthter* a line is written above the cluster of letters representing the consonants, but it has been treated as empty.

In line 1 the abandoned attempt at *be t[hys]* is written at the end of a line, and is
accidentally left undeleted by the writer when she writes the words fully at the beginning
of the following line.

Glossary

(6)	*persawe*	=perceive
(7)	*Anarretans*	=inheritance
(8)	*hwr*	=hurt
(9)	*A bowth*	=about
(10–11)	*no noder*	=none other, no other
(11)	*both*	=but, except
(11)	*custum londe*	See note
(11)	*Wrothe*	=wrote

(14)	*resawe*	=receive, deal with the financial administration of
(14)	*to*	until
(15)	*A cowtte*	=account
(17)	*mynde*	intention
(19)	*senyt*	=sent
(25)	*youre*	=our
(29)	*renabull*	=reasonable
(30)	*a nonswarre*	=an answer
(32)	*soker*	=soccour, help
(33)	*gyff*	=if
(33)	*tennens*	=tenements?
(35)	*ponttit*	=appointed
(35)	*commande it*	=commandit, commanded
(37)	*boune* †	ready
(42)	*youre ... bedde womon*	woman who prays for you (*bedde* =bead, prayer)

Explanatory notes

(24–5) *the nateuite of youre lade*: Feast of the Nativity of Our Lady, 8 September.

(11) *custum londe*: Alice Radcliffe's explanation is far from clear, but the term appears to refer to land on which dues have to be paid, being held by a trustee while the owner (her young son) is a minor.

Background

The writer is probably the Alice Radcliffe (née Gerard) who was the wife of Thomas Radcliffe of Winmarleigh, in Lancashire, about ten miles South of Lancaster. It is from Winmarleigh that she writes (l. 41). She was also from Lancashire, the daughter of Sir Thomas Gerard of Brindle, a few miles south of Preston. Her husband (born 1483) died in 1521, his eldest son then being aged five. Winmarleigh, together with other Radcliffe properties, was settled on her at her marriage. If this letter is dated [1524] the references to her son seem appropriate to a boy of nine. The daughter *of renabull hage to gyf a nonswarre for hwr selfe* (ll. 29–48) could be a year or so older or younger. Alice Radcliffe would presumably have been in her late twenties.

However, Hardy, *Hist. MSS Commission*, dates the letter [1549], identifying the writer as Lady Alice Radcliffe, the widow of Sir Alexander Radcliffe (1475–1548/9). She was a Lancashire woman, the daughter of Sir John Booth of Barton, and at this time would presumably have been in her sixties or early seventies, her eldest son being aged forty-six. This age, together with the fact that the family home was at Ordsall, Nottingham-shire, makes this ascription unlikely.

The language looks early, however this could be consistent with a young woman writing in 1524 or an elderly woman in 1549.

The family of Sir Andrew Windsor, the recipient of the letter, had estates close to Winmarleigh. The wording of the letter (l. 6) implies that he is either bringing Alice Radcliffe's child up at his home, and/or that he is his godfather.

Topics for linguistic investigation

1. The use of the characters ʒ, *y* and *th*; and of *w*.
2. The evidence relating to the pronunciation of vowels in the spellings
   (9) *ony*, (9) *mon*, (11) *londe*, (21) *knawe*, (21) *trawthe*, (30) *gud*, (37) *loncaschyre*.
3. The evidence relating to the pronunciation of consonants in the spellings (5) *is*, (7)
   Anarretans, (4) *Wyche*, (6) *qwere*, (9) *sall*, (10) *hawe*, (26) *swlde*, (28) *cumhynge*, (29)
   hage.
4. The verb-forms (6) *Dyssyryt*, (7) *be*, (8) *lys*, (10) *has*, (14) *cum*, (20) *be*, (23) *is*, (33) *cum*,
   (33) *be longys*, (35) *commande it*, (39) *be longys*.
5. The writer's perception of what constitutes a word.
6. The extent to which it is feasible to describe some of the syntax in this letter as 'bad'.

Text 47

Kate Ashley: Devon (London) 1549

(Public Record Office Manuscript SP 10/6, Item 22)

[f. 59r] .4°. ffebruarij M^ris Ashleye vnto master secretary

[f. 58r] thes I haue talked at su*m* certayne tyme {w^t hyr grace} y^t hyt was yn possybel for my lorde admyrall to haue hyr {grace} ~~duryng~~ {tel} the kynges maigestes came to hys nowne rule for: I was sure y^t my lorde protectors grace
5   nor the co*n*sel wold not soffer a subiec to haue hyr but hys grace at ful age myght do hys pleasuer

al so I thynke I had the same talke w^t pary at the delyuere & redyng of hys leter I thynke y^t {thes} was my talke to hyr grace for y^t purpose y^t sche shuld not set hyr mynde on hyt seyng the vnlekelyowde of hyt

10   I haue no nother thyng y^t I canne as now reme*m*ber but yf I coude I wold not hyde hyt as the lorde knoweth who moue your harttes to haue pety on me & good master secretary spke y^t I maye change my preson for by my trothe hyt ys so cowlld y^t I can not slepe yn hyt & so darke y^t I can not {yn the daye} se for I stope the wendo w^t strowe thar ys no glase

15   [f. 58v] I moust beseke you good master secretary to bere w^t my want of memory wyche ys neuer good whan I am yn best quiet {as my lady & al my feloues & hysbond can tel yow}: & thes soro has made hyt moche worsse thys I ende the lorde be w^t you: desyryng you for the loue of schrist to moue my lordes grace to haue pety on me & forgeue thes my gret foly y^t wold ether talke or spke of
20   maryage to such a p*er*sounage as sche ys: for ponyschment whare of I haue sofered gret soro & ponysschment & shame y^t neuer wel out of my hart hyt I do thyink my selfe worthy: trustyng y^t my lordes grace who has marcy on al wel not deny me for thes ~~my first~~ {my first} foute: for yf hyt whare possyble y^t I myght be w^t hyr {grace} agayne wyche I loke not for: neuer wold I spke noe
25   wyse of maryage no not to wyne al the woreld & as tochyng my lordes boldenes yn hyr chamber the lorde I take to recorde I spke so oughte to hym ye & sayd y^t hyt was co*m*playned on to my lordes of the co*n*sel: hyt he wold sware what do I I wold the al sawre hyt y^t I coude not make hym leue hyt at last I told the quene

of hyt who made a small mater of hyt to me & sayde sche wold co*m* w^t hym hyr
30   selffe: & so sche ded euer affter

kateryn aschyly

Notes

Text

The document is noted, along with other material relating to the same person, in Robert
Lemon, *Calendar of State Papers, Domestic Series, of the Reigns of Edward VI, Mary,
Elizabeth 1547–1580* (HMSO, London, 1856), pp. 13–14.

Manuscript

The unlikely spelling (12 etc.) *spke*, is repeated several times, so is presumably
intentional. The final *d* (5) *wold* is possibly *e*. Since the letter-shape is ambiguous, there
is insufficient evidence to support the less conventional spelling.

Glossary

Familiar words are sometimes obscured by spelling, especially (21, 27) *hyt* (=yet), (26)
oughte (=oft), (28) *the al sawre* (=they all saw).

(5)	*soffer*	allow

People

(1)	*master secretary*	Principal Secretary of State, Sir Thomas Smith
(2)	*hyr grace*	the Princess Elizabeth
(3)	*my lorde admyrall*	Thomas Seymour
(3–4)	*the kynges maigeste*	King Edward VI
(4)	*my lorde protector*	Edward Seymour
(7)	*pary*	Thomas Parry, Cofferer of Elizabeth's Household, also suspect and imprisoned at this time

Background

Katherine (Kate) Ashley or Astley was nurse-governess to Elizabeth I from her early
childhood.

She was in her forties at the time of these letters. Her father was Sir Philip Champernowne of Modbury, Devon, and Gawen Champernowne, whose divorce is featured in
Text 24, was a nephew, as were also Sir Walter Raleigh and Sir Humphrey Gilbert. She
was probably Philip's eldest child, born c.1505. She was unmarried when she took up
the post of governess to the three-year-old princess in 1536, but made a late marriage in
1545, to John Ashley or Astley (1507–95) who also held a high position in Elizabeth's
household. She continued to serve the adult Elizabeth, being appointed her principal
Lady of the Bedchamber at her succession in 1558.

As governess to the future queen she was concerned with initial education as well as
general upbringing and welfare, but it is noticeable that Roger Ascham, who recom-

mended her for the post and was a close friend of both Kate and her husband, wrote letters to her in English only, rather than in the Latin he employed to others.

She seems to have been the one person to whom Elizabeth was truly attached, and her own loyalty was unswerving. Before Elizabeth came to the throne, however, Kate's imprudent words led to several imprisonments on suspicion of treason. In this letter she is answering charges that she countenanced sexual frolics between Elizabeth and Thomas Seymour at the period when Elizabeth lived in the household of Henry VIII's widow Katharine Parr, whom Seymour married, and that, since Katharine's death, she has encouraged the Princess to consider marrying Seymour.

Kate Ashley died in 1565, having had no child herself, but her great formative influence on Elizabeth is spoken of in all contemporary comments, including those of the Queen herself.

The fullest account of her is in C. E. Champernowne, *The Champernowne Family*, Unpublished typescript in Westcountry Studies Library, Exeter.

Topics for linguistic investigation

1. Reasons for making the following equations with PDE: (4) *nowne* (=own), (1, 17) *thes*, *thys* (=thus), (21) *hyt* (=yet), (23) *foute* (=fault), (28) *sawre* (=saw).
2. Supply the text with present-day punctuation, and analyse what you have done.
3. The evidence relating to pronunciation in the spelling.
4. The forms: (2) *hit*, (11) *moue*, (17) *has*, (21) *do*.
5. Re-write the text in the way a clerk of the same period would record a deposition (cf. texts in Depositions section above).
6. Is it possible to read the writer's character from the language of a text of this kind?

Text 48

Lady Katherine Paston: Lincolnshire 1624/1625

(British Library Manuscript Additional 27,447)

Text A (1624)

[f. 232v] To my beloued sonne will Paston these at Cambridge spede:/

[f. 232vr] My good will: the Lords blessinge be euermor vpon the. I haue
receiued two letters from the this weeke w^t a booke, all which are most wellcom
to me: I am glad to heer by good m^r. Roberts that thow hetherto {h}aste
5   demeaned thy self well and as it is meet thow shooldest {haue} giuen good
respect to all; all good news of the, and from the, cheers me more then any
thinge in this world; and I know thow dost Loue to haue me cheerly. goe on still
my good chilld in all well doinge and be then as mery as mery maye be:/ m^r
Parker I hope by this time haue deliuered my letter and token to the, he was to
10   be at Cambridge on munday or tusday Last: I doe Like that thow doest inditt
thy owne letters thy selfe. for thow weart wont to know how to speake to me.
and euen so wold I haue the wright. and hetherto I doe Like exedingly of them
and of the well wrightinge of them: the vse of wrightinge will perfict your hand
very much: I am so strayted of time as I can not tary Longer to talke w^t the now:
15   but bid the farwell. besechige god to keepe the in all thy ways now and
euermore:/

                    thy most louinge Mother
                    Katherine Paston

at the Commencment I will send a beaver hat to the but I feare it will be to bigge
20   ore to Littell or too broad verged or sumthinge amis:/ but if it shold not doe
Comly send it me then a gayn. and I will send for an other for the:/
farwell and euer more well:/

good will tell tom Hartstonge that I doe Like well of his wrightinge. I wold
haue written to him to put him in minde of sum thing*es* but I haue now no
25   time:/

Text B (1625)

[f. 262v] To my most beloued sonne william Paston thesse I pray ye at Corp Christ Coledge Cambridg

[f. 262r] My good chilld the Lord blesse the ever:/ I was glad to heer by Phillup
of thy good healthe and allso by m^r Roberts letter to vnderstand of thy wellfare
5   every way: the hope of {the continuanc of} which, dothe {still} cheer me every
way:/ thy father haue bine very ill. w^t his owld truble in his Legge so that he
haue kepte his bede w^t it this 5: or 6: days, but now god be thanked it is on the
mendinge hand but yett he can not indure to sitt vp:/ your brother and all good
frindes heer are well, I hope thow doest keep good fiers. this cowld wether. for
10   it is bothe comfortable and howlsum: heer haue bine much Losse heerabout w^t
thesse great windes and ill wether; diuers botts w^t wheat wch was to be deliuered
for the kinges provision at Yarmouth are sunke in the riuer, which is the owners
Losse and not the kings:/ I was sory to heer of tom harstons beinge ill, but hope
well of his recouery: I did wright to the the last satterday when I had very littell
15   time to say any thinge for hast: Commend me very kindly to good m^r Roberts I
doe not know whether he shall ~~not~~ need ~~off~~ a new supply: yett before our Lady:
I will sende so soon as the wether breake vp to know how the squars goe in the
mean time I pray god blesse the farwell sweet harte to thy owne selfe:/ thy most
louinge Mother Katherine Pasto<n>

20   my Neec knyvett hathe a yonge sonne and is very well:/

Notes

Text

The texts have been edited by Ruth Hughey (ed.), *The Correspondence of Lady Katherine Paston 1603–1627*, Norfolk Record Society, Vol. 14 (1941), No. 43 (p. 73) and No. 49 (p. 77).

Manuscript

The writer uses a single symbol for *ss*, as in (A2) *blessinge*, and (B13) *Losse*, and it is also employed in (B11) *thesse*.

In (A4) {*h*}*aste* the inserted *h* virtually obscures the *a*. In (A15) *besechige* there is no abbreviation mark to indicate an omitted *n*.

In Letter A lines 23–5 are written in the left-hand margin, turning the sheet on its side, and similarly line 20 in Letter B.

Glossary

(A5)	*demeaned*	behaved, conducted
(A5)	*meet*	appropriate
(A7)	*cheerly*	cheerful

(A10)	*inditt*	compose (see note)
(A14)	*am strayted of*	am short of
(A19)	*Commencment*	Graduation Ceremony
(A20)	*verged*	?brimmed
(A21)	*Comly*	nicely, suitably
(B5–6)	*every way*	in every respect
(B7–8)	*on the mendinge hand*	?in the process of mending
(B16)	*our Lady*	Lady Day, 25 March (see note)
(B17)	*how the squars goe*	how things are going (OED SQUARE)

People

Identifications from Hughey, *Correspondence*:

(A4 etc.)	*m^r Roberts*	Tutor to William Paston
(A8–9)	*m^r Parker*	a Norfolk friend whose son was also at Cambridge
(A23 and B13)	*tom Hartstonge*	a fellow-undergraduate from Norfolk
(B3)	*Phillup*	Phillip Alpe, employed by Lady Katherine
(B20)	*my Neec knyvett*	Katherine Knyvett, wife of Lady Katherine's nephew

Explanatory notes

(A10) *inditt*: Like *wright* this could refer to either composition or penmanship, but seems to be the former.

(B16) *our Lady*: In pre-Reformation times any Festival of the Virgin Mary could have this title; by the seventeenth century it referred only to the Feast of the Annunciation, which as well as a church festival was one of the four Quarter Days on which rent etc. fell due.

(B20) *a yonge sonne*: The birth of this child, baptised February 1624/5, dates this letter.

Background

Lady Katherine Paston (1578–1628) was the daughter of Sir Thomas Knyvett and married Sir Edmund Paston, descendant of the Pastons whose fifteenth-century letters are well known. Lady Katherine's family home was at Ashwellthorpe, Norfolk, about ten miles south of Norwich, and her married home about thirty miles away at Paston, near the Norfolk coast. She was at this time aged 46.

Her son William was born in 1610, and was an undergraduate at Cambridge at the age of 14, usual at this time.

Topics for linguistic investigation

1. The evidence relating to pronunciation in the spellings (A4) *hetherto*, (A12) *wright*, (A13) *perfict*, (B6) *bine*, (B8) *frindes*, (B9) *fiers*, (B10) *howlsum*, (B20) *yonge*.
2. A survey of other texts for the choice of second-person pronoun between family-members.
3. The possibility of local usage in the verb-forms *haue* (A9, B6, B7 and B10) and (B17) *breake*.

4. The contrasts in function between (A10) *doe* and (A20) *doe*, (A2) *haue* and (B20) *hathe*, (A5) *is* and (B7) *be*, (A12) *wold* and (A23) *wold*.

5. A survey of other texts in regard to the currency of verb-groups of the type (A24–5) *wold haue written*, (B12) *are sunke*, (B16) *doe not know*.

Text 49

Florence Smyth: Bristol [1629] and 1639

(Bristol Record Office Manuscripts AC/C60/16 (Text A) and AC/C60/7
(Text B))

Text A

[f. 1v] To My best frend M^tr Thomas Smyth this
At Ashton

[f. 1r] Deere Tom

I am glad to heare thou art well and that thou likes so well of my aduice as to
5   falo it I hope it will not be the wors for ether of us if it ware I showld be ueri
sori since it was my desire but I trust in god we shall do well enufgh/

all maters heare are well past ⚓ though it were my hard fortune to stand for a
god mother for want of abeter and so one might sware to se how litel they
estemed me I was no wis ambitious of the place had not my father spoken to me
10   I think the child had had but halfe her baptism

I must now bid the godnight for I sat up so long at cards last night with my pa
the Barnit and M^tr Bluet that I can scarce se yet If thou wart in the bed I should
kepe my eyes open I still looke for the this day senight acording to your promies

                                                          thine
15   Flo Smyth
Hinton this Ash wensday

Text B

[f. 1v] To my Best frend Thomas Smyth Esquier at Henri Betes at the sine of
the Raindeare ouer {a}gainst Eseks Hous in the Stran this
in London

[f. 1r] My Deare Hart

5   My Brother Frank kame in on tuesday as I had nuli dined and told me he left

243

thee well wch was welcom nues to me he & I went isterday and dined wth the captaine Ford and brought my cosen florance home wth vs whare she has leaue to stay till Miels day and by that time I hope you will be torning homeward whare you are motch wanted bot most by mee Frank went hence to day and I

10   haue {bin} at corch at the bering of long ashton whar M^{tr} Tok preched For the tenshelinges M^{tr} Foster was not willing to be destorbed for he is to prech at wels on sonday, as wee ware going to courch I hard 14 pes of ordinance go of to welcom my Lord cotington into Bristol how long he stais I know not, for our one afaires our corne is all home I thank God exsept som tith our hops will be

15   all in this week I hope and for the leting of them I haue don nothing your sister Smyth is dayli expected for our infantri thay are all in helth I prays God and {I} Gor as big as a beare all your frends at loer kour are well and so is thy best frend that prays for thy quick & saf retorne

Flora Smyth

20   Ashton ye 26th of sep 1639

Notes

Text

Among the papers of the Smyth family of Ashton Court, near Bristol. The letters are summarised by J. H. Bettey (ed.), *Calendar of the Correspondence of the Smyth Family of Ashton Court 1548–1642*, Bristol Record Society, Vol. 35 (1982), pp. 99 and 149.

Manuscript

In Text A the writer, having reached the bottom of the page, writes lines 11 (*for I sat up* …) – 15 in the margin. Line 16 is written upside-down at the top of the page. Similarly in Text B lines 17 (*all your frends* …) – 20 are written in the margin.

Glossary

(A13)	*this day senight*	a week today
(B1)	*sine*	shop–sign (see note)
(B5)	*nuli*	=newly, immediately before
(B8)	*Miels day*	Michaelmas, 29 September
(B10)	*corch*	=church
(B10)	*bering*	?rush-bearing (see note)
(B12)	*pes of ordinance*	canon
(B12)	*of*	=off
(B14)	*one*	=own
(B14)	*tith*	=tithe, small fraction (not necessarily a tenth)
(B15)	*leting*	?=leaching. soaking (see note)
(B16)	*infantri*	youngsters
(B16)	*prays*	=praise
(B17)	*Gor*	See note

Placenames

(A2)	*Ashton*	Ashton Court, the Smyth estate
(A16)	*Hinton*	Hinton St George, Florence Smyth's parents' estate
(B2)	*Eseks Hous in the Stran*	Essex House in the Strand
(B10)	*long ashton*	Long Ashton, village near Ashton Court
(B11)	*wels*	Wells
(B13)	*Bristol*	Bristol
(B17)	*loer kour*	Lower Court, also in Long Ashton, where Thomas's mother Elizabeth and her second husband lived

People

(A11)	*my pa*	John, Lord Poulett, Florence's father
(A12)	*the Barnit*	Bettey, *Calendar*, suggests Sir William Portman, Baronet, a neighbour of the Poullets
(A12)	*Mr Bluet*	Bettey, *Calendar*, suggests John Blewet of Holcombe, Devon
(B1)	*Henri Betes*	Henry Betty's, the Smyth family's London tailor
(B5)	*My Brother Frank*	?Frank Poulett
(B7)	*captaine Ford* and (B10) *Mr Tok*	Not identified
(B7)	*my cosen florance* and (B15–16) *your sister Smyth*	Not identified
(B11)	*Mr Foster*	Tutor to the Smyths' eldest son, Hugh; presumably ordained
(B13)	*my Lord cotington*	Frances, Lord Cottington

Explanatory notes

(A7–10) Florence has agreed to act as god-parent at the child's baptism, being called upon as a last-minute stop-gap, since two god-parents are required.

(B1–2) *at the sine of the Raindeare*: Pictorial signs outside premises were used to indicate shops as well as inns. Henry Betty was the London tailor patronised by the Smyth family.

(B10) *the bering*: Many churches had rush-bearing ceremonies, especially on their Patronal Festival, where rushes and garlands were brought in to decorate the church. Although in the North these were the occasion of general holidays, in Southern England they were simply a service.

(B15) *leting*: Perhaps for *leaching* with reference to the procedure of soaking the hops, or possibly *letting*, with reference to leasing out the hop-fields for the coming year.

(B17) *I Gor as big as a beare*: *Gor* could be *go*, the spelling perhaps suggesting linking *r* to the following word, or a form of *grow*. She is commenting on the progress of a pregnancy – she had nine children by Thomas Smyth and six from a second marriage.

Background

Both letters are to the writer's husband, the same Thomas Smyth who is the recipient of the letters from his mother printed as Text 50 below.

Florence, or Flora, Smyth (1612–76) was 17 at the conjectural date of Letter A and 27 at the date of Letter B. She was the daughter of John, Lord Poulett, of Hinton St

George, near Crewkerne in Somerset. In 1627, at the age of fifteen, Florence married Thomas Smyth of Ashton Court, Long Ashton, near Bristol, Somerset, the Poulett and Ashton families already being close friends. Her husband (1609–42) was only seventeen, the early marriage being arranged because his father was on the point of death. At the age of eighteen he inherited the estate, and was also MP for Bridgwater. Later he was Knight of the Shire for Somerset.

Topics for linguistic investigation

1. The evidence relating to pronunciation in the spellings (A5) *falo*, (A6) *enufgh*, (A7) *heare*, (B2) *Stran*, (B5) *nuli*, (B6) *isterday*, (B8) *Miels*, (B10) *corch*, (B11) *destorbed*, (B12) *hard*, (B17) *kour*.
2. The verb-forms (A4) *art*, (A4) *likes*, (A7) *were*, (A12) *wart*, (B13) *stais*, (B16) *prays*.
3. How do other letters reflecting relationships compare with this one in the use of second-person pronouns?
4. The verb-groups (A10) *had had*, (B8) *will be turning*, (B11) *is to prech*, (B12) *ware going*, (B13) *stais*, (B13) *know not*.
5. The part of speech and syntactic role of (A4) *of*, (A9) *no wis*, (A12) *scarce*, (A13) *senight*, (B14) *home*, (B14) *som*.
6. The history and status at this period of the word *pa* (A11).

Elizabeth Gorges: Bristol 1635 and 1640
(Bristol Record Office Manuscripts AC/C48/Items 19 and 23)

Text A

[f. 1r] Deare Tom, I am glad to heare that your selfe wyfe and littel Hugh are
so well returned to Henton, much douteinge that it would haue bine a very
wearisome iourney to my daughter and Hugh, and haue acordeinge to your
desier sent our .3. hourses the souner to bringe you home, hopeing they will
5   perform the iourney as well as grase horses may. littel Florance was with me
this afeternone, and is very well, she hath a toothe broken the flesh wch made
her some thinge ile and not of quiete, before it came out. I beliue she will haue
more very shortly. So wisheinge you and yours a good returne hether, with m^r
Gorges loue and myen to my daughter and your selfe assureinge you. wee shall
10   not thincke it boldnes, but assurance of your loues, to comand any thinge that
is ours, to doe you or your seruise, Thus prayeing god to blese you with yours
I rest

Your euer loueing mother
Eilizabeth Gorges

15   Aishton Phelips this .12. of Iuly .1635

Franck Rogers and your sister desiers me to returne ther loue and respectes to
you bothe.

Text B

[f. 1r] Deare Tom, I hope my daughter and your selfe came well to your
Iourneys ende, and haue ere this meett and discoursed with many frends, and
well reconsiled formor pasages, wch when your leasure serues, I shall be glad to
vnderstand of, all our swette Iwells at Aishton are very well, as you lefte them
5   I prays god, as soune as Edwards comes hether I hope to sette forward your
derections for Elminton bisines, trusteing you haue fully resouled what shall
be done ther, the two bakers haue bine hire againe to know what to doe, I
comanded them to see there wher no more lose by ther negligence, vntel your
seruantes returne, and if then I reseued, no other order frome you, if Phellip

10   would pase his word for the rente this one yeare I thought they myte holde it,
and he seemes to be very willinge to giue as the old man heth offerd for a finne
hireafter if you please. what you derecte shall be carefully obcerued by me, to
call vppon those you Imploye, or any waye elss with in my power, I long to be
at Aishton, with my littel ones, wch I intend as soune god willing as E.P. his gone,

15   tel my daughter her great cofer could not be caried by horse, I thought to haue
put it into two trounks, but Harald doth asure mee that you maye better forbear
what is in it, then to send it any way but by waygen, or wayine, as yet ther
is none hard of, and I haue the cofer hire in the house in a readiness. So
with my deare loue to you bothe prayinge god to bless you bothe with all yours

20   I rest

Your Euer loueing mother
Eliza: Gorges

Bristow this .22th. february .1640

Notes

Text

Among the papers of the Smyth Family of Ashton Court, near Bristol. The letters are summarised by J. H. Bettey (ed.), *Calendar of the Correspondence of the Smyth Family of Ashton Court 1548–1642*, Bristol Record Society, Vol. 35 (1982), pp. 123 and 154.

Manuscript

Neither letter is endorsed on the verso, though in Text A there may have been an endorsement now lost, since the relevant part of the page is torn off.

Glossary

(A5)	*grase horses*	=grass horses, horses kept at grass
(B3)	*reconsiled*	settled
(B3)	*pasages*	disputes
(B4)	*Iwells*	=jewels, darlings
(B10)	*pase his word*	make a personal promise
(B11)	*finne*	=fine, financial settlement
(B14)	*his*	=is
(B15)	*cofer*	trunk
(B16)	*forbear*	do without
(B17)	*wayine*	=wain, heavy cart

Local placenames

(A2)	*Henton*	Hinton St George
(A15 and B4)	*Aishton Phelips*	Ashton Philips
(B6)	*Elminton*	Elmington
(B23)	*Bristow*	Bristol

People

(A16)   *Franck Rogers*   Frances Rogers, son-in-law to Elizabeth
(B14)   *E.P.* (also (B9) *Phellip*)   Edward Phelips of Montacute, lawyer and friend

Background

Elizabeth Gorges, in her late forties at the time of these letters, is writing to Thomas Smyth, her son by her first marriage. Since her husband's death she has changed her surname by a second marriage.

   Elizabeth Gorges (c.1590–1658) was born Elizabeth Gorges, daughter of Sir Thomas Gorges of Langford, Wiltshire. Elizabeth married Sir Hugh Smyth in 1604, Hugh having been the ward of Elizabeth's father. His mother's letters to their son Tom as a young Oxford student survive, and also some, as exemplified here, written when he is an adult with wife (see Text 49) and children of his own, Florence and Hugh being two of nine. Elizabeth's second marriage was to her cousin, Sir Ferdinando Gorges. She and her husband lived mainly at Lower Court (Ashton Philips), Long Ashton, only a mile from Ashton Court, now Thomas's.

   When Letter A is written, Elizabeth is at Lower Court and Thomas is at his father-in-law's house at Hinton St George, but travelling home shortly. When Letter B is written, Thomas is home, but Elizabeth is away at the Gorges' Bristol house.

Topics for linguistic investigation

1. The evidence relating to the pronunciation of vowels in the spellings (A4) *desier* and (A9) *myen*, (A8) *hether* and (B8) *vntel*, (B5) *soune*, (B12) *hireafter* and (B18) *hire*, (B18) *hard*.

2. The evidence relating to the pronunciation of consonants in he spellings (B8) *wher*, (B10) *myte*, (B14) *his*, (B23) *Bristow*.

3. The constructions (A6) *she hath a toothe broken the flesh*, (A7) *some thinge ile*, (B3–4) *to vnderstand of*, (B13) *any way elss*, (B16) *Harald doth asure mee*, (B16–17) *you maye better forbear what is in it, then to send it*.

4. *Our swette Iwells* and *my littel ones*: Ways women (and men?) refer to children at this period.

Memoirs

My hed & hart woe than at worck how
to Eßcape a prison knowing thes prison
to be som of ye worst for Kellefa —
I being aquanted with ye natur of ye
Spaniards Apperted Litell Chariti from
them . . . My being vn Easie had my
Ey toward ye shore knowing I had —
but Litell tim before I should be
deliuerd vp to ye Jaylor. I asked the
purser which thay Cald ye Steduan
whother J.smith not goe on shore he
tould me he would Ashe ye Capton
It being don ye Captaine toull him
I must firßt goe to ye Gouerpor —
A Bad in Coradgment I not being —
willing to stand to his kind nor still
watcht for an Opertunatie at Laßt
I had a boate Com abord with two
wimon pasend to be hoers: rouning
to wellcom hurk os migh be for —
ther Turnes One stoping out of ye
boate to Com vp ye ships side fill ouer
abord in ye water there was presently
a hobbob I hoeing ye mon kon oude

Plate VII

Plate VII

Text 54
Edward Coxere: Dover 1681

Religious Society of Friends Library MS. Vol. S.281, page75
Edited text 54/40–52

My hed & hart was then at work how
to Escape a prison knowing there priso<n>s
to be som of ye worst for Rellefe – –
I being aqwainted with ye Natur of y^e
5   spaniards Axpacted Litell Chariti from
them .. My {mind} being vn Easie had my
Oÿ toward ye shore knoweing I had –
but Litell tim be fore I shoulld be
deliuerd vp to ye Iaylor. I asked the
10   purser which thay Calld ye skreuan
wether I. mith not goe on shore he
Toulld me he woulld Aske ye Capten
It being don ye Captaine toull him
I must first goe to ye Gouerner – –
15   A Bad in Coradgment I not being –
willing to stand to his kindness still
watcht for an Opertunetie at Last
I sae a boate Com a bord with two
wimen Rakend to be hoors: coming
20   to wellcom such as migh be for –
there Turnes One steping out of
ye boate to Com vp ye ships side fell ouer
a bord in ye water there was presentlÿ
a hobbob I seeing ye men Ron ouer

Handwriting: Mixture of old shapes, e.g. *c*, (17) *watcht*, *e* and *d*, (4) *aqwainted*, and new ones, especially *h*, (1) *hed & hart*.

Characters: Use of *y* in (3) *y^e*, and marked as *ÿ* when representing vowel, (7) *Oÿ*, (23) *presentlÿ*.

Allographs: Long and short *s*, (2) *prison*, (5) *spaniards*. Characters *u* and *v* operating as allographs, (9) *deliuerd vp*.

Capitals: Clear and frequent, (2) *Escape*, (4) *Natur*, (5) *Axpacted Litell Chariti*.

Abbreviations: None, apart from *y^e*.

Punctuation: None in normal function. Full-stops used adjacent to pronoun *I* (9, 11), and dashes to fill spaces at end of lines (3, 7 etc.). Dots in uncertain use in line 6.

Alterations: Insert in line 6, with position indicated by caret mark. At end of line 2 lack of space leads to the final -*s* being written above (edge of page has subsequently worn away, wih loss of the <*n*>.

Typical spellings: (5) *Axpacted*, (11) *mith* and (20) *migh*, (13) *toull* but (12) *Toulld*, (15) *in Coradgment*. Single items written as two words, (6) *vn Easie*, (8) *be fore*.

Introduction to Memoirs

Someone who writes memoirs is making a story out of some particular past time in his or her life. This is why memoirs are different from both journals and letters.

In a journal the writer, looking back over the day, notes down those things which have been done, seen or heard of, and which he expects to look back to at some future time. Whether in the long run they will turn out to have had significance is not known to him as he writes. In memoirs, the writer looks back from some distance and writes about the things he experienced, selecting incidents which he remembers and which, in retrospect, he assesses as important to him, and setting them together as a developing story. This may be simply at the end of the journey or the adventure, or it may be at some later point in life, looking back across many years.

In the extracts chosen here, four men tell stories of something that has happened to them. Thomas Dallam (Text 52), is a designer and builder of organs, who having safely returned from an incident-packed journey by sea and land to Constantinople where he had to deliver and install an organ as a gift from Queen Elizabeth to the Sultan of Constantinople, writes down what he calls *A brefe Relation of my Travell from The Royall Cittie of London towardes The Straites of Mariemediteranum, and what hapened by the waye*. Thomas Mowntayne (Text 51), writing in the early years of the reign of Elizabeth I, describes how, as a Protestant member of the clergy during England's recent Catholic time under Queen Mary, he coped with bullying from the Church, personified in the Bishop of London. James Melville (Text 53) in his mid-forties, recalls the time seventeen years earlier when as a young Professor at St Andrews University in Scotland his opinions made him a hunted man, forcing him into a rough and hazardous sea journey to England. Edward Coxere (Text 54), a fifty-year-old seaman and formerly a ship's gunner, now a Quaker, frequently imprisoned for his religious non-conformity, looks back over his *seuerall Adventures By sea with the daingers Difficulties and hard ships I met for seuerall years* and writes the story of danger and survival at sea thirty years before, when he was crew-member of a ship which escaped total wreck in the Straits of Gibraltar only to be captured by a Spanish man-of-war.

The fact that the memoir is dealing with events in one's past, however recent, results in language which is different from what is used in writing about events as they happen. A letter written during an on-going experience will employ present tenses, such as where Kate Ashley (Text 47) describes the prison she is in, by my trothe hyt ys so cowlld y^t I can not slepe yn hyt & so darke y^t I can not yn the daye se for I stope the wendo w^t strowe thar ys no glase (47/12–14).

In contrast, memoirs employ the past tenses which are appropriate for experiences now over,

> ye dore was verrie litle & opened verrie straitly, into ye gallarie/ the wynde blowed marvalus strongly/ & made a greate noyse, for ye house Lay verrie open/ to ye sea & wether (52/19–21).

In the same way a letter from Ames Steynings (Text 42), written to his uncle while the Siege of Maastricht is in progress, uses simple presents and present-tense perfects when he describes what has been happening,

> there is Lately come downe to the army an enimy who is tiled magna de sancta crusia who thinckes to releeue the towne with 15 thousand foot and horse, wee haue had hard duety of it ever since … the enimy hath Lost many of his people all ready and many wee haue taken prisoners (42/22–6),

but past tenses are used in memoirs for describing what happened,

> a cusing of my awin name … offerit to me/ be the assistence of God to put me saiff in Bervik w^{t}in twenti foir houres be sie/ To this also my vncle Roger and vther frinds aggreit sa efter consultation at my God and finding of his warrand in my hart I concludit to go (53/1–5).

Moreover, this generally past-tense presentation produces a background against which an occasional dramatic narrative-present form can be used,

> bot the youngman being verie skilfull and able starts to his kist (53/37–8),
> Bot being af and on w^t dumbar about ane efter noon/ comes of the hilles of lamermure age a grait mist wt a tempesteus schoure and drow (53/33–4).

Unlike virtually all the other kinds of document in this collection, memoirs have a printed counterpart. At this time, autobiography was establishing itself as a literary genre, and various autobiographies were printed before 1700.[1] Publishing the account of one's own life or of a physical or spiritual journey became an increasingly popular undertaking as the sixteenth and seventeenth centuries progressed, and by the beginning of the eighteenth century autobiography was familiar enough to readers for Daniel Defoe to use it as the covert mode for writing fiction.

Occasionally, 'ordinary' people without literary skills or pretensions did see their memoirs published, but there was a high, and publicly ackowledged, level of ghosting. When someone was less than confident about his skill to write in English acceptable for publication, the writing was done for him, and was welcomed. This is clear from prefaces such as that in the printed memoirs which are 'written by' seaman William Okely,[2] the story of his escape in a home-made boat from slavery in Algiers,

> I was conscious to my self of the great unfitness to recommend it to publick view, in such a garb as might vindicate it from Contempt; for though it has been drawn out

many Years with my own hand, and many have had the perusal of it, have approved it, and desired it; yet till I could prevail with a Friend to teach it to speak a little better English, I could not be perswaded to let it walk abroad: The Stuff and matter is my own, the Trimming and Form is anothers, for whom I must vouch, that he has done the Truth, my self, and the Reader, Iustice.

However, where a personal story was a private document only, no ghost-writer improved its grammar, and no printing-house imposed on it the improved spelling or punctuation which virtually always replaced idiosyncratic orthography when a text appeared in print.[3] Coxere's memoirs are written in an assured style, and he tells us that he had command of several languages, often being called upon to act as ship's 'lingwister'. Only his mastery of spelling conventions is poor, and with no-one to standardise his orthography, his holograph manuscript retains spellings which would have been lost in a printed version, such as *wether I: though it wear* 'whether I thought it were', *pouering of holle broad sids* 'pouring of whole broadsides', and *wimen Rakend to be hoors* 'women reckoned to be whores'. His use and perception of verb-forms would also have been tidied up in print, such as his *should a fell* for 'should have fallen'. Moreover, Coxere's story in print would have had the punctuation it, like all other documents, manifestly lacks in manuscript. In the same way a printed text of Thomas Mowntayne's memoirs would do away with spellings such as his *crwell*, *trubule* and *porpoose*.

In a manuscript, too, a better-educated writer was able to relax into less standardised language than would appear above his name in a printed work. James Melville is a University Professor, and his *Life* is principally a religious-political polemic. However, he allows himself in the extract printed here to be led astray into sheer story-telling. His extremely competent narrative is also homely, as he chooses to use Scots, albeit in a watered-down form, and so he has available to him Scots lexical items such as *keaue ower*, *drow*, *a prettie pirhe of weund* and *viuers*, and forms such as *quhilk*, as well as a Scots orthographic system giving spellings such as *sweit* and *saiff*, and a Scots vowel-system reflected in *maist* and *awner*.

Where memoirs or autobiographies are published, a readership is clearly anticipated. With unpublished documents there remains the question of whether a reader was envisaged, or whether the memoirs were totally personal. Typically, there are no *you* pronouns or sections directly addressed to a reader. Again, this is in contrast with letters, where someone recounting an adventure may write a comment directly to his addressee, such as where Ames Steynings writes about the progress of the Siege of Maastricht and then comments,

> good vncle it is a great deale of misery that a soildier doth endure besides danger every minight of his Life (42/47–9).

However, it is possible that at least some of the documents quoted here were meant for others to read. Coxere may well have been writing with an eye to being read by circulation to fellow-Quakers with whom he has a common experience of conversion, and Melville, other than in the quoted extract, was making serious political and religious statements in his writing. In the case of Mowntayne, we know that the aim was, in fact, publication. His manuscript is among those gathered by his contemporary John Foxe, when compiling the record of Protestant sufferings in Queen Mary's time which was published in the various editions of his *Book of Martyrs*, popular and officially-recommended anti-Catholic reading in the years that followed. That Mowntayne wishes to make his account as telling as possible is evident from his detailed correction of his manuscript, extra words and phrases being added to hammer home the attitudes he wants his reader to share,

> thys hastye bushop {& crwell man} (51/22).

Memoirs are, by definition, written in the first person singular,

> I rowit my selff till the hyd com af my fingars (53/48)
> I perseuing of it Toulld my Conserts I: woulld get vp & see if perhaps I: migth get a can of wine in yᵉ Croude (54/14–16)
> when we had Layne about halfe an houre// we yᵗ had oʳ weeden pillowes/ weare sodenly wonderfully Tormented wᵗʰ a varmen yᵗ was in or pillowes (52/8–9).

Third person pronouns and verbs are of course used where other people's actions are described, but 3rd person passages often contain oblique 1st person pronoun forms, since other people's actions are included in the narrative specifically because they had some effect on the narrator himself,

> This my Cusing being a mariner conducit a bott to carie a Town of his portage wyn about to Carell/ and decking me vpe in his se attyre betymes in the morning about the Simmer solstice/ tuk me in down vnder dondie as a shipbroken sie man (53/8–11).

Variety of pronoun and verb forms, and sentence structures, may be introduced where speech is incorporated into the narrative by direct quotation. Mowntayne uses this method extensively,

> Than yᵉ bushop callyd me vnto hym & sayed: thow herytycke how darste thow be so bowlde: toyvse that sysmatycall saruys styll (51/5–7),
> godys pasyon sayd yᵉ bushop: dyd not I tel yow my lorde deby. howe yow sholde knowe an heretyke (51/15–16).

A different way with speech is to transfer it to indirect reporting, a less dramatic mode which Coxere prefers,

> I asked the purser which thay Calld yᵉ skreuan wether I. mith not goe on shore he Toulld me he woulld Aske yᵉ Capten (54/44–6).

It is interesting to speculate about this difference in the ways in which the two memoir-writers handle speech. It might be because Mowntayne is thinking back only a few months while Coxere is recalling things said thirty years previously, but this is not a very convincing explanation. We need, rather, to examine why each writer wishes to introduce speech into his narrative. In Coxere's case, his exchange with the purser leads on to the next part of his story, as he tells us that finding he will get nowhere by asking, he cleverly seizes an opportunity and makes a daring escape. It is the content of the speech that counts, not the wording. However, Mowntayne is far more self-aware in his style. His intention is not only to describe what happened, but to demonstrate how well he acquitted himself in argument, and to emphasise how loathsome, vindictive and hypocritical these members of the ecclesiastical establishment are. So he puts direct speech in their mouths, intending that the speakers should be shown as condemning themselves by their own words,

> godys pasyon sayd ye bushop: dyd not I tel yow my lorde debytye howe yow sholde knowe an heretyke? he ys vp w^t ye lyuynge god: as thoo ther were a dead god they haue nothynge yn ther mowthes thes herytykys but ye lord lyuythe: ye lyuynge God rwlythe: ye lorde: ye lorde/ & nothyng but ye lorde (51/15–19),
>
> the lord debytye sayed/ my good lorde chaunseler: trobyl not yor selue w^t thys herytyke: I thynke all the worlde ys full of them god bles me from them: but as yor lordshyp sayed euen nowe full well: hauynge a chrystyan quen nowe raynynge ouer vs: I truste ther wylbe shortyly a refformasyon an an order taken for thes herytykes & I truste god hathe presaruyd yor honorable lordshyp euen for y^t very same porpoose (51/22–8).

However recent the incident Mowntayne is recalling here, it is extremely unlikely that he is recalling actual speeches; there is a great difference between the order of recall needed for utterances of this length and that demonstrated by witnesses to a few items of verbal abuse. Rather he is fictionalising, inventing the kind of things he wants the Bishop and his cronies to have said and to have betrayed themselves with. This means, of course, that the direct speech which he presents has the same status as the direct speech of a fiction-writer or a dramatist. It tells us a great deal about the way people spoke at the period, but it is not primary evidence.

The use of imagined dialogue and careful selection of loaded language makes Mowntayne's memoirs the least artless of the four texts quoted here. However, there is one syntactic feature which they all have in common, and which challenges the assessment of their language which their spelling might lead a modern reader to make. This is the constant use of constructions subordinated not by clause patterns with *when*, *because*, *after* and so on, but by the employment of present-participial phrases. This may be modelled on Latin style, but it is interesting that it is used not only by the priest and the professor but by the organ-maker and even more frequently by the gunner,

> hauynge a chrystyan quen nowe raynynge ouer vs: I truste ther wylbe shortyly a refformasyon (51/25–6)
> Sa coming hard to the steppes of the Archbishops peare at Sttandr// we lossit our skleattes (53/20–21)
> passinge awaye ye time/ wth such Lyke talke, ye moste parte of vs fell a sleepe (52/16)
> thay being in a horie not minding of me we being Iust by the shore put ye boat a shore I being be twene hope & dispare Lest I shoulld be discouerd being at ye shore thay minding The woman more then me I as sliely as I coulld got a shore and

being well a qwainted there I Run a bout a qwarter of a mille and got in to yᵉ towne
(54/54–8).

This, they are surely indicating, is the kind of syntax in which memoirs should be
written; even if the stories of their adventures are for their eyes only.

Notes

1. For an extensive list of both texts and discussions of the genre, see George Watson (ed.), *The
   New Cambridge Bibliography of English Literature* (Cambridge University Press, Cambridge,
   1974), Vol. I (600–1660), Section 6.II 'Letters, diaries, autobiographies and biographies', and
   Vol. II (1160–1800), Section 5.VI, 'Letters, diaries, autobiographies and memoirs'. Also Paul
   Delany, *British Autobiography in the Seventeenth Century* (Routledge, London, 1969).
2. William Okely, *Eben-ezer, or a small monument of great mercy appearing in the miraculous
   deliverance of W. Okely … from slavery* (Nat. Ponder, London, 1675).
3. For discussion of the extent to which printers regularised authors' orthography, see Ronald B.
   McKerrow, *An Introduction to Bibliography for Literary Students* (Clarendon Press, Oxford,
   1927 and later imprints), pp. 246–51; for a particular example, D. G. Scragg, *A History of
   English Spelling* (Manchester University Press, Manchester, 1974), p. 70.

Text 51

Thomas Mowntayne: London 1559

(British Library Manuscript Harley 425)

[f. 106r] nowe whan I cam ynto yᵉ greate chamber: at S marye ouerys ther I
fownd the bushp standynge {at a baye wyndowe} wᵗ a great {compane} aboute
hym/ & many swter� bothe men and wemen: for he was gooynge to the courte
amonge home ther was one mʳ ~~ssylmmmmd~~ {ssellynger} a kynghte and lord
5   debytye of Iyerland beynge a swtter also: to my lorde [f. 106v] Than yᵉ bushop
callyd me vnto hym & sayed: thow herytycke how darste thow be so bowlde:
toyvse that sysmatycall saruys styll. of late set forthe: seynge yᵗ god hathe sent
vs {nowe} a catholycke quene: whose lawys thow haste broken as yᵉ reest of
{thy} fellowse hathe don: & yow shall knowe the pryse of {yt} yffe I do lyffe:
10 ther ys suche abomynable companye of yowe? as ys able to poyesyn a hole
realme wt yor herysys/ my lorde sayed I: {I} ham none heretyke: for yᵗ waye yᵗ
yow cownte herysy? so worshupe we ye lyuynge god: {&} as oʳ fore fatherys
hathe done {& beleuyd}? I men<e> habraham: Isaake: & Iacob: wt yᵉ reste of
yᵉ holly prophetys & apostyllys: euen soo doo I beleue {to be sauyd & by no other
15 meanys/} godys pasyon sayd yᵉ bushop: dyd not I tel yow my lorde debytye
howe yow sholde knowe an heretyke? he ys vp wᵗ yᵉ lyuynge god: as thoo ther
were a dead god they haue nothynge yn ther mowthes {thes herytykys} but ye
lord lyuythe: yᵉ lyuynge God {rwlythe}: yᵉ lorde: yᵉ lorde/ & nothyng but yᵉ
lorde/ her he {chaffyd} lyke a bushp: & as hys manar was many {tymys}: he
20 put of hys cape & rubbyd to & froo {vp and don}: the fore parte of hys heed:
wher a locke of hare was alwayes standynge vp: and yᵗ as sume saye wase hys
grace/ but to passyffye thys hastye bushop {& crwell man}: the lord debytye
sayed/ my good lorde chaunseler: trobyl not yoʳ selue wᵗ thys herytyke: I thynke
all the worlde ys full of them {god bles me from them}: but as yoʳ lordshyp
25 sayed euen nowe full well: hauynge a chrystyan quen nowe raynynge ouer vs:
I truste ther wylbe shortyly a refformasyon {an an order taken} for thes
herytykes & {I truste} god hathe presaruyd yoʳ honorable lordshyp euen for yᵗ
{very} same porpoose/ {than sayed mʳ selynger vnto me: submyt yoʳ selue vnto
my lorde & {{so}} yow shal fynd fauor at hys hnad I thanke yoʳ syr sayd I: plye
30 yoʳ owne swete: & {{I pray yow}} let me alon for I neuer offendyd my lord
neyther yet wyll ~~make~~ I make any suche submysyon has he uolde haue me to
doo be assueryd of yᵗ god wyllynge wel sayd he: yow are a stuburne man} than
stode ther one by: mvche lyke vnto docter martyn & sayed: my lorde the tyme

260

pasythe a waye: trubule yor selue no longer w^t thys herytyke? for he ys not onlye
35   an herytyke? but also a traytor to ye quene{*ys* magesty}: for he was one of them
y^t wente forthe w^t ye ducke of northeth*u*mberland & was yn opyn felde a gaynste
here grace: & therfor as a traytor he ys one {of them} y^t ys exsemte {owte} of
the {generall} pardon and hathe loste ye benyfytt of ye same/ ys yt: euen so
saythe ye bushope? feche me ye boke y^t I maye see {yt}? than was ye boke
40   broughte hym: weryn he loked: as one Ingnora*n*te what had ben done/ and yet
he beynge ye cheffe doere hym selue ther of than asked he of me whate my name
was/ I sayed my name was thomas mownttayne/ thow haste wronge saythe he?
{why so my lorde} y^t thow haste not mow*n*tyd to tyborne or to {soche} a lyke
place [f. 107r] than sayed I vnto hym: I beseche yor lordshyp be so good lored
45   vnto me: as to let me knowe myn acusar*es* whoo they be: for I truste y^t I haue
not desaruyd nother to be hangyd as a theffe: nor yet to be burnyd as herytyke/
for I onely beleue yn one god {yn trynyty}: & as for the lawes of the realme {I
truste} I haue not offendyd or brokyn {anye of them} no sayd ye bushop: I wyll
make thee {to} synge a newe songe or thow & I haue don for thes ij: be alwayes
50   lynked to gether: treson: & herysy: & thow haste lyke a shamles ma*n*: offendyd
yn bothe & y^t shalte thow knowe: I wyl scole ye my selue/ than he callyd for the
marshall or some of hys me*n*: & ther was non of them ther: than calyd he for
one m^r hu*n*gerford: on of hys {owne} Ientellmen; hyme he row*n*dyd yn ye eare
a prety whyele: & than opynly {t}he {bushop} sayed w^t a loude woysce: I praye
55   yow m^r hu*n*gerford: take thys {trayterus} herytke & haue hym to ye marshallsee:
& reme*m*ber {wel} whate I haue sayed vnto yow: for thys ys one of ~~them~~ {or
{{new}} brochyd bretheryn} that spekethe agayenste al good work*ys*/ no my
lorde sayed I I never prechyd {or spake} a gayenste anye of thos good workys
{w^{ch} be} comawndyd of god yn the {holy} scryptur*ys* {to be don} for yn thos
60   {good} workys: euery chrystyan man awghte to exsersys hym {selue} al y^e
dayes of hys lyffe: & yet not to thynke hym selue to be Iustyffyed therby: but
rather to cownte hym selue an vn prouytable seruant whan he hathe don the
beste he can y^t {ys} trwe qothe the bushop yn ded: yor fraternytye was: ys: &
euer wyll be al to gether vn p*r*ophytabull yn al agys & good for nothynge but for
65   ye fyere/

Notes

Text

Extract only. The complete text was edited in John Gough Nichols (ed.), *Narratives of the Days of the Reformation, Chiefly from the Manuscripts of John Foxe the Martyrologist*, Camden Society, Original Series, Vol. 77 (1859, and reprint by AMS Press, New York 1968), pp. 177–217.

Manuscript

There is extensive and interesting revision of the text by the writer's insertion of additional words and phrases. The long inserted passage in lines 28–32 is added in the margin.

Some smaller alterations show second thoughts on spelling: (2) *compane* is altered from *companye*, (3) *wemen* is earlier *wyemen*, (13) *Iacob* is altered from *Iakob*. Grammatical alterations are made in (60) *hym{selue}* and (49) *{to} synge*.

Suspect, as probable mistakes, are: (4) *kynghte*, (29) *hnad*, (29) *yo*.

The letters *m* and *n* in word-final position are given a looped-back flourish which has been considered empty. Also deemed empty is the frequent use of a stroke above an *m* or *n*. Although it might represent a second nasal-letter, *mm* and *nn* spellings are not confirmed from elsewhere in the text.

In (4) *ssellynger* a now illegible name, beginning with *ssyl* but without *g* and ending in *d*, has ben scored out, and the present reading inserted above. Another hand has confirmed this by writing *ssellenger* below.

Glossary

(2)	*swterys*	petitioners
(19)	*chaffyd*	grew angry (see note)
(22)	*grace*	attractive feature
(26)	*an order*	(repressive) measures
(43)	*tyborne*	Tyburn gallows (see note)
(49)	*or †*	before
(51)	*scole*	= school, discipline
(53)	*rowndyd*	whispered to (transitive)
(54)	*a prety whyele*	briefly
(55)	*yᵉ marshallsee*	the Marshalsea, a London prison
(57)	*new brochyd*	recently begun

Proper names

(1)	*S marye ouerys*	St Mary Overy's Church, London
(4)	*mʳ ssellynger a kynghte*	Sir Anthony St Leger
(33)	*docter martyn*	Thomas Martyn, keen opponent and persecutor of Protestants

Explanatory notes

(2) *the bushp*: The Bishop of Winchester, Stephen Gardiner, also Lord Chancellor under Queen Mary.

(7) *that sysmatycall saruys … of late set forthe*: the forms of Anglican worship set out in Edward VI's time in *The Booke of Common Prayer* (1549 and 1552), and now, in Mary I's reign, illegal under the 1553 Act of Repeal.

(16) *the lyuynge god*: Biblical phraseology frequent in both the Old and New Testaments (e.g. Psalms 42 and 84), here stigmatised as Protestant cant.

(19) *chaffyd*: Not the much later verb *chaffed* 'bantered', but earlier *chafed* simultaneously in its figurative sense 'grew angry', and in awareness of its literal sense 'rubbed'.

(36) *yᵉ ducke of northethumberland*: John Dudley, Duke of Northumberland, married his son to Lady Jane Grey and campaigned for the succession to fall to her rather than to

Mary. His defeat led to his execution in 1553. Known active participants on the Dudley side were still at risk.

(43) *thow haste not mowntyd to tyborne*: Tyburn gallows was also the place where heretics were burned. It was on a hill-top and *to mount the gallows* was also a common description of the hanging procedure. The Bishop's pun on Mowntayne's name is matched by a possible Shakespearian pun (*Love's Labour's Lost* IV.i.4) on *mountain/mounting*.

(48–9) *I wyll make thee to synge a newe songe*: The Bishop is parodying the opening of Psalm 96, again mocking Protestant Biblical quotation.

(58–63) Mowntayne's final speech on *good works* and *justification* is heavily loaded with Protestant thinking and phraseology; for his use of the phrase *an vn prouytable seruant* see Luke 17:10.

Background

From among the papers gathered c.1559 by John Foxe when compiling for his *Book of Martyrs* material about Protestants persecuted during Mary's reign. Mowntayne was a priest who, having embraced Protestant views, refused to switch back to Catholicism, and his continued public use of Anglican forms of Service led to his arrest.

Topics for linguistic investigation

1. Mountayne's changes to his first version of the manuscript.
2. The function of the question marks.
3. The evidence relating to pronunciation in the spellings (5) *bushop*, (11) *ham*, (26) *an*, (40) *weryn*, (44) *lored*, (45) *desaruyd*, (54) *whyele*, (54) *woysce*.
4. The forms: (51) *shalte*, (13) *hathe*, (34) *pasythe*, (55) *haue*, (59) *be*, (63) *qothe*.
5. The use of *do*-support.
6. The constructions: (17) *they haue nothynge yn ther mowthes thes herytykys but* …, (39) *y^t I maye see yt*, (39–40) *than was ye boke broughte hym*, (48–9) *I wyll make thee to synge a newe songe or thow & I haue don*, (53–4) *hyme he rowndyd yn ye eare a prety whyele*.
7. How Mountayne manipulates the language to make the Bishop detestable.

Text 52

Thomas Dallam: Lancashire (London) 1599

(British Library Manuscript Additional 14,780)

[f. 47r] growinge towardes nyghte/ & rememberinge whate hard Lodginge we
should haue in oᵣ new In// findinge a thicke softe weed, that growed by yᵉ wood
sid everrie one of vs yᵗ was thare/ gathered a bundle of it to Laye under oᵣ
headₑₛ/ when we should sleepe/ nyghte beinge come/ & oᵣ supper ended,

5   everie man chalked out his Ristinge place vpon yᵉ bare bordₑₛ/ oᵣ Ienisarie
placed him selfe vpon aborde yᵗ Laye louse vpon ye Ieistₑₛ:/ everie man had his
sorde Reddie Drawne Lyinge by his side, tow of oᵣ company had musketₑₛ,
when we had Layne about halfe an houre// we yᵗ had oᵣ weeden pillowes/
weare sodenly wonderfully Tormented wᵗʰ a varmen yᵗ was in oᵣ pillowes yᵉ wᶜʰ

10   did bite farr worss than fleaes/ so yᵗ we weare glad to throw awaye oᵣ pillowes/
and sweepe yᵉ house clene/ but we could not clense oᵣ selues so sowne/ Thus
as we Laye wakinge in a Darke vncomfortable house/ mᵣ glover tould vs what
strainge varmen & beastₑₛ he had sene in yᵗ contrie/ for he had Lived Longe
thare/ he spoake verrie mvche of Aderₑₛ: snaykₑₛ: & sarpentₑₛ/ yᵉ Defferance,

15   & yᵉ bignes of som wᶜʰ he had sene

passinge awaye yᵉ time/ wth such Lyke talke, yᵉ moste parte of vs fell a sleepe,
& som yᵗ could not sleepe/ Laye still & sayd nothinge for disquietinge of yᵉ
Reste/ all being whyshte// mᵣ baylye, had occasion to goe to the dore to make
water/ yᵉ dore was verrie litle & opened verrie straitly, into yᵉ gallarie/ the

20   wynde blowed marvalus strongly/ & made [f. 47v] a greate noyse, for yᵉ house
Lay verrie open/ to yᵉ sea {&} wether,/ mᵣ baylle when he Lay downe to sleepe,
had vntied his garterₑₛ a Litle/ so yᵗ when he came into yᵉ gallarie, yᵉ wynde
blew his garter yᵗ was Louse & trayled after him/ Rovnde aboute yᵉ other
Legge, it was a great silke garter, & by yᵉ force of yᵉ wynde/ it fettered his

25   Leggₑₛ bothe faste together/ oᵣ talk a Litle before; of Aders snakes & sarpentₑₛ
was yeat in his Rememberance/ & yᵉ place neare wheare mvche varmen was//
he Thoughte they had swarmed aboute him// but aboute his Legge/ he
Thoughte he was sur of a sarpente/ so yᵗ soddonly he cried oute wᵗʰ all the voyce
he hade/ a sarpente/ a sarpente: a sarpente, & was so frighted yᵗ he could not

30   finde yᵉ Doore to gitt in/ but made a greate buslinge/ & noyse in yᵉ gallarie,//
on yᵉ other side/ we yᵗ weare in yᵉ house// did thinke yᵗ he had saide, assalted,
assalted/ for before nyghte we doubted yᵗ some tritcherie would hapen vnto us

264

in y^t towne/ so y^t we thoughte ye house had bene besett wth people to cvtt o^r
Throte*s*/ thare was .15. of vs in ye house & it was bute a litle house/ everie man
touke his sorde in hande, one Reddie [f. 48r] to spoyle another/ not any one
knowinge the Cause, one y^t could not finde his sorde, goot to ye Chimnay &
offeringe to climbe vp, Downe fell a parte of ye chimnaye tope vpon his heade/
& hurte him a Litle/ another y^t was sodonly awakede/ strouke aboute him wth
his sorde/ & beate downe ye shelfe & broke ye pitcher*es* & plater*es* wch stood
thar on/ ye Rovme being verrie dark for it was a boute mydnyghte/ other*es* did
thinke y^t they weare pullinge Downe ye house over our head*es*/ o^r janisarrie who
should haue bene o^r garde & haue proteckted vs from all Dainger*es*/ he
Lykewyse doubtinge ye people of ye towne/ & hearinge suche a noyse/
sododonly/ he touke vp ye louse borde wheare on he Laye/ & sliped Downe
into ye valte/ as we weare thus all a mayzed, at ye Laste m^r bayllye fovnde y^e
waye in at ye Doore/ when m^r glouer saw him com in/ he sayd vnto him/ how
now man what is ye matter/ who do yow se/ m^r baylle was even bretheless w^th
feare/ cryinge out, & wth struglinge to gitt in at ye Doore, so y^t he could not
answer him at ye firste/ at Laste he sayd, a sarpente a sarpente had trubled him/
when m^r glouer harde him say so/ than feare was gone/ & he wente to ye Dore/
& thare he founde m^r. bayllis garter/ Reddie to be carried away wth ye wynde
[f. 48v] After we hade a litle wondered, at o^r great amayzmente, for so smale a
cause// m^r glouer caled everie man by his name/ to se yf any man weare slayne
or wounded// for thare was sixtene of vs in all/ o^r weaperns all drawne & y^e
Rovme was but Litle, everie man beinge caled/ we weare all alive/ & but smale
hurte done/ At laste we found o^r Ianisarie wanting who myghte well be
ashamed/ to make it knowne wheare he was// but mr glouer callinge him
verrie earnestly/ he answeared in ye valte, he could not git out any way/ but m^r
gosnal Touke vp ye borde y^t Lay wheare he wente downe/ & Lyinge a longe
vpon ye floure, he could but hardly Reatche him to take him by ye hande/ wth
mvche adew theye puled him vp// when he Leaped into ye valte/ beinge verrie
sore frighted/ he caste of his vper garmente/ and lefte behind him in ye valte//
but no man could p*ar*swade him to goo Downe againe & fetche it// for ye place
was Lothesom// & it should seme y^t he was thare frighted wth somthinge, in
y^t kinde m^r baylye was/ so his garmente Remayned thare till ye morninge y^t he
who aved the house did fetche it

Notes

Text

Extract only. The complete text was edited by J. Theodore Bent (ed.), *The Diary of
Master Thomas Dallam 1599–1600*, as Section I of *Early Voyages and Travels in the
Levant*, Hakluyt Society, Vol. 87 (1893). This extract (in Bent's version) has appeared
in John Julius Norwich, *A Taste for Travel* (Macmillan, London, 1985) pp. 340–41.
Dallam's life and adventures are discussed and his diary quoted at length in Stanley
Mayes, *An Organ for the Sultan* (Putnam, London, 1956).

Manuscript

There is a clear error in (44) *sododonly*. For the reading (66) *aved* see explanatory notes below.

Some initial letters transcribed as capitals (especially *L*) may be intended as lower-case variants in initial position.

Glossary

(2)	*In*	lodging (not necessarily public house)
(8)	*weeden*	made of weeds (OED's only example of this word)
(9)	*varmen*	noxious creature
(15)	*bignes*	size
(17)	*disquietinge*	disturbing
(18)	*whyshte*	silent
(19)	*straitly*	narrowly
(32)	*doubted*	feared
(33)	*besett*	surrounded
(35)	*spoyle*	injure
(37)	*offeringe*	attempting
(46–7)	*how now*	interjection, usually preceding question
(56)	*wanting*	missing
(64–5)	*in y^t kinde*	in the same way
(66)	*aved*	?owned (see note)

Explanatory notes

(5 etc.) *Ienisarie, Ianisarie*: Member of the Turkish army, forcibly recruited from Russian or African slaves or by a one-in-five levy of Christian boys. Here he is the official escort assigned to the party.

(58–9) *m^r gosnal*: J. T. Bent, *Diary*, suggests that this man is called *Gonzale*.

(66) *aved*: J. T. Bent, *Diary*, reads *oved* and equates with *oued/owed* 'owned', which is the meaning demanded by the context. However, the manuscript has *aved*. This might be a non-standard *a* for *o* spelling, normally a Northern feature, but there is no parallel spelling elsewhere in the text (despite Dallam's Lancashire roots). There is also the possibility of interpreting it as *(h)aved*, but there is no other dropping of initial *h* here.

Background

Dallam (born in Lancashire but working in London) was a noted designer and maker of organs and was, in his late twenties, commissioned by Queen Elizabeth I to make and take an organ to the Turkish Sultan Mohammed III in Constantinople. This incident in his account of the journey is set in Cannosea, modern Ganos, in Greece, then part of the Ottoman Empire, where the party has been driven ashore by bad weather.

Topics for linguistic investigation

1. The evidence relating to pronunciation in the spellings: (6) *Ieistes*, (7) *sorde*, (9) *varmen*, (14) *spoake*, (30) *gitt*, (30) *buslinge*, (54) *weaperns*, (61) *adew*.

2. The evidence for pronunciation that is offered by the story that people misheard 'assaulted' as 'a serpent'.

3. Verb-forms used by Dallam.

4. The constructions (17–18) *for disquietinge of y*ᵉ *Reste*, (27) *he Thoughte they had swarmed aboute him*, (37) *Downe fell a part of y*ᵉ *chimnaye tope*, (44) *y*ᵉ *louse borde wheare on he Laye*, (45–6) *at y*ᵉ *Laste mr bayllye fovnde y*ᵉ *waye in*

5. The derivational morphology of: (1) *Lodging*, (5) *chalked*, (8) *weeden*, (15) *bignes*, (17) *disquietinge*, (29) *frighted*, (33) *besett*, (64) *Lothesom*.

Text 53

James Melville: Scotland 1601
(National Library of Scotland Manuscript Advocates 34.4.15)

[p. 121] Sa seiking resolution cairfullie of my God what to do/ a cusing of my awin name/ of his awin frie mocion and accord offerit to me/ be the assistence of God to put me saiff in Bervik wᵗin twenti foir houres be sie/ To this also my vncle Roger and vther frinds aggreit sa efter consultation at my God and finding

5   of his warrand in my hart I concludit to go. albeit noᵗ wᵗout grait tentationes and mikle heavines/ yit on the part reioysing yᵗ God gaiff the hart to leaue natiue countrey house and sweit lowing new maried wyff and all for the loue of him and his Chryst. This my Cusing being a mariner conducit a bott to carie a Town of his portage wyn about to Carell/ and decking me vpe in his se attyre

10 betymes in the morning about the Simmer solstice/ tuk me in down vnder dondie as a shipbroken sie man, and rowing about behouit to go to the heavin of Sttandr/ to los a certean of skleatt steanes/ and because it was law water ~~and~~ we behoued to ly a whyll in the road till the water grew/ whare the bott wanting ane owerlaft/ the seall was cassen ower hir ta end and ther I leyed vpe lest I

15 shuld be spyed of sum shipes rydding besyde/ bot wᵗin short space partlie be rokking in the sie and partlie for want of eare I grew sa extream seik/ yᵗ manie {a} tyme I besaught my Cowsing to sett me a land/ schesin rather ane sort of dethe for a guid cause nor sa to be tormented in a stinking holl. and yit whowbeit it was extream peanfull/ I gatt ther notable medicin of vomitine quhilk was

20 a preseruatiue to my helthe all yᵗ yeir. Sa coming hard to the steppes of the Archbishops peare at Sttandr// we lossit our skleattes and tuk in viuers and rowit out agean immediatlie and cam yᵗ night to Pitmillie burn mouth wher I gead a land and reposit me in my sie abbit/ and efter offers of grait kindnes be the Lard/ and furnitour of a rubber of stark merch eall/ betymes in the

25 morning we rowit out about the ness/ the day was hat/ ther was bot twa men in the bott/ by twa Cusings of myne wᵗ my selff/ of these twa we haid an at our deuotion/ the vther was the awner of the bott and verie euill affected/ bot the hat rowing and the stope wᵗ the stark eall laid besyd him/ maid him atteans to keaue ower a slipe/ and it pleisit God to send a prettie pirhe of weund wherby

30 getting on a seall vpon hir or ever our schipper wakned we was a guid space besouth the May/ wha seing he could noᵗ mend him selff was fean to yeild and agrie wᵗ his merchant for a hyre to Bervik. Bot being af and on wᵗ dumbar about ane efter noon/ comes of the hilles of lamermure age a grait mist wᵗ a

tempesteus schoure and drow/ quhilk or we could gett our sealles taklit/ did
35   cast ws about and or my Cusing [p. 122] was awar caried ws bak almaist to the
May wᵗ sic a how wa and spin drift yᵗ the bott ~~in~~ being opin he lukit for grait
danger giff the stormie shoure haid continewed/ bot the youngman being verie
skilfull and able starts to his kist and tuk out a compas and finding ws contrare
our course/ wᵗ mikle ado wanting helpe/ and schipping of mikle water he cust
40   about and pykit on the wind, halding bathe the helme and scheit/ susteining in
the mean tyme euill langage of the schippar in stead of helpe/ till it pleasit God
mercifullie to luik vpon ws and wᵗin an houer and an halff to dryve away the
schoure and calme the drow/ sa yᵗ it fell down dead calme about the sune
drawing leache. To keipe the sie all night in an opin litle bott it was dangerus/
45   and to go to dumbar we durst not/ sa of necessetie we tuk ws toward SᵗTabs
heid/ bot we haiffing but twa eares and the boot slaw and heavie/ it was about
alleavin houres of the night or we could win thar/ whowbeit na men was ydle/
yea I rowit my selff till the hyd com af my fingars mair acquented wᵗ the pen
nor working on an are/ Coming vnder the crag we rowit in wᵗin a prettie lytle
50   holl betwix the mean and the head/ whare easelie going a land we refreschit ws
{wᵗ} could water and wyne and returning to our boot sleipit the dead of the
night/ but neidit nan to wakin ws, for soone be the day light piped thar was sic
a noyse of foulles on the crag and about ws because of thair young annes, that
we war almaist pressed to lainche out/ now we haid Cawdingham bay and hay
55   mouth to pas by and yᵗ bot slawlie rowing be the land whar was the residence of
Alexʳ home of Manderston an of our cheiff confederat enemies and wha haid
intercepted a bott of the Erle of Angus coming about from Tantallon to Bervik
noᵗ long befor/ this put ws in grait feir/ but our guid God gardit ws making a
sweit thik mist till aryse wherby we might bot skarslie gis at the sight of the land,
60   and yᵗfra nane could sie ws/ sa we cam on hulie and fear till we was wᵗin the
bounds of Bervik/ whar we was in graitest danger of all vnbesett in the mist be
twa or thre of the Cobles of Bervik qˡᵏ war sa suift in rowing yᵗ they ged round
about ws/ bot we being fyve wᵗin burd and haiffing twa pistolets wt thrie
swordes and they na armour they war fean to let ws be, nemlie when they
65   vnderstud yᵗ we was making for Bervik. Thus gretiuslie pretected be my guid
God I cam to Bervick.

Notes

Text

Extract only. The complete text was edited as *The Diary of Mr James Melvill* (Bannatyne
Club, Vol. 34, Edinburgh, 1829), and by Robert Pitcairn (ed.), *The Autobiography and
Diary of Mr James Melville* (Wodrow Society, Edinburgh, 1842). Short extracts are
printed, using Pitcairn's text, but with the title which appears in the manuscript itself,
in J. G. Fyffe (ed.), *The Historie of the Lyff of James Melvill* (Saltire Society, Edinburgh,
1948).

Manuscript

Capital *L* is much used word-initially, but since it also appears medially in (63) *pistolets* it has been considered as a variant on lower-case *l*, and is transcribed as such here.

The full form (34) *quhilk* is also represented by (62) *qlk*. No expanded form of the item *no'* occurs, though other Scots texts suggest that it represents *nocht*.

Glossary

Familiar words obscured by spelling

(7)	*lowing*	=loving
(8)	*Cusing*	=cousin
(9)	*Town*	=tun, large cask
(11)	*heavin*	=haven, harbour
(12)	*skleatt*	=slate
(14)	*ta*	=two
(16)	*eare*	=air
(17)	*schesin*	=choosing
(21)	*peare*	=pier
(23)	*abbit*	=habit, clothes
(24)	*merch eall*	=March ale (noted for its strength)
(28)	*atteans*	=at once
(29)	*a slipe*	=asleep
(29)	*weund*	=wind
(46, 49)	*eares, are*	=oar(s)
(65)	*gretiuslie*	=graciously

Other items

(5)	*warrand*	authorisation, approval
(8)	*conducit* †	hired
(9)	*portage wyn*	wine for export
(10)	*the Simmer solstice*	midsummer, 21 June
(11)	*shipbroken* †	shipwrecked
(11)	*behouit*	was obliged
(12)	*los* †	unload
(12)	*certean* †	quantity
(13)	*road*	sheltered water near shore
(13)	*wanting*	lacking
(14)	*owerlaft* †	overdeck
(14)	*cassen*	thrown (past participle of *cast*)
(21)	*viuers* †	provisions
(22)	*burn* †	stream
(24)	*furnitour*	supply
(24)	*rubber*	cask, barrel
(24)	*stark* †	strong
(24)	*betymes*	early

(25)	*ness*	headland
(28)	*stope*	flagon
(29)	*keaue ower* †	topple over
(29)	*pirhe* †	sudden breeze
(30)	*or ever*	before
(31)	*besouth*	to the south of
(31)	*fean*	glad
(32)	*af and on* †	approximately
(34)	*drow* †	drizzle
(34)	*or* †	before
(34)	*taklit* †	reefed
(35)	*cast ws about*	drive us in the other direction
(36)	*how* †	deep
(36)	*wa* †	wave
(36)	*spin drift*	whipped-up spray driven over surface
(38)	*kist* †	chest
(38)	*contrare*	contrary to
(39)	*schipping*	taking on board
(39)	*cust*	=cast, turned
(40)	*pykit on the wind* †	brought (the boat) sharply into the wind
(44)	*leache* †	=laigh, low
(50)	*holl*	cove
(50)	*mean* †	mainland
(60)	*hulie* †	slowly; the phrase *hulie and fear* (=fair) slowly and gently but steadily
(61)	*vnbesett* †	surrounded
(62)	*Cobles* †	small boats
(63)	*pistolets*	pistols

Local placenames

(3)	*Bervik*	Berwick-upon-Tweed
(9)	*Carell*	Crail
(11)	*dondie*	Dundee
(12)	*Sttandr*	St Andrews
(22)	*Pitmillie*	Pitmilly
(25)	*the nes*	Fife Ness
(31)	*the May*	Isle of May
(32)	*dumbar*	Dunbar
(33)	*lamermure age*	Lammermuir Edge
(45–6)	*St Tabs heid*	St Abbs Head
(54)	*Cawdingham*	Coldingham
(54–5)	*hay mouth*	Eyemouth
(56)	*Manderston*	Manderston House, nr. Duns
(57)	*Tantallon*	Tantallon Castle, nr. Dunbar

Background

Melville (1566–1614) born in Montrose, Scotland, was Professor of Hebrew and Oriental Languages at the University of St Andrews, and an ordained member of the clergy. His use of Scots is particularly interesting in the light of this. His outspoken voicing of strong Presbyterian views made him a hunted man in Scotland when power in ecclesiastical matters was restored to Bishops and King in 1584. His tale of his escape to England stands out from the religio-political polemic of the rest of his *Life*.

Topics for linguistic investigation

1. The mixture of Scots and Southern English spellings.
2. The mixture of Scots and Southern English verb inflexions.
3. The use of constructions which begin with present participles.
4. The constructions: (8) *This my Cusing*, (13) *we behoued to ly*, (15) *spyed of some shipes*, (33) *comes of the hilles of lamermure age a grait mist*, (44) *To keipe the sie all night … it was dangerus*, (49) *nor working on an are*.
5. The etymology of: (8) *conducit*, (12) *los*, (21) *vivers*, (22) *burn*, (29) *keaue*, (29) *pirhe*, (30) *schipper*, (34) *drow*, (38) *contrare*, (59) *till*, (60) *hulie*, (62) *Cobles*.
6. Where Melville uses Scots words, were there Southern English words with similar meaning available at this date which he could have used instead?

Text 54

Edward Coxere: Dover, Kent 1681

(Religious Society of Friends Library Manuscript MS. Vol. S.281)

[p. 72] we now being taken the spanyards made. to wards there owne shore and
anchord be tweene Mallago: and vells Mallago both prise & man of war I being
ther prisoner in yᵉ man of war The spanish Captaine spied a ship he calld me
to him & bid me Luck in his skrie glas to see wether I: though it wear an Inglish

5   man of war or a Marchant man It being in Cromwells time thay dreded our
frigats I Toulld him yᵗ I though it was noe man of war but did soe pose it was
one yᵗ did not mater him with yᵗ he sed he woulld trie) {&} Comanded yᵉ
Anchor to be got vp and made to wards him I was presently securd down in yᵉ
houlld & 3 or 4 more of my consorts when got Close to gether these 2 ships The

10   Great gons be gan to Ratell pouering of holle br{o}ad sids in to Each other vere
smartlÿ a Considerabell time I being in yᵉ holld: sae throw yᵉ Creuases of yᵉ
bords the spaniards hand wine vp to the men be twene dakes & bred to Refresh
them sellus be twene whills thay hauing ocation for som thing wear I was shut
vp [p. 73] Opend yᵉ skutell but did not shut it a gain I perseuing of it Toulld my

15   Conserts I: woulld get vp & see if perhaps I: mi{g}th get a can of wine in yᵉ
Croude thay wisht me not to goe fearing thay woulld knock me at hed I being
then not ouer Care full in ~~ts~~huch maters got mee vp and went diractly in to yᵉ
gon Rume whear .I. though .I shoulld find most frends If any shoulld a fell one
me I seing one Lay ded which was my frend I being vn ~~Ease~~ Ease in my mind

20   kept moueing in fear & willing to get a Can of wine I turnd back a gaine to yᵉ
maine hat{c}h and in yᵉ hobob Got a great can of wine and bred and got sudenly
a way with it to my holle a gaine wear lay a ded man by yᵉ skotell ~~wen~~ I went
downe to my Conserts a gaine and toock a hat & dented it in yᵉ Crown pouerd
wine in and sapt the bisket & made mere{i}) thoe honger be sharp yet yᵉ haserd

25   was great and we were Refreshed when yᵉ spanyards Lay ded and bleding in
there wounds and there gons shot out of the caradges till at last I perseued Les
noise ouer my hed {&} the gons not soe qwick of motion [p. 74] The Inglish
man had soe plied him with shuch vn pleasant baales ~~that~~ that yᵉ proud
spanyard was forst to Lay downe yᵉ Codgells The Inglish man perseuing him

30   willing {to} fet{c}h Breth & to be quiet hoised vp his saills and Left yᵉ spaniard
to fit his ship a gaine and went a way with flieing Cullers which site pleased
me vere well for I was Calld vp to hellp them & yᵉ first work I was set to was to
hellp Care a ded spaniard out of yᵉ Rownd howce & what Ells I was Comanded

to doe

35   Our ship yᵉ prise Laying at Anchor all this whill for want of Mast but was not
Idell soe long as there gons did Reach yᵉ Inglishman
The wind Coming faier we sailld) for Mallago and geting boath ships in to the
Moalld The Gouerner of yᵉ Towne Came downe in his Coach The spaniards
Reiosing with fiering of guns for there safe a Riuall with a braue prise But pot

40   a shore there ded & wounded men [p. 75] My hed & hart was then at work how
to Escape a prison knowing there priso<n>s to be som of yᵉ worst for Rellefe I
being aqwainted with yᵉ Natur of yᵉ spaniards Axpacted Litell Chariti from
them .. My {mind} being vn Easie had my Oÿ toward yᵉ shore knoweing I had
but Litell tim be fore I shoulld be deliuerd vp to yᵉ Iaylor. I asked the purser

45   which thay Calld yᵉ skreuan wether I. mith not goe on shore he Toulld me he
woulld Aske yᵉ Capten It being don yᵉ Captaine toull him I must first goe to yᵉ
Gouerner
A Bad in Coradgment I not being willing to stand to his kindness still watcht
for an Opertunetie at Last I sae a boate Com a bord with two wimen Rakend to

50   be hoors: coming to wellcom such as migh be for there Turnes One steping out
of yᵉ boate to Com vp yᵉ ships side fell ouer a bord in yᵉ water there was
presentlÿ a hobbob I seeing yᵉ men Ron ouer [p. 76] The ships side in to yᵉ Boate
to hellp har I being as Actiue then as som of them was sune in yᵉ {boate} with
them as If I had gon to saue life thay being in a horie not minding of me we

55   being Iust by the shore put yᵉ boat a shore I being be twene hope & dispare Lest
I shoulld be discouerd being at yᵉ shore thay mindin{g} The woman more then
me I as sliely as I coulld got a shore and being well a qwainted there I Run a bout
a qwarter of a mille and got in to yᵉ towne: being thear I sune got to yᵉ water
side wear yᵉ ~~bo~~ flemens boats Laÿ fearing a heue & Croie I hauing yᵉ

60   Lan{g}widg as duch as wel as french & spanish preuaill{d} with one to Care
me of a bord of there ship being a bord I gaue them a full a count of my
Condition and If thay woulld but Entertaine me I woulld worke & be vere much
obliged to them for Libertes sake [p. 77] It was granted me to Remaine there by
the skiper: My Next work was to har{k}en out what Entertainment our

65   Captaine & companie I Left be hind me woulld meete with
At Last I herd yᵉ spanyards weare soe kind as to giue them Liberti thay being
but feu & thay hauing Left be hind them a good ship well Laden with wheat
pillchers & Tin yet it was more then was Axpacted

[p. 72a Text accompanying illustration]

70   An Inglish marchant man
A spanish man of war in which I was A prisoner in yᵉ time of the figh
The Dilleience of London of which I was Guner
After we got of from the shore we had ~~we had~~ fitted our ship with Ieure Mast
then the spanish man of war a boue tuck vs

Notes

Text

Extract only. The complete text has not been edited in its original spelling, but there is a modernised-spelling text with notes and helpful introductory discussion, by E. H. W. Meyerstein (ed.), *Adventures by Sea of Edward Coxere* (Clarendon Press, Oxford, 1945).

Manuscript

A photograph of lines 40–52 from this document, together with a commentary, appears as Plate VII on pp. 252–3 above.

The text is illustrated with sketches of ships described.

Coxere sometimes sets two dots over the letter *y* (11, 43, 52).

He frequently uses some mark of punctuation near the pronoun *I*, sometimes a colon after it, sometimes a dot before and after, and sometimes a single dot. In one instance (the second example in l.15) the colon has been carefully added as a correction in darker ink. However some of the instances of *I* followed by colon (e.g. in line 4, and the first example in l. 15) are slightly suspect, since they occur at the ends of lines, and it is Coxere's habit to put colons and other dots at the end of lines which do not totally fill the available space. Paragraphing is dubious.

There are several instances of the writer correcting his own spelling by inserting a letter omitted earlier, (10) *br{o}ad sids*, (15) *mi{g}th*, (56) *mindin{g}*, (60) *Lan{g}widg* etc. The deletion of initial *t* in (17) *tschuch* is likely to be not a correction, but a false start crossed out, probably *these*.

In (28) *baales* the *aa* is altered from earlier *oa*; in (24) *yet* the initial *y* has been written over an earlier *y* which had a stroke going up to superscript *e*, as in the *y^e* that follows; in (45) *skreuan* the *re* is written over an earlier *ee*.

In (41) *prisons* the word is written at the extreme edge of the page, and the letter *s* is written above the line for lack of space, however the edge of the leaf has subsequently worn away so that the letter after *o*, which may be reconstructed as *n*, is no longer present.

Glossary

The Man of War: Coxere and other prisoners are confined in the *hold*, below the water-line, his exit from which is via the *scuttle*, a small hatch covered with a trapdoor. One or more gun decks are over their heads, also the *gun-room*, the living-quarters of the junior officers. The *round-house* is the quarters of the senior officers on the top deck.

(4)	*skrie glas*	spy-glass, telescope
(8)	*presently*	immediately
(9)	*consorts*	colleagues
(13)	*hauing ocation for*	needing
(16)	*at hed*	on the head
(24)	*sapt*	=sopped, dunked
(24)	*bisket*	ship's biscuit, hard-tack
(26)	*caradges*	wheeled stands for canon
(28)	*plied*	kept on supplying

(28)	*baales*	=(canon) balls
(29)	*Lay downe yᵉ Codgells*	give up the fight
(30)	*hoised*	hoisted
(31)	*fit*	put in order
(31)	*with flieing Cullers*	with flags flying
(38)	*Moalld*	= mole, harbour enclosed by breakwater
(45)	*skreuan*	See note
(50)	*for there Turnes*	in need of them
(51)	*ouer a bord*	overboard
(59)	*flemens*	Flemings, Dutchmen
(59)	*heue & Croie*	=hue and cry, shout of pursuit
(60–61)	*Care me of aboard of there ship*	=carry me off aboard their ship
(62)	*Entertaine*	employ
(64)	*harken out*	find out by enquiry
(68)	*pillchers*	=pilchards

Placenames

(2)	*Mallago, vells Mallago*	Malaga, Velez Malaga

Explanatory notes

(44–5) *the purser which thay Calld yᵉ skreuan*: The ship's purser kept accounts and organized supplies, so Spanish *escribano* 'clerk'.

Background

The bulk of the autobiography of Edward Coxere (1633–94) is about his adventures as a gunner under the flags of various nations, and the last section deals with his conversion to Quakerism. He says that Dover is both his birthplace and his home. He does not mention formal education, but does tell us that he was often called on as ship's 'lingwister' since he has a command of French, Dutch and Spanish, and even 'Lingwa frank', useful in Tunisia. In this extract his storm-damaged ship, the *Diligence*, has been captured by a Spanish man of war in the Straits of Gibraltar, and he has been taken on board the Spanish ship.

Topics for linguistic investigation

1. Coxere's corrections to his own spelling.
2. The spelling-evidence relating to the pronunciation of vowels.
3. Supporting evidence from other texts for the pronunciations suggested by the spellings: (4) *wether*, (18) *a*, (28) *shuch*, (46) *toull*, (59) *flemens*.
4. Evaluation of the evidence concerning pronunciation in the spellings (6) *though*, (15) *mi{g}th*, (24) *thoe*, (31) *site*, (45) *mith*, (50) *migh*.
5. The use of participial constructions in lines 48–61.
6. Survey other texts for the use of *which* in reference to people.
7. How reasonable would it be to describe Coxere's language as sophisticated English in naïve spelling?

Presentments

Dorchester Bill October the 5 1657

305 104

Alsoe presente Robert Lane of Dorchester
ye labourer for comeing drunke from molendge
upon the foure and twenty day of iune
and for cuting of a new hare rope in
flaxlands in Dorchester feild the same
time of William Mellor and turninge the
horse luse when hee was upon his owne
ground

This Lane when hee was worned to watch
ye did say that hee would watch when hee
listed but hee did the same for he was
much complaynd of by his naibors

Constables
William Mellor
Nathaniel May

Plate VIII

Plate VIII

Text 581
Constables of Irchester: Northamptonshire 1657

Northamptonshire Record Office Manuscript QSR 1/6 No. 104
Edited text 581/1–11

Irchester Bill October the 5 1657

Wee present Robert Lane of Irchester
laborer for coming druncke from weling{bore}
upon the foure and twenty day of iune
5   and for cuting of a new hare rope in
flexlands in Irchester feild the same
time of William Bletsoe and turning the
horse luse when hee was upon his owne
                        grownd
10   This Lane when hee was wornd to watch
hee did say: that hee would watch when hee
listed and so hee did the seruis for he was
mutch complaynd of by his naibors
          Constables
15   William Bletsoe
           Nathaniel May

Handwriting: Traditional letter-shapes, especially *h*, (1) *Irchester*, *c* (5) *cuting* and *x* (6) *flexlands*, but style of *e* is Greek rather than reversed circular.
Allographs: Long and short *s*, (11) *say*, (9) *horse luse*, (9) *was*.
Capitals: Clear, and used consistently for proper names and to begin sections.
Abbreviations: None.
Punctuation: None. Marks which appear are almost certainly unintended, in line 7 apparent bracket between *William* and *Bletsoe* is the tail of the *h* above, in line 11 apparent comma after *watch* is probably an accidental mark.
Alterations: Letters above line at end of line 3 because of lack of space. Run-on in lines 8–9 differently solved.
Typical spellings: (8) *luse*, (13) *naibors*.
Problems of interpretation: Uncertainty about whether the document is written by one of the constables who has signed his own names and written in his colleague's, or whether text and names have been written by an amanuensis.

279

Introduction to Presentments

Presentments are the paperwork by which constables, churchwardens and holders of other offices reported to the appropriate authorities those matters which fell within their remit. In the course of the two hundred years 1500–1700 these areas of responsibility were multiplied, and also changed because of social and religious developments, seventeenth-century constables, for example, having to report on Roman Catholics and Non-conformists in their villages (Text 58).

The job-description for constables, who were unpaid appointees, usually two for a parish, was extremely wide-ranging.[1] They were primarily concerned with the preservation of the peace, and had powers of arrest. They were called on to report not only breaches of the peace but matters ranging from unlicensed ale-houses to the state of the highways and the expulsion of vagrants after the deterrent whipping for which they themselves were responsible. Some constables' presentments, such as Text 55A and B, give detailed narrative about local incidents and people, while others are brief. Some derive from a specific set of articles to which the constables have been instructed to respond. One such questionnaire,[2] from Bedfordshire in 1616, includes items such as,

> Item what Ryetous owtregious or unlawwfull. Assemblyes tendinge to the breache off his majessties pease
> Item what recuzantes Popishe or sectary. That com not to Churche to heare Devyn servise According to the law: by whom harbored. And how longe they beine recusantes
> Item what Alhowsseis or Typplinge howsses be with in yowr parishe lyssensed or not lyssensyd and who they bee and whether those lysensed Do observe the orders to them latlye prescrybed yee or no And what ponishement hayth ben Don them unlysenced
> Item what Commun Dronkirdes or Commen hawnters off allhowses be with in yowr parishe

together with instructions to look for other matters such as beggars, unauthorised building and illegally high wages paid to servants. The 1657 Southwick constables' presentment (Text 58F) is clearly derived from some similar list. Village constables, termed 'petty' constables, made their presentments to the Quarter Sessions via the Chief Constable of the administrative area (hundred) to which their village belonged. The 1616 list quoted above is headed by the instruction,

Theis Articles to Be Enqwyred. off And Seirtyffied From tyme to tyme: Especiallye Syxe Days beffore Everye general Assyzes particularlye … by A Commandemente From the Judgeis.

The Chief Constable was probably a local gentleman and himself a Justice of the Peace.

Every Parish also had two or more churchwardens, elected and normally unpaid. Several sets of churchwardens' annual accounts appear earlier in this collection (Texts 9, 12 and 17). As well as being accountable to parishioners for their management of church property during their year of office, they were required to make presentments[3] to the local diocesan authorities, through the Archdeacon, who held consistory courts to which they were summoned. Their reports dealt with offences against canon law and church discipline.[4] The presentments reported by the churchwardens of Stratford-upon-Avon for 1628 (Text 57) are fairly typical in including blasphemy, drunkenness, sexual harassment, an alehouse open for business during the Sunday Service, fisticuffs and defamation alleging witchcraft, irreverence in church and insulting body-language and backchat to the churchwarden. Examples from elsewhere mix the reporting of sexual irregularities (especially where they might result in unsupported women and children becoming a drain on the parish poor-relief) with the noting of repairs needed to the church fabric,

> we present our church yard wall as much as is now in decay
> we like wise present one bell in decay.
> we like wise presnt degory secombe for not Cohabiting with his wife like wise we present michall trease for he & his wife doe not Cohabit to gether
> wee like wise present ffrances dan to be the Reputed father of a base childe by the bodey of Annis cortis with in our parich.[5]

In New England the churchwardens of Virginia were given detailed notes on what to present,

> You shall sweare that you shall make true presentments of all such persons as shall lead a prophane or ungodly life, or such as shall be common swearers, drunkards or blasphemers, that shall ordinarilie prophane the saboth dayes or contemne God's holy word, or sacrament; you shall also present all adulterers or fornicators, such as shall abuse their neighbours by slanderings, tale carryeinge or backbiting, or that shall not behave themselves orderlie in the church during devine service. Likewise you shall present such masters and mistresses as shall be delinquent in catechizing of the youth and ignorant persons, so help you God.[6]

Like constables, English churchwardens had a set of articles, issued by the diocese, to which they were expected to respond. Presentments often refer to these, and the reference-numbers indicate the number of items sometimes included,

> Ye present George Pennye for a recusant papist According to the 45 Article. We presnt Richard Waterer for carrying a load of hay on newe years daye last Article 27.[7]

In the course of the seventeenth century the distinction between secular and ecclesiastical matters became less clear, and the presentments made to the local Petty Sessions in the hundred of Plympton, Devon, in 1683 (Text 59) are made jointly by the constables and churchwardens of each parish, and deal both with masterless men and licensed alehouses and also with dissent from the established church, and with legal but scandalous behaviour,

> As for any profan swarers or Coursers or Common Ale house hantters drunkards or Lewd parssons we know none with in our pirsh (59A/18–19).

As this nil return indicates, the agenda of their report must be determined by a questionnaire which has been sent to them.

Constables and churchwardens were not the only people from whom presentments were demanded. The papers of a 1675 Manor Court at Bullwick, Northamptonshire,[8] include presentment documents from various manor officials, including the pinder, who presents William Cunington *for keeping luse his Cowe*, the field-searcher, who makes a presentment *for ouechargein the Common with 2 beast*, the ale-taster, who also deals with bread, and who complains,

> I haue noe weights to whey there bread and for our Alehouses they sell there Ale as they list,

and the leather-searcher, who smugly reports *Omne Bene*. There are also minutes of many other kinds of courts whose business was to receive presentments and to note and take action about the information received. From these records, in the absence of the original presentment documents, the nature of such documents can be reconstructed. Ports, for example, had Admiralty Courts, dealing with maritime business. The Admiralty Court of Southampton met at Leape in September 1574, and minuted various matters presented to it, such as,

> Item they present that Robert West of Remhall found a pece of Tymber driving in the Sea a quarter of an yere past.
> Item Thomas Haills of Leape founde a boye virkin driving in the Sea.
> Item they present that Robert Tucker of Itchin very hath a nett called a drawght nett an ynche in the narrowest and two inches on the meases.[9]

Similarly, towns had courts dealing with municipal business. As well as the Admiralty Court, Southampton had a Court Leet which met regularly and minuted presentments concerning public health and safety, such as,

> Item we present there are many inhabitantes in S[t]. micheles parishe and other parishes of the Towne of the meaner sorte that vsually doe washe and rinnce there Clothes, Lynnen/ &/ wollen at the Counduits, in the Towne, most vnseemly, and hange there clothes vppon Lynes in the streats
> Item we present there is no reformation of the daungerous bakehowses, and places for the fewell namely. broome/ heath, and virses. wherw[th] they heat there ovens: w[ch] is a great abuse and Likly to endaunger the whole Towne wth fyer, (w[ch] God forbidd).[10]

Although some enjoyed the power, very few people welcomed election or appointment to any of the offices where they had to watch and report on their neighbours, and reluctance had to be countered by a system of fines for refusing to serve. Snooping and reporting was not only distasteful, but made you an object of dislike and insult,

> Item we present those whose names followe for railinge uppon the Churchwardens & abusinge them with euill termes.[11]

In fact the attempted enforcement of discipline was often dangerous, as many complaints suggest,

> William Risdon of S[t] togumber yeoman deposeth that about six yeares sithince he beinge then one of the Churchwardens of S[t] togumber aforsd came with Alawfull warrant to take A distresse vpon the lands of the widow Luckis Mother of the sd Nicholas Luckis for her refusing to pay her rate for the Church & driveing Ahorse out of the grounds of the sd widow Luckis the sd Nicholas violently assaulted & wounded him with Acorne Pyke.[12]

There were no qualifications for being either a churchwarden or a constable, apart from residence in the parish. Literacy was not a condition of appointment. But this, naturally, raised huge problems when so much paperwork was involved in the job, not only with presentments to be written, but also with instructions being sent in writing. A Wiltshire constable in 1616 petitioned his local Quarter Sessions asking for release from his office,

> forasmuch as I am unlearned, and by reason thereof am constrayned to goe two miles from my howse to have the help of a scrivener to reade such warrants as are sent to mee, and am a very poor man.[13]

Just as many church wardens regularly got someone else to write their accounts (see Introduction to Accounts page 43 above), so too presentments were written by a more literate person at the request of those who had to submit the necessary documentation. Thus Text 58G describes itself as

> A Bill mad ffor the Cunstables of Desborrow Anno domino 1657,

and even the names of the Desborough constables are written for them. The ever-helpful Roger Lowe (Text 35) records in his journal how he wrote on behalf of local constables, and joked about doing it without payment,

> saturdaij Constables of Hadocke and Goleborne came to have me write theire presentmts for assizes and when I had done I writt poore is provided highwaijes repaired these querijs answerd and clarke vnrewarded att which they laughed most heartily (35/44–7).

As in the writing of churchwardens' accounts, the literacy of the constables' helpful friend might be low-level. Where the parish officials themselves felt competent to write their own presentments they too might be far from skilled.

The outcome for the present-day historical linguist is that presentments are documents of very great interest, since so many are written in naïve English.

They are especially valuable in regard to spelling, and the information it yields in regard to pronunciation. Even six lines of a single text from the constables of the Essex parish of Wickham St Paul's in 1652 contain many spellings which are informative for the reconstruction of the writer's pronunciation, such as *thether* 'thither', *akayne* 'again', *bey* 'by', *worttelle* 'worthily', *recayued* 'received', *huse* 'us', *mytte* 'might, *sofvered* 'suffered', *onne* 'any' and *reme* 'realm' (55A/8–13), and at roughly the same date a short presentment from a constable of Southwick in Northamptonshire is equally characteristic,

> sowick bill 1657/
> I present weedo stiuen for briwing with out a licance
> Item our pore ar preuided for
> Item our Charch is in good repare
> Item our hiwaes ar in good repare
> Item our wach and ward ar duly cape
> Item wee haue no recusantes/ in our toune or paresh
> Item wee haue no new eracted tanemantes
>   Edmun Ierland. Canstabel (Text 58F).

The spelling abilities of the writers of presentments are particularly stretched when they are required to deal in official gobbledygook. Evidence points to the everyday use during the seventeenth century of the word *papist* when referring to a Roman Catholic, as in the words for which the Barking fishwife Margaret Edwards is in trouble in Text 8,

> hee heard Margarett the wife of the said Thomas Edwards say; That … shee would haue holpe to haue torne him in peices like a Papist dogg as hee was (8/24–29)

or the comment reported in Text 55,

> he ys a were fellen & ase Ranke a papeste as onne ys wette In the Reme of yngellond (55A/12–13).

Most people could make a fair stab at spelling that. However, where officialdom asked about Catholics who refused to attend Anglican services they employed the term *recusant*. When some of the Northamptonshire parish constables dealt with this query, they felt obliged to use the 'official' word, but had only a hazy idea what the word was, so for *recusants* we have the variants *a qusantes* (58C/3), *a cusants* (58H/3) and *Accusance* (58G/3). Similarly, the constables sending in presentments about how people of no fixed abode have been moved on from parish to parish have great difficulty with the official word *vagabond*, writing *wacabons* (56A/2), *facabones* (56C/1) and *ffacabandes* (56D/2). An unfamiliarly tough Christian name causes parallel problems for another writer, despite the fact that he has been called in to help his local constables, when he sets down *Ferdinando* as *ffarthing nando* (58G/4).

Interestingly, the presentments of village churchwardens are for the historical linguist one of the few sources of spellings reflecting pronunciation which continue into later centuries, as parishioners elected wardens for their common sense rather than their educational standard. Two Cornish presentments surviving among Exeter Diocesan papers read,

I Present the Saits the North Side of the Church & I Now Nothing Moar Presentable Whitness my hand John Horswell [1779]

and,

I do Sicertifey that I have Nothing two Persent to your Lordship Court at Truro Witness my hand this 17th of July 1805.[14]

Vocabulary is another area in which the language of Early Modern English presentments repays investigation. The mis-analysis of difficult words has already been mentioned. Also of interest is the way in which lexical items which do not show any markedly mangled form are nevertheless derived from official usage. When constables write

Wee know no profane swarers nor Common: drunkards nor alehous hanters with-in our parrish (59C/18–19)

the adjective in *profane swarers* is striking, and the phrase *alehous hanters* is a lively compound. It becomes apparent, however, that the language of the Bere Ferrers constables and churchwardens is far from innovative, when the same words are seen to appear in the presentment written by their opposite numbers in Yealmpton,

As for any profan swarers or Coursers or Common Ale house hantters drunkards or Lewd parssons we know none with in our pirsh (59A/18–19).

The responses from both parishes have been derived from phrasing in their questionnaire of articles to be answered, as the introductory *As for* in the second example confirms. Other terms such as *a night Whalker* (59B/12) and the adjective *storde* (='sturdy') applied to a vagrant (56A/15) are probably similarly derived. Being given a list of offenders to be looked out for was used by some cunning churchwardens as an opportunity to avoid presenting anybody from their parish, since they were able to claim that the terms were not sufficiently clearly defined,

To the 39th: 40th: 41th we cannot define a blasphemar swearer or drunkard and therefore craue aduice (how to present such) untill the next Courte.[15]

It is perhaps lexical divergence between presentments which is even more notable. Often we find words which are local to the area where the presentment is written, and this shows up particularly clearly in relation to those matters which are constantly being dealt with in a number of reports. For example, one recurring matter for presentment is dung-heaps in the street. In Stratford-upon-Avon Francis Harbadge is presented for having *hys mukhyll at chamburs doore*, and in nearby Coventry John Allcut is reported *for a muckil lying in the street*. But in Winchester Nicholas Cripps *hathe kepte A dunge myxton befoore his doore*, while a few miles away at Southampton, a presentment is made that *there is no reformation of the noysome gutter and mixon wᵗʰout posterne gate*.[16] Even where we are unable to make a direct comparison between texts from different places, local words can be identified. Thus Cornish churchwardens in 1665[17] make a presentment that *the Planching* ('floor') *of the tower* is in need of repair. In Yorkshire in 1501[18] someone is presented as having *pylled hollynnes* ('cut wood from holly trees') *in diverse places*. In

Shetland in 1602[19] it is reported that *twa lytill pellokis* ('dolphins') and *ane selchie* ('seal') have been washed ashore. The Stratford-upon-Avon churchwardens in 1628 present Richard Johnson who comes to church late and *there sits verie vnreverentlie ther sometymes lawfing & Romling* ('making a disturbance') (57/27–8).

Morphology needs careful setting into context within a presentment. Conservative forms are often associated with officialdom. Thus although by the second half of the Seventeenth Century the past participle of *hold* was generally *held*, as in

> We know none within our parrish that doth premit any unlawfull Assimbleys to bee held in thare houses (59C/16–17),

the older *holden* was used in the formulaic heading,

> Slipton bill for the quarter sesions holden at Northampton for the hundered of huckslow (58C/1–2).

Context also affects our assessment of the non-standard form *herne* ('hers') in the Stratford-upon-Avon text (57/32), for it is not from the churchwardens themselves but from their direct quotation of old *goodie bromlie* who has been complaining that another woman has accused her of casting the evil eye on her family.

The most marked feature of the syntax of presentments is the not-infrequent struggle to produce structures that hang together, as with the various changes of grammatical direction in

> Item Richard Iohnson the yeonger for late Coming to Church & as wee thinke hee hath noe imploiment but lasines & there sits verie vnreverentlie ther sometymes lawfing & Romling & a vsuall werer of his hat in Church in Contempt for I see him goe barehed Comonlie athome & in the streetes & a vsuall goer forth of Church before sermon be doone (57/26–30),

or the repeated subject in *This Lane when hee was wornd to watch hee did say* ... (58I/6). There are also constructions worth checking against less naïve texts, such as the handling of negation in constructions such as *he nor his wiffe was not at home* (55B/9) and *wee haue noe Ale house nor no profeaine swearers nor saboth breakres* (58H/5), and the employment of *a* before the present participle in

> her selfe a servinge three persons wth provision & a takinge monie of them (57/15–16).

There are particular difficulties in making a satisfactory analysis of the high incidence of verbs with *do*-support used in non-negative statements. One could argue that the writers of presentments are using the construction with formal weightiness, or an attempt at it, or that what is on record here reflects common and everyday usage.

It has often been observed[20] that in the Early Modern period the literary stereotype of the village constable depicts him as a comic and incompetent dolt. Real-life presentments occasionally suggest to the modern reader that the popular view had at least some basis, the presentment from Devon in 1683, for instance, which says that church attendances have probably been lowered by Reasson of a Late distemper of the small pox which happened amoungst vs and proued very mortall to many of our parishoners (59A/11–12).

But we need to check the phrase *very mortall* against the data in a historical dictionary before we dismiss it as clownish. On the other hand, that naïveté of English can be allied with engaging naïveté about their role as presenters of formal reports is sometimes abundantly clear, as in

Item edward wakeland for putting his handes vnder the Coates of marie west & hath told her husband he woold a doone the other thing in a more bestlie manner wch shee will be in Court to tell tis to longe to write (57/42–4).

Notes

1. For summaries of the constable's role see W. E. Tate, *The Parish Chest* (Cambridge University Press, Cambridge, 1946, reprinted Phillimore, Chichester, 1983), pp. 176–87; W. T. Mellows and D. H. Gifford, *Elizabethan Peterborough*, Northamptonshire Record Society (Anthony Mellowes Memorial, Volume No. 2 and Tudor Documents III) (1956, for 1953–4), Introduction, pp. xlii–xliv; Carl Bridenbaugh, *Vexed and Troubled Englishmen 1590–1642* (Oxford University Press, London, 1968), pp. 248–50.
2. Quoted in Tate, *Parish Chest*, pp. 178–9.
3. For a detailed account of churchwardens and their presentments see the Introduction (pp. vii–lxxv) to Sidney A. Peyton (ed.), *The Churchwardens' Presentments in the Oxford Peculiars of Dorchester, Thame and Banbury*, Oxfordshire Record Society, Vol. X (1928).
4. See Tate, *Parish Chest*, pp. 95–6.
5. Churchwardens of North Petherwin, Cornwall, August 1665; Devon Record Office Manuscript, Churchwardens' Presentments Box 23/6, Item 2.
6. Virginia Colony 1632; quoted by Paul Hair (ed.), *Before the Bawdy Court* (Elek, London, 1972), p. 202.
7. Churchwardens of Benson, Oxfordshire 1624; Peyton, *Oxford Peculiars*, p. 29.
8. Northampton Record Office Manuscript, TB390.
9. Edwin Welch (ed.), *The Admiralty Court Book of Southampton 1566–1585*, Southampton Records Series, No. 13 (1968), pp. 46–7.
10. Southampton City Archives Office Manuscript SC/6/1/27 f. 15v–16r.
11. Churchwardens of Banbury, Oxfordshire 1619; Peyton, *Oxford Peculiars*, p. 214.
12. Case at Somerset Quarter Sessions 1657; Somerset Record Office Manuscript Q/SR/95.III f. 201r.
13. Quoted in Bridenbaugh, *Vexed and Troubled*, p. 251.
14. Devon Record Office Manuscript, Churchwardens' Presentments, Cornwall, Box 23, 4/32 and 1/5.
15. Stratford 1560: Shakespeare Birthplace Trust Manuscript BRU/15/7/32, f. 59r. Coventry 1657: Levi Fox (ed.), *Coventry Constables' Presentments 1629–1742*, Dugdale Society, Vol. XXXIV (1986), p. 6. Winchester 1589: Hampshire Record Office Manuscript W/K5/8/B, f. 1r. Southampton 1603: Southampton City Archives Office Manuscript SC/6/1/27, f. 15v.
16. Churchwardens of Kingsutton, Oxfordshire 1619; Peyton, *Oxford Peculiars*, p. 294.
17. Devon Record Office Manuscript, Churchwardens' Presentments, Cornwall, Box 23/4/3 (Parish of North Hill).

18. James Raine, *A Volume of English Miscellanies Illustrating the History and Language of the Northern Counties of England*, Surtees Society, Vol. LXXXV (1890), p. 30.

19. G. Donaldson (ed.), *The Court Book of Shetland 1602–1604*, Scottish Record Society, Vol. 84 (1954), pp. 18 and 32.

20. See the studies by Hugh C. Evans, 'Comic Constables – Fictional and Historical' in *Shakespeare Quarterly*, Vol. XX, Shakespeare Association of America, New York, 1969, pp. 427–33, and by Louise D. Frasure, 'Shakespeare's Constables' in *Anglia*, Vol. LVIII (1934), pp. 384–91.

Text 55

Parish Constables: Essex 1562

(Essex Record Office, Manuscripts Q/SR4/13 (Wickham St Paul's) and Q/SR4/14 (Great Maplestead))

Text A (Parish of Wickham St Paul's)

Thes bethe wordes thatt Iohn northe of wyckame Constabell & thomas edwardes of the same town ded here ellesabette fettes say Commyng thether to examyne theme for ther a parell as thay whar commanded by the quennes komessioner ferst they acced hem wossarwante he wase and he sayde my lorde
5 Roberdes man and thei ded acce hem wotter he war of howsholld or arettayner and he sayd of howsholld butt he wase notte In wages butt {sayed} he mytte & yf he wollde then they sayd to heme you haue holld owtte att the coorte well and he sayd I {kame} frome thence I kame yester daye & thether I well akayne bey & bey & they ded saye master fettes we ded her say here grace wase worttelle
10 recayued att my llorde Recces and ~~ge~~ grette resortte & he sayed no nott huse the resortte thatt wase att sere Ihon wenfordes for they mytte notte be sofvered & then she sayred thuse he ys a were fellen & ase Ranke a papeste as onne ys wette In the Reme of yngellond

Text B (Parish of Great Maplestead)

The presentmente of Richard Grene and Iohn payne constables And Iohn parker and Robarte Bryannte parisshoners there

ffurste vppon Crestmas even Laste we the said constables withe dyuerse other of the parishe willinge to see thinges well ordrede in or said parishe acordinge
5 vnto oure othe/ Becausse Alettell before we dede heare of matters myche nedfull & wourthie to be amended/ we the said inhabitauntes dede Serche dyuerse howsses beinge suspecte Amonge whiche we came vnto one/ who namethe hymselfe Newcome other name we knowe not/ And when we cam to his howsse/ he nor his wiffe was not at home And the we went vnto one
10 Smethes howsse/ And ther we met the saide Newcome at smythes gate/ ~~vnto~~ vnto whome we said/ Newcome we haue bene at your howsse as we haue bene at others to see se what order or Rewle you do kepe/ And then he made vs this answer/ what haue you to do to serche my howsse you shall not com ther/ I am as honest as the beste of you all/ ffor you are all Churles & that ys the Allmosse

15   that you do geue Morou*er* abought Michaellmas laste this Newcomes wyffe ded
       dwell in Sibble heding*ha*m withe hur husbonde to our*e* knoledges and as we
       haue vnderstande while she was ther/ this newcome chaunsede wher this
       woman was. And claymed her for his wiffe. vppon whiche thinge the man that
       came with hur to heding*ha*m sodenly was gone. and none cold tell wher*e* he
20   became. And so ~~th~~ syns that tyme this newcome and she haue contenewede to
       gether & still doo. whether she be his wiffe or no we cannot tell. very susspecte
       p*er*sons they be bothe and howe they leve we cannote tell. And therfore we
       desyre your good counsell or Order in this behalffe And Remedye for the same

Notes

Text

From Session Roll for Essex Quarter Sessions. The texts are edited and discussed briefly, with a facsimile and transcription of Text A, by F. G. Emmison, *Elizabethan Life: Disorder, Mainly from the Essex Sessions and Assize Records* (Essex County Council, Chelmsford, 1970), pp. 33–4.

Manuscript

The two texts are in different hands.

Text A

The letters *u*, *v* and *w* are very similar, and it is possible that (A6) *butt*, (A10) *recayued* and (A11) *sofvered* have *w* instead of *u/v*.

Also confusable are *e* and *o*, and (A7) *holld* might be argued to be *helld*.

As often in hands of the period, *t* and *c* are very similar. For (A9) *worttelle* 'worthily' Emmison, *Elizabethan Life: Disorder*, reads *worccelle*, explaining it as an adverb based on *wassail* and so meaning 'with riotous festivity'.

Text B

In (B12) *see se* the clear error of dittography is made where *see* ends one line and *se* begins the next.

(B9) *the* has no mark indicating that it is an abbreviation for *then*, but it seems very likely that this is the word intended.

Glossary
Familiar words obscured by spelling

(A3)	*a parell*	=apparel, clothes, livery
(A4)	*wossarwante*	=whose servant (see note)
(A5)	*acce*	=ask
(A5)	*wotter*	=whether
(A5)	*arretayner*	=a retainer (see note)
(A7)	*holld owtte*	=held out, ?lasted
(A8)	*akayne*	=again

(A9)	*bey & bey*	=by and by, very soon
(A9)	*here grace*	=Her Grace (the Queen)
(A9)	*worttelle*	=worthily (see note on Manuscript)
(A10)	*huse*	=us
(A11)	*sofvered*	=suffered, permitted
(A12)	*sayred*	=said
(A12)	*were*	=very, utter
(A12)	*fellen*	=villain (or possibly ?felon)
(A12)	*papeste*	=papist, Roman Catholic
(A12)	*onne*	=any
(A12–13)	*wette In*	=within
(A13)	*Reme*	=Realm
(B14)	*Allmosse*	=alms
(B22)	*leve*	=live, make a living

Other items

(A6–7)	*& yf*	if
(A7)	*wollde*	wanted
(A10)	*resortte*	gathering, crowd
(A12)	*Ranke*	out-and-out
(B3)	*Crestmas even*	Christmas Eve
(B3)	*dyuerse*	various
(B4)	*willinge*	wishing
(B4)	*ordrede*	conducted, regulated
(B6)	*wourthie*	deserving
(B12)	*Rewle*	conduct, behaviour
(B13)	*what haue you to do*	what business have you
(B14)	*Churles*	peasants
(B15)	*Michaelmass*	Feast Day of St Michael, 29 September
(B23)	*counsell*	advice

Explanatory notes

(A1) *bethe*: The present plural beth 'are' has almost certainly died out by this time, so this represents *be the*.

(A3) *theme*: Fettes and his wife.

(A4) *wossarwante*: The interpretation is Emmison's, *Elizabethan Life: Disorder*.

(A5) *of howsholld or arretayner*: The distinction is whether or not his service involves living in (see OED RETAINER 2).

(B16) *Sibble hedingham*: The adjacent Parish to Great Maplestead.

Background

Wickham St Paul's and Great Maplestead are two Essex villages, about twenty miles to the North of Chelmsford. Both Parishes were in the Hundred of Hinckford, so the Constables' reports are for the Petty Sessions for that Hundred.

Text A

The circumstantial narrative is merely to give a setting to the Constables' report of Elizabeth Fettes' *wordes*, alluding to someone's Catholic faith in terms unacceptable in 1562, when Queen Mary is on the throne.

On instructions from a Royal Commissioner the village Constables are checking the local big house for illegal livery and maintenance. The Fettes are employed by the Rich family, *my llorde Recce* and his son *my lorde Roberd*. The Rich's have recently entertained the Queen, as has neighbouring *sere Ihon Wenforde*, identified by Emmison, *Elizabethan Life: Disorder*, as Wentworth.

Text B

The Constables' report here is about suspected sexual immorality, but also about Newcome's disrespectful language to them while acting in their official capacity.

Topics for linguistic investigation

1. Punctuation in the two texts.
2. Text A spellings relating to the pronunciation of consonants.
3. Do the texts demonstrate any shared features from which one might begin to discuss North Essex pronunciation?
4. The use of the auxiliary *do*.
5. The syntax of (A8) *thether I well akayne*, (A10–11) *no nott huse the resortte that was att sere Ihon wenfordes*, (B9) *he nor his wiffe was not at home*, (B18–19) *vppon which thinge the man ... was gone*.
6. The linking of clauses and sentences in Text B.
7. The different basis of insult in *papist* and in *churl*.

Text 56

Parish Constables (Vagrancy): Essex 1566

(Essex Record Office, Manuscript Q/SR 19A)

Text A (Parish of Littlebury)

[No. 24; f. 1r] Esex Lytelbere anno domini 1566
Me memoran dom Resaived of the connstables of worlden xiiij wacabo{n}s o
ther wyse callede e Iepcyanse the xvijth day of agost{e} and de ly verede them
to the connstables of Lytell chesterde{forde} the same daye to Iohn Rynolde
5   the Connstable of lytel chesterde **X**

xpian Laurence	edmonde Lavrance
Iohan Lavrance	dora the Lavrance
Katcheryn peter	elyzabethe peter
wyllim balse	{Locmicke ker}
10 agnes penko	barberes dego
mari symond	margrgret Robeth
willim Robth	Cristoferde Lavrance
Jackey dego	

[f. 2v] me moran dom Re cay vede of the connstables of adele ende on Rycherde
15   felove ye viijth daye of a{o}gost a storde va ga bonnde and de ly ve rede hym that
same daye to the connstables of lytele chesterforde

Robrt gepson

me moran dom Re cey vede of the Connstables of wenden on Ione glove^r
the xxxith daye {of} iuly a storde va gabonde and dely werrede her to the
20   connstables of lytell chesterforde that same daye

Text B (Parish of Bradwell-juxta-Mare)

[No. 6] 1566 Bradwell iuxta mare

Sy^r ou^r dutyes Remembred &c/ This may be to sertyfye yow that sythe the
tyme of ou^r beinge in offyce wch hath bene sence the xxixth of Iulye Laste paste
there hathe bene no vagabondes wthin ou^r Tounnshipp/ but All thinges hathe

293

5   bene in good order accordynge to the wholsome Lawes of this Realme/ & this
for this tyme we Leaue trooblynge of yow &c/

Your Louynge ffrendes to vse and Commande Thomas Love and Henrye Laye
Constables of Bradwell next the Sea

Text C (Parish of Southminster)

[No. 10] the constales of sem outere ass consarnyng facabones we haue hade
none of a longe tyme

Text D (Parish of Roxwell)

[No. 44] Iohn strustell constable of the hamlet of Rausell

Thys schall be to ssartefi yowe that we had no ffacaband*es* ssen*es* the last quartar
ssesschen*es* In owre hamlet But on stewene tolle & heme we toke as a ffacabond
& careded hem a ffoare my lord Rothe the xv of Iune be cawes we ffownd
5   ffellonie In hem ffor brekeyenge of the quenes *proclam*ossen

Notes

Text

From Vagrants' Roll for Essex Quarter Sessions. The texts have not been edited before.

Manuscript

Each text is a separate document in a different hand.

Text A

Word-division in this text is a problem, but has been retained as in the manuscript, since
there seems to be a strong link between the gaps and syllable boundaries.

The series of minims transcribed as *nn* might represent *un*; thus (A2 etc.) *connstables*
and (A15) *va ga bonnde*.

Text D

In (D1) Identification of the name of the Parish is less than certain, since it may be
written *Ransell*.

Glossary

(A3)	*e Iepcyanse*	=egyptians, gipsies
(A14)	*on*	=one
(A15)	*storde*	=sturdy, able-bodied and violent
(B2)	*sythe*	since
(D4)	*a ffoare*	=afore, before

(D5)   *ffelonie*   serious crime
(D5)   *proclamossen*   =proclamation

Local placenames

(A1)   *Lytellbere*   Littlebury
(A2)   *worlden*   Saffron Walden
(A4 and variants)   *Lytell chesterdeforde*   Little Chesterford
(A14)   *adele ende*   Audley End
(A18)   *wenden*   Wenden Ambo
(B1)   *Bradwell iuxta mare* (also (B8) *Bradwell next the Sea*)   Bradwell-on-Sea
(C1)   *sem outere*   Southminster
(D1)   *Rausell*   ?Roxwell

Explanatory notes

(A19) *xxxi*[th.] the superscript letters reflect the numeral *one and thirtieth*.
(D4) *Lord Rothe*: Sir Thomas Wrothe, Essex Justice of the Peace.

Background

Vagrancy, unemployment and poverty were concerns throughout the Early Modern period, principally because of the threat they posed to society. Various Acts set out legislation aiming to deter vagrants by punishment and, later, addressing the problem by employment on public works and by financial help for the incapable.

In 1566 Constables were operating under the provisions of a 1531 Act which instructed Constables to arrest vagrants, refer them to local Justices of the Peace, have them whipped, and move them out of the Parish to their birthplace. When this was some distance away, vagrants were handed over to the Constables of the neighbouring Parish, who in turn passed them to the next Parish.

An Act of 1547 had laid down more severe punishments, but Constables and JPs had been unwilling to enforce its harsh provisions, and the 1531 Act had been reinstated in 1550.

The Constables of each Parish were required to make regular reports, including nil returns such as Text C, on their dealings with vagrants.

Text A is from a Parish in the North-west corner of Essex. Littlebury has boundaries with the neighbouring Essex parishes of Saffron Walden (A2), Little Chesterford (A4 etc.) and Wenden Ambo (A18). Audley End (A14) is a village within the Saffron Waldon area.

Texts B and C are from the Hundred of Dengie, the area in the West of Essex lying between the Rivers Blackwater and the Crouch. Text D, if the identification of the place-name is correct, is from a Parish in the central area, near Chelmsford.

Topics for linguistic investigation

1. The evidence relating to pronunciation in the spellings (A1) *Resaived*, (A2) *worlden*, (A12) *Cristoferde*, (A15) *storde*, (A19) *dely werrede*, (C1) *consarning*, (D2) *ssartefi*, (D3) *sesschenes*, (D3) *stewene*, (D4) *a ffoare*.

2. Reasons why *vagabond* is spelled in so many ways (See OED for some of them).
3. The perception of words and syllables in Text A.
4. The constructions (A2) *of the connstables*, (B6) *of yow*, (C2) *of a longe tyme*, (D5) *of the quenes proclamossen*.
5. The history and development of the word *egyptians*.
6. Ways in which the style of each presentment reflects each set of constables' different perceptions of what kind of document a presentment is.

Text 57

Churchwardens of Stratford-upon-Avon: Warwickshire 1628

(Shakespeare Birthplace Trust Record Office Manuscript BRU 15/1/160 and fragment ER51)

[f. 221r] It*em* wee pr*es*ent all thees names vnder written

the 8th of Iune

It*em* Iohn whittell loder for loitering forth of Church sermon tyme & seeing the pariter & my selfe vntrussed wth his pointts

5   It*em* Iohn burman of shotterie the yeonger for the like went homward*es* {Iune the 15th} I speaking to him aske mee what I made forth & what {I} had I to doe

It*em* {will*iam* Greene} the widowe greene sonn the same day for sleeping in the belfrie wth his hat on his head

It*em* the 8th of Iune the sabboth day after eveninge prayer

10   {Tho Ainge sergantt for keepinge drinkynge in his house ~~in~~ vpon the saboeth day} It*em* thomas Iellfe {abram fisher} will ange the bucher Robert butler the y{e}onger at the house of thomas ange e sargant drinkinge in the howse in & w^{the} the Companie of Christopher knight an excomunic{t}ated p*er*son

the 22 of Iune

15   {a nawtie house} It*em* will*iam* <   wife> wth twoo maydes a<t> home her selfe a servinge three <per>sons wth provision & a takinge monie of them

It*em* harr<y> mace & his wife at home wth nawtie Companie wth them but ru<n> away throw the back sides

It*em* Richar<d> sand*er* Collermaker & wiffe at home & straungers drinking wth
20   them

It*em* wth the<m> th<omas> h<   > on that wears his hat Comonlie in

297

Church ~~w~~ & is a Comon Romlor & lauffer in Church & goer forth of Church
before tys doone

25   {wheeler} It*em* Iohn wheeler for late Coming to Church & was in the towne
abroade seene by the Constabls the 28 of ~~I~~ maye sermon tyme

It*em* Richard Iohnson the yeonger for late Coming to Church & as wee thinke
hee hath noe imploiment but lasines & there sits verie vnreverentlie ther
sometymes lawfing & Romling ~~w~~ & a vsuall werer of his hat in Church ~~there~~ in
Contempt for I see him goe barehed Comonlie athome & in the streetes {& a
30   vsuall goer forth of Church before sermon be doone}

{holder} It*em* the wife of Anthonie holder sayth ~~gooddie~~ goodie bromlie is on
ill looke wooman an I woold over looke her & herne as I had over looke others
& bid me arent the wich & sayde I was a whore & my basterd*es* mayntayne me
& bid me get me home howe wolld brushe the motes forth of my durtie gowne

35   her witnes: patiens ford: prudence wright: & goodwiffe asson:

{dawes} It*em* the 26 of Iune the wiffe of vmprie dawes did fflie in the face of
old widowe bucke & threw her downe Calling her old hore & wiche in the
hearing of my selfe & manie other*es*

It*em* sanders the Cooke ~~the Coo~~ a drinkinge at moses {evening} sermon tyme

40   {wakeland} It*em* edward wakeland for vsing beastlie behavior toward*es* ann
greene a littell before Crismas that shee was fayne to fall downe to save her selfe

It*em* edward wakeland for putting his hand*es* vnder the Coates of marie west &
hath told her husband he woold a doone the other thing in a more bestlie
manner wch shee will be in Court to tell tis to longe to write & shee sayth her
45   husband doth vse a wearie liffe {w^{th} her} & sayth it shall be a breach while hee
liveth

It*em* this marie west sayth that {hee sayd} on greatithes wiffe pulled vp her
Coates but shee was such a ~~pokkte~~ {filthie} whore hee Coold not finde on his
hart to meddell wth her

50   It*em* {more} hee sayth that on plimor of assencontlie ~~sayd the mayd~~ was noght
wth her a gainst the seston wch is the wiffe of on Arter seetens

It*em* vppon the information of ~~marie~~ {Ales} smith & marie west wee pr*esent*
him for a Comon swerer & blasphemer of god

It*em* wee p*res*ent him for a Comon drunkard

55   It*em* wee p*res*ent thomas pace of shotterie for keeping back the poores monie
whereas the p*ar*ties hawe at warrick before the Iustices {take their oathes} to
the Contrarie

the p*ar*ties deceved are on mils on belcher & twoo fatherles & motherles
Children

60   [f. 221v] The 15 of Iune – at Tho. Anges serjant being Saboth day after
Eveninge Prayer Abraham Fisher
Tho. Felse
William Ange bucher
Robert Butler the younger
65   Christopher knight wch is an excomunicat person and they drinkinge in his
company

Io Hall
Antonie smithe
George X Bartin his marke

70   It*em* wee p*res*ent thomas tibbitts for not paying the Clarks wages

Notes

Text

From records of Stratford-upon-Avon Town Council. The text has not been edited
before.

Manuscript

This document has suffered from its containing the signature of Dr John Hall, the
Stratford-upon-Avon physician who was Shakespeare's son-in-law. His distinctive
signature was cut out by a collector, possibly Edmund Malone, the eighteenth-century
editor of Shakespeare. In 1899 the fragment, found in Malone's copy of John Hall's
Select Observations on English Bodies, was returned, to be kept with the document,
though it is still a separate fragment. Since the signature was on the verso side of the
sheet, text on the recto side was affected. This is still readable on the fragment, but
some text has been totally lost by trimming. Lines 15–21 of the text are affected, where
most gaps may be filled by conjectural restoration, but not the surnames in lines 15
and 21.

Lines 60–66 are roughly crossed through. They are written at the top of the verso of
the sheet, in a different hand from the text on the recto. The incident is dealt with in
lines 10–13.

Marginal notes, printed here within insert brackets in lines 10–11, 15, 24, 31, 36 and 40, draw attention to some entries.

In l. 6 the pronoun *I* has been inserted before *had*, but the *I* originally written after *had* has not been deleted.

In (13) *excomunictated* the inserted *t*, written above the word, might be intended to precede the *c*, giving *excomunitcated*.

In l. 7 *sonn* the minim strokes could be read *soun*.

In l. 12 the isolated *e* does not appear to be the end of Thomas A(i)nge's surname.

Glossary

(3)	*loder*	=loader, carrier (see note)
(3)	*forth*	outside
(4)	*pariter*	=apparitor, summoner to Church Court
(4)	*vntrussed*	unfastened
(4)	*pointts*	laces holding up hose
(6)	*made*	was doing
(15)	*nawtie*	wicked
(18)	*back sides*	back yard
(21 etc.)	*on*	=one
(22)	*Romlor*	someone who makes a disturbance
(22)	*lauffer*	=laugher
(24–5)	*in the towne abroade*	out in the town
(29)	*athome*	=at home
(31)	*goodie*	courtesy-title for elderly woman of lower class
(32)	*ill looke*	with the evil eye
(32)	*over looke*	bewitch with evil eye
(32)	*herne*	hers
(33)	*arent the*	=aroint thee, begone
(34)	*howe*	=who
(34)	*motes*	dust-particles (see note)
(41)	*fayne*	forced
(42)	*Coates*	skirts
(45)	*wearie*	See note
(45)	*breach*	separation
(48)	*pokkte*	infected with the pox
(49)	*meddell w^th*	have sex with
(50–51)	*was noght w^th*	had sex with
(51)	*a gainst*	beside
(51)	*seston*	=cistern, pond
(56)	*hawe*	=have

Local placenames

(5)	*shotterie*	Shottery
(50)	*assencontlie*	Aston Cantlow
(56)	*warrick*	Warwick

Explanatory notes

(3) *loder*: Probably Whittell's occupation as *loader* 'carrier', but possibly, in view of the charge, *lodder* 'layabout'.

(4) *vntrussed*: As in several of the entries which follow, the syntax switches uneasily from '[We present] so-and-so for doing such-and-such' to '[So-and-so] did such-and-such'. Thus *vntrussed* is a preterite of which John Whittell is the [implied] subject, not a past participle post-modifying *the pariter & my selfe*.

(34) *howe*: loosely linked to what precedes, the 'who' referring back to the implied subject of *bid ... & sayde ... & bid*. Mrs Holder's wish to brush the dust out of her gown is a vivid way of saying she would like to give her a thrashing.

(45) *wearie*: The adjective could mean 'depressed' or 'depressing' (see OED). The overall sense here is that Marie West is claiming that her marriage is on the point of breakdown because of the effect on her husband of Wakeland's behaviour and boasting.

(50–51) The relative clause depends on the pronoun *her* in l. 51, 'had sex beside the pond with the woman who is the wife ...'.

Background

The Churchwardens of Holy Trinity Parish Church, Stratford-upon-Avon, are jointly setting down all known misdemeanours for the month of June 1628. Their statutory role is to look for, note and report breaches of church discipline rather than to deal with crimes. Serious matters will go forward to the Church Court (see line 44).

At this time attendance at worship and preaching in the established church is obligatory. A man who attends but keeps his hat on is indicating dissent from the Church of England, because he is a Non-conformist or a Roman Catholic.

Topics for linguistic investigation

1. What this text tells us about the 3rd person singular indicative form of verbs.
2. The form and use of the pronouns (4) *my selfe*, (32) *her & herne*, (33) *the*, (34) *me*, (51) *w^{ch}*.
3. What parts of the verb are (6) *aske*, (18) *run*, (33) *mayntayne*, and (32) *over looke* (56) *take*, (65) *excomunicat*?
4. The evidence of other texts of the period for the currency of (16) *a servinge*, (23) *tys*, (36) *did fflie*, (43) *woold a doone*, (50) *on plimor*.
5. The intrusion of 1st person singular forms used by one or other of the church-wardens.
6. Why does the writer have particular difficulties in handling Goody Bromley's complaint?
7. What does this text suggest about the history of *aroint* as set out in OED?
8. A comparison with the vocabulary of sexuality used in other texts.

Text 58

Parish Constables: Northamptonshire 1657
(Northamptonshire Record Office Manuscript QSR 1/6)

Text A (Spratton)

[No. 86] Spraton Bill

Wee doe present M Elizabeth Blisworth ffor not lodging Travilers sent by the Constabl<es>

Also we doe present William fasser for a suerer
we doe present william ffasser for serving a suppena on the saboth day

5

Constables
Thomas Pearson
Iohn Chadwick

Text B (Lowick)

[No. 87] We the Cunstables of Luffwick whose names are Heer vnder written doe present Clement Tarry. and Susana Tary widdo^s Ann Childs widd^o. and Mary Childs. Robert Tippin and his wiffe Ann the wiffe of daniell Banks and Ann Smith the wiffe of William Smith. all thes for being Popishly affected, and for not comming to church this Last 3 weekes, as for any thing ells we know nothing, but. Omne Bene.

5

October the 6th Thomas Branford
1657   William Smith   Cunsta{bles}

Text C (Slipton)

[No. 88] Slipton bill for the quarter sesions holden at Northampton for the hundered of huckslow

I persent m^{er} william preston and his wife for a qusantes: and Robbert Lion And his wife for the Like: and beteris Mesers for the Like/ our hie wayes ar in sofishant repare

5

302

the 6 day of october   Thomas Nickolas
1657   Constaball

Text D (Whittlebury)

[No. 90] Whittlebury bill ~~Sep:~~ {October} 6th: 1657

I the Cunstable Accordinge to the Articles given mee in charge with the concent
of some of the Inhabitants whose names are heare vnder written present
Edward Richards for erectinge p*ar*te of a kill howse vppon the Comon streete
5 and a hey way leadinge to the p*ar*ishe Church

                            Richard Hood   Cunstable
                            Iohn Iackman
                            Thomas Clarke
                            Iohn Savage
10   Iohn Burtone
                            Edward Ayres
                            Robert Bignill

Text E (Pytchley, Orlingby Hundred)

[No. 94] October the 6 – 1657

at the sessions then I present Henry Hasslewood of Pichly for causing a
disorder at Pichly aforesaid by baiting of a bull vpon the 24 day of septem*ber*
last when I had somened my deuission to apeare at the pettie sessions or statutes
5 for the rateing & recording of wages & did their by draw a way the companie in
the prime of the statutes that those that wanted saruants could not hire them &
would & did continnew the dissorder though I sent the baily to discharge him

I present william vnderwood of the same for not coming to Pichly church but
onse this 3 or 4 yeare nor to anie other {church or} priuat plase of meeting for
10 the worsheep of god soe far as I knowe or doe beleeve

                            Henry Wine on of the
                            cheif constables of the
                            hundred of orlingbury

Text F (Southwick)

[No. 95] sowick bill 1657/

I present weedo stiuen for briwing with out a licance

Item our pore ar preuided for

Item our Charch is in good repare

5   Item our hiwaes ar in good repare

Item our wach and ward ar duly cape

Item wee haue no recusant*es*/ in our toune of or paresh

Item wee haue no new eracted tanemantes

Edmun Ierland.   Canstabell

Text G (Desborough)

[No. 100] A Bill mad ffor the Cunstables of Desborrow Anno domino 1657

Ouer Watch is duely kept And our high waies in good Repaire

wee doe present m^r polton the elder ffor being Accusance

wee doe present m^r ffarthing Nando polton And Mary his wife ffor Being
5   Accusants

wee present Giles Chapman Katthierne Chapman And Elizebeth Chapman
Mary Chapman Ann Wod ffor beinge Accusance

Edward Silby
Thomas Stephens
10   Cunstables

Text H (Aldwincle)

[No. 101] Aldwinckle Bill

wee present willam ffoster and his wife margaret for Acusants

wee present Richard Renere and his wife for a cusants

we present mary Thurlby the wife of Henry Thurlby for an a Cusant

5   wee haue noe Ale house nor no profeaine swearers nor saboth breakres our wach

is keept our hie ways and brig^es ar mayntined our pore ar prouided for our Churches are in Repaire

Edward Lawford
Iohn Maunsell   Counstables

Text I (Irchester)

[No. 104] Irchester Bill October the 5 1657

Wee present Robert Lane of Irchester laborer for coming druncke from weling{bore} upon the foure and twenty day of iune and for cuting of a new hare rope in flexlands in Irchester feild the same time of William Bletsoe and
5   turning the horse luse when hee was upon his owne grownd

This Lane when hee was wornd to watch hee did say: that hee would watch when hee listed and so hee did the seruis for he was mutch complaynd of by his naibors

Constables
10   William Bletsoe
Nathaniel May

Notes

Text

Constables' Presentments for Northampton Quarter Sessions. The texts, with others from the same set, have been edited by Joan Wake (ed.), *Quarter Sessions Records of the County of Northampton. Files for 6 Charles I and Commonwealth (A.D. 1630, 1657, 1657–8)*, Northamptonshire Record Society, Vol. 1 (for 1921–2) (1924), pp. 172–8.

Manuscript

A photograph of Text I lines 1–11 from this document, together with a commentary, appears as Plate VIII on pp. 278–9 above.

Each text is a separate document from the village concerned.

Text E comes from the Chief Constable of the Hundred to which Pytchley belongs, since one of the people being presented is accused of having disrupted an official meeting called by him; the second accusation in the same presentment may be simply a transfer of the report of the village Constable.

Text G is specified as written on behalf of the Constables rather than by them, and the signatures are both written in the same hand as the text.

Glossary

(A4)	*suerer*	=swearer
(A5)	*suppena*	=subpoena, summons to appear in Court
(B6)	*omne bene*	=omnia bene, (Latin) all well
(C3)	*a qusantes* (also *accusance, accusants* etc.)	=recusant(s), Roman Catholic(s) refusing to attend Anglican worship
(D4)	*kill howse*	=kiln-house, building with a kiln
(E4)	*deuission*	=division, administrative area
(E4)	*pettie sessions*	minor Court convened for local area
(E4)	*statutes*	Statute Sessions, for formal announcement of fair wages and for the hiring of servants
(E5)	*rateing*	fixing the financial level
(E5)	*their by*	=thereby, by this means
(E5)	*companie*	people present
(E6)	*prime*	beginning
(E7)	*baily*	bailiff
(E7)	*discharge him*	stop him doing it
(E8)	*but*	except
(I4)	*hare rope*	rope made of (horse)hair (cf. OED HAIR–LINE)
(I6)	*watch*	act as watchman
(I7)	*listed*	wanted

Personal names

(C4)	*beteris*	=?Beatrice
(G4)	*ffarthing Nando*	=?Ferdinando

Local placenames

(A1)	*Spraton*	Spratton
(B1)	*Luffwick*	Lowick
(C1)	*Slipton*	Slipton
(C2)	*huckslow*	Huckslow (Hundred)
(D1)	*Whittlebury*	Whittlebury
(E2)	*Pichley*	Pytchley
(E13)	*Orlingbury*	Orlingbury (Hundred)
(F1)	*sowick*	Southwick
(G1)	*Desborrow*	Desborough
(H1)	*Aldwinckle*	Aldwincle
(I1)	*Irchester*	Irchester
(I3)	*welingbore*	Wellingborough
(I4)	*flexlands*	?local field name

Background

Village Constables were required to submit reports to Quarter Sessions held at or near Epiphany, Easter, Trinity and Michaelmas. These are from various Northamptonshire villages for the Michaelmas Quarter Session 1657 (the Feast of St Michael actually falling on 29 September).

The presentments are based on formal lists of matters on which a report is required. The identification of Roman Catholics evidently figured prominently at this time, as the Commonwealth knew itself increasingly threatened by Royalists, many of whom would be Catholics, in the years immediately before the 1660 Restoration.

Topics for linguistic investigation

1. The evidence relating to the pronunciation of consonants in the spellings (B1) *Luffwick*, (C2) *hundered*, (C5) *sofishant*, (D4) *kill*, (F1) *sowick*, (F6) *cape*, (F9) *Edmun*, (G4) *ffarthing Nando*, (I8) *Naibours*.

2. The evidence relating to the pronunciation of vowels in the spellings (D3) *heare*, (E6) *saruants*, (E10) *beleeve*, (F2) *briwing*, (F4) *charch*, (F8) *eracted*, (F8) *tanementes*, (G2) *Ouer*, (H5) *profeaine*, (H6) *mayntined*, (I5) *luse*.

3. Why the writers had special problems in spelling *constable*, *highway* and *recusant*.

4. The constructions (E9) *this 3 or 4 yeare*, (E2) *baiting of a bull*, (H5) *noe Ale house nor no profeaine swearers nor saboth breakres*, (I3) *the foure and twenty day of iune*, (I6) *This Lane when hee was wornd to watch hee did say*.

5. The use at, before and after this period of compounds with a similar syntactic basis to that in (H5) *saboth breakres*.

6. The degree to which writers of presentments approximate to a common formulaic syntax and phraseology.

Text 59

Parish Constables and Churchwardens: Devon 1683
(Devon Record Office Manuscripts DQS 15/255/2 (Yealmpton), DQS 15/66
(Buckland Monachorum) DQS 15/44/1 (Bere Ferrers))

Text A (Yealmpton)

Devon sh^r. Plympton Hundred Yealmpton pirsh

the presentmants of the Constabls and Chruch wardenes of the pirsh and
County aforsaid made the .9th day of Aprill 1683

5   As for such as doe not dewly Com to Chruch Every sabath day and att the
begining of divine service we know none but are Reddie to com except those
whome we haue hear after presentd

Concerning that Latte order of sissions that we Received to present all disenters
from the sacrament of the Lord Supper itt hath meett with such good affect in
our said parish that att our Late Communion of Easter we had present about
10   :200: passons who did Receiue and if any did absent wee suppose the might
keep of by Reasson of a Late distemper of the small pox which happened
amoungst vs and proued very mortall to many of our parishoners we know non
that doe scruple to Receiu vpon the account of Consianice except those whose
names are vnderwritten Richar Browne: Iohn Alger: Nathaniell: Elliot Robart
15   velle: ~~Margery Elliot~~

As for any Nonconformist ministers ~~or othe~~ or other that take vpon them to
preach or teach in Convinticls we know none with in our said pirsh

As for any profan swarers or Coursers or Common Ale house hantters
drunkards or Lewd parssons we know none with in our pirsh

20   As for any other misdemeaners or offences committed and don since the Last
sessione one punished or presented we knowe none with in our pirsh

Wm Adams	vic
Ieffery Scobell	Church warden
Iohn Spicer	
Thomas Edwards	Constabls
Iohn: Champernowne	
Richard Hillersdon	

Text B (Buckland Monachorum)

The 10th day of Apprill. Anno dominij 1683. A true: Pressentmentte of the
Parrish: of Buckland monachorun

ist we knowe noe decentters: ffrom Church in the time of dervine service in the
Parrish. Nether know we of any that preach in Convinttecolls: or vnlawfull
5 assembbles in ouer Parrish:

we doe Pressentte the person*es* ffolowinge for not Reseauinge the Saccramentt:
in our Parrish: ~~William Stevens the Ellder and William~~ {stet} ~~Stevenes the
younger~~ and Iohn Stacy: William dingell and Nichollas dingell: Thomas White
and his wife Blanch Scobbell: and Richard dundrige: the younger:

10 wee doe Pressentt Edmond Cortter of our Parrish for A masterles idell and
disorderly person and a night Whalker: and a verye dangerus ffellowe:

The pe^rsons that are fite to sill beer in our Parrish are Thesse ffollowinge
William Dauy: Thomas Chubbe: Ellizabath Slenime Rabbish Sprye:

The purson*es* that are Chossen in our Parrishe to be ouerseer*es* for the poore
15 are Nichollas Sprye the Elder Iohn Tallder Ellis dundrige:

	Iohn Haynes		Ellis Stevens
	Phillip dawe		Iohn ffoote
	Counstabbles		Churchwardens:
sworne before of	Nicholas Hanning		
20 | | Iohn Bran | | |

Text C (Bere Ferrers)

[f. 1r] {xijth: day of Aprill Anno d*omi*ni 1683./}

Hear shewith the presentments of Beereferris by the Con*sta*bles and Churchwardens whos names are under-Svbscribed: According to the best of our
knowledge

5 Wee doe present as Absenters from Church Robin Wakeman and Elezebeth
Wakeman his wife: & Magdelen Wakeman: & Mary Wakeman: for Absenting
from Church ~~ever since the Last Sessions~~ {for two moneths last past} The
Same for not Reseuing the Sacrament

Wee doe present ffransis Boaden John Boaden: & Nicolas Clarke for not

10   Reseauing the Sacrament But they haue promised to Reseve the next Sabboth
      day

      All-so wee doe present Henrey dondrig for Absenting him Selfe from Chorch
      & Sacrament {for 3 Sundays last past}

      Wee know none within our parrish that doth take upon them to teach or preach
15   in Conuentikels
      We know none within our parrish that doth premit any unlawfull Assimbleys
      to bee held in thare houses

      Wee know non profane swarers nor Common: drunkards nor alehous hanters
      with-in our parrish

20   Wee doe Retorne the names of Such as haue Setiuicats from the Minister and
      Church-wardens as followith Ioseph: Doidge: Huge Clarke: Mary Burgis:
      Nathaniell Blagdon: Iames Toule

      Wee haue giuen notis to the poor wardens to parfick thar accounts And haue
      Nominated fit parsons to Stand in thare Rume

25   Wee know no other misdemeniers With-in our parrish Since the Last Sessions:

      the number of our Alehous Keepers with in our parrish haue bin Eight

              Christopher Edgcombe
              Thomas X ffoot   Robert Stephens
                 Con*sta*bles   Church warden

Notes

Text

Presentments by Constables and Church Wardens for Devon Petty Sessions. The texts
have not been edited before.

Manuscript

Each presentment is a separate document.

Text A

The signature of the vicar (l. 22) appears to match the hand in which the document is
written. Other signatures are added in different hands, except that a single hand writes
the names of both constables.

Text B

In l. 13 the minim-strokes transcribed *nim* in the surname rendered as *Slenime* are totally confusable.

The Christian name transcribed as *Rabbish* in the same line also seems unlikely.

Text C

The main text is written in a semi-calligraphic hand which matches that of the signature of Constable Christopher Edgcombe (though see below). But the insertions in lines 1, 7 and 13 are scribbled in in a very different style. Note the correction of *non* to *no* in l. 18.

Glossary

(A7)	*Latte*	=late, recent
(A7)	*sissions*	Quarter Sessions
(A7–8)	*disenters from*	people who refuse to partake
(A10)	*Receiue*	take Communion
(A10)	*the*	=they
(A11)	*distemper*	illness
(A16)	*Convinticls*	Non-conformist meetings for worship
(A18)	*Coursers*	people who set their dogs to chase game, especially hare
(A18)	*hantters*	=haunters, habitual frequenters
(A21)	*one punished*	=unpunished
(B10)	*masterles*	See note
(B11)	*night Whalker*	=night walker, person out after dark with criminal intentions
(B12)	*fite*	=fit, properly qualified
(B14)	*ouerseeres for the poore*	parish officials concerned with poor relief
(C3)	*under-Svbscribed*	written or signed below
(C20)	*Setiuicats*	=certificates (see note)
(C23)	*parfick*	=perfect, complete
(C24)	*Stand in thare Rume*	replace them

Explanatory notes

(B10) *masterles*: Frequently used at this period to refer to a vagrant (see OED MASTER-LESS). Statutes against vagrancy distinguished between disreputable vagabonds and people who travelled with the backing of a patron, such as a company of actors entitled to call themselves Lord Such-and-Such's Men.

(C20) *Setiuicats*: From 1673 until 1828 the holding of public office or employment was open only to those who could prove their adherence to the established Church of England by producing annually for the Quarter Sessions a Sacrament Certificate confirming that they had taken Communion in an Anglican church.

Background

The Devon parishes from which these documents come are all in the Hundred of Plympton, but not close neighbours.

By this date Church and State have made Constables and Churchwardens jointly responsible for presentments, and each return has to be sworn before local Justices of the Peace whose counter-signatures are added (in Text A, Sir John Champernowne of Modbury and Richard Hillersdon of Membland; in Text B Nicholas Hanning and John Bran; Text C not countersigned, though it it possible that Christopher Edgcombe, who signs and writes out the document (see Account of Manuscript above) is himself the Justice of the Peace, since his surname is that of a local gentry family.

Each presentment is evidently going through the itemised list with which they have been provided. The focus on dissent from the Church of England, characterised by refusal to take Holy Communion, appears to be concentrating on Non-conformist groups who prefer their own alternative worship in *Conventicles* and *Assemblies*, but the term *dissenter* can also apply to Roman Catholics at this time, and not only legislation but strong popular opinion was anti-Catholic.

Topics for linguistic investigation

1. The evidence relating to pronunciation in the spellings (A6) *hear after*, (A13) *Consianice*, (A18) *hantters*, (A21) *one punished*, (B7) *Reseauinge*, (B11) *Whalker*, (B12) *sill*, (C20) *Setiuicats*, (C23) *parfick*.
2. The significance for pronunciation in the variants (A10) *passons*, (A19) *parssons*, (B11) *person*, (B14) *pursones*; (A16) *Convinticls*, (B5) *convinttecolls*, (C15) *Conuentikels*; (B4) *assembbles*, (C16) *Assimbleys*; (A4) *Chruch*, (B3) *Church*, (C12) *Chorch*.
3. On what grounds can one say whether (C2) *shewith*, (C14) and (C16) *doth* and (C26) *haue* are singular or plural?
4. The constructions (A5) *we know none but are Reddie to com*, (B4) *Nether know we*, (B19) *before of Nicholas Hanning*, (C2) *Hear shewith the presentments*, (C6–7) *Absenting from Church*.
5. The use of auxiliary *do*.
6. The development of the specialised seventeenth-century meanings of *assembly*, *conventicle*, *dissenter*.

Wills

... followinge ...

Item I gieve ... nine & twenty sheepe ... borrow ...
Item to ... nine pownd ... & borrowdon of ...
Sneddon keepe of ... to pay ...
money towards my debts ...

Item I gieve ... fower & twenty sheepe
& ... to keepe ... payment ... pske ...
my Rent

Item I gieve in to ward of my Rent & my debts
to be payd as afore sayd & out of ... stock
Item I gieve my ... to my ... for
our boote food & ... payne

Item all y Remonder ... plainly and wises
& all ... belonging to my two dowghters Eliza & Mary ...

Item I make my two dowghters Eliza & Mary
my Lawfull executors

Item I make ... my wealth & bonds &c for
my Lawfull ord law

Item it is my will & testament to goe ... &
of all y aforesayd goods & ... be ... & ...
& two ... the ... ... to keepe it
till y accomt be given up
witnesse to it   y marke of Richard

Edmond Wood
y marke of Elizabeth Wodworth
y marke of Margery Millard
John Wodworth

1637/102 (ii)

Plate IX

Text 64A
Richard Fewster: Gloucestershire 1636

Gloucestershire Record Office Manuscript GDR WILL 1637/102,
Version A, f. 1v
Edited text 64A/25–46

this is ffollowing/
Item I giue &c/ nine & twenty sheepe {bought} of edward Bale
cost nine pound wch I Borrowed of Iohn
Gooddenow these I Leaue to pay him & ye re
5   maynder toward my Rente
Item I giue &c ffo for {wintering} humphery hewettes sheep
cost cometh to thirty two shillinges eyght pence toward
my Rente
Item I giue wt do want of my Rent & my debtes
10   to be payd as affore sayd & out of the stock
Item I giue my towales to my executors for
ouerseers for theyr paynes
Item all ye Remoueables & planckes are mine
& all thinges be longinge
15   Ittem I Make my two daughters Eliza: & Mary
my Lawffull executors
Item I make Ierremy walkly & thomas ffewster
my Lawffull ouer seers   {to my ouerseers}
Item it is my will & testament to sell & disspose of
20   all ye afforesayd goodes & chattle by ye ouerseers
& ye two executors to Receiue ye munny & to keepe it
till ye account be giuen vpp
witnesses to it   ye Mark of Richard ffewster
                               RF
25   Iames Moody
ye Mark x of Elizabeth wodrooffe
ye Mark x of marger<e>t Millerd
Iohn Woodrooffe

Characters: Use of *y* in (4) *y*^e.

Allographs: Long and short *s*, (19) *sell*, *testament*, *is*. Characters *u* and *v* operate as allographs, (22) *vpp*, (2) *giue*. Use of *i* in (17) *Ierremy*, (28) *Iohn* (cf. pronoun (2) *I*).

Capitals: Not consistently used for proper names. Each clause begins with capital, but others used apparently randomly, e.g.(3) *Borrowed*, (15) *Make*.

Abbreviations: (3) *w*^{ch}, (4) *y*^e, (9) *w*^t (=what). Also (9) *debtes* and (14) *thinges*; (18) *ouer*; (4–5) *remaynder* and (21) *munny*. Abbreviation for (7) *toward* combines mark for *ar* and superscript *d*. Major abbreviation in (21) *Receiue*.

Punctuation: Marks (slashes/?commas) after introductory phrases (1 and 2). Colon marking shortened name (15) *Eliza*.

Alterations: Extensive insertion and deletion.

Special note: A very battered original document. At the bottom, marks instead of signatures, and seal.

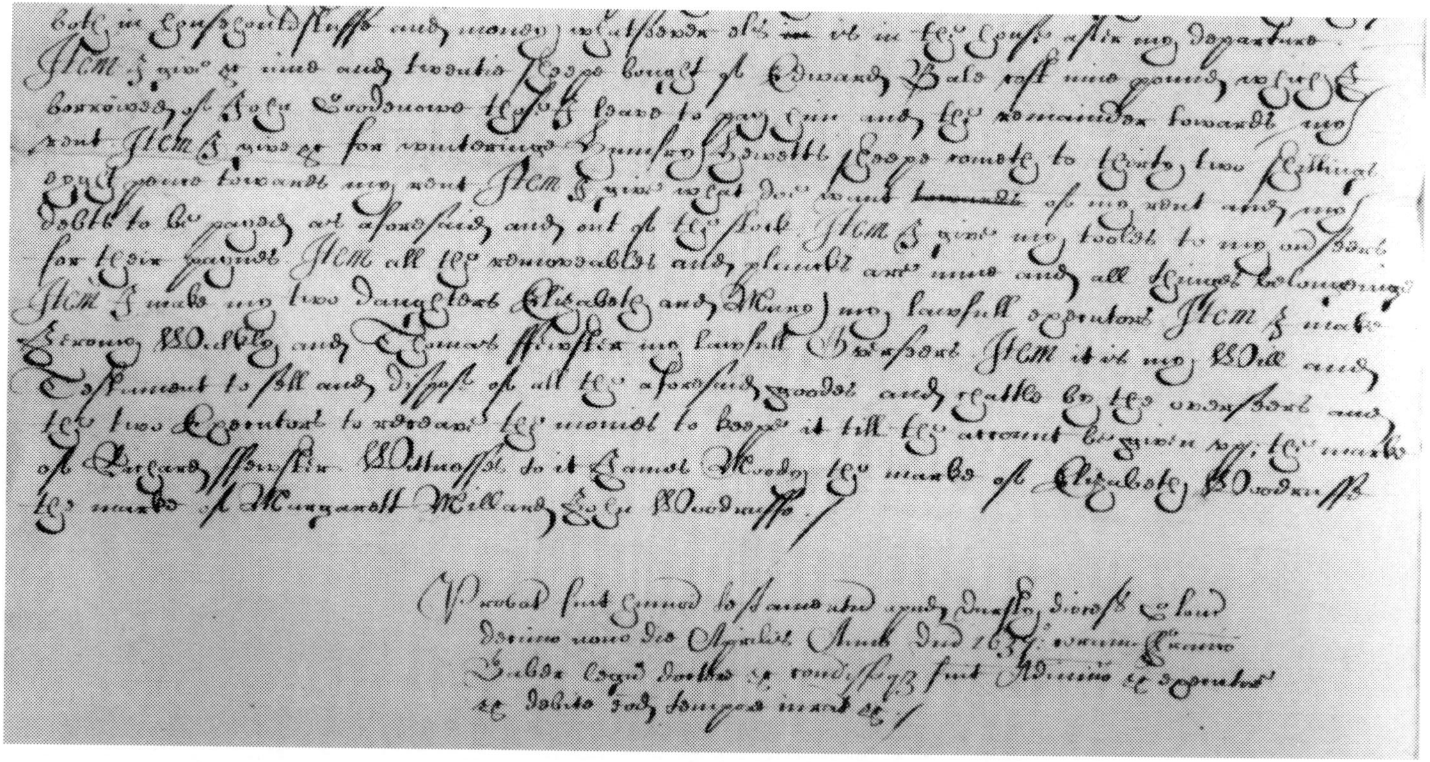

Plate X

Plate X

Text 64B
Richard Fewster: Gloucestershire 1636

Gloucestershire Record Office Manuscript GDR WILL 1637/102, Version B
Edited text 64B/19–37

Item I give &ᶜ nine and twentie sheepe bought of Edward Bale cost nine pound which I borrowed
of Iohn Goodenowe those I leave to pay him and the remainder towards my
rent. **Item** I give &ᶜ for winteringe Humfry Hewetts sheepe cometh to thirty two shillings

5 eyght pence towards my rent. **Item** I give what doe want ~~towards~~ of my rent and my
debts to be payed as aforesaid and out of the stock. **Item** I give my tooles to my ouerseers
for their paynes. **Item** all the removeables and plancks are mine and all thinges belongeinge< . >
Item I make my two daughters Elizabeth and Mary my lawfull executors. **Item** I make
Ieremy Walkly and Thomas ffewster my lawfull Overseers. **Item** it is my Will and

10 Testament to sell and dispose of all the aforesaid goodes and chattle by the overseers and
the two Executors to receave the monies to keepe it till the account be given vp; the marke
of Richard ffewster. Witnesses to it Iames Moody the marke of Elizabeth Woodruffe
the marke of Margarett Millard Iohn Woodruffe./

Probat*us* fuit hoc testament*um* apud dursly diocesis G°loucesteri
15 decimo nono die Aprilis Anno d*omi*ni 1637°: coram ffrancisco
Baber legum doctore &ᶜ condissaque fuit Administratio &c executor
&c debite e*odem* tempore iurat*us* &c./

Handwriting: The overall effect of greater sophistication than Version A of the same text (see Plate IX) is not because a different
hand is used (except in the word *Item* throughout), but because letters which are basically similar in shape are here written carefully.
Allographs: Long and short *s*, (9) *sell and dispose* (with virtual identity of the long *s* and the *f* in (9) *of*), (9) *goodes*. System for *u* and
v retained in (10) *vp*, but see (8) *Overseers*, (10) *receave*. Use of *i* in (8) *Ieremy*.
Capitals: For all proper names (use of *ff* in (8) *ffewster* equates with capital), but not for random nouns or verbs except important
terms, e.g. (8) *Overseers*, (8) *Will*, (9) *Testament*.
Abbreviations: In English only in (5) *ouerseers*. Extensive use of abbreviation in formulaic Latin added at end.
Punctuation: Full-stops at end of each item, and combined with slash to mark major end-points in lines 12 and 16. Semi-colon in
line 10 where text ends and record of signatures begins.
Alterations: Only a single deletion in line 4, with correct text immediately following.

Introduction to Wills

Wills from the Early Modern period have been studied for various reasons. Since the first bequest by virtually all testators is to bequeath their soul to God many investigations[1] have surveyed the terms in which this is formulated, monitoring the changes in religious belief which underlie the different formulations in 1542,

> I be qveythe my sovle vnto alle myty god my makar & redemar & to the gloryous wyrgen ov[r] lady sent marry & to alle the holy company off heven (62/7–9)

and in 1640,

> I leave my saule to god, and beleives to be saveit be the mercie of god onlie in the merites, obedience, satisfaction of Cryst Iesus my savior and Redemer.[2]

Other research[3] has used wills and the inventories that so often accompany them as sources of information on the living conditions of the period, as demonstrated by the clothes and household furnishings possessed by people in various classes of society. An affluent Somerset widow, for example, makes her bequests,

> To the said Alce my doughter my stonding cup and the cover and vj spones of siluer, my best girdill, my bedis of corall, a fetherbed with thappurtenances and the hanging of grene say that hangeth in my night chamber, a materas, ij couerlettes, ij pair of blankettes, ij pair of shetes, a fyne new shete, one of my best twoells, one of my best tableclothes, a pair of gret shetes that hir name is market thereupon with blue threde, ij of my best smoks, ij of my best kercheffs of lowne, iiij of my best kercheffs of holande, viij nysettes, a bonet of velvet, ij pannes, my gret chaffer, ij crokes, ij plates, vj potengers, vj sawcers, one bason of laten with thewer, ij candelstickes, a broche with an aundire, one of my best forsetts of spruce, a table that stondith in the hall, a shep cofer also ij gownes, ij kertills.[4]

For historical linguists, too, they are documents of value.

Wills are written documents which express the testator's personal wishes in regard to the distribution of property after his or her death. The older technical difference between a will (bequeathing land and buildings) and a testament (bequeathing personal property) is rarely maintained, and even the earliest document below, dating from 1504, describes itself as *my testament & last Wille* (60/3). By definition a will must be capable of being shown to set out what the testator truly wished, and must be so clear as to admit

318

of no arguments about interpretation, since it will have to be dealt with by other people after the death of the person who made it. Elaborate safeguards existed to prevent fraud. If he wrote the will himself, not only was the testator's signature needed, but those of witnesses who were present at the time it was written. If he asked someone else to draw up the will, the finished document had to be read over to him in the presence of witnesses and then signed and sealed and signed by the witnesses. If the will was merely expresed verbally but no document formally made, then a nuncupative will was drawn up, describing the dying man's spoken wishes about his property and signed by witnesses who had heard his words. All wills had to be proved, that is, officially confirmed as true records, and this probate process was at this time, except during the Commonwealth period, done by church (Archdeacons') courts, where business arising from disputed wills was also handled.[5] When the will was proved a register copy would be made, to be filed among the Diocesan probate records, while the original document was normally handed back to the executors who had been named by the testator and whose job was to bring the will to probate and then to administer its provisions. Sometimes a will appointed overseers to help with this job.

There are therefore two matters which the linguist considering a will has to attempt to settle: Who actually wrote the original will, the testator or an amanuensis? And is the copy that survives the original, a copy, or the register copy?

Obviously, you could only write your own will if you were literate. But this problem would never arise for a large proportion of the population, since wills were needed only by people with sufficient possessions to justify one. The illiterate poor did not die intestate because of their lack of education but because of their lack of property. Where a person of property wished, he could write his own will, and that of Londoner William Chamberlayn (Text 62) states that it is a holograph,

I have wreton thys w^t myne hovnd (='own') hand the daye & the yer a bove sayd (62/42–3).

Far more frequent are wills written by amanuenses. People without the necessary literacy called on local clergy or schoolmasters or a skilled friend. Thus a will from the Bristol area begins by stating that it is

writen by me Richard Martine vicar there the 18th day of February Anno Domini 1599 as followeth …

while another is witnessed by

Thomas Iames, parson and writer hereof.[6]

Joshua Baudon, the Mayor of West Looe (writer of the accounts in Text 16) is minuted in the borough records as making a deposition about having written a will for a Looe man,

in or about the yeare of oure Lord God one thowsand six hundred fifty three, George Cloake then of the said Burrough was sicke in body, but in perfecty minde & remembrance. then sent for this deponent to write his will, wch this deponent shortly after did.[7]

Amanuenses could also be family, friends or neighbours of no special local standing. Roger Lowe (writer of Text 35) has already been mentioned as the writer of accounts for churchwardens, presentments for constables and letters for friends. He was happy to write wills too, recording his skills in his journal,

> I was sent for to Whitleige greene this night to one William Marsh who lay sicke and had seaverall times sent for me to write his will which I did. John Hasledon went with me in night and William Knowle was there and I composed the mans will somewhat handsomely.[8]

In other words, he was acting as more than an amanuensis, taking down William Marsh's words from dictation; he was setting down the sick man's wishes in the proper way which he was aware was appropriate for a will. Lowe's expertise we can only guess at, but that wills were often written on behalf of people who were themselves literate but who acknowledged that they needed professional help with such an important document is clear. In 1505 the will of Robert Widewe, Canon and Sub-dean of Wells Cathedral, ends,

> In witness whereof I have desired Mr. Robert Williamson, notary to write this my last will with his own hande the day and yere above rehersed.[8]

There is always the possibility, in addition, of a normally competent writer calling on someone else's services because he wishes to make a will at a time when he himself is incapable of writing because of grave illness. A will from Cornwall in 1646 says that it is being *written by my brother* and the preliminaries set out that the testator is

> often visited with sicknes & thereby the rather moved to consider the uncertainetie and frayltie of mans lief yet perfect and whole in minde & memorye.[10]

Many wills were written when the testator was *cike in bodey but wolle in miende* (63/2–3).

The question of who a will was written by is important to our assessment of the linguistic information contained in it. Wills usually give the testator's place of residence, and very often his occupation, and since the provisions of the will roughly indicate the level of prosperity we begin to build up a picture of the testator as a prosperous city tradesman or a poor village labourer and so on. If the language in the will is the testator's own then we have material of particular sociolinguistic value. If, on the other hand, the local vicar is the writer, then the spelling will be his, and possibly other features of the language too, as Lowe's comment above suggests. At the same time, it may well be that, clergy and schoolmasters apart, the testator and the amanuensis may well both have lived in the same town or village all their lives, sharing the same local dialect, so that a spelling such as *sawle* or a form such as *childer* may characterise the English of both people. The difficulty is compounded by the fact that most amanuenses are anonymous.

Where a will is nuncupative, witnesses swear to the dead person's last words concerning his property,

> The Lattir will testament and legasie of Vmq[le] Iohnne duncane elder burgis of Dundee Maid & spokin be his awin mouth In presens of Iohnne Andersoun merchand Iames thomsoun walter broun william duncane.[11]

Witnesses usually claim verbatim recall of what was said,

> ffirst he said, I knowe I shall nowe dye and not recover and there is but one way wth me/ And therfore concernyng my worldly goodes, So it is that I broughte litle or nothinge to my wyffe Katheryn, And therfore I will not take or geue any thinge from her, but do referre all to her discretion.[12]

How accurate the witnesses were we can never know, but certainly the quotations in many nuncupative wills give the impression of speech, such as a Darlington man's bequest to his son,

> a yonge black calfe, to be brong up a bout house whel saint tillinmas, com a twelmunth.[13]

There is no certainty that this is not the non-standard language of the witnesses rather than of the testator, but the likelihood of their being his close family and neighbours is even stronger here than when someone calls on another person's services to write a will on his behalf.

Where the original document has been lost over the centuries but the register copy has been kept in Diocesan records, now safely lodged in a local record office, a will presents the further problem as to how close to the original was the copy the clerk of the church court made. Internal evidence, such as extremely idiosyncratic or extremely conventional spelling may suggest an answer in some cases. Otherwise, a comparison between texts where the same clerk copied out the wills of a number of people could be informative, or an examination of such wills as have survived both in original and in copied form.

When working on wills from the Leeds area preserved in the probate registry at York, one editor[14] found so many similarities in spelling that he concluded that the wills were not only copied by one clerk, using his own spelling preferences, but that he was copying from dictation. While the second half of this conclusion can be challenged, the first part is confirmed by examples from various registries from which books of copies of wills have survived. For example, two wills made in April 1532 and proved in June of that year, entered one after the other in the register books at Lincoln,[15] share identical spellings for *buryed*, *yerde*, *doughter*, *wyff*, and *whome*, all items for which different writers at this date might use considerable variation. Both also employ the non-etymological spelling *whytnes/whyttnes* for 'witness'.

As for those rare wills for which both original and copy have survived, Text 64 (also Plates IX and X), the will of Richard Fewster, made in 1636 and registered at Gloucester a few months later, provides a classic example. For some reason both documents were filed, and both have been kept. The clerk replaces with more bland spellings the idiosyncratic versions of words used by the testator's friend in writing the will for him, making changes such as,

yearth	earth
eleauen	eleven
coults	colts

shipp	sheepe
howsell	household
munny	money
towales	tools.

However, it is noteworthy that the clerk's preferences also lead him to introduce a few spellings which are less conventional than his original, such as *wiefe* and *receave*.

The spelling of a copied will is far more likely to give us information about the language of the clerk than about that of the testator or his amanuensis. However, there is no evidence that the clerks felt free to alter wording, grammar or morphology, except in an extremely minor way. Thus the original document has,

> Item I giue &^{c}/ nine & twenty sheepe bought of edward Bale cost nine pound wch I Borrowed of Iohn Gooddenow these I Leaue to pay him & ye remaynder toward my Rente (64A/26–8)

of which the copyist retains virtually everything,

> Item I give &^{c} nine and twentie sheepe bought of Edward Bale cost nine pound which I borrowed of Iohn Goodenowe those I leave to pay him and the remainder towards my rent. (64B/19–22)

He does alter *these* to *those* and *toward* to *towards*, but does not, for example, insert a relative pronoun before *cost*. With other features illustrated here, such as the style of numeral, the zero-inflexion on *pound* and the use of *of* where present-day usage would employ *from*, the clerk would have no motivation for making changes as he copied, since these usages are common to all speakers and writers at the time. There are other instances where forms and words from local dialect appear in register copies, but we have no way of telling whether this is because of reluctance to make substantial changes or because the copyist himself shares the dialect. The common use of local spellings in register copies certainly suggests that the latter might well be the case.

That wills, original or copied, can be a source of dialect material is one of the factors which makes them worth investigating. Thus Robert Goodyere of York uses *whye* for 'heifer' and *garth* for 'piece of enclosed land' (61/9 and 11). Another York will of the early sixteenth century has,

> John my son shal be myn executor; and for God's sake, rule all wisely as I have done, & ȝe shall have moch menske ('honour') thereof,[16]

while a will from Wells leaves a friend of the testator *a sparke* ('speckled') *kowe*.[17]

Even more striking are the number of spellings suggesting local pronunciation, as all the texts edited here demonstrate, illustrating the English of Lincolnshire, Yorkshire, London and Gloucestershire. For comparative purposes it is especially helpful that wills so often include mention of the same things, so that the same lexical items crop up constantly, many of which happen to be words where the pronunciation is of special interest, either for dialect, or for development during the Early Modern period, or for both. For example, most wills have a bequest of the soul to almighty God. The vowel of *soul* illustrates an important North/South difference. Whether the spelling suggests that there is or is not a consonant before the *t* of *almighty* is important, as is the related sequence in *daughter*, another frequent word. Testators normally give directions for the interment of their body; the vowel in *bury* is of interest, as is that in *church*. The verb *bequeathe* itself is worth watching for the spelling of its final consonant.

Local inflexional morphology may also be recorded, such as the weak plural *housen* (Somerset 1543[18]) for 'houses' or the mutation plural *breder* for 'brothers' (60/51). In bequests of livestock, the plural of *cow* occurs in various forms, and some plural of *child* appears in almost every will: *chylderyn* (60/50), *childer* (61/14, *cheldarne* (62/19), *cheldringe* (63/21).

Of particular interest is the morphology of what is usually the first verb in a will. The historical context for this is important, as well as the contemporary dialect situation. When someone, whether testator or helper, made a will he or she was producing a document for which many models of form existed. Wills were regularly written in Latin in the Medieval period, and their marked formulaic style was carried over into vernacular use in the sixteenth century. A typical will of 1400 might read,

> In Dei nomine Amen. In vigilia Sanct Jacobi Apostoli A.D. millesimo cccmo, ego Nicholaus Westerne, ville de S., grocer, compos mentis licet eger in corpore, condo testamentum meum in hunc modum. Inprimis lego animan meam Deo omnipotenti, beate Marie virgini et omnibus sanctis eius, corpusque meum ad sepelendium in ecclesie parochiali Sancti Michaelis de S ...[19]

The phrasing of the totally English will of William Chamberlayn, written by him in London in 1542, is closely based on this same stereotype,

> In the name of god amenn & In the yere off ov^r lord god a thovsand CCCCC xlij ... & the xx day off maye I William chambarlayn setesan & skynar off lvndon beyng hole off mynde & off parfeyt remembrance ... make & orden thys my present testament & laste wylle In manar & fovrme as here aftar folovthe/ fyrste & formoste I be qveythe my sovle vnto alle myty god my makar & redemar & to the gloryous wyrgen ovr lady sent marry & to alle the holy company off heven & I wyll that my body be bvred inn the chvrche yard (62/2–10).

Most wills of the Early Modern period do the same. The item of special interest here is the construction,

> ego Nicholaus Westerne, ville de S., grocer, compos mentis licet eger in corpore, condo testamentum meum,

and its English calque,

> I William chambarlayn setesan & skynar off lvndon beyng hole off mynde & off parfeyt remembrance ... make & orden thys my present testament & laste wylle.

The subject of the verb *make* in this traditional formulation is an elaborate noun phrase headed by the pronoun *I*, so that the word *I* and the verb are separated by a lengthy stretch of text. In Northern English and Scots at this time first person singular verbs in the present tense had two possible inflexions; zero-inflexion was used where the pronoun *I* was immediately adjacent, but *-(i)s* was used where pronoun and verb were separated, even by a few words. So in Text 44, an early sixteenth-century letter from Westmorland, Anne Clifton writes *And her I ly and kepys hows* (44/23), and in Text 43, a late seventeenth-century Scottish letter, James Stewart has *I desayr yrfor to be at sobmesion* (43/29) alongside *I sell seay nomor at present bot desayrs yow & all to be seriows* (43/35). In wills, therefore, the words which the traditional formulation places between *I* and the verb *make* demand, for Northern and Scots writers, the employment of the form *makes*. Thus we find *makys* in Coppuldyke, writing in Lincolnshire (60/3) but *make* in Chamberlayn the Londoner (62/6). In a number of texts, however, the situation is complicated by what may be awareness on the part of the writer that to use an *-(i)s* ending here is a provincialism. The wills of sixteenth-century clergy from the diocese of Durham show that many were happy to employ the Northern inflexion, as in,

> I William Bennett, Doctor of Dyvinitie and Vicar of Ayclyf, in the countie of Durham, weike in bodie but of good and perfect understandinge and memorie, thankes be to Almightie God, maikes this my last Will and Testament.[20]

Others preferred to use the non-Northern form, either simply,

> I Robert Lyghtton, Vecar of Horslae, being sek in my bodie and holl in my mynd, make this my laste Wyll and Testament,[21]

or with *do*-support,

> I William Birche, Pastor of Stanhop, of perfect memorye in a dekeyed bodie, do maike my last Will.[22]

But there were also a large number who in order to avoid an *-(i)s* ending, substituted the *-eth* which does indeed equate in Southern usage with Northern *-(i)s*, but only in the third person singular and not in the first. So we find texts such as,

> I Thomas Myddletounn, Clarke, and Vickarr of Bushoppmydlam, beinge of good and perfecte remembrance, maketh heere my last Will and Testament.[23]

Hypercorrection seems the most likely explanation of the form, though it was possibly influenced by the number of official documents of other kinds, such as indentures and petitions which often began with the third person form *witnesseth* or *sheweth* without any preceding noun or pronoun to justify its use.

One further matter arises from the fact that before the sixteenth century wills were normally in Latin. Sometimes a will mixes Latin and English sections, as in the 1521 will (Text 61), which begins by using the standard Latin formula, then transfers into equivalent English. Moreover early in the sixteenth century those wills still written in Latin sometimes demonstrate extreme macaronic usage, with the names of household objects bequeathed being rendered in English, as in a Buckinghamshire will of 1517 where a daughter is bequeathed vnum par le Blankettes vnum materas cum le bolstare vnum pelowghe vnum candelsteke le laten vnum basson de laten ... duos siscos et duos sausers de le pewter.[24]

Notes

1. Such as A. G. Dickens, *Lollards and Protestants in the Diocese of York 1509–1558* (Oxford University Press, London, 1959).

2. Will of James Rigg, Carberry, Scotland; Scottish Record Office Manuscript CC8/10/11. Reproduced in Grant G. Simpson, *Scottish Handwriting 1150–1650* (Bratton, Aberdeen, 1973 and later reprints), doc. 28.

3. Such as F. G. Emmison, *Elizabethan Life: Home, Work & Land, From Essex Wills and Sessions and Manorial Records* (Essex Record Office, Chelmsford, 1991). There are also many booklets dealing with the names of household items, such as Rosemary Milward, *A Glossary of Household, Farming and Trade Terms from Probate Inventories*, Derbyshire Record Society, Occasional Paper No. 1 (1977, rev. edition 1986).

4. Will of Alice Clayton, Kingsbury, Somerset 1501; F. W. Weaver (ed.), *Somerset Medieval Wills*, Somerset Record Society, XIX (1501–1530), (1903), p. 22.

5. See Anne Tarver, *Church Court Records: An Introduction for family and local historians* (Phillimore, Chichester, 1995), Chapter 3, 'Probate and Testamentary Business', pp. 56–81.

6. Sheila Laing and Margaret McGregor (eds), *Tudor Wills Proved in Bristol 1546–1603*, Bristol Record Society, Vol. XLIV (1993), Docs 134 (1600) and 182 (1602).

7. Cornwall Record Office Manuscript B/WLO/158, records for 1668.

8. Ian Winstanley (ed.), *The Diary of Roger Lowe* (Picks Publishing, Ashton-in-Makerfield, 1994), p. 5.

9. Weaver, *Somerset Wills*, Vol. XIX, page 88.

10. Will of Thomas Hordon of Callington, yeoman; *Guide to Cornish Probate Records* (Cornwall Record Office, Truro, 1996), pp. 38–9.

11. Nuncupative will of John Duncan 1577; Scottish Record Office Manuscript CC/8/1.

12. Nuncupative will of Harry May 1573; Bristol Record Office Manuscript, Bristol Wills No. 8.

13. Nuncupative will of William Dockera, 1610; J. A. Atkinson, B. Flynn, V. Portass, K. Singlehurst and H. J. Smith (eds), *Darlington Wills and Inventories 1600–1625*, Surtees Society, Vol. CCI (1993), p. 105.

14. George Denison Lumb (ed.), *Testamenta Leodensia: Wills of Leeds, Pontefract, Wakefield, Otley and District 1539–1553*, Thoresby Society, Vol. XIX (1913), Preface, p. 5.

15. The wills of John Leke and John Rowme; C. W. Foster (ed.), *Lincoln Wills*, Vol. III 1530–1532, Lincoln Record Society, Vol. 24 (1927), p. 229.

16. Will of John Alayn 1509; James Raine (ed.), *Testamenta Eboracensia: A Selection of Wills from the Registry of York*, Vol. V, Surtees Society, Vol. LXXIX (1884), p. 3.

17. Will of Edmond Carter 1529; Weaver, *Somerset Wills*, Vol. XIX, p. 284.

18. Will of Richard Chaplinge; Weaver, *Somerset Wills*, Vol. XXI, p. 78.

19. Formulary in Eileen A. Gooder, *Latin for Local History* (Longmans, London, 1970), p. 74.

20. Will of William Bennett 1583; James Raine (ed.), *The Injunctions and other Ecclesistical Proceedings of Richard Barnes, Bishop of Durham, from 1575 to 1587*, Surtees Society, Vol. XXII (1850), Appendix X, 'Wills of beneficed and other clergymen within the Diocese of Durham, from 1559 to 1603 ... From the Registry of Durham', p. cxviii.

21. Will of Robert Lyghtton 1584; *ibid.*, page cxxviii.
22. Will of William Birche 1575; *ibid.*, page cx.
23. Will of Thomas Myddletounn 1584; *ibid.*, page cxxv.
24. E. M. Elvey (ed.), *The Courts of the Archdeaconry of Buckingham 1483–1523*, Buckingham-shire Record Society, No. 19 (1975), p. 232.

Text 60

William Copulldyke: Lincolnshire 1504
(Lincolnshire Archives Manuscript LCC Wills 1506–1525)

[f. 4v] In the name of god Amen*n* the xx day of the monethe of april in the yere
of o*r* lord god m° ccccc° iiij° I Will*ia*m Cupuldyke of haryngton*n* hawyng my
hole mynde & gud memore makys my testament & last Wille in this maner and
forme folyng ferst I gif my So{a}wle to almyghty god & o*r* blissed lady Saynt

5   mare & to all the Sanct*es* in hewne & my body to be bereed where as yt shall be
thowthe most conuenyent by myne executor*es* Also I will that the hy awter of
harynton hawe for tythes forgotyn vjs viijd also I gif to the chirche of
haryngton*n* vjs viijd also I gif to o*r* lady of lincoln xijd also I gif to chirche of
aswardby xxd also I gif to the chirches of Sutterby Enderby and Brynkell eu*ere*

10 of them xijd also I will that if eny ma*n* or woma*n* canne clayme eny det or dewte
& make Suffycyent pr*o*we ther of that thej be content & payed and if I hawe
wronged eny ma*n* by acc*io*n or ether wyse I will he be recompensed acordyng
to gud co*n*cyence Also I will that A noneste preste be fonde A yere to pray for
my Sawle in the chirche of haryngton*n* And all this to be had takyne & p*er*sawyd

15 of my gud*es* moweabull & wnmoweabull Also I will there be A nobet keped in
the chirche of haryngton*n* yerly withowt ende for my fader Sawle & myne and
my antecessores my moder Sawle my wywes Sawle & all cristen Sawles w*t*
prestes clerkys ryngyng of bellys and pore folke to be at the same And there to
be disposed yerly x s by the discresc*io*n of myne executor*es* feoffer*es* Also I will

20 that my wyffe hawe hyre Iwnter without eny interrupc*io*n terme of hyre lyfe
Also I will that Iohn Cupuldyke my neldeste son*n* hawe yerly to his fyndyng vi
marke to he cu*m* to ~~h~~age of xv yer*es* and after from that age to he cu*m* to lawfull
age x li And if it be Soo that ~~eche m~~ [f. 5r] eche vi marke yerly benot Spent of
hym fully in the Space of the Seid xv yeris then I will y*t* the rewenes be keped

25 ~~& keped~~ & spent of hym to his best promoc*io*n in the other yer*es* thenne nexe
ensewyng also I will ~~also I will~~ that hamond Cupuldyke my sone hawe to his
fyndyng yerly to he cu*m* to the age of xxi yere v marke and tobe orderrede in
man*er* & forme as it is afore rehersed for his broder Iohn also I will y*t* Thomas
my sone hawe to his fyndyng yerly to he cu*m* to the age of xxi yer*es* iiij marke

30 and it to be orderred in man*er* & forme os it is afore rehersed for his brod*er* Iohn
and if my wife be with a sonne thenne I will that yt hawe yerly to the fyndyng
to it be of the age of xxi yere iiij marke and it tobe orderred in man*er* and forme
os yt es afore rehersed for this broder Iohn and all thise to be p*er*sawyd and

327

takyn of the Isewss & p*ro*fett*es* of all my land*es* & teneme*n*tes rent*es* reu*er*ciones
35   & s*er*uec*es* beyng in the handes of my feoffes also I will that my wiff hawe iij
Silu*er* gobilett*es* p*ar*sell gylte with a cou*er*yng the terme of hyre lyfe & aftere to
remayne to my sonne and myn here os a nare lome for ewre Also I will that my
sonne hamond hawe all my p*ur*chessed land*es* the whiche I bowthe of George
Ienkynson in Enderby to hym and his heres male of his body cu*m*yng also I will
40   that my son*n*e hamond hawe xx li Also I wyll that my sonne Thomas hawe xx
li Also if my wyfe be wyth a sonne thenne I will that yt hawe xx li Also I will
that my dowght*er* Elizabeth haw to hyure mareage .C. marke3 And if sche be
disposed to be A woma*n* of relegion I will sche hawe xx marke3 or more os yt
schall be thowthe resnabull by ye discrec*i*on of myn executor*es* Also I will that
45   Cecyll my dowght*er* hawe to hir mareage .C. marke3 And if my dowght*er*
Elizabethe dy or Sche be maryed or yf sche be a woma*n* of religion thenne I will
that my dowght*er* Cecyll hawe of hyre mareage mony .l. marke3 also if my wyf
be with a dowght*er* I will yt hawe .C. marke3

*   *   *   *

Also I will that my brod*er* Iames hawe for a rewarde xl S also I will that my
50   brod*er* leonard haw to a reward xl S and all this mone vnto my Seid chylderyn
& breder to be had [f. 5v] taken*n* & p*er*sweyd of all my land*es* & ten*emen*tes rent*es*
reu*er*sonis & s*er*uyc3 beyng in the hand*es* of my feoffe3 And also I will that the
seid*es* land*es* rest Seyll in the hand*es* of my seid feoffe3 to thiss my lest will be
p*er*formed

*   *   *   *

55   Also I will that marget my wyffe ~~my~~ haw all my hostelmente3 of howssold & all
my gud*es* catall moweabull & wnmoweabull my fen*er*allis keped my dett*es* payed
my dowght*er* browthvp myne executor*es* & s*er*uand*es* rewarded Also I will that
all my chelderen be rewled by there moder if Sche be wnmareed and by myn
executor*es* & feoffe3 for the cause that yf Sche be mareed Sche most be rewled
60   & not rewle & thenne I will y*t* my Said Schilderen be rewled by myne executor*es*
& feoffe3 And also if my Said dowghterS will not be rewled by ther moder &
myne executor*es* & feoffe3 thenne that dowght*er* or dowghteres that soo es
disposed to haue nothyng of thir my last will The resedew of my ~~d~~ gudes not
beqwethed nor disposed I pwtt to the disposisc*i*on of myne exceutor*es* whome
65   I make & ordeyne marget my wiffe will*ia*m boucher of willughby Gentilman s*er*
Iohn byllyngay the p*ar*son of the chirche of Aserardby that they dispose them
for my Sawle os Shall be most plesewre to god & to my last wyll Also I humely
beseke my lord chanceller of England for the tyme beyng to be the Sup*er*vosor
yf it plesse hyme of this my last will & testament In vitnis wherof I hawe
70   Subscrybed my name the xxi^te day of the moneth aboueseid the xix of the reigne
of kyng henr*i* the vij^th

per me will*ia*m Copulldyke

Notes

Text

From the Probate Register of the Diocese of Lincoln. The text has been edited by C. W. Foster (ed.), *Lincoln Wills registered in the District Probate Registry at Lincoln*, Vol. I (1271–1526), Lincoln Record Society, Vol. 5 (for 1912) (1914), pp. 20–22.

Manuscript

Final -*g*, as in (2) *hawyng*, has an additional curl which has been treated as empty.

The sequence -*on*, with curled-back final *n* normally indicates abbreviation for *ion*, as in (44) *discrecion*. In the case of (46) and (43) *religion*, where the *i* is already written, the curl has been treated as empty, but expansion to *religioun* could be argued for.

In (33) *persawyd* the letter *y* is written on top of some other letter; to clarify the correction, the writer has inserted a further *y* above the word, but this has been omitted here.

In l. 33 *this* is almost certainly an error for *his*. as in the parallel phrase in l. 28.

There is an problem in regard to plurals where the inflexion is abbreviated. Unabbreviated plurals show a mixture of *es* and *ys* or *is* forms, as in (17) *Sawles*, (18) *clerkys*, (24) *yeris*. Since *es* spellings are marginally more frequent, abbreviated words have all been expanded in this way, as (5) *Sanctes*, but the effect is to give the *ys*/*is* spellings an unjustifiable appearance of being outnumbered. The abbreviation rendered *er*, however, has only *er* parallels in unabbreviated words.

Glossary

(4)	*folyng*	=following
(5)	*hewne*	=heaven
(6)	*thowthe*	=thought
(11)	*prowe*	=proof
(14)	*persawyd*	=perceived, obtained
(15)	*moweabull & wnmoweabull*	See note
(15)	*a nobet*	=an obit, Requiem Mass on anniversary of death
(18)	*clerkys*	men in minor orders
(19)	*disposed*	distributed
(19)	*executores feofferes*	executors acting as trustees (see note)
(20)	*Iwnter*	=jointure, financial provision for widow
(20)	*terme of hyre lyfe*	as long as she lives
(21)	*to his fyndyng*	for his maintenance
(22)	*to*	until
(23)	*li*	(Latin abbreviation) pounds
(24)	*rewenes*	=revenues, income
(25)	*to his promocion*	to help him
(28)	*in maner & forme as*	just as
(28)	*rehersed*	described
(31)	*with a sonne*	pregnant with a son
(33)	*os*	=as

(33)	*es*	=is
(33)	*thise*	=?these
(34)	*Isewss*	=issues, proceeds
(34)	*tenementes*	holdings
(34)	*reuerciones*	properties reverting to my estate at my death
(35)	*serueces*	lands let in return for service
(35)	*feoffes*	trustees
(36)	*parsell gylte*	=parcel-gilt, gilded on the inner surface only
(37)	*here*	=heir
(37)	*a nare lome*	=an heirloom
(37)	*ewre*	=ever
(38)	*bowthe*	=bought
(39)	*heres male of his body*	male heirs, provided they are his children or grand-children
(42)	*hyure*	=her
(42–3)	*be disposed*	wish(es)
(43)	*woman of relegion*	nun
(46)	*or*	before
(50)	*mone*	=money
(51)	*breder*	brothers
(53)	*rest*	remain
(53)	*Seyll*	?profitable, ?safe (see note)
(55)	*hostelmenteʒ*	household furniture
(56)	*catall*	property
(56)	*fenerallis*	=funerals
(63)	*thir*	this
(65)	*ser*	=Sir, courtesy-title for Priest

Local placenames

(2)	*haryngtonn*	Harrington
(8)	*lincoln*	Lincoln
(9)	*aswardby* (and (66) *Aserardby*)	Aswardby
(9)	*Sutterby*	Sutterby
(9)	*Enderby*	Bag Enderby
(9)	*Brynkell*	Brinkhill
(65)	*willughby*	Willoughby

Explanatory notes

(15) *gudes moweabull & wnmoweabull*: The distinction is between unmovable property, which is land, houses etc. and movable property, which is everything else possessed. Simple use of *gudes* would be ambiguous.

(19) *executores feofferes*: Both words are nouns. The use of *feofferes* appears to be an instance of the writer using *feoffor* in the sense of *feoffee* (see OED FEOFFOR in regard to this use).

(53) *Seyll*: It appears to be an adjective, related to the noun *sele* 'happiness, prosperity'. To read the item as the adverb *Styll* would be attractive, but is not justified by the manuscript.

(68) *my lord chanceller*: The office was held 1504–15 by William Warham, Archbishop of Canterbury and previously Bishop of London.

Background

The Copledykes were a gentry family living at Harrington Hall in the village of Harrington, about twenty-five miles East of Lincoln. In the Parish church of St Mary's there is a brass of Margaret Copuldyk, c.1480, with the indent for a now-missing brass of her husband. If the dating is correct this must be the testator's mother and father, otherwise it could be his wife and himself. Another monument is for Sir John Copledyk who died 1552, probably William's eldest son, still a minor in 1504 (lines 35–6). The other villages mentioned are within a mile or so of Harrington, and about seven miles East is Willoughby, home of Copulldyke's executor William Boucher (line 65).

Topics for linguistic investigation

1. The use of the characters ȝ and *ƿ*.
2. The evidence relating to the pronunciation of vowels in the spellings (3) *gud*, (4) *blissed*, (7) *chirche*, (12) *ether*, (16) *Sawle*, (30) *os*, (53) *lest*.
3. The evidence relating to the pronunciation of consonants in the spellings (6) *hy*, (6) *awter*, (6) *thowthe*, (25) *nexe*, (36) *gobilettes*, (50) *chylderyn*, (67) *humely*.
4. The different patterns of change in the history and subsequent development of the spellings (10) *det*, (58) *moder*, (68) *beseke*.
5. The forms (3) *makys*, (6) *myne*, (16) *fader* and (17) *moder*, (22) *marke* and (22) *yere*, (22) *cum* and (69) *plesse*, (51) *breder*, (53) *seides*, (63) *thir*.
6. The use of *to the fyndyng* in l. 31, as contrasted with *to his fyndyng* in l. 29.
7. *Tythes forgotyn*: Why this text has so many phrases where adjectives post-modify the nouns they qualify.
8. Differences from present-day English in the selection of prepositions.

Text 61

Robert Goodyere: Yorkshire 1521

(University of York, Borthwick Institute of Historical Research Manuscript
York District Probate Register, Vol. 9)

[f. 176v] In dei nomine Amen xxvj^to die mensis aprilis anno d*o*m*i*nj Mill*e*s*i*mo
quingentesimo xxj^mo Ego Robertus goodyere de Stillingflette compos mentis et
sane memorie condo et ordino testa*mentu*m meu*m* in hunc modu*m* In primis I
gif my saull to god almyghty to o^r lady seynt mary and to al the saynt*ys* in heuyn
5   and my body to be beryed with{in} the chirch yerd of Stillingflete It*e*m I gif for
my mortuary my best beast It*e*m I gyf xx^d to haue a dirige song for my saull.
and my nebowres which doith hono^r god the day of my beriall w^t oblac*i*on to
co*m*me home to my house and take parte w^t a potte w^t ale to pray for my saull
and al cristen saull*ys*. It*e*m I gif a yong whye to stillingflete kirke and to the welle
10   of the same towne It*e*m I gif to Alison Johnson a yong whye and a whete land
y^t buttys of tipplyng hedland at his garth end It*e*m to Isabell Iohnson a tithe
land in gawtresse It*e*m I gif to Robert Iohnson my best bonnett The Residew of
my good*ys* my dett*ys* paid I gif to Elisabeth my wif and to Iohane goodyere and
Elisabeth goodyere my childer whome I make my executo^rs and they to dispose
15   for thelth of my saull as they thynke best and this I make my last will Thes being
witnes Sir George Bukle my curat Iohn bentley Richard Talio^r and Robert
Iohnson

Notes

Text

From the Probate Register of the Diocese of York. A short extract from the will appears
in James Raine (ed.), *Testamenta Eboracensa: A Selection of Wills from the Registry at
York*, Vol. V, Surtees Society, Vol. 79 (1884), p. 129.

Glossary

(6)	*mortuary*	gift to incumbent of church
(6)	*beast*	farm-animal
(6)	*dirige*	Office for the Dead
(6)	*song*	=sung
(7)	*oblacion*	offering (see note)
(8)	*take part w^t*	share in (see note)
(9)	*whye* †	heifer (OED QUEY)

332

(9)	*welle*	public fountain
(11)	*buttys of*	adjoins (see note)
(11)	*garth* †	piece of enclosed land
(8–9)	*tithe land*	plot of land, the income of which is used for paying the owner's tithes
(12)	*bonnett*	hat
(15)	*thelth*	=the health, well-being
(16)	*sir*	courtesy-title for priest

Latin

(1–3) In the name of God, Amen. The 26th day of the month of April AD 1521, I, Robert Goodyere of Stillingfleet, being of sound mind and good memory, make and ordain my testament in this manner: First ...

Local placenames

(2)   *Stillingflette*   Stillingfleet

For *tipplyng hedland* (11), *garth end* (11) and *gawtresse* (12), see under Background below.

Explanatory notes

(7) *oblacion*: it is not clear whether the sense 'offering' in this case refers to money, or is being used with wider reference to worship.

(8) *take part w^t*: Almost certainly 'share in', although the usual sense when followed by the proposition with is 'side with, take (someone's) part' (see OED PART).

(11) *buttys of*: The verb is usually followed by *on*, *upon* or *against*.

(11) *his garth end*: Since his can scarcely refer back to *Alison Johnson* the form is probably the early-sixteenth-century possessive of *it*, referring back to *hedland*. The following *garth end* is thus a descriptive phrase rather than the field-name it later became (see under Background below).

Background

Stillingfleet is about six miles south of York. The names *garth end* (11) and *gawtresse* (12) match local field-names cited in Stillingfleet records of the mid-eighteenth-century as *Garth End field* and *Gawtrees field*; *tipplyng hedland* (11) may be presumed to be another field-name.

Topics for linguistic investigation

1. The evidence relating to pronunciation in the spellings (4) *gif*, (4) *saull*, (5) *chirch*, (7) *nebowres*.
2. The forms (6) *song*, (7) *doith*, (11) *buttys*, (14) *childer*, (14) *whome*, (15) *thynke*.
3. The difference in origin and use between the two groups of loan-words (6) *mortuary*, (6) *dirige*, (7) *oblacion*, and (9) *whye*, (9) *kirke*, (11) *garth*.
4. How far is it possible to assess whose language is on record here?

Text 62

William Chambarlayn: London 1542

(Greater London Record Office Manuscript DL/C/418, Bundle II, Item 60)

Ih*esus* R*ex*

In the name of god amen*n* & In the yere off ov^r lord god a thovsand CCCCC
xlij & in the xxxiij yere off ov^r soferay*n* lord kyng henry the viijth & the xx day
off maye I W<illiam> chambarlayn setesan & skynar off lvndon beyng hole off
5   mynd*e* & off parfeyt remem<brance> lavd*es* & thank*es* be to my maker cryste
Iesu ~~& &~~ make & orden thys my present testamen<t> & laste wylle In manar &
fovrme as here aftar folovthe/ fyrste & formoste I be qveythe my sovle vnto alle
myty god my makar & redemar & to the gloryous wyrgen ov^r lady sent marry &
to alle the holy company off heven & I wyll that my body be bvred in*n* the
10   chvrche yard nex to mastars popes walle as nythe as may be I be qvethe to the
heye halter to the blesed sacramente xj^d I wyll aftar my fynyal expenses done &
my det*es* wyche off ryght*e* I do hove any parson or p*ar*sons be well & trvely payd
then I wyll & orden thys my pr*es*ent testament & laste wyll y^t alle svche gvd*es* &
monye off myne as then shalbe ~~I~~ remaynyng shalbe devyd<ed> in tov to egalle
15   partes y^t ys to saye the one ~~to~~ parte theroff to ~~Iohane~~ Ione ~~my~~ my wyfe therw^t
to do hare fre wyll & plesare a cordyng to the cvstome off the citey off lvndon
& the other partey shalle remayne vnto my selfe & to the parformans off my
legases here vndar wreten that ys to saye I be qveythe to hevery on off my god
cheldarne xij^d apes I be qvethe to reynold pytman vj^s viij^d I be qveythe to
20   wyll*ia*m penden iij^s iiij^d I be qveythe to Iarge taylefer*es* dovtar my kynsevomane
& god dovtar att the day of har marage x^s I be qveythe to my cosen Ihon franke
berebrvar xx^s for a blake gvne ~~I be qveythe to my cosen hys wyfe my golde rynge~~
~~w^t a selle~~ I be qveythe to my lady hyll a crvsado for a Iemy I be qvethe to my
spesyall frend syr rovland hylle a byge hovpe off gollde I be qveythe to myster
25   leye a crvsado I be qveythe to mysteres colte a golde rynge w^t a dyamond I be
qveythe to mastar colte a crvsado I be qveythe to my brodar robard chambarlayn
my best gvne fvrd w^t blake boge my best dobelet my best gaket my best hoson
my best shert & cape & my best pvche w^t a loke off selver & to hys wyfe a crvsado
I be qvethe to the yemenry off my company xl s to make them a recrasyon att
30   my beryall daye I be qvethe to the fvndars xxs so that the cvm to my beryall I
wyll that ther shall be geven to my nebvrs that wyll take ytt & in the parys iiijs
{among them} I wyll that shalle be geven in sent oloves in the holde Iury to pvr

334

hovsholdrs v^s I be qvethe to syr nykolas Iaxson ij dosen bogy pryse xij^s I be
qvethe to syr hare koxe ij dosen boby xij^s ~~I be qvethe to me~~ < > ~~leser vs a~~
35 ~~sarvyes~~ I be qvethe to ~~halle~~ that hathe ben my sarvant*es* for a remembrans xx^d
a pes I be qvethe to the iiij presen hovses lvdgatte neve gat the kyng*es* benche
the marsha<l>seye to hether off them iiij d a pes & halle the resedeve off my
parte that ys lefte I wyll y^t Ione my {wyfe} shalle have ytt ~~wyll the~~ {wyche}
I make & ordan myne exseketryx off thys my last wyll & syr rovland hyll
40 {knyght} ~~marchant venterar~~ & {~~marsar~~} Iohan ffranke berebrvar myne
overseayars <prayi>ng myne exceketryx & oversears to be lovers to my sole as
the wollde that I shold be to thars beyng in lyke kasse In wetnes were off I have
wreton thys w^t myne hovnd han<d> the daye & the yer a bove sayd I be qvethe
mastar dobes dovtars heche off them a crvsado in wetenes I have set to my sell

45 By me wyll*i*am chambarlayn skynar ~~I be qvethe my mastar davy my nyte govne~~
~~fvrd w^t besant*es* bake*s*~~

wyttenys to this will I s*ir* Rowlland hill the xviij day of octobr an^o 1545
p*er* me Roland hill

Notes

Text

From the Probate Register of the Diocese of London. Most of the text has been edited
by I. Darlington (ed.), *London Consistory Court Wills 1493–1547*, London Record
Society, Vol. 3 (1967), pp. 142–3.

Manuscript

William Chamberlayn wrote his own Will *w^t myne hovnd hand* (l. 43); lines 47–8, as the
content confirms, are by a different hand, presumably Sir Rowland Hill's.

There are some problems associated with abbreviation conventions. The conventional
abbreviation-mark for final -*es*, as in (5) *thankes*, also occurs after *e*, as in (5) *lavdes*. An
idiosyncratic final -*s* symbol is also used, as in (31) *neburs*, (42) *wetnes* and also the strange
form (10) *mastars*.

The ends of lines are sometimes lost from the document, but can usually be restored,
(41) *praying* being the most conjectural reading.

Glossary

(1)	*Rex*	(Latin) King
(4)	*setesan*	=citizen, freeman of city
(4)	*skynar*	=skinner, dresser of furs
(5)	*lavdes*	praise(s) (see note)
(11)	*fynyal*	=funeral
(14)	*to*	=two
(14)	*egalle*	equal

(18)	*hevery on*	=every one
(19)	*apes*	=apiece, to each
(20)	*Iarge*	=George
(22)	*berebrvar*	=beer-brewer
(22)	*gvne*	=gown
(23)	*crvsado*	a portugese coin
(23)	*Iemy*	double ring (OED GEMEL and GEMEW)
(26)	*boge* (also (33) *bogy*)	lamb-skin (OED BUDGE)
(27)	*gaket*	=jacket
(27)	*hoson*	=hosen, hose
(28)	*cape*	=cap (see note)
(28)	*pvche*	=pouch
(29)	*yemenry*	=yeomanry, general body of freemen of Livery Company
(29)	*company*	Livery Company
(29)	*recrasyon*	=recreation, refreshments
(30)	*fvndars*	=founders
(30)	*so that*	provided that
(30)	*the* (also in (42))	=they
(31)	*parys*	=parish
(33)	*pryse*	=price(d)
(34)	*hare*	=Harry
(34)	*boby*	=?bobac, marmot
(37)	*hether*	=either, each (of four)
(40)	*marchant venterar*	member of one of the associations of Merchant Adventurers
(40)	*marsar*	=mercer, dealer in luxury fabrics
(41)	*overseayars*	=overseers, people appointed to help executors
(42)	*wollde*	wish
(42)	*in lyke kasse*	=in like case, in a similar situation
(43)	*hovnd*	=own
(44)	*set to*	affixed
(44)	*sell*	=seal
(45)	*nyte govne*	=night-gown, dressing-gown
(46)	*besantes backes*	sheepskin (see note)

Explanatory notes

(5) *lavdes*: The noun *laud* 'praise' is a non-count noun. The plural form used here is either by analogy with *thankes* or because of the influence of the name of the Service of *Lauds*.

(10) *the chvrche yard nex to mastars popes walle*: On the City wall were a chapel and hospital known as St Augustine Papey, so named after its community of poor priests. That Chambarlayn is thinking of this, rather than the churchyard of All Hallows on the Wall, is also suggested by the location between the chapel and hospital of the Old Hall of the Curriers ('leather-dressers').

(15) *parte(s)*: In view of (17) *partey*, these spellings could represent *party* rather than *part*; cf. (34) *hare =Harry*. Similarly, the name *Dobes* in l. 44 possibly *=Dobby's*.

(28) *cape*: The loanword *cape* is not recorded as early as this, so this is almost certainly a spelling for *cap*.

(32) *sent oloves in the holde Iury*: The church of St Olave Upwell was in the street called Old Jewry.

(36–7) *the iiij presen hovses* etc.: Ludgate, Newgate, the King's Bench and the Marshalsea.

(46) *bezantes bakes*: OED has BASAN/BAZAN, tanned sheepskin used in bookbinding, but here evidently in reference to sheepskin used in clothing for warmth.

(47 etc.) *sir Rowlland hill*: A distinguished businessman, Master of the Mercers' Company and Lord Mayor in 1549.

Topics for linguistic investigation

1. The history and subsequent replacement of the spellings (5) *parfeyt*, (12) *detes*, (14) *egalle*, (26) *brodar*.
2. The evidence for the pronunciation of vowels in the spellings (28) *selver*, (36) *presen* etc., (30) *beryall*, (36) *neve* and (22) *berebrvar*, (35) *sarvantes*, (29) *yemenry*.
3. The evidence for the pronunciation of consonants in the spellings (7–8) *alle myty*, (21) *dovtar*, (31) *neburs* etc., alongside (10) *nythe* and (12) *ryghte*; (12) *wyche* and (42) *were off*; (8) *wyrgen* and (20) *kynsevomane*; (11) *halter*, (32) *holde* etc.; (24) *spesyall*.
4. The evidence for the pronunciation of consonant clusters in the spellings (10) *nex*, (43) *hovnd*, (27) *dobelet*, (18) *hevery*, (25) *mysteres*.
5. The forms (7) *folovthe*, (35) *hathe*, (5) *be*, (9) *be*, (12) *be*; (27) *hoson*; (40) *myne*.
6. The writer's handling of the syntax in (11–15) *I wyll … egalle partes*.
7. The etymology of (23) *crusado*, (27) *boge*, (34) *boby*, (46) *besantes*.
8. Compare the evidence on sixteenth-century London English offered by this text with that provided by Text 33.

Text 63

Thomas Maertemer: Gloucestershire 1593

(Bristol Record Office Manuscript Bristol Wills No. 77)

In The name of god Amen I Thomas maertemer of Ackeley in the Pariche of
ovlueston and in The Couentey of Gloirsiter houes bane mane Am cike in
bodey but wolle in miende Thinkes be to all mitye God of This I make my Last
Wille & Testiment the xj daye of avgust an Adomni 1593 & in The xxxv yeare
5 of the Rayne of overe Souerrayn{e} Ladey ~~qewene~~ {queene} Elizabethe bi The
grase of god queene of Eingland franc*e* and Erland defender of The faythe &
fereste I geue & be quefe my souell To all miti god & my bodey To be bured in
ovlueston Chorch haye Item I geue & be queue To my son Thomas martimer
iij^li & my best Coefer Item I geue To my son willim mertimer iij^li mi nexe
10 best{e} Coefer Iteme I geue To my Doteter Anes mertimer my nexte beste
Coue my beste floke bede & A payer of blancketes my beste Ceuerled & my next
best bouester & To pillibers & A payere of {my} beste Chestes & A beare in
chete of the beste & my beste bras pone & iiij platteres ij pottengers ij Sacers ij
canstekes one Sl{o}uteseler ij selfer spones ij Carchars ij neckegers her
15 Motheres Tachoches her motheres Coefer her motheres beste cassoke & A you
& A Lame Item I geue To my Sester in Laue margret Wodshall A you & A
coeffer Item I geue to my wife Aules merttimer A pese of de mayene groune
{called more helle} by estimacion vij ackeres or Ther A bout bet more or Les
Soe Longe as my coessen gaimes mertimer do soe Longe Leuese paiinge the
20 Som of ij^s iiij^d A yare {Rate} ~~for~~ {to} Touardes the breddeinge ovpe of my To
yonger cheldringe Thomas & Willim all the reste of my godes mofebele & ovn
mofebele I geue To my wife Aulles mertimer whom I make my excexetoer Item
I ove to my sone gorge mertimer for A pese of grouene If I do houelde ete three
yeares Then I moste I moste paie xxx^s for et & of this my Laste well and
25 Testetimente I make Iohn h<   >ester Willi*a*m horte of tokenton & ~~Iohn Waker~~
{Thomas Segear} my oveser Seieres witnes of this my Laste well & Tesstiment
Thomas segare Aulles waker margrete wod shalle withe otheres

T

Probat*us* xxiij° Septem 1593

338

Notes

Text

From the Probate Records of the Diocese of Bristol. The text has not been edited before.

Manuscript

In l. 24 the repeat of *I moste* is an error of dittography.

In (10) *beste* the final *e* is not a true insertion, but has been written above the word for lack of space at the end of a line.

The gap in (25) *h<   >ester* is because of a hole in the document.

The note confirming that the will has been proved (29) is in a different hand.

Glossary

(2)	*houes bane mane*	=husbandman, farmer
(3)	*wolle*	=whole
(4)	*an Adomni*	=anno domini (Latin)
(7)	*fereste*	=first
(8)	*haye*	enclosure (see note)
(9)	*Coefer*	?=coffer, strong-box (see note)
(10)	*Anes*	=?Agnes
(11)	*flocke bed*	mattress stuffed with woollen flock
(11)	*Ceuerled*	=coverlet
(12)	*bouester*	=bolster, pillow
(12)	*pillibers*	=pillow-beres, pillowcases
(12)	*Chestes*	=sheets
(12–13)	*beare in chete*	See note
(13)	*pone*	=pan
(13)	*platteres*	flat dishes
(13)	*pottengers*	soup-bowls
(13)	*Sacers*	=saucers, small dishes
(14)	*canstekes*	candlesticks
(14)	*Slouteseler*	=salt–cellar
(14)	*selfer*	=silver
(14)	*Carchars*	kerchiefs, head-coverings
(14)	*neckegers*	neckerchiefs
(15)	*Tachoches*	clasps (OED TACHE)
(15)	*cassoke*	loose gown (for either sex)
(15)	*you*	=ewe
(17)	*de mayene groune*	=demesne ground, freehold land
(18)	*bet*	=but
(19)	*gaimes*	=James
(19)	*Leuese*	=?lease
(20)	*yare*	=year
(20)	*Rate*	rent

(20)	*breddeinge ovpe*	bringing up
(21–2)	*godes mofeble & ovn mofeble*	=goods movable and unmovable, possessions and land/buildings
(26)	*oveser Seieres*	=overseers, people appointed to help executors
(25)	*waker*	=?Walker
(27)	*wod shalle*	=Wodshalle (cf. l. 16)
(29)	*Probatus*	(Latin) proved

Local placenames

(1)	*Ackely*	Awkley
(2)	*ovlueston*	Olveston
(2)	*Gloirsiter*	Gloucester
(25)	*tokenton*	Tockington

Explanatory notes

(8) *haye*: OED records this sense only from the mid-seventeenth century.

(9 etc.) *Coefer*: This appears to be *coffer* 'strong box', though the context also supports identification with *heifer*, especially in (16–17) *A you & A coeffer*. It is possible that it represents *heifer* in l. 17, but *coffer* elsewhere.

(12–13) *A beare in chete*: Evidently a special sheet: the phrase could represent either *burying-sheet* 'winding sheet' or *bearing-sheet* 'sheet for wrapping a baby at birth or at its christening'.

Background

Awkley, Olveston and Tockington are Gloucestershire villages a few miles north of Bristol, towards the Severn.

Topics for linguistic investigation

1. The writer's difficulties in regard to syllables, as in (25) *Testetimente* and (2) *houes bane man*.

2. The evidence relating to the pronunciation of vowels in the spellings (3) *miende*, (8) *Chorch*, (2) *Couenty*, (11) *payer*, (13) *Sacers*, (14) *selfer* and (16) *Sester* etc., (20) *yare*.

3. The evidence relating to the pronunciation of consonants in the spellings (3) *wolle*, (7) *be quefe* and (8) *be queue*, (7) *all miti*, (9) *nexe*, (12) *bouester*, (12) *beare in* and (21) *cheldringe*, (17) *groune*, (20) *Touardes*.

4. The derivation of (14) *canstekes*, (14) *Carchars*, (14) *neckegers*.

5. *Pillibere* and *Pottinger*: obsolete names for household articles still in use.

6. *Saucer* and *Cassock*: words with less specialised meanings in the Early Modern period than in Present-day English.

Richard Fewster: Gloucestershire 1636
(Gloucestershire Record Office Manuscript GDR WILL 1637/102)

Version A

[f. 1r] The will of Richard ffewster of yᵉ parrish of Boxwell december yᵉ tenth Anno 1636

In yᵉ name of god Amen/ first I giue and bequeath my Body to yᵉ yearth & my soule vnto god yᵗ gaue it

5   Item I giue and bequeath my eleauen kine to be ~~giuen to my wi~~ sould & equally deuided betwene my wyffe & my two daughters at home

Item two coults & a mare to be sould & deuided as affore sayd

Item I giue &ᶜ eyghte{e}ne shipp be sould & deuided {as affore sayd}

Item I giue &ᶜ the cowe called hewes to be sould & giuen to my Little grandchild
10   Iane gooddenow

Item I giue &ᶜ/ to Eliza: yᵉ biggest pott & my daughter Mary yᵉ ~~Lesser~~ greate kettle

Item I giue yᵉ Little pott to my wife

Item I giue &ᶜ/ to my wiffe & my two daughters 4 peeces off pewter to each

15   Item I giue &ᶜ a Bed to my wife & all thing*es* belongeng to ~~mmm~~ it

{Item I giue all my cheess in yᵉ howse to be sould to pay my Rente}

Item I giue &ᶜ a bed & all thing*es* be Long to it to my da{u}ghter Elizabete

Item I giue &ᶜ/ a bed to my daughter Mary & all that be Long to it

Item I giue &ᶜ an o{a}ken coffer to {my daughter} Eliza

20   {Item one greate ould kettle to my two daughters}

Item I giue my daughter Mary A nother coffer

Item I giue to my wiffe two Little kettles

Item I giue & be queath to my wife & two daughters all other thing*es* both in howsell stuff mun*n*y wᵗ soeuer elce is in yᵉ howse affter my dep*ar*ture

25   [f. 1v] this is ffollowing/

Item I giue &ᶜ/ nine & twenty sheepe {bought} of edward Bale cost nine pound wᶜʰ I Borrowed of Iohn Gooddenow these I Leaue to pay him & yᵉ remay*n*der toward my Rente

Item I giue &ᶜ ~~ffo~~ for {wintering} humphery hewett*es* sheep ~~cost~~ cometh to
30   thirty two shilling*es* eyght pence tow*ard* my Rente

Item I giue wᵗ do want of my Rent & my debt*es* to be payd as affore sayd & out of the stock

Item I giue my towales to my ~~executors~~ for ouerseers for theyr paynes

Item all yᵉ Remoueables & planck*es* are mine & all thing*es* be longinge

35   Ittem I Make my two daughters Eliza: & Mary my Lawffull executo*r*s

Item I make Ierremy walkly & thomas ffewster my Lawffull ou*er* seers

Item it is my will & testament {~~to my ouerseers~~} to sell & disspose of all yᵉ afforesayd good*es* & chattle by yᵉ ouerseers & yᵉ two executo*r*s to Rec*eiue* yᵉ mun*n*y & to keepe it till yᵉ account be giuen vpp

40   yᵉ Mark of Richard ffewster
                                           RF

witnesses to it
Iames Moody
yᵉ Mark **X** of Elizabeth wodrooffe
45   yᵉ Mark **X** of marger<e>t Millerd
Iohn Woodrooffe

Version B

The Will of Richard ffewster of the parrish of Boxwell december the tenth
Anno 1636./
In the name of God Amen. ffirst I give and bequeathe my body to the earth
and my soule vnto God that gave it. **Item** I give my eleven kine to be sould and

5   equally devided betweene my wiefe and my two daughters at home. **Item** two
colts and a mare to be sould and devided as aforesaid. **Item** I give &ᶜ eyghteene
sheepe to be sould and devided as aforesaid. **Item** I give &ᶜ the cowe called
Hewes to be sould and given to my little granchild Iane Goodenow. **Item** I give
&ᶜ to Elizabeth the biggest pott and my daughter Mary the greater kettle. **Item**

10 I give the little pott to my wiefe. **Item** I give &ᶜ to my wiefe and my daughters
fower peeces of pewter to each. **Item** I give &ᶜ&ᶜ a bed to my wiefe and all
thinges belongeinge to it. **Item** I give all my cheese in my house to be sould to
pay my rent. **Item** I give &ᶜ a bed and all thinges belongeinge to it to my
daughter Elizabeth. **Item** I give &ᶜ a bed to my daughter Mary and all thinges

15 that belonge to it<.> **Item** I give an oaken coffer to my daughter Elizabeth.
Item one greate ould kettle to my two daughters. **Item** I give my daughter
Mary another coffer. **Item** I give to my wiefe two little kettles. **Item** I give and
bequeath to my wiefe and two daughters all other thinges both in househould
stuffe and money whatsoever els ~~in~~ is in the house after my departure. **Item** I

20 give &ᶜ nine and twentie sheepe bought of Edward Bale cost nine pound which
I borrowed of Iohn Goodenowe those I leave to pay him and the remainder
towards my rent. **Item** I give &ᶜ for winteringe Humfry Hewetts sheepe cometh
to thirty two shillings eyght pence towards my rent. **Item** I give what doe want
towards of my rent and my debts to be payed as aforesaid and out of the stock.

25 **Item** I give my tooles to my ou*er*seers for their paynes. **Item** all the removeables
and plancks are mine and all thinges belongeinge<.> **Item** I make my two
daughters Elizabeth and Mary my lawfull executors. **Item** I make Ieremy
Walkly and Thomas ffewster my lawfull Overseers. **Item** it is my Will and
Testament to sell and dispose of all the aforesaid goodes and chattle by the

30 overseers and the two Executors to receave the monies to keepe it till the
account be given vp; the marke of Richard ffewster. Wittnesses to it Iames
Moody the marke of Elizabeth Woodruffe the marke of Margarett Millard Iohn
Woodruffe./

Proba*tus* fuit hoc testamentu*m* apud dursly diocesi*s* Gᵒlo*u*c*esteri* decimo nono

35 die Aprilis Anno d*omi*ni 1637ᵒ: coram ffran*cis*co Baber legu*m* doctore &ᶜ
condissaq*ue* fuit Admin*istrati*o &c executor &c debite eod*em* tempore iurat*us*
&c./

Notes

Text

From the Probate Records of the Diocese of Gloucester, Version A is the original will, version B is an official copy. The text has not been edited before.

Manuscript

Photographs of lines A25–46 and B19–37 from these documents, together with commentaries, appear as Plates IX and X on pp. 314–15 and 316–17 above.

Version A is the original will, to which the testator, either illiterate or too ill to write his name in full, has shakily written his initials as his mark. Two of the witnesses have signed by their marks, two have signed their names, and the hand of one of these, John Woodrooffe, matches that of the text. The document is cramped on to both sides of a small sheet, creased and stained, a scribbled working version with many corrections. Version B is a fair copy, carefully written with a degree of calligraphic sophistication, and tidying up various aspects of the language of the original.

Glossary

(A3)	*yearth*	=earth
(A5)	*kine*	cows
(A8)	*shipp*	=sheep
(A12)	*kettle*	cauldron
(A24)	*howsell*	=household
(A29)	*wintering*	tending and providing for during Winter
(A33)	*towales*	=tools
(A34)	*Remoueables*	movable items

Latin

(B34–7) This will was proved at Dursley in the Diocese of Gloucester on the 19th day of April AD 1637, before Francis Baber, Doctor of Law etc. and administration was decreed etc. the executor etc., sworn at the time in regard to the debt etc.

Background

Boxwell is a Cotswold village about three miles east of Wotton-under-Edge. Dursley, where the will was proved, is a larger town about eight miles away.

Topics for linguistic investigation

1. The evidence relating to pronunciation in the spellings (A3) *yearth*, (A8) *shipp*, (24) *howsell*, (24) *munny*, (33) *towales*, (B5) *wiefe*, (B8) *granchild*.
2. Which aspects of the language does the copyist feel free to change, and which does he feel obliged to retain? Why?
3. Interesting linguistic features of Text A which would be lost if only Text B had survived.
4. Names given to animals in the Early Modern period.

Indexes

Index of Texts by Date

Notes

* Text location known, but uncertainty about area of writer
† Place of birth of writer, but no longer resident there

Index of Texts by Area

Notes

* Text location known, but uncertainty about area of writer

† Place of birth of writer, but no longer resident there

Texts: Areas and Counties

SCOTLAND:
2. 7. 21. 22. 23. 36. 43. 53

NORTH WEST
Lancashire: 28. 35. 46. 52†
Westmorland: 13. 44

NORTH EAST
Durham: 3
Lincolnshire: 60
Yorkshire: 4. 10. 19. 61

WEST MIDLANDS
Gloucestershire:
   17. 49. 50. 63. 64
Wiltshire: 1

MIDLANDS
Buckinghamshire: 41
Leicestershire: 20. 39
Northamptonshire: 15*. 58
Oxfordshire: 38
Peterborough: 18
Warwickshire: 57

EAST
Norfolk: 48

LONDON
33. 34. 51. 62

SOUTH WEST
Cornwall: 16. 26. 37
Devon: 5. 6. 9. 11*.
   24. 27. 45. 47†. 59
Somerset: 42†

SOUTH
Hampshire: 31
Sussex: 14. 25

SOUTH EAST
Essex: 8. 30. 55. 56
Kent: 12. 40. 54

AMERICA
Massachusetts: 32
Virginia: 29

Alphabetical Index of Texts